JAPAN
THE STORY
OF A NATION

JAPAN
THE STORY OF A NATION

FOURTH EDITION

EDWIN O. REISCHAUER

Alfred A. Knopf, Publisher
NEW YORK   *1989*

THIS IS A BORZOI BOOK
PUBLISHED BY ALFRED A. KNOPF, INC.

Library of Congress Catalog Card Number:
ISBN 0-394-58527-5

Manufactured in the United States of America

Previously published under the title of: Japan: Past and Present.

Fourth Edition

ABOUT THE AUTHOR

Edwin O. Reischauer came to Harvard as a University Professor in September 1966 after serving with distinction as U.S. Ambassador to Japan from 1961 to 1966. That diplomatic post was the culmination of long experience and study in East Asia. Born in Tokyo in 1910, he lived in Japan until 1927. He received his A.B. degree from Oberlin College in 1931 and his Ph.D. from Harvard in 1939. In the interval he studied at the Universities of Paris, Tokyo, and Kyoto, as well as in Korea and China. He became an instructor at Harvard in 1939, an associate professor in 1945, and professor of Japanese history in 1950. During World War II he served in the Military Intelligence Service of the War Department General Staff. From 1955 to 1956 he was president of the Association for Asian Studies. He was director of the Harvard-Yenching Institute from 1956 to 1961 and served as chairman of its Board of Trustees from 1970 to 1983. Among his books are *The United States and Japan; Wanted: An Asian Policy; Ennin's Travels in T'ang China; East Asia: Tradition and Transformation* (with J. K. Fairbank and A. M. Craig); *Beyond Vietnam: The United States and Asia; Toward the 21st Century: Education for a Changing World; The Japanese; My Life Between Japan and America;* and *The Japanese Today: Change and Continuity.*

To My Brother Bob
The first American casualty in World War II
Shanghai, August 14, 1937

CONTENTS

PREFACE

This book on the history of Japan has acquired quite a history itself. It had its inception in a series of four or five hours of lectures which I, as a lieutenant-colonel in the United States Army, occasionally gave to officer candidates in the army intelligence training program conducted in the Pentagon Building in Washington during World War II. It occurred to me that, if I could present a reasonably useful picture of Japanese history orally in four or five hours, I should be able to do the same in brief written form. This I undertook to do during the few weeks following the Japanese surrender in August 1945, when my intelligence activities suddenly lost their meaning and while I was waiting for a special release from the army in order to join the Department of State for policy planning work on Japan and Korea. I wrote virtually without reference to books, believing that the forgetting of minor details about Japanese history during my years of war service would help make the essentials stand out in my mind all the more clearly.

The result was a very thin, small volume entitled *Japan: Past and Present*. As the years passed, however, Japan changed rapidly, and the "present" became quite different from Japan at the time of the surrender. There was clearly a need to bring the book up to date. Lengthening perspective on the war and prewar years also kept showing Japan in new lights, and I had learned more about the whole of Japanese history. As a consequence, I started on a long series of revisions and extensions of the original work.

Japan: Past and Present appeared in revised and expanded editions in 1952 and 1964, the second written while I was recuperating in a hospital in Hawaii from an almost fatal stabbing I experienced while serving as the American ambassador to Japan. When I wrote still another updated and expanded revision in 1970, I made such extensive alterations throughout the book that I changed its title to *Japan: The Story of a Nation*. This I brought up to date again in revised editions in 1974 and 1981. In the 1981 revision I made the greatest changes of all, rewriting practically the whole of the book. Since 1981 the rate of change in Japan has slowed considerably while the attitude of the outside world toward Japan has changed enormously and at remarkable speed. This has necessitated in the present edition an extensive rewriting of large parts of the book as well as an addition of almost a decade of new materials.

To attempt to thank all those who have given me aid in the many editions of this book or the host of scholars on whose work I have drawn would be quite impossible. I shall limit myself to mentioning two people who have been particularly helpful in this latest revision. They are Professor Albert Craig, who has given me several very useful suggestions, and Ms. Ellie Rutledge, who bore the brunt of typing the manuscript and checking points of detail.

Edwin O. Reischauer

JAPAN
THE STORY
OF A NATION

PART ONE

TRADITIONAL
JAPAN

1

LAND AND PEOPLE

Japan has long had one of the world's most distinctive and sophisticated cultures, and today it is an economic giant—the second or third largest in the world, standing at or near the forefront of many of the great advances of human civilization. This record is all the more remarkable when one considers Japan's smallness in size and population as compared to the United States, Soviet Union, China, and India. Japan was all but ignored by the world at large only a century and a half ago. Thus the amazing story of its rise to its current prominence must be attributed largely to the Japanese people themselves.

Japan is not as large as France or even the single American state of California, though it is only fair to point out that it is larger than either Italy or the British Isles, the homes of the two greatest empires the Western world has ever seen. It is extremely mountainous, rising to the beautiful volcanic cone of Mt. Fuji, 12,389 feet high. Less than a fifth of its not particularly fertile terrain is level enough for cultivation. Thus it is much smaller in usable land than it appears on the map, and it is not blessed with many mineral resources either. Today it is dependent on foreign imports for more than 90 percent of its energy resources, mostly in the form of oil, almost all its minerals, and much of its food.

Japan's chief natural assets are its plentiful rainfall and temperate climate, which encourages an energetic way of life. In latitude, it parallels the East Coast of the United States from New England to

Georgia, with most of the larger cities at about the level of North Carolina. The climate is comparable to that of the American East Coast, except that, being located several hundred miles out in the ocean, Japan experiences somewhat less extreme temperatures in both winter and summer and receives considerably more precipitation as rain or snow.

Making full use of this abundant water, the Japanese, during the past two millennia, have laboriously constructed an intricate system of channels to convert wherever possible every piece of cultivatable land into irrigated rice paddies. These irrigated fields, combined with a long growing season, hot summers, hard work, and great agricultural skills, have made the Japanese the most productive farmers per acre in the world. About half the country can grow two crops a year—one of rice, the other of some other grain or vegetable. This intensive agricultural pattern has permitted Japan to maintain a larger population than any Western European nation since at least medieval times. Extensive irrigation controls of large river systems, as in Mesopotamia, India, and China, are thought by some to have contributed to centralized, despotic systems of government. In Japan the river systems are small, and irrigation instead appears to have helped foster the notable Japanese propensity for cooperation and consensus decision making in small groups.

Plentiful rainfall means that Japan is a verdant land, with a heavy forest cover on its mountains. The combination of rugged coastlines, precipitous but forested mountains, and a lush countryside makes Japan a most beautiful land wherever people and industry have not despoiled it. All this natural splendor may have contributed to the great sensitivity the Japanese have shown throughout history to the wonders of nature and to their great love of its beauty.

Japan's location cannot be considered to have been any great asset, particularly in early times. It lies at the extreme eastern edge of the Asian-European "ancient world" of high civilization, considerably farther out to sea than the British Isles on its western edge. Japan was no crossroads of world trade but lay at the veritable end of the earth, the most isolated of all the major countries that enjoyed a high civilization in premodern times. External influences for long came to it slowly and only as filtered through the nearby continental lands of China and Korea.

There were important compensations, however, for this insularity. For a land cut up into small pieces by innumerable mountain ranges,

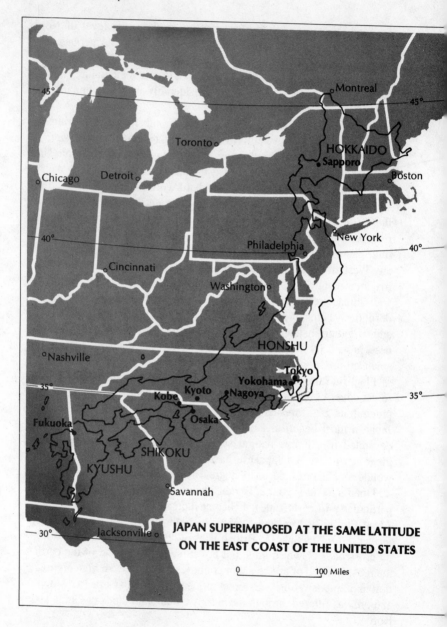

**JAPAN SUPERIMPOSED AT THE SAME LATITUDE
ON THE EAST COAST OF THE UNITED STATES**

0 ———————— 100 Miles

the waters surrounding Japan permitted relatively easy communication between the islands and also along the coast. This was particularly true of the Inland Sea, which cut through the middle of western Japan. The sea also provided ample supplies of fish, which remain the chief source of animal protein in the Japanese diet. Their insular position also spared the Japanese from the conquests and pillage by foreign hordes inflicted on many other lands and from incessant warfare along their frontiers. Isolation thus gave the Japanese relatively greater peace and more opportunities than most peoples have had to develop their own special talents and produce a remarkably distinctive way of life.

Japan is part of the East Asian zone of civilization, which centers around China and includes Korea and Vietnam. This is the part of the world that has derived most of its basic culture from the civilization developed in ancient times on the plains of North China. Although the home throughout history of a large part of the human race—roughly a fifth to a quarter—the East Asian cultural zone has been the most isolated of the great spheres of early civilization. It was cut off from the other centers of ancient culture in India, the Middle East, and the Mediterranean Basin by the great land barrier of the mountain ranges and deserts of Central Asia and the jungles and rugged terrain of Southeast Asia. In this relatively isolated zone, Japan was the most isolated area of all. In contrast to the 20 miles of the Straits of Dover separating England from France, it is 100 miles from Japan to Korea and 500 to China.

Japan nonetheless is culturally a daughter of Chinese civilization, much as the countries of North Europe are daughters of Mediterranean culture. The story of the spread of Chinese civilization to the peoples of Japan during the first millennium after Christ is much like the story of the spread of Mediterranean civilization to the peoples of North Europe during the same period. But the greater isolation of the Japanese from the home of their civilization and from all other peoples meant that in Japan the borrowed culture had more chance to develop along new and often unique lines. One popular concept is that the Japanese have never been anything more than a race of borrowers and imitators. The truth is quite the contrary. Although geographic isolation has made them conscious of learning from abroad, it has also allowed them to develop one of the most distinctive cultures to be found in any area of comparable size. Take, for example, things as basic as their traditional clothing, their cuisine, or their domestic architecture and the manner in which they live at home. The thick straw floor mats, the sliding paper panels in place of interior walls, the open, airy structure of the whole house, the recess for art objects, the charcoal-burning braziers (*hibachi*), the peculiar wooden or iron bathtubs, and the place of bathing in daily life as a means of relaxation at the end of a day's work and, in winter, as a way of restoring a sense of warmth and well-being—all these and many other simple but fundamental features of daily life in traditional Japan are unique to the country and attest to a highly creative culture rather than one of simple imitation.

Japan's cultural distinctiveness has perhaps been accentuated by its linguistic separateness. Although the Japanese writing system has been derived from that of China and innumerable Chinese words have been incorporated into Japanese in much the same way that English has borrowed thousands of Latin and Greek words, Japanese is basically as different from Chinese as it is from English. Its structure is strikingly like Korean, but even then it appears to be no more closely related to Korean than English is to Russian or the Sanskrit-derived languages of India. Possessing a writing system more complex than any other in common use in the modern world and a language with no close relatives, the Japanese probably face a bigger language barrier between themselves and the rest of the world than any other major national group.

Geographic isolation and cultural and linguistic distinctiveness have made the Japanese highly self-conscious and acutely aware of their differences from others. In a way this has been a great asset to them in the modern age of nation-states, for they have faced no problem of national identity. Indeed, Japan constitutes what may be the world's most perfect nation-state: a clear-cut geographic unit containing almost all the people of a distinctive culture and language and virtually no one else. On the other hand, extreme self-consciousness bred of isolation has become a serious handicap in the current age of international interdependence. It has made the Japanese somewhat tense in their contacts with foreigners, and they have shown relatively little sensitivity to the feelings and reactions of other peoples. At times they appear obsessed with a sense either of superiority or inferiority toward the outside world. Japan's isolation may help explain some of the extremes in its international relations and also, perhaps, the uneasiness Japanese feel even today about their place in the world.

The Japanese are basically Mongoloid in race, closely related to their neighbors in Korea and China; but like all modern peoples, they are the product of extensive racial mixture. Many different groups found their way into Japan, a few as early as paleolithic times. During the last ice age, which continued until about 11,000 years ago, Japan was joined by land to the rest of Asia. Since Japan was the geographic end of the line, peoples who wandered into it could not move on but stayed and mixed with those who came later.

One interesting racial ingredient was provided by the Ainu. These may be a proto-Caucasoid people—that is, a group that split off from the white race so early that not all the characteristics of this race had as yet developed. At one time the Ainu may have occupied most of Japan, or they may have been only relatively late intruders from the north. In any case, some twelve centuries ago their ancestors lived in the northern island of Hokkaido and the northern third of the main island of Honshu. Since then they have been slowly pushed north and all but some 20,000 have been culturally and racially absorbed by the Japanese. Today they are on the point of vanishing, but they have left behind a genetic legacy that may account for the relative abundance of facial and body hair of some Japanese as compared with other Mongoloids, and possibly helps to explain the great variety of facial types among the Japanese.

There is a popular theory that some early immigrants to Japan were carried there by the Japan Current, which flows from Southeast Asia past Taiwan, the Ryukyu Islands, and Japan, much like the Gulf Stream off the East Coast of the United States. Strong similarities in mythology, social customs, and early architecture between Japan and Southeast Asia and the South Pacific are cited in support of this concept. There is, however, no archeological evidence to back it up. A better explanation of these similarities is that they resulted from very early waves of cultural influence and, possibly, people who moved outward from South China, some to Southeast Asia and others to Japan, perhaps by way of Korea.

The archeological record clearly shows that a large number, if not most, of the early inhabitants of Japan came to the islands from Korea and areas farther away in Northeast Asia, and there is indisputable historical evidence that a considerable flow of people from the peninsula into Japan continued until the eighth century A.D. An early ninth-century book attributes recent continental origin to more than a third of the aristocratic families at the Japanese court at that time. By then, however, the mixing was almost complete, and the Japanese were well on their way to becoming the homogeneous people we know today. They also already occupied most of what we now call Japan. Only in the extreme north were the culturally alien Ainu still to be absorbed, and in southern Kyushu there were still some groups that may have been culturally as well as politically distinct, but were in any case on the verge of complete assimilation.

Paralleling the flow of people and probably carried in part by it, a series of cultural influences also spread from the Asian continent to Japan. Pieces of the world's oldest known pottery, dating from around 10,000 years ago, have been found in Japan as well as China. From around 10,000 B.C. there developed in Japan a primitive hunting, fishing, and gathering society, known as *Jomon* from its mat-patterned pottery, which shows great variety, boldness, and originality in its designs.

Although Jomon culture lingered on until comparatively modern times in the extreme north, it was beginning to be displaced or absorbed by a more advanced agricultural society by around 300 B.C. This new culture, called *Yayoi*, is identified by its relatively simple, thin, wheel-shaped pottery, but its outstanding feature was its irrigated rice cultivation, much like that in use today. It also possessed bronze and iron; bronze artifacts, including obvious imitations of Chinese bronze mirrors, were used primarily for ceremonial purposes. Starting in north Kyushu, the area closest to Korea, Yayoi culture spread rapidly up the Inland Sea to central Japan and on to the Kanto Plain in the east. This plain, where modern Tokyo is located, is the largest relatively level area in Japan. The metallurgy and agriculture of the Yayoi culture were ultimately derived from China, but only indirectly. They probably came to Japan as the result of waves of culture and movements of peoples from Korea and areas north of China, most likely pushed eastward into Japan by the unification of China in the third century B.C.

A new archeological era, the tumulus period, named for the large earth mounds erected over the graves of dead leaders, began around 300 A.D. In time these mounds came to be of huge size, indicating the existence of relatively large political units capable of marshaling a great deal of manpower. The largest mound, located in central Japan

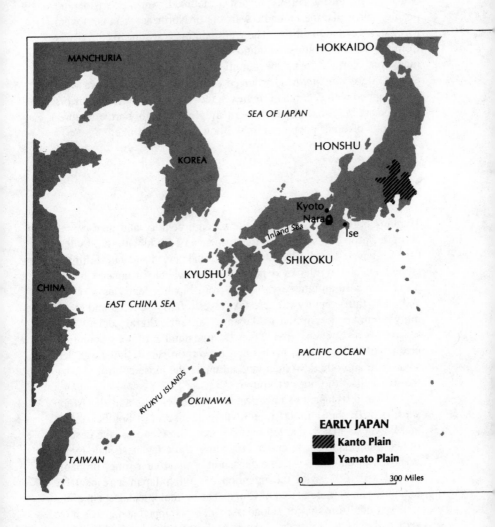

MANCHURIA

HOKKAIDO

SEA OF JAPAN

KOREA

HONSHU

Kyoto
Nara

Inland Sea

Ise

SHIKOKU

KYUSHU

CHINA

EAST CHINA SEA

PACIFIC OCEAN

RYUKYU ISLANDS

OKINAWA

TAIWAN

EARLY JAPAN

▨ **Kanto Plain**
■ **Yamato Plain**

0   300 Miles

and dating probably from the late fifth century, is almost 2,700 feet long and surrounded by moats. Many were of keyhole shape—square in front and round behind. The arms and horse trappings associated with finds from this period suggest a mounted, warlike, aristocratic people, much like the nomadic warriors of Northeast Asia who were invading Korea at that time. The wall paintings on some of the tombs from the seventh century are almost identical to contemporary paintings from North Korea. The tumuli often had cylindrical pieces of pottery, known as *haniwa*, arranged on them in rings. Haniwa were often capped with decorative figures, a few of which depicted warriors and horses, but most of which were simple and highly artistic representations of other people, animals, houses, and the like.

Tumulus burials lasted through the seventh century and then ceased abruptly, probably because of the influence of Buddhism, but by that time we have entered fully into the historical period and can shift from archeological to written evidence for our knowledge of Japan. Chinese histories record an emissary coming from Japan as early as A.D. 57, and a late third-century Chinese text gives a fairly detailed and seemingly accurate description of Japan as an agricultural society with sharp class distinctions, divided into a large number of petty countries, presumably tribal units, each ruled over by a semireligious leader, some men and others women, and all under the loose control of what the text calls "the queen's country."

The earliest Japanese histories, the *Kojiki* of 712 and the *Nihon shoki* of 720, start with creation myths reminiscent of Southeast Asia and Polynesia. They also tell of a supreme Sun Goddess, the descent of her grandson to earth, and the founding of the Japanese state by his grandson in 660 B.C.—a date chosen at a much later time, probably around A.D. 600, with the intention of giving Japan a respectable antiquity comparable to that of China. The mythological descent of the imperial line from the Sun Goddess, still worshipped at Japan's most sacred shrines at Ise, east of the capital region, and the Chinese account of the supremacy of the "queen's country," suggest an originally matriarchal people who became the strongly male-dominated society of later history only through subsequent influences from the highly patriarchal society of China. The histories then go on to recount a confused but somewhat plausible story of conquest from Kyushu up the Inland Sea to central Japan and on to the Kanto Plain. By the fourth or fifth century, Yamato, one of the tribal units in the central area, had clearly established its control over most of the others, and this political unit grew into the completely historical nation of Nihon or Nippon, known to us through its South Chinese pronunciation as Japan.

The concentration of the largest tumuli in central Japan around the modern cities of Osaka and Nara corresponds well with the rise to supremacy of Yamato, and some are traditionally identified with early priest-chiefs of that state. The traditional symbols of authority of these priest-chiefs, the so-called Three Imperial Regalia, also tie in well with the archeological record. They are a long iron sword like those common throughout Northeast Asia, a bronze mirror representing the Sun Goddess but clearly derived from China, and a so-called curved jewel (*magatama*), a small comma-shaped stone, perhaps originally representing a bear claw and common also in Korean archeological finds.

The Japanese state that emerged into history in the fifth and sixth centuries was clearly a further development of the tribally divided country described in the early Chinese records. Under the leadership of Yamato, the country was divided into a number of local hereditary units called *uji*, sometimes translated as "clans." These had their hereditary chiefs and their own *uji* deities. Under the controlling family and tied to it by pseudofamily bonds were hereditary functional groups called *be*, which consisted mostly of farmers but also included pottery makers, weavers, and other specialized groups. The *uji* were ranked in hierarchical order under the ruling Yamato group, which also had certain *uji* under its direct control to perform various functions, such as military service, the manufacture of various goods, ritualistic divining, and supervision of the Yamato group's lands, which were scattered throughout Japan.

Yamato by this time controlled most of modern Japan, except for the northern part of Honshu and Hokkaido, and until 562 it maintained some sort of foothold on the south coast of Korea. Though explained in the Japanese histories as the result of conquest by a warrior empress, the Korean foothold was more probably connected with the movement of peoples from Korea to Japan and the resulting close relations between certain groups on both sides of the straits separating the two countries. In any case, Japanese armies were active on the peninsula in the fifth and sixth centuries, and Yamato did not finally give up the attempt to reestablish a foothold in South Korea until 663, shortly before the unification of Korea by the southeastern state of Silla in 668.

Many characteristics of *uji* society were to remain typical of Japan in its later history. This was certainly true of the strong emphasis on hierarchy and hereditary authority. The aristocratic mounted warrior of the tumulus period was also to emerge again as a dominant figure in feudal times. And of particular significance, the early Yamato priest-chiefs developed into the imperial line, which served as the sacerdotal source of political authority throughout history and is today by far the oldest reigning family in the world.

The religious beliefs and practices of *uji* times have also continued as one of the main religious streams of Japan. Nameless, at first, these beliefs were subsequently called *Shinto,* "the way of the gods," to distinguish them from Buddhism. The worship of the Sun Goddess and other *uji* ancestors and deities was part of a much broader worship of fertility and the wonders and mysteries of nature. A waterfall, a mountain crag, a mysterious cave, a large tree, a peculiarly shaped stone, or an unusual person might inspire a sense of awe. Such objects of worship were called *kami,* a term somewhat misleadingly translated as "god" but obviously not comparable to the Judeo-Christian concept of God. This simple Shinto notion of deity should be borne in mind when trying to understand the "deification" in modern times of emperors and of soldiers who died for their country.

Early Shinto had almost no ethical content, except for an emphasis on ritual purity, which may have contributed to the Japanese love of bathing. On the other hand, it had numberless places of worship and countless festivals and ceremonies. Places where people felt a sense of awe became cult spots and eventually shrines. Today tens of thousands of such shrines dot the landscape of Japan, each with its characteristic *torii* gateway. Some are great institutions dating back to antiquity; thousands are village shrines still identified as the abode of the local *uji* deity; and others are merely miniature edifices of stone or wood recently erected in front of a gnarled old tree or on a mountain top.

The underlying stream of Shinto today remains little changed since prehistoric times, although much has been done during the past thousand years to make it into a more organized religion. In modern times it was consciously used, through an emphasis on the early mythology connected with it, as an inspiration for national solidarity and fanatical patriotism. But despite these later uses, Shinto remains basically unchanged: It still centers around the worship of nature, fertility, reverence for ancestral deities, and a sense of communion with them and the spirits of nature.

2

THE ADOPTION OF THE CHINESE PATTERN

The peoples of North Europe have always been conscious of their double heritage—their primitive Teutonic roots and the cultural legacy of ancient Greece and Rome. Similarly, the Japanese have a double heritage—the native culture of early Japan and the higher civilization of classical China. As in North Europe, true history started for Japan only when the broad stream of a highly developed civilization reached its shores and, in a different geographic setting, combined with the simpler traditions of the local people to form a new culture, based directly on the old civilization but differentiated from it by a richer and more complex superstructure.

The Japanese had long had some contact with Chinese civilization. Envoys and traders had gone back and forth between the two countries since at least the first century A.D. Immigrants from Korea brought with them the arts and sciences of the continental civilization. Knowledge of Chinese writing, for example, had become well established in Japan by the fifth century. These early borrowings from China, however, were made only very slowly and almost unconsciously, as has been the usual pattern in the spread of civilization throughout the world. But an abrupt acceleration in the rate of learning from the continent started in the second half of the sixth century, when the Japanese suddenly became conscious of the advantages of the superior cõntinental civilization and the desirability of learning more about it. Why this spurt in the process of learning from China should have come at just this moment in Japanese history is not certain. The Japanese may have reached a level of cultural attainment and political organization that for the first time permitted more rapid and more conscious learning from abroad. And the renewed vigor displayed by Chinese culture at that time may have facilitated the process.

China's history as a highly civilized part of the world reaches back into the second millennium before Christ. Its first great period as a colossal military empire came during the time of Rome's greatness, roughly from about 220 B.C. to A.D. 220. The era of political disruption that followed came to an end in the second half of the sixth century, when a new and greater Chinese empire emerged from the chaos of three centuries of civil war and barbarian invasions. This new empire was far richer and stronger than the first. In fact, during the seventh and eighth centuries China was, with little doubt, the richest, most powerful, and technologically most advanced country in the world. This period, which was known by the dynastic names of Sui (581–618) and T'ang (618–907), was a time of unprecedented grandeur, might, and brilliant cultural attainment.

It is small wonder that the Japanese felt the reflected glory of the new Chinese empire and attempted to create a small replica of it in their own isolated islands. Other petty states in Korea, Manchuria, and on the southwestern borders of China, dazzled by the grandeur and might of Sui and T'ang, were attempting to do the same. A millennium or more later, the borrowing of political, social, and economic institutions from more advanced countries was to become commonplace throughout the world; but it is surprising that the Japanese at this early date went about transplanting the more complex Chinese institutions and techniques with such great zeal and in so systematic a way. The result during the next two centuries was a cultural surge forward in Japan that stands in sharp contrast to the slow, fumbling progress of North Europe at this time. This difference may not have been due so much to the tribal people of Japan and North Europe, who were actually somewhat similar, as to the attractiveness of their respective models. While Rome was falling completely to pieces, China was rising to new heights of grandeur.

The start of the heavy flow of Chinese influences to Japan is usually dated as 552, the year the Buddhist religion is said to have been officially introduced to the Yamato court from Paekche, a kingdom in southwestern Korea. Actually, Buddhism had probably entered Japan even earlier, but this official introduction affords a convenient date to mark the time when the Japanese first started consciously to learn from the Chinese. During the next few centuries, Buddhism served as an important vehicle for the transmission of Chinese culture to Japan, just as Christianity served as a vehicle for the transmission of Mediterranean civilization to North Europe. Buddhism is by origin an Indian religion, but it had slowly spread to China and won a place of importance in Chinese culture during the troubled era between the two great periods of empire. It was a vigorous proselytizing religion at that time, and missionary zeal carried it beyond China to Korea and from there to Japan. From the sixth to the eighth centuries, continental priests occasionally came to Japan, and scores of Japanese converts went to China to learn more about the new faith. Returning from the continent, these student priests, even more than foreign missionary teachers, took the lead in transmitting to Japan the new religion and many other aspects of Chinese civilization.

In the second half of the sixth century, Buddhism and other new influences from abroad so affected the Yamato court that clashes broke out between a faction favoring the acceptance of Buddhism and other continental ideas and an opposition group that resisted the new religion and all change. More fundamentally, this was a battle between leading *uji* groups for dominance of the Yamato court and its priest-chiefs. The pro-Buddhist Soga *uji*, which was closely intermarried with the reigning family, emerged victorious in 587, and under its dynamic leader Umako embarked on a series of significant innovations. Most of these were later attributed to Prince Shotoku, the regent for the reigning empress from 593 to 622, but Shotoku was probably at most only a partner in these enterprises. In large part of Soga blood himself, he was made regent only after Umako had murdered his own reigning nephew and put his niece Suiko on the throne. Umako, until his death in 626, was clearly the most powerful figure at court.

Suiko was the first of several women who reigned between 592 and 770, usually as compromise candidates chosen to head off succession disputes. When the last of these women rulers fell so much under the influence of a Buddhist monk that it was feared he would usurp the throne, feminine leadership was permanently abandoned, except for two much later cases in the seventeenth and eighteenth centuries, by which time the position lacked any semblance of power. Another and probably more basic reason for the switch to purely male rule was growing Chinese influence and the Chinese abhorrence of women rulers. Japanese women, who in earliest times may have enjoyed a position of social and political dominance over men, gradually sank to a status of subservience. Their rights and influence in the early feudal society of medieval times were still considerable, but eventually even these were lost as they were turned into mere handmaidens to men.

Among the most significant innovations carried out by Umako and his associates in the early seventh century was the reinstitution of embassies to China. One may have been sent in 600, and three more certainly went between 607 and 614. These were followed by periodic embassies during the next two centuries, until 838. The immediate political results of these embassies were slight and their economic significance was not much greater, but they were of the utmost cultural importance. Buddhist monks as well as scholars, artists, and technicians of all sorts accompanied these missions, some staying in China for years of intensive study. Upon their return to Japan they became leaders in their respective fields, the men most responsible for the successful transmission to this isolated land of the science, arts, philosophy, and institutions of the great continental civilization. Japanese leaders showed extraordinary wisdom in sending students to China in this way; it was, in a sense, the world's first program of organized study abroad.

Another innovation of this period was the creation in 603 of twelve court ranks for courtiers. This probably was an effort to strengthen central power by emulating the system of bureaucratic rule in China and lessening the prestige of the *uji* ranks. Eventually, *uji* ranks, along with the *uji* themselves, shrank into insignificance, while the court ranks gained in importance, becoming an exceedingly complex system of twenty-six grades that was to last, at least in outward form, until modern times. The Chinese calendar was adopted in 604, and in the same year a so-called Seventeen Article Constitution, consisting of general Buddhist and Chinese Confucian precepts, was issued. Although the remaining text is probably of later date, the original document, like the remaining one, probably manifested the desire of the leaders for more centralized political power and the adoption of Buddhist concepts.

Prince Shotoku appears to have had a genuine interest in Buddhism, and some of the Buddhist writings attributed to him may be genuine. He definitely was associated with the founding of the beautiful Horyuji monastery near Nara. Some of its present buildings, which date from late in the seventh century, are the oldest wooden buildings in the world, and they are crammed with superb Buddhist art from those early times. While the Japanese were perhaps slow in grasping all the intricacies of Buddhist doctrine, they showed an amazing skill in mastering the continental art that accompanied these teachings and soon were producing masterpieces to rival those of their Korean and Chinese teachers.

Meanwhile, dissatisfaction with Soga dominance and fear of a Soga usurpation of the throne mounted at the Yamato court and resulted in a coup d'état in 645, in which the Soga were destroyed. There were two leaders of this coup. One was Nakatomi Kamatari (the surname is always given first in Japanese), whose family, under the newly acquired name of Fujiwara, was in time to dominate the court completely.

The other was a prince of the reigning family who, though occupying the throne only briefly from 668 to 672 under the name of Tenji, was one of the few Japanese emperors who seems to have ruled as well as reigned. Among the very few others were Tenji's brother Temmu (reigned 673–686), who also had to fight to gain the throne, and Tenji's great-grandson Kammu (reigned 781–806). In fact, it was not until Tenji's time that the part played by the Yamato priest-chiefs began to mirror the role of Chinese emperors. Although the idea of the centralization of power around an emperor in the Chinese manner had obviously been present in Umako's time, and the embassies of 607 and 608 to China bore messages referring to the Japanese ruler on equal terms with the emperor of China, it was only in the second half of the seventh century that an effort was made to convert the Yamato priest-chiefs into the all-powerful monarchs of the Chinese system. They did not, however, lose their religious role in the process, but combined thenceforth the two roles of Japanese high priest and Chinese secular ruler. In the long run, the religious role was to reemerge as the dominant one.

The coup d'état of 645 was called the Taika (Great Change) Reform. The name Taika was the first Japanese attempt to adopt the Chinese system of counting years by arbitrarily named "year periods." In 1368 the Chinese made their year periods correspond to reigns, and the Japanese followed suit in 1868. According to this system, the first few days of 1989 are known as Showa 64 for Hirohito, whose reign was the longest in authenticated history, and with his death 1989 became Heisei 1 for Akihito, his son and successor.

Later historians attributed to the years 645–646 a series of great political and economic changes that remade Japan according to the Chinese model, but these reforms were actually achieved only piecemeal over the remainder of the century and into the next. The chief motivation for these reforms was the desire to make Japan a more centralized and powerful state, but a certain urgency was given to this task by China's invasion of Korea at this time and the destruction of a large Japanese army and fleet dispatched there in support of Japan's ally, Paekche. In this stimulus to change produced by an external military menace one can see a small parallel to the much greater change forced on Japan by the threat of Western imperialism in the nineteenth century.

In the seventh century the Japanese sought to create a theoretically all-powerful emperor surrounded by an elaborate bureaucratic government modeled after that of T'ang China, which was the most highly developed and complex system of government the world had as yet seen. They made some conscious adjustments, however, to fit their own special circumstances. Outranking the Central Council of State, with its prime minister and ministers of the left and right, which paralleled the Chinese secular government, they created an Office of Deities to represent the religious functions of the emperor. Also, instead of the standard six ministries of the Chinese system, they created eight to include one for the imperial household and another for a central secretariat. These ministries and many other bureaus and offices were staffed with officials, each with an appropriate court rank.

The creation of a central government based on Chinese models was an easier task than the development of a Chinese type of provincial administration. Communications were still too imperfect and the spirit of local autonomy too strong to permit direct rule of all parts of the land by a bureaucracy dispatched to the provinces from the court. But the Japanese adopted at least the outward forms of the Chinese system. The land was divided into sixty-six provinces. Each province was divided into counties, and each county into villages. Central government officials were sent out to rule the provinces, but the lesser officials were drawn from among the local leaders.

The Japanese even attempted to adopt the extraordinarily complex Chinese system of land ownership and taxation. In early T'ang China, agricultural land was in theory nationalized and distributed equally among the peasants, so that each adult tax paying male could carry an equal share of the tax load. This he paid partly in produce and partly in labor, or in military service, which was considered a form of labor for the state. The whole system depended on detailed census records and land surveys.

Even in China, despite the long tradition of centralized bureaucratic rule, this cumbersome system did not work well and tended to break down completely every few generations. That the Japanese should have attempted to apply it in their *uji*-dominated land was remarkable; nonetheless, it was put into practice, probably for the most part in areas long under direct Yamato control. It actually operated fairly well for a century or more and left traces throughout the country until the fifteenth century. But the conscript army, which was part of the Chinese tax system, never took on real life in Japan. After the threat of China's seventh-century conquest of Korea subsided, Japan, as an island country, had no pressing need for large armies to defend it against invaders. The Japanese levies soon degenerated into little more than labor gangs, while the true fighting man seems to have remained the aristocrat on horseback.

One major aspect of the adoption of the Chinese political pattern was the establishment for the first time of a permanent capital—Japan's first city. Hitherto the capital had shifted, usually with each reign, to the estate of the new ruler, in part to avoid the pollution of his predecessor's death. The first capital, called Heijo but now known as Nara, was located in the Yamato Plain. It was laid out in 710 in ambitious imitation of Ch'ang-an, the great T'ang capital, as a rectangle of checkerboard streets, with the palace and government buildings at the north end of the great central north–south avenue. It was 2.5 by 3 miles in size, as compared with Ch'ang-an's 5 by 6 miles. Unlike Ch'ang-an, a world metropolis of more than a million people, Nara, even in its reduced size, was far too large for Japan's small population and backward conditions; its western half was never built up, nor were the great city walls, characteristic of all Chinese cities, ever constructed. They simply were not needed in insular Japan. Despite its shortcomings, this ambitious effort was impressive for the Japan of that time, and the old capital area is still dotted with many stately tile-roofed monasteries dating from that period and representing the best remaining architecture from the T'ang period anywhere in East Asia.

Toward the end of the eighth century the emperor Kammu, possibly with the intent of escaping the influence of the great Buddhist temples that ringed Nara, decided to abandon this first city and build a new capital. In 794 this second city, called Heian, was laid out 30 miles north of Nara. Again the scale was ambitious, a rectangle some 3 by 3.5 miles, and again the city wall and the western half of the city never materialized. But this second capital, later to be known as Kyoto, remained the imperial capital of Japan until 1868, and the checkerboard pattern of its principal streets still accurately reflects the Chinese-style city laid out over a thousand years ago. The time when the capital was at Heijo is known as the Nara period (710–784) and the early centuries after its removal to Kyoto as the Heian period (794–1185).

Most of the changes in government, economics, and life carried out during the great transformation of Japan that took place between the sixth and ninth centuries were embodied in elaborate Chinese-type law codes. The earliest remaining one is that of 701, drawn up during the Taiho year period but known to us only through later commentaries. The Japanese also adopted the Chinese concept that a major duty of government was to maintain a clear historical record of the past as a guide to political action. Such efforts to compile official histories were continued until 887. From this idea stemmed the two early Japanese histories already mentioned, the *Kojiki* of 712 and the *Nihon shoki* of 720. These first two histories are fairly reliable accounts of the period after about A.D. 400, but they also preserve the naive and primitive mythology of antiquity. They were clearly used to shape both the mythology and early historical traditions in a manner that would enhance the prestige of the Yamato court. At times in later periods these early histories and their mythology were also utilized to whip up among the Japanese people a sense of uniqueness and ultranationalist fervor, as during the wars of the late nineteenth and early twentieth centuries.

The process of learning and borrowing from China was, of course, not limited to politics. In fact, what the Japanese were learning culturally and intellectually at this time was to have a deeper and more lasting influence than the borrowed political institutions. For the most part, the latter decayed within a century or so and eventually disappeared in all but name. But many of the religious concepts, artistic skills, and literary forms learned during these centuries, far from losing their vigor, continued to develop and shaped the basic cultural patterns of later ages.

Buddhism grew greatly in strength in the capital area and enjoyed even higher official favor than the native Shinto cults, but it remained much weaker in the provinces. The emperors and noble families built splendid temples and monasteries and sponsored impressive Buddhist ceremonies. One emperor, Shomu, conceived the idea of erecting a monastery and nunnery in each province and a great central monastery at the capital to symbolize religiously the whole concept of political centralization. The 53-foot seated bronze Great Buddha (or *Daibutsu*) at the central Todaiji monastery, which was dedicated in 752, remains one of the largest bronze figures in the world, though it has been somewhat disfigured by later repairs. The personal effects of Shomu and other artifacts and fine works of art from this period are preserved in great quantity in the Shosoin storehouse, which stands nearby. Many Japanese emperors, tiring of the heavy burdens of their dual religious and secular roles, began to abdicate the throne and retire to the quiet life of a Buddhist monk.

Besides Buddhism, the Japanese absorbed a great many other Chinese concepts and ideals, such as Confucian philosophy, the historical lore of that ancient land, its rich literature, and many Chinese myths and superstitions. They also learned a great deal of China's advanced technology in textiles, metalwork, bridge building, architecture, and the like. The Buddhist temples themselves were architectural masterpieces. They housed beautiful and deeply spiritual bronze, lacquer, clay, or wooden statues of divinities, exquisite religious paintings, and other magnificent works of art. Some of these art treasures had been brought from the continent, but others of equal beauty and artistic merit were produced in Japan. They attest to the amazing success with which the Japanese absorbed much of the best in the Chinese artistic tradition and indicate the early development of a happy combination of artistic taste and superb craftsmanship that ever since has characterized the Japanese.

In art, the Japanese could have had no better teachers than the Chinese; but in the field of writing, Chinese influence was less fortunate. Japanese is a language of simple phonetic structure but polysyl-

The Five-Storied Pagoda and, to its right, the Kondo (Golden Hall) of the Horyuji Monastery near Nara, dating from the seventh century and probably the oldest wooden buildings in the world.

labic, highly inflected words. It can be written easily by phonetic symbols. The Chinese writing system is not adapted to phonetic transcription or the representation of inflections, however. It lacks inflections, and in ancient times the words were mostly monosyllabic. As a consequence, the Chinese found it possible to develop and hold to a writing system in which all the individual words were represented by unique symbols, originally of pictographic origin, which we usually call characters and are known in Japan as *kanji* ("Chinese writing"). These characters range from a single line ⎯⎯• to represent "one" to the calligraphic monstrosity in twenty-five strokes 灣 representing the word "bay" and forming the *wan* of Taiwan.

The Chinese student has always been faced with the grim necessity of mastering several thousand of these characters before he could be considered literate. In addition to this problem, the ancient Japanese were faced with the added difficulty that the Chinese writing system was not suited to the writing of their language. Had Japan been the neighbor of some Western or South Asian country using a phonetic script such as our own alphabet, the Japanese would have quickly learned to write their native tongue with efficiency and ease. Unfortunately, geographic accident decreed otherwise, and the Japanese were burdened with the most cumbersome of writing systems. Like the youth of China, the young people of Japan were sentenced generation after generation to years of mentally numbing memory work simply to learn the rudiments of writing.

Because of the tremendous prestige of all things Chinese and the difficulty of adapting Chinese characters to the writing of Japanese, the early Japanese made little effort to write their own language. Proper names and brief poems in Japanese were spelled out laboriously with one Chinese character used phonetically for each syllable, but little else was attempted. Instead, the Japanese wrote in straight and often reasonably good classical Chinese. Using Chinese much as medieval Europeans used Latin, they wrote their histories, geographies, law books, and official documents of all sorts. They even attempted to imitate Chinese literary forms, and men of education prided themselves on their ability to compose poems in Chinese.

The great transformation of Japan from the late sixth until the early ninth centuries is all the more remarkable for having been achieved through the difficult medium of the Chinese writing system. This writing system, more than anything else, gave an unmistakably Chinese, or East Asian, cast to Japanese civilization, and even today the use of Chinese characters appears to Westerners to be among the most colorful and distinctive aspects of Japanese culture.

3

THE DEVELOPMENT OF
A NATIVE CULTURE

The period of greatest learning from the continent lasted from the late sixth century until the middle of the ninth, but then a subtle change began to take place in the Japanese attitude toward China. The prestige of all things Chinese remained great, but the Japanese were no longer so anxious to learn from China or so ready to acknowledge Chinese superiority. After three centuries of borrowing, elements from the Chinese system had become so thoroughly familiar to the Japanese as to have taken on a life of their own. There existed, at least in the capital district, a cultured society with its own political and social institutions, patterned of course after Chinese models, but changed to fit Japanese needs by conscious experimentation and slow, unconscious modification. The Japanese were no longer a primitive people, overawed by the vastly superior continental civilization and eager to imitate anything Chinese. Japan was reaching a state of cultural maturity that made it ready to develop along its own lines. The emphasis shifted from borrowing more new things to adapting and assimilating what had already been acquired.

A contributing reason for the lessened interest in learning from China was the political decay that became marked in the T'ang dynasty as the ninth century progressed. In 894 it was decided not to send a proposed mission to China because of the turmoil in that land.

Merchants and Buddhist monks continued to travel between the two countries, but there was a decided lessening of contact between them for the next few centuries, and the resulting increase in Japanese isolation hastened the cultural modifications already well under way in the islands.

One of the clearest signs of increasing divergence from Chinese patterns was the development during the ninth and tenth centuries of an adequate way of writing Japanese. The new writing system evolved from the use of certain Chinese characters in greatly abbreviated form as simple phonetic symbols devoid of any specific meaning in themselves. Since the Chinese characters each represented one monosyllabic word, the phonetic symbols derived from them stood for a whole syllable, such as *ka, se,* or *mo.* The result was a syllabary rather than an alphabet. Except for a final *n,* Japanese syllables all end in vowels, limited to the five basic vowels, *a, e, i, o,* and *u,* pronounced as these are in Italian.

The Japanese syllabary, or *kana* as it is called, was at first a confused affair. For one thing, the Chinese characters used were abbreviated in two different ways. In one system, called *hiragana,* the whole character was written in a stylized or cursive form. Thus the Chinese character 奴 meaning "slave" became the *hiragana* symbol ぬ standing for the sound *nu.* In the other system, called *katakana,* some element of a character was chosen to represent the phonetic value of the whole. Thus this same Chinese character for "slave" became the *katakana* symbol ヌ, also standing for *nu.* Another complexity was that the choice of characters for abbreviation as *kana* was at first quite haphazard, and usually several were used for any one syllable. In fact, both *hiragana* and *katakana* became standardized only about a century and a half ago, and variant forms are still sometimes used in everyday correspondence.

The Japanese syllabaries formed more clumsy writing systems than alphabets, but they were reasonably efficient for writing Japanese, and with their development there appeared a literature in the native tongue. As noted before, even at the height of the Chinese period, poems had been composed in Japanese and laboriously written down by the use of unabbreviated Chinese characters to represent each syllable phonetically. It was in this way that the 4,516 poems collected around the year 760 in a great anthology known as the *Man'yoshu (Collection of a Myriad Leaves)* were recorded. The new *kana* were much simpler, and the courtiers and their ladies developed a veritable craze for jotting down poems on almost every conceivable occasion and exchanging them in their frequent love letters. The best of these poems were collected by the court in the *Kokinshu (Ancient and Modern Collection)* of 905 and in twenty later imperial anthologies over the next five centuries.

Most of the poems were quite brief, following a strict pattern of thirty-one syllables called the *tanka* (short poem). The *tanka* was too slight to do more than suggest a natural scene and, by some deft turn of phrase, evoke an emotion or some sudden insight. Within its narrow limits, however, it could be both delicate and moving.

The *kana* syllabaries also made possible more extensive literary works in Japanese. In the tenth century stories, travel diaries, and essays appeared, written in a Japanese that sometimes achieved considerable literary distinction. For the most part, educated men, much like their counterparts in medieval Europe, scorned the use of their own tongue for any serious literary purpose and continued to write histories, essays, and official documents in Chinese; but the women of the court, who usually had insufficient education to write in Chinese, had no medium for literary expression other than their own language. As a result, while the men were pompously writing bad Chinese, their ladies consoled themselves for their lack of education by writing good Japanese—and created, incidentally, Japan's first great prose literature.

The golden age of the first flowering of Japanese prose was the late tenth and early eleventh centuries. Most of the writers were court ladies living in ease and indolence, and the commonest form of literary expression was the diary, liberally sprinkled with "short poems." Some of the diaries told of travels, but more often they concerned the intrigues, ceremonials, and constant flirtation and lovemaking that characterized court life at this time. The outstanding work of the period, however, was not a diary but an extremely lengthy novel, the *Genji Monogatari (The Tale of Genji),* written by Lady Murasaki early in the eleventh century. This is an account of the love adventures and psychological development of an imaginary Prince Genji. It is not only the earliest example of a major genre of world literature but, both in the original Japanese and in the magnificent English translations by Arthur Waley and Edward Seidensticker, it constitutes one of humanity's major literary achievements. The diaries and novels by

Sekai Bunka Photo

Section of one of the Genji Scrolls, illustrating the early eleventh-century novel The Tale of Genji.

court ladies were clear evidence of the development of a true native Japanese culture. They had no prototypes in Chinese literature and were entirely Japanese. The transplanted Chinese civilization had flowered into a new culture, and the Japanese, a people only recently introduced to the art of writing, had produced a great literature of their own.

One may wonder why Japanese writing is still burdened with Chinese characters, if a thousand years ago the Japanese had already developed a phonetic script well suited to their language. The only explanation is the continuing prestige of China and the Chinese language. Most learned men continued to write in Chinese, but as their knowledge of the foreign tongue declined during the period of lessened contact with China, *kana* additions crept increasingly into their bastard Chinese texts. Others inserted Chinese words written in characters into Japanese *kana* texts. The result of both tendencies was the development of a hybrid writing system that has become the standard written Japanese of modern times. In it, nouns and other uninflected words and the roots of verbs and adjectives are represented by characters insofar as possible, leaving for *hiragana* the inflections and whatever else cannot be conveniently written in characters. *Katakana* is reserved for foreign names and words not deriving from Chinese characters or for terms we might put into italics.

The inevitable complexities of such a system of writing have been compounded by other factors. Chinese characters, having come to Japan over a prolonged period of time and from different dialectical areas in China, often are pronounced in more than one way in Japan, few of them very close to the original Chinese pronunciations. In addition, they are used not just for borrowed Chinese words, but also for Japanese words of corresponding meaning. It is as if the Chinese character for "water" 水 were to be used in English to represent the word "water" and also to represent the element "aqua" in "aquatic." Many characters also represented Chinese words that corresponded in meaning to several different Japanese words. For example, the Chinese word *shang,* written by the character 上, has Japanese equivalents variously read as *ue, kami, agaru, ageru,* and *noboru,* to list the commonest, just as it has such English equivalents as "on," "above," "upper," "to mount," and "to present."

The coexistence of both Japanese and Chinese readings for most characters and the multiplicity of Japanese readings for many means that every line of modern Japanese presents a series of miniature problems in reading and interpretation. Moreover, thousands of technical and scholarly words have been manufactured out of Chinese lexical elements, though often in Japan itself, much as North Europe has coined words like "telephone" out of Mediterranean word roots. Unfortunately, many of the word compounds produced from Chinese words in this way are identical as pronounced in Japanese. For example, an abridged dictionary lists no fewer than twenty distinct words of Chinese type all pronounced *kōkō.* This is one reason why new words in Japanese and many substitutes for older ones are now often taken from more distinct English words and written in *katakana.*

The current Japanese writing system is dismayingly complex, and this situation cannot be easily corrected. Chinese characters have worked themselves deeply into the whole culture and have acquired for the Japanese artistic and psychological values they would be loath to abandon. Since World War II the number of characters in common use has been drastically reduced, and the writing of many of them has been considerably simplified. Although the use of characters seems on the whole to be slowly declining, the system remains probably the most difficult and cumbersome in common use anywhere in the world and is not likely to be changed significantly in the near future.

The spectacular development of a native Japanese literature was accompanied by equally profound changes in other fields. The arts of painting, sculpture, and architecture began to show distinctive Japanese characteristics. In art, the Japanese displayed a flair for abstract design and for narrative scroll paintings, which depicted court ceremonials and the histories of monasteries and of warfare. In architecture, they showed a clear preference for buildings set in natural surroundings, instead of the stately, balanced architecture of China.

Significant changes also began to occur in borrowed Chinese political and economic institutions. The whole system from the start had been much too complex and sophisticated for the needs of the relatively small and backward land Japan still was. The wonder is not that the system began to break down, but that the Japanese had succeeded in adopting as much of it as they had. Even in China, the central government was constantly fighting the natural tendency of taxpaying peasants and lands to gravitate to the estates of influential families or for power to slip into the hands of factions at court or of semiautonomous local magnates. In only recently centralized Japan, these tendencies were even harder to resist, and a breakdown of the system was all the more inevitable.

The key defenders of central government power in the Chinese system were the bureaucratic scholar-officials. The system of selecting these men mainly through competitive scholastic examinations was only just being perfected during the seventh century. Because of the newness of this system even in China and the especially strong sense of hereditary aristocratic rights in Japan, the Japanese could not bring themselves to adopt wholeheartedly the Chinese concept of a bureaucracy based on educational merit. They used this system mostly for the selection of minor clerical functionaries and normally left the top government posts open only to those of high birth. This meant that a powerful bureaucracy did not develop and actual control remained in the hands of those families in the best position to misuse it for their own benefit. The court nobles also proved reluctant to leave the pleasant life at the capital to take up assignments in the provinces. Already in the eighth century they began to send deputies in their place, thus leaving the provinces much less closely regulated by the court than they should have been

A more deep-seated problem was the keeping of tax lands in production and equitably divided among the peasants who bore the tax burden. The introduction of agriculture as part of Yayoi culture had produced a veritable population explosion, which kept the islands comparable to or ahead of the major countries of Western Europe from then until today. The economic and administrative innovations absorbed from China from the sixth century on seem to have continued this trend of rapid population growth at least through the first third of the eighth century, but then an unwelcome import from the continent reversed the picture. Japan's maritime isolation and sparse contacts with the outside world seem to have kept it relatively free from serious worldwide epidemics, but now increased intercourse with the continent suddenly brought waves of diseases to which the Japanese had not yet built up immunities. Between 735 and 737 smallpox swept the land, in much the way the Black Plague ravaged medieval Europe, killing perhaps a quarter or a third of the people. Subsequent epidemics periodically repeated the tragedy, until by the end of the twelfth century the islanders had developed adequate immune systems.

During these centuries of fluctuating population, it was difficult to maintain the rigid Chinese type of land ownership and taxation. Because of epidemics, dikes, sluices, and other water works needed for paddy rice farming would fall into disrepair, and as a consequence cultivated fields would be abandoned. Rapid population growth between epidemics would necessitate the restoration of the fields by any means possible. Before the adoption of the Chinese system, the large work units of the *uji* may have adequately met comparable situations on a local scale. The nationalized Chinese system, however, was less flexible. What was needed was more local initiative and variation.

The government attempted various countermeasures. Most important was its decree in 743, shortly after the great smallpox epidemic, to permit land ownership in perpetuity to families that restored fields to productivity, but this measure, of course, undercut the whole Chinese system. In 749 some great monasteries at the capital were granted estates, known as *shoen,* to help defray their expenses. Such *shoen* proliferated, particularly in areas where much of the agricultural land had been abandoned, and some of them fell into the hands of nonclerical officials.

From the original adoption of the Chinese land holding and tax system, the aristocratic families of the capital region and the provinces had retained the bulk of their lands as tax-free rank, office, and special merit fields (the same system had applied in the early T'ang). Since these families controlled the large numbers of peasants needed to restore fallow fields and open new lands, they, together with the great capital monasteries and Shinto shrines, took the lead in establishing new *shoen*. The aristocrats were also well placed to win official recognition of their new holdings and increase their tax-free status, sometimes obtaining for them the right to immunity from official inspection.

One way the *shoen* grew was through the commendation of lands to them by harried taxpayers, much as happened in early feudal Europe. Commendation was resorted to because the rental payments to the new proprietors were less than the earlier tax payments had been, and the powerful new owners had the influence and know-how at court to arrange such legal changes.

In this way between the ninth and twelfth centuries much of the agricultural land was gradually transformed from taxpaying public domain into *shoen*. Often made up of scattered tracts of ricefields, these estates were sometimes owned by powerful provincial families, but more commonly by the great court families and major Buddhist and Shinto institutions of the capital region. The *shoen* system was quite complex. Rights to income from the estates, called *shiki*, were divided among a whole hierarchy of persons or institutions. At the bottom was the actual cultivator, with his family workers and hired hands. Above him was the controller of the estate, usually a family of local prominence acting, in theory, merely as the manager for the proprietor. The latter, as we have seen, was usually a great court family or religious institution. In many cases, above the proprietor would be a protector, that is, some even more powerful family or religious institution. This system of multiple incomes from a single piece of land is reminiscent of conditions in medieval Europe.

Even those areas that were not turned into *shoen* but remained part of the public domain and were under the control of the provincial governments took on many of the characteristics of the estates. Appointments as governors of certain provinces became the hereditary right of particular families and were looked on as a fixed source of family income. The governors in turn often assigned the functions of local control over their lands to aristocratic provincial families, often on a semihereditary basis. Thus the control of these lands and income from them were privatized in much the same way as those of the estates.

The net result of all this was a steady loss of income and functions on the part of the central government. Most of the movement of goods throughout the country was no longer based on tax payments to the central government but on the payment of rents and fees on private estates or on public lands to the noble families and religious institutions of the capital area. The elaborate Chinese-style central government had progressively less to do, and as a result increasing emphasis was placed instead on the ceremonial aspects of government. From the late eighth century on, a few relatively simple organs of government were developed to handle more efficiently the remaining functions that the government did perform. From time to time, efforts were made to recapture the control once exercised by the central government and to stem the growth of *shoen,* but always without success in the long run.

Although the power and institutions of the central government gradually atrophied and a number of noble families and religious institutions became its multiple successors as the real controllers of the land, Japan's insularity saved it from foreign conquest, and the antique religious aura of the imperial family saved it from usurpation, as might have occurred under comparable conditions in China or elsewhere in the world. One of the noble families, however, did win almost complete control over the imperial line, much as the Soga had a few centuries earlier. This was the Fujiwara, descended from Nakatomi Kamatari, one of the two main leaders of the Taika coup of 645. The family was nearly snuffed out when Kamatari's four grandsons all fell victim to the smallpox epidemic of 737, but subsequently their descendants returned to prominence and by the ninth century had come to hold most of the top government posts. Like the Soga, they also intermarried with the imperial line, and in 858 Fujiwara Yoshifusa became the regent for the child emperor, who was the son of one of his daughters. This was the first time anyone outside the imperial family had occupied this position. Yoshifusa's adopted son and heir, Mototsune, likewise became regent in 876, and in 884, when an adult came to the throne, he invented for himself the new post of *kampaku,* or chancellor, to describe the position of a regent for an adult emperor.

The Fujiwara family so dominated the court during the next two centuries that the period from 858 to 1160 is commonly called the Fujiwara period. The family was at its height from 995 to 1027 under the leadership of the glorious Michinaga. At this time Lady Murasaki described in her *Tale of Genji* the culturally sophisticated and languorous life of the court aristocracy.

Nothing could have been further from the imperial autocracy and bureaucratic power of the centralized Chinese political system than the picture Lady Murasaki gives of the heyday of the Fujiwara. Nor did the Japanese described in her novel bear much resemblance to those of the *uji* system of primitive times. But the life, culture, and political system of the Fujiwara period clearly derived a great deal from both of these earlier societies. It was a welding of the two into a new and distinctively Japanese culture.

Occasionally the imperial family challenged Fujiwara leadership, but never with lasting success. The emperor Uda, who was not born of a Fujiwara mother, made a valiant effort in the late ninth century, and from 1069 up to the thirteenth century abdicated emperors frequently had the final say at court. Since the headquarters of retired emperors were known as *in,* their rule was called *insei.*

Despite the efforts of some retired emperors, the Fujiwara retained the posts of regent and chancellor and normally had control over the court, which they maintained until the great political transformation of 1868. The rise to power in the late twelfth century of a provincial military aristocracy greatly curtailed the authority of the Fujiwara and their government, but a surprising degree of prestige and authority lingered on, with the court remaining important until the sixteenth century. Only in an isolated, tradition-bound country like Japan could a powerless government have continued to exercise so much influence for so long or a purely symbolic imperial line have survived usurpation. In fact, it was during the Fujiwara period and its aftermath that a typically Japanese pattern of rule through figureheads became normal: It became the rule rather than the exception for the person or group in nominal control to be the pawn of some other more directly powerful person or group.

4

THE BIRTH OF A FEUDAL SOCIETY

During the tenth and eleventh centuries, while the spotlight was on the Fujiwara and the brilliant literary and artistic accomplishments of the court they dominated, others offstage were preparing the next acts in the drama. The capital aristocrats had transformed the borrowed civilization of China into a native culture, but they had lost control over the political and economic life of the country. While they were going through the forms and ceremonies of little more than a sham government and devoting their energies more to the arts of poetry-writing and lovemaking than to governing, local military aristocrats were gaining practical experience managing the provinces and *shoen*, and controlling the peasants on them, with little direction from the capital. The somewhat decadent, effeminate courtiers at Kyoto were producing a literature and art that future generations would look back to with pride, but their less sophisticated and hardier country cousins were laying the foundations for an entirely new Japan.

The decline of Chinese-type political institutions and the weakening of the central goverment's control over the provinces make the period of Fujiwara supremacy appear to have been one of unmitigated political decline. In reality, the political decay at court was offset by the growing political experience and general sophistication of the once-backward provincials. During the height of the Chinese period, they had hardly participated in the brilliant culture transplanted from T'ang to the capital district, and they had been completely overshadowed by the noble families at court. Little by little, however, they absorbed many of the basic skills and much of the culture of the continental civilization, and by the eleventh century they had reached a stage of development that permitted them to start laying the foundations for a new society and a new political structure. The population's increased immunity to most epidemic diseases by this time also set the stage for renewed population growth and a resultant surge in the economy.

The central figure in the new society, as in the *uji* society that had preceded the period of borrowing from China, was the aristocratic fighting man on horseback. In ancient times he had been the warrior leader of the *uji*. Now, in the twelfth century, he was a local official or the manager of a tax-free *shoen*, defending his lands from marauders by his skill as a horseman and his prowess with bow and sword. Dressed in loose-fitting but efficient armor made up of small strips of steel held together by brightly colored thongs, he had become a close counterpart of the knight of early feudal Europe.

As late as the twelfth century, these provincial warriors accepted the capital at Kyoto as the source of all legitimate rights to land or to local government positions. Their chief economic contacts with other areas were still based on the payment of rent to estate proprietors and protectors in the capital area and the shipment of tax payments from public lands. But the central government was no longer in a position to give them protection from banditry and lawlessness, and for this purpose they began to join together to defend their own interests. Such bands were often only small family or local groupings, but larger units gradually formed around particularly prestigious leaders. The most obvious source of prestige was close association with the court, especially the imperial family. Distant branches of the imperial family had been reduced to the status of commoners by being given family names and had often gone to the provinces as officials to make their fortunes. Families of this type were in a particularly advantageous position to build up warrior bands personally loyal to them. The usual names given such imperial offshoots were Taira (also called Heike) and Minamoto (also known as the Genji). Some of these Taira and Minamoto branch families attained considerable local prominence.

Early signs of the rise of warrior cliques were to be seen in the wide-scale fighting in both the Kanto region in the east and in the

Inland Sea area that culminated in 940 and 941 in the destruction of so-called rebel forces. Between 1028 and 1087 a particularly distinguished line of Minamoto gained prominence in eastern Japan, first by crushing a "rebel" Taira family and then by crushing two other prominent warrior families in northern Honshu. At times, these particular Minamoto were called on by the Fujiwara to protect their interests in Kyoto from great religious institutions nearby, which had developed their own military forces on the *shoen* they owned and which sought, through a joint display of Buddhist relics and military might, to overawe the court. Similarly, a line of Taira warriors that had its seat of power in the Inland Sea area was relied on by those retired emperors who challenged Fujiwara power in the eleventh and twelfth centuries.

Despite their virtual monopoly of military power, the provincial warriors did not question the authority of the Kyoto court until the middle of the twelfth century, when they were called into the capital area to decide by force succession disputes within the imperial and main Fujiwara families. Brief military encounters occurred in 1156 and in the winter of 1159–1160 between various leading members of the two prominent Taira and Minamoto lines. These left Taira Kiyomori the victor in unchallenged military control of the capital. He took advantage of this situation to settle down in Kyoto, have himself and family members appointed to high court posts, marry his daughter to the emperor, and in 1180 put his own grandson on the throne. Thus

Mounted and armored warriors, attacking a Kyoto palace in the fighting that took place from 1159 to 1160, as shown in a thirteenth-century picture scroll of the war.

he established his dominance over the court in much the same way the Fujiwara had done three centuries earlier.

Kiyomori, however, failed to build up and consolidate his own warrior band, relying instead on his control over the traditional seat of authority. But the warrior class, particularly in the distant Kanto, was eager to gain complete control over its lands, free of interference from Kyoto. Kiyomori had also failed to stamp out the rival main line of the Minamoto. The heir to it, Yoritomo, grew to manhood in the custody of a minor Taira family, called the Hojo, in the mountainous Izu Peninsula on the edge of the Kanto Plain. Taking advantage in 1180 of a call for help from a rebellious imperial prince, Yoritomo challenged the authority of the Taira and the Kyoto court. He did this simply by asserting his own right to appoint local government officials and estate managers in the Kanto region. Most of the leading warriors of the area, who were largely of Minamoto stock, responded quickly by shifting their allegiance to him, seeing in him a local source of authority better able and more likely to protect their interests than the distant court. Military leaders from all over the country soon followed suit.

This sudden break with tradition gave rise to a wave of lawlessness throughout the country, as local warriors saw a chance to increase their authority and wealth at the expense of absentee proprietors and protectors. Minamoto bands closer to the capital than Yoritomo's attacked Kyoto, eventually seizing the capital in 1183 and driving the Taira back to their strongholds along the Inland Sea. The imperial court then appealed to Yoritomo to restore order. His younger brother, Yoshitsune, quickly seized Kyoto and then, after a pause, drove the Taira westward, annihilating them early in 1185 in a naval battle at Dannoura at the western extremity of the Inland Sea. All the remaining military bands of western Japan quickly bowed to Minamoto supremacy. Four years later Yoritomo dispatched a large force against a Fujiwara family that controlled most of northern Honshu from its brilliant provincial capital at Hiraizumi, north of the present Sendai, and through its destruction completed the conquest of the whole country.

Yoritomo was now in unquestioned military control of the whole land, but he carefully avoided the mistakes Kiyomori had made. He eschewed high posts in the imperial government, and by taking for himself in 1192 the title of *shogun*, an old term for commanders in wars against the Ainu in the north, implied that he was merely the general of the central government's army. He also remained at the headquarters he had established at Kamakura, now a seaside resort and suburb of Tokyo, building there, in the heart of his area of power, his own military government. In a sense, Japan now had two separate governments, each handling its own sphere of activities and not inter-fering with the other. But Yoritomo's government, in reality if not in theory, was clearly the controlling power. It came to be known as the *bakufu*, or "tent government." This term, commonly translated in English as "shogunate," became the generic name for all later gov-ernments of the warrior class. Since Kamakura was the only real locus of power, people soon brought to it all legal cases, even though they involved rights to governorships and estates derived in theory from the imperial court.

Yoritomo's *bakufu* had a quite simple structure, even though it bore a heavy burden of litigation. A legal code for warrior families, known from the "year period" as the Joei Code, was drawn up in 1232, but basically the new regime depended on the customary law that had been growing up throughout Japan. The whole basis of government was the rather one-sided bond of personal feudal loyalty to Yoritomo on the part of the members of the Kanto warrior class who had joined his cause and other local military men who had been allowed to enlist as his "vassals" or "honorable housemen" (*go-kenin*). The reward for their loyalty was his guarantee of their rights to property and posts as managers of estates or as local officials. To many of them he gave the new position of *jito*, which also carried with it rights to *shiki*, or income. *Jito* was a term just coming into use and signified various degrees of managerial, police, judicial, and other authority over es-tates or public lands. Land and positions confiscated during the war against the Taira and in later disturbances provided ample openings for positions of this sort; other openings were created by confiscations from warriors of dubious dependability or simply by giving *jito* as a new title to existing local officers.

The *jito* differed from the earlier managers and local officials in that their authority derived exclusively from Kamakura, not Kyoto. Since they had the military and judicial power of Kamakura behind them, they had a good chance to increase their income and authority at the expense of absentee proprietors and protectors, as well as the local

SEA OF JAPAN

HOKKAIDO

Hiraizumi •

HONSHU

KOREA

Kamakura
Mount Fuji
IZU

Kyoto •
(Osaka) • Nara
Yoshino

INLAND SEA

HAKATA BAY

SHIKOKU

PACIFIC OCEAN

KYUSHU

MEDIEVAL JAPAN

0   200 Miles

officials who lacked Kamakura's backing. Starting in the 1190s, the *bakufu* also began the regular appointment of *shugo* (the word means "protector") in most of the provinces. Their duties were to lead the other local "housemen" of Kamakura in suppressing crime and rebellion and in providing guard services in Kyoto. Throughout the country, the bulk of the most desirable posts as *jito* and virtually all the appointments as *shugo* went to warriors from the Kanto. There was also a clear policy of favoring families of relatively lowly origin but unquestioned loyalty over families of older or more distinguished lineage who seemed more likely to challenge Kamakura's authority.

At first the Kyoto court welcomed the suppression of the lawlessness let loose by the five-year war between the Taira and Minamoto, but soon it realized that inevitable erosion of its own authority was being caused by the new system. An emperor, believing that much of the warrior class was chafing under the control of the *bakufu* and would join his cause, "revolted" against Kamakura in 1221 in what has been called the Jokyu Disturbance, but he was easily suppressed and exiled from court. Kamakura took this opportunity to expand greatly its control throughout western Japan, and a *bakufu* headquarters was established within Kyoto itself.

The Kamakura *bakufu* remained throughout a thinly spread, small organization. It consisted of only a few thousand personal vassals of the shogun, scattered mainly as *jito* throughout the country and organized under the loose supervision of the provincial *shugo*. Above the *jito* and *shugo* were a few small administrative and judicial bodies at Kamakura, supervising this whole fragile system of rule. Despite its simple structure, however, the Kamakura system proved quite effective; it survived two major crises and lasted a century and a half, until 1333.

One crisis was the disappearance of the Minamoto line of shoguns. In theory, the whole system depended on the personal loyalty of the "housemen" to the shogun, and yet the Hojo family, which had been the custodians of Yoritomo, managed to do away with the Minamoto and take over control of the Kamakura government as regents for a purely symbolic shogun. Yoritomo himself, fearing the rivalry of his close relatives, had had them destroyed, including Yoshitsune, the chief general in the fighting against the Taira. After Yoritomo's death in 1199, his Hojo widow, Masako, together with her father and later her brother, became the chief powers in Kamakura. Together they engineered the deaths of Yoritomo's two sons and placed an infant

Fujiwara in the post of shogun in 1219. After 1252, imperial princes were used in place of Fujiwara nobles to play this symbolic role.

The Kamakura period thus demonstrated in extreme form the tendency for rule from behind the scenes. An emperor at Kyoto was merely the puppet of a retired emperor or a Fujiwara regent, whose sham government was in fact controlled by the private military government of a shogun, who in turn was the puppet of his Hojo regent. The Hojo also demonstrated another lasting characteristic of the Japanese political system—the tendency for joint rather than individual rule. The regent was joined from 1224 on by another leading member of the Hojo family who acted as a "co-signer." Other key posts, such as the controller of the Kyoto headquarters, were shared by two men, while most key decisions were made by boards of councilors in Kamakura.

The other great crisis of the time was the most serious threat of aggression from abroad that Japan was to experience before the twentieth century—the attempted Mongol invasions of 1274 and 1281. The Mongols, a nomadic people of the steppe lands north of China, conquered in the first half of the thirteenth century all of Central Asia, southern Russia, and much of the Middle East, and their armies penetrated through Hungary to the Adriatic Sea. At the eastern end of this vast empire, they completed the subjugation of Korea in 1259 and crushed the last organized resistance in China itself in 1276. In the east, only Japan remained free of their rule. When the Mongol emperor Kublai Khan sent emissaries to Japan demanding capitulation, the terrified courtiers of Kyoto were ready to accede. But the warriors of Kamakura refused and made their stand unmistakably clear by beheading some of the emissaries.

Such a direct affront could not go unpunished; in 1274 a strong Mongol force set out on Korean ships to subdue Japan. Certain small islands were seized and a landing was made at Hakata Bay near the modern city of Fukuoka in northern Kyushu. Before any decisive engagement could be fought, however, the Mongols decided to withdraw their fleet to the continent because of the threat of the inclement weather. That they would return was a foregone conclusion. For the next several years Kamakura kept many of its vassals from the western part of the country on guard in northern Kyushu and busy constructing a wall around Hakata Bay to contain the vaunted Mongol cavalry.

The Mongols did come again in 1281, this time with a great joint armada of Korean and Chinese ships, and again a landing was made at

Mongol soldiers aboard ships in their invasion of Japan in 1281, as portrayed in a picture scroll by a Japanese artist of the time.

Hakata Bay. The invading forces are estimated to have numbered about 140,000 men, the greatest overseas expedition the world had as yet seen. The Mongols were accustomed to large-scale cavalry tactics, which had met no match anywhere in the world, and they had superior weapons at their disposal, such as the gunpowder bomb hurled by a catapult. Against this overwhelming force, the Japanese had a mere handful of knights accustomed only to single combat. But the Mongols were slowed by the wall the Japanese had built and by the attacks of smaller Japanese boats, which maneuvered more easily in the narrow waters of the bay. Before the Mongols could deploy their full forces ashore, a typhoon descended upon the fleet and destroyed it, bringing the invasion to a disastrous end. To the Japanese, the typhoon was the *kamikaze*, the "divine wind," protecting the land of the gods from foreign invaders. The incident has, of course, loomed large in Japanese historical memory and contributed to the irrational conviction many Japanese once had that their land was sacred and inviolable.

The period between 1156 and 1221 marked an epochal change in Japan and the start of seven centuries of rule by military men. Until 1180 the old imperial government and the estate system it had produced had remained basically intact, despite the shifting of much of the real military power to local warrior bands and the Taira usurpation of power at Kyoto. The Minamoto, however, created a new source of authority and, while outwardly recognizing the legitimacy of the old imperial government, developed new institutions that, like a cancer, were consuming the old body politic. An entirely new type of government was growing up within the increasingly empty shell of the old, making use of the old institutions but based on fundamentally different principles—those of feudalism. The basic cement of government had become the lord-vassal relationship of personal loyalty on the part of one man or family to another; political positions were becoming identified with the relationship of persons to control over and income from agricultural land; most positions were becoming openly hereditary; and a new aristocracy of warriors, while paying deference to the old court elite, was clearly in control of the country.

The theoretical supremacy of the imperial government and the survival of many of its functions and rights make the Kamakura period not fully feudal, but the resemblance to the feudalism of Western Europe was striking and was to become progressively more so. The origins of the two systems were also probably much alike. In both cases, they seem to have grown out of a special blending of concepts of centralized imperial rule with native traditions of tribal organization and personalized bonds of loyalty. In Europe these two ingredients came from the Roman Empire and the Germanic tribal background of the peoples of North Europe; in Japan they came from T'ang China and the *uji* form of organization of primitive Japan. Apparently this exact blend is an unusual one in world history, because Japan affords the only close and fully developed parallel to Western feudalism.

There were, however, many differences between the two systems. Feudalism came a little later in Japan than in Europe, paralleling between the late twelfth and sixteenth centuries much the same course Western Europe followed from the ninth through the thirteenth, and the conditions of high feudalism, corresponding, say, to eleventh- and twelfth-century France, were not achieved in Japan until the beginning of the sixteenth century. This lag in Japan may have resulted from the lack of external pressures, which allowed a slower and more spontaneous transition from imperial to feudal institutions. In both areas, however, the feudal system was strongly legalistic at first, and at their heights both stressed the obligations and promises of the lord as well as the vassal, in order to try to keep the allegiance of the latter during an age of constant warfare. But the difference in the backgrounds of the two feudal systems—the strong legal concepts of Rome versus the emphasis on ethics in Confucian China—perhaps made the tone of feudalism more legalistic in the West and more moralistic in Japan. As a result, Japanese feudal relationships were commonly phrased in absolute terms and described like the relations between father and son, while in the West an emphasis on feudal rights proved to be the background for the later development of democratic institutions.

Japanese feudalism was to survive, at least in outward form, far past the sixteenth century—in fact, until the middle of the nineteenth. As we shall see, this late feudalism, which again was probably attributable to Japan's relative isolation, was quite different from anything Europe ever experienced. Because of the long duration of feudal rule in Japan, it is small wonder that the impress of feudalism lay heavily upon modern Japan. It can be seen in the strong military traditions of the Japanese in the late nineteenth and early twentieth centuries and in their unconscious assumption as late as the 1930s that military men were somehow less selfish and more honest than civilians and therefore had a right to political authority. Even today there are survivals in the strong master-disciple and boss-client relationships to be found in certain areas of Japanese society.

The warrior class brought with it an ethos quite different from that of the previously dominant court nobility. The military man gloried in a life of warfare, in the Spartan virtues, and in the ascetic practices of self-discipline and physical and mental toughening. He put great store on loyalty and personal honor and prized bravery, valor, and frugality. He made a cult of his sword, a cult kept alive as late as World War II by Japanese officers who proudly lugged cumbersome traditional swords into the jungles of Southeast Asia. His outstanding virtues— endurance in adversity, a great capacity for unswerving personal loyalty, and dogged perseverance in achieving a goal—became characteristics that still are observable among the Japanese. While the sensitive and slightly effete society of the late Fujiwara period seems quite remote from modern Japan, even the early feudal system is clearly recognizable as the ancestor of the Japan we have come to know in modern times.

Although the Gempei War, as the Taira–Minamoto conflict was called, came at the very beginning of the Japanese feudal age, it has always been looked back on as the time when the ideals of warrior society were established. Its incidents became a major theme of much of later Japanese literature. The custom for warriors to commit suicide in a hopeless situation, at first to avoid disgrace and torture but later more to demonstrate loyalty, started at this time and became a sort of ideal. The approved method of suicide, known as *seppuku* (or more vulgarly *harakiri*, "belly slitting"), was a particularly painful way to die but was well calculated to display contempt for the enemy and loyalty to one's lord. It has been glorified and romanticized ever since and even today may help account for the Japanese fascination with the subject of suicide.

The ascendancy of the warrior class naturally brought with it cultural as well as political shifts, but much less markedly so. There was naturally a new emphasis in literature and art on war and the value system of the military man, but otherwise most of the trends in poetry, prose, architecture, and painting went on little affected by the political transformation, and in the field of sculpture there was a renaissance of the classic traditions of the Nara period. For example, the 49-foot bronze Great Buddha (*Daibutsu*) of Kamakura, which is of virtually equal size but far greater beauty than the Great Buddha dedicated at Nara in 752, dates from the middle of the thirteenth century. Basically, there was a continuity of cultural trends between the Fujiwara and Kamakura periods. This was probably because the rising military society lived so long side by side and in close contact with the old court. The warrior leaders of Japan, unlike many of their European counterparts, were not cultural boors but prided themselves on their literary talents, fine calligraphy, and poetic skills. It is not surprising, therefore, that the classic arts and literature continued to have a major influence on Japanese society throughout the feudal period and until modern times.

A profound shift in Buddhism, however, was going on during this period, though for the most part quite independently of the political changes. Buddhism had come from India to China and then to Japan as a highly intellectualized philosophy with a rich literature, glorious art, and colorful ceremonies that appealed to the upper classes. Early Indian Buddhism had stressed the pain and vanity of human existence. It accepted the common Indian belief that the individual is reborn again

The Great Buddha (Daibutsu) *at Kamakura, cast in the middle of the thirteenth century. The temple building housing it was swept away by a tidal wave.*

and again into this world, with his status in each life depending on his actions in previous existences. The Buddha taught that this endless and painful chain of causality, or *karma*, could be broken only by overcoming the desire for life and, through this enlightenment, achieving a sort of salvation, known as *nirvana*. This was the merging of the individual ego with the cosmos, much as a drop of water loses its identity in the vastness of the sea.

These concepts, which seemed unduly pessimistic to most Chinese and Japanese, had become considerably modified during their long journey across Asia from India to China and were further modified in China itself. This more diverse set of beliefs was known as Mahayana, or the Greater Vehicle, but even these concepts appealed at first to the Japanese much less than the art, ceremonies, magical powers, and general Chinese culture that accompanied Buddhist philosophy. Up through the eighth century, the six so-called Nara sects of Buddhism were largely confined to the court aristocracy, but two new sects introduced from China early in the ninth century proved to have a more popular appeal. Both were brought back by monks who had accompanied the embassy of 804 to China.

One of these monks was Kukai, better known as Kobo Daishi (Daishi means "great teacher"), who introduced the Shingon, or True Word, sect, establishing it at his headquarters on Mt. Koya, on the southern rim of the capital area. Shingon was an esoteric (meaning "secret") sect, emphasizing magic formulas, incantations, masses for the dead, and other ceremonials, as well as an elaborate iconography and pictorial representations of Buddhist philosophy. Under Shingon leadership, the deities of Shinto were identified as the local Japanese manifestations of universal Buddhist deities. The two religions became so thoroughly intertwined, theologically and institutionally, that it was not possible to disentangle them from each other until the nineteenth century, and then only by government fiat.

The other monk returning from the embassy of 804 was Saicho, better known as Dengyo Daishi, who introduced the Tendai sect at the great Enryakuji monastery he established on Mt. Hiei just northeast of Kyoto. Tendai teachings were all-inclusive; they treated esoteric Shingon and all other forms of Buddhism as differing levels of Buddhist truth, fitted to different levels of individual understanding. Because of its broad intellectual base and the strategic location of its chief monastery, which looked down on the capital, Tendai became the source of most later sectarian developments in Japanese Buddhism.

Through these two new sects, Buddhism began to spread much more widely among the people. Starting in the late tenth century, strong emphasis was placed on the concept that history was entering a degenerate age when people could no longer achieve salvation themselves but had to rely on faith, particularly in the Buddha Amida. The nature of salvation also shifted from the extinction of self as in the original idea of *nirvana* to a belief in an afterlife in the Pure Land Paradise of Amida. Such concepts of achieving salvation through faith, curiously enough, were closer to basic Christian tenets than to original Buddhism. But they were strong enough to predominate not only among the common people but also at the court.

The spread of this emphasis on salvation through faith may have fitted the age of serious epidemic diseases, and the decline of epidemics by the Kamakura period and the resultant increase in population and improvement of economic conditions also fit in well with a great social and geographic spread of Buddhism. There seems to have been a general heightening of culture at this time among the lower classes throughout the country. This is suggested not only by their increased participation in Buddhism but also by the fact that commoners, who had been notably absent from the classic art and literature of the earlier Chinese age, began to be depicted in painting and then in literature from the eleventh century on.

The belief in winning salvation by calling on the name of Amida became embodied in sectarian form in the Jodo, or Pure Land, sect, founded by the monk Honen in 1175. The teachings of his greatest disciple, Shinran (1173–1262), led to the founding of another sect called the True Pure Land sect, or simply Shinshu, the True Sect. Shinran taught that there was no way to salvation except through faith and the wholehearted calling on Amida's name, known as *nembutsu*. He preached "the equality of all in Buddhism," saw no special role for the monkish life, and thus advocated marriage for the clergy. Later followers emphasized writing Buddhist texts for the common people in Japanese rather than traditional Chinese. They also made the sect the largest one of all and built its lay congregations into powerful secular bodies, which at points in the fifteenth and sixteenth centuries challenged the warrior class for political leadership.

Another popular sect was founded in 1253 by Nichiren (1222–1282) and bears his name. Of very plebian origin, Nichiren was intolerant of all other forms of Buddhism, insisting that the only way to salvation was by calling not on Amida but on the *Lotus Sutra*, a Buddhist scripture that promised the ultimate salvation of all living creatures. Naturally, his followers frequently came into conflict with other sects and with the political authorities. He also showed a strong nationalistic streak, claiming that Buddhism had degenerated in India and China and that his brand of Japanese Buddhism was the only truth. The intolerance and fighting spirit of Nichiren is still reflected today in the vigor of Soka Gakkai, a recent Nichiren offshoot which is the largest of the post-World War II religious movements.

While the faith sects were popular with all classes and served in particular as mediums of self-expression for the lower classes, there was also at this time another new and distinctive Buddhist movement, which was significant in another way. This was Zen, which means "meditation." Meditation as an important Buddhist practice goes far back in India and China and had been introduced much earlier into Japan, but in the Kamakura period it was given sectarian expression by two monks who had studied in China. In 1191 Eisai brought the Rinzai sect of Zen, which emphasized sudden enlightenment through *koan*, or meditation on insoluble or even nonsense problems. Dogen introduced the Soto sect in 1227; he emphasized enlightenment through *zazen*, or long periods of "sitting in meditation." Zen received special favor from the Kamakura *bakufu* and its successors, perhaps because it was institutionally new and not connected with the powerful and rich earlier sects. Its character-building disciplines also came to appeal to the warrior class and became a lasting element in the Japanese personality.

5

GROWTH AND CHANGE IN THE FEUDAL SYSTEM

The Kamakura system, however effective for a while, was peculiarly susceptible to the ravages of time and change. It depended on the personal loyalty of a band of warriors who had originally come for the most part from the Kanto and were knit together by old ties and the fact that Kamakura, not Kyoto, was the source and guarantor of most of their property and power. As the generations passed, this sense of personal loyalty declined among their descendants, now considerably increased in numbers and scattered as *jito* throughout the whole land. Loyalty for them was more likely to be directed toward personally known strong local leaders, particularly the families holding the post of *shugo*, rather than toward distant Kamakura and its purely symbolic shogun.

Another factor in the decay of the system was the custom of dividing a warrior family's income, which was normally in the form of *shiki* revenue from the office of *jito,* among all the sons and even daughters. As a result of such divided patrimonies, many knightly families, while still owing service to Kamakura, could ill afford the military equipment of a mounted warrior and the feudal services expected of them. Long years of preparation against the actual and anticipated Mongol invasions made the situation particularly severe for the warriors of Kyushu, on whom the main burden had fallen. There was deep dissatisfaction because defense against external enemies, unlike the defeat of internal foes, produced no rewards in the form of new lands to be parceled out to deserving warriors. The financial situation of some of Kamakura's vassals had become so bad by the late thirteenth century that many were seriously in debt. On occasion the *bakufu* tried to aid them by ordering the cancellation of warrior debts, as was most notable in the sweeping order of 1297, which was euphemistically called *tokusei,* or "virtuous government."

Because of the gradual erosion of the loyalty of the warrior class to the Hojo-dominated *bakufu* and resentment at the increasing domination of Kamakura by that family, the whole system collapsed quite suddenly when it was challenged in 1333. An emperor known as Go-Daigo (or Daigo II) had developed the anachronistic idea that the emperors themselves should rule, and Ashikaga Takauji, the head of a Kanto *shugo* house of distinguished Minamoto lineage who was sent to suppress him, simply shifted sides. Another Kanto leader of similar lineage and status then marched on Kamakura and destroyed the Hojo.

While Go-Daigo futilely attempted to restore imperial rule, these two generals fought each other for military supremacy, and Takauji emerged victorious. Meanwhile he had broken with Go-Daigo, who fled from Kyoto in 1336 and set up his court at Yoshino in the mountains on the southern edge of the capital area. Takauji placed a member of a rival branch of the imperial family on the throne, giving Japan two imperial courts, a "northern" one at Kyoto and a "southern" one at Yoshino. The half-century during which this situation existed is known as the period of the Northern and Southern Courts, a term taken from a similarly named period in Chinese history. It was ended only in 1392, when the third Ashikaga shogun, Yoshimitsu, persuaded the southern court to return to Kyoto on a promise—which was never honored—that it would alternate with the other line on the throne.

Meanwhile Takauji and his successors had been busily attempting to restore a new *bakufu* to exercise centralized control over the military class. Takauji made Kyoto his headquarters and obtained for himself the title of shogun in 1338, but there could be no thought of rewelding the whole warrior class into a single band of vassals loyal to the Ashikaga in the manner of the Kamakura system. Instead, the Ashikaga attempted to create a three-tier form of feudalism in which the various *shugo,* assigned the control of one or more provinces, would be the shogun's vassals, and they in turn would control the lesser warriors of their repsective provinces, while also staffing the few simple organs of central government set up in Kyoto.

Many of the *shugo* were cadet branches of the Ashikaga family, and for a while in the late fourteenth and early fifteenth centuries the *bakufu* did operate as a reasonably effective central government. It was at its height under Yoshimitsu, who became shogun at the age of ten in 1368 and dominated the *bakufu* until his death in 1408, even though he abdicated the position of shogun in 1394. He and some of his successors tried to exercise despotic rule and achieve a position like that of the kings of early modern Europe. The shogunate, however, started to decline seriously after the ruling shogun was assassinated in 1441, and it lost all control over the country during the Onin War, which swept all of Japan from 1467 until 1477. For the next century Japan was plunged into incessant warfare. The Ashikaga shoguns, however, continued to occupy their now largely symbolic post until 1573, much like their powerless fellow Kyoto residents, the emperors and Fujiwara regents. The whole period from 1333 to 1573 is commonly known either as the Ashikaga period or as the Muromachi period from the location in northern Kyoto of the Ashikaga headquarters.

Apart from a short period of apparent stability, the Ashikaga shogunate was far from being an effective central government for most of the more than two centuries that bear its name. It exercised little or no control over distant *shugo*, and it was usually under the domination of the powerful *shugo* near the capital, who developed hereditary rights to the top *bakufu* posts. These families frequently fought one another for domination of the shogunate or were engaged in internecine succession wars of their own. In fact, it was succession disputes among some of the leading *shugo* families that were chiefly responsible for the outbreak of the Onin War, which marked the end of all effective central control.

The weakness of the government and the almost incessant warfare during the Ashikaga period suggest the possibility of general economic and cultural decline, but this was far from the case. There was a marked growth in technology and in the economy as a whole throughout the Kamakura and Ashikaga periods, both undoubtedly stimulated by growing population and increased contact once again with the continent. There had never been an end to the movement of traders and monks between Japan and China, but it seems to have expanded rapidly from the late twelfth century on. A sign of this was the introduction of the Zen sects in the early Kamakura period by monks returning from China, and Zen monks played a large part in both commercial and cultural contacts with China during the Ashikaga period. Japanese merchants also began to play a larger role than before. Coming as they did from a militarized, feudal land, it is not surprising that their activities often shaded off into piracy. They would simply take by the sword what they could not get by trade. These Japanese pirate-traders, known as *wako,* laid waste the coasts of Korea during the fourteenth century, and then shifted their main area of activity to China during the next two centuries.

Because of the Ashikaga hope of reaping the benefits of the lucrative trade with China and the desire of the Ming dynasty in China to put a stop to Japanese piracy, a system was worked out in 1404, after several decades of diplomatic overtures on both sides, for a limited number of Japanese ships to go periodically between the two countries with tallies provided by the Chinese court attesting to their legitimacy. Between 1404 and 1547 some eighty-four Japanese ships went to China as part of this so-called tally trade. The Chinese saw the system as fitting into their concept that the other nations of the world were subservient to the Chinese empire and had to pay it tribute if they wished to be considered part of the civilized world. To the lasting shame of Japanese historians, Yoshimitsu and his successors not only sent "tribute" but were willing to accept investiture by the Chinese emperors as "kings of Japan." The Ashikaga, however, did not in fact control much of the tally trade, except during the first few years. Most of the ships were financed by other prominent warrior families or religious institutions, particularly Zen monasteries, as well as by private merchants. The Japanese had little regard for the Chinese concept of a controlled tributary trade and were intent only on making profits, and so they continually sent more ships on more occasions than the official agreement called for. The bulk of the exchange of goods with China, moreover, was carried on by unauthorized ships and pirates, and a flow of trade also grew up with Korea by way of Tsushima Island and with China by way of the Ryukyu Islands, the modern Okinawa.

Foreign trade was only one of the aspects of economic growth during this time. The indebtedness of the Kamakura *jito* was a sign of a growing money economy. There was a marked decline of barter in favor of the use of currency, which was largely in the form of copper coins from China. But money drafts also came into wide use. The slow breakdown of the *shoen* also gave rise to wider trade patterns within the country and the development of periodic marketplaces all over the land, as well as trading ports along the coast. Pawnbrokers, moneylenders, and wholesale merchants became prominent elements in the society of the time. The political fragmentation of the country led to the creation of toll barriers on the roads, set up by petty feudal authorities. But such fragmentation was at least in part offset by the development of manufacturing and trading guilds, known as *za,* which protected themselves through monopoly rights, guaranteed by the patronage of prestigious families and institutions associated with the old imperial court. Such guilds flourished particularly in the environs of Kyoto, the economic as well as political heart of the country.

Marked technological advances were also evident during this period in increased rice yields per acre and in the development in all parts of Japan of many small specialized centers of production for papermaking, weaving, metalworking, and the like. While raw materials, such as copper, remained the fundamental Japanese exports to the continent, and imports were largely manufactured goods, such as minted coins, silks, art works, and books, the export of some manufactured items to China, chiefly swords and painted folding fans and screens, showed that Japan was catching up with China technologically. The finely laminated steel swords of Japan, in fact, were the best the world has ever seen and were in great demand abroad. Some 30,000 are recorded to have been shipped to China in a single tally mission, to the consternation of the Chinese authorities.

The location of the *bakufu* in Kyoto, together with the continued decline of the imperial court, resulted in the transfer of leadership in cultural matters from the court to the Ashikaga. In fact, some of the shoguns proved much more noteworthy as cultural than military leaders. Even the strong Yoshimitsu set the artistic tone of his day, and his monastic retreat in the northern hills of Kyoto, with its gorgeous Golden Pavilion (Kinkakuji) built in 1397, made Northern Hills (Kitayama) the name for the culture of his time. Similarly, the Eastern

Hills (Higashiyama) culture of the eighth shogun, Yoshimasa (1436–1490), derived its name from his monastic retreat in the eastern hills of Kyoto, where he built his smaller but subtly beautiful Silver Pavilion (Ginkakuji) in 1483.

The Ashikaga shoguns strongly favored the Rinzai sect of Zen, probably seeing it as a balance to the rich, landed monasteries of the older sects. Takauji relied heavily on a Zen cleric, Muso Soseki, in religious, artistic, and even political matters. The Ashikaga, following a Chinese precedent, designated five great Zen monasteries in the capital to be the official Gozan or Five Monasteries, and this practice developed into an elaborate system of ranking Zen monasteries throughout the country, centering around what grew to be eleven major ones in Kyoto.

Zen monks were active in the official tally trade with China, and they were the carriers of many new influences that reflected the cul-

Late sixteenth-century garden at the Sambo-In temple in Kyoto.

Consulate General of Japan, New York

tural achievements of China during the Sung dynasty (960–1279). They revived Japanese interest and skills in the Chinese language and literature, introduced the revised Confucian teachings of Sung times known as Neo-Confucianism, popularized Sung styles of monochrome landscape painting, and took the lead in the type of landscape gardening that reached its perfection in the gardens of the Kyoto Zen monasteries of this period and is now copied around the world. They also introduced Japanese to the drinking of tea, which at first was looked on as an aid in meditation but by the late sixteenth century had become an elaborate esthetic ritual. The so-called tea ceremony, together with flower arrangement, which also derives from medieval times, were to become part of the training of every cultivated girl in modern Japan.

The refined artistic taste of the Ashikaga court and its Zen monks left a lasting impression on Japanese esthetics. It emphasized what was natural, irregular, small, and simple in preference to things that were artificial, shaped by man, large, and grandiose. It displayed a disciplined cultivation of the essence—the handful of blossoms or branches in a flower arrangement; the simple instruments and spare, graceful movements of the tea ceremony; the sometimes austere design of the gardens, which in limited space called to mind the vast wonders of nature; and the few bold lines of paintings that suggested sweeping landscapes and vast cosmic powers. It was an esthetic that complemented the emphasis on discipline and self-cultivation the feudal Japanese had derived from Zen and the warrior ethos. It was also an esthetic peculiarly suited to the relative simplicity and poverty of medieval Japan. It is interesting that in recent years it has proved to have worldwide appeal in our own more complex and affluent age.

While the Ashikaga court was dominated by Zen esthetic tastes and new Chinese artistic influences, an even greater part of the culture of the time grew from native and often quite popular roots. The domestic architecture of the age, with its entranceway, sliding paper doors, *tokonoma,* or recess for the display of art objects, and thick reed mats (*tatami*) covering the whole floor space of rooms, is essentially the domestic architecture of modern times. In literature the traditional forms continued, though with declining vigor, while new and more plebian trends became more typical of the age. Well-known stories and historical incidents recited by blind lute players and others became popular, as did tales of ghosts and goblins. Great epic accounts of warfare were particularly popular, such as the *Heike monogatari*

("Tale of Heike") of the early thirteenth century, which recounts the rise and fall of the Taira family, and the *Taiheiki* ("Record of the Great Peace") of around 1370, which tells of the incessant conflict of the period of the Northern and Southern Courts. In poetry the practice of linking endless chains of verses composed in turn by two or more persons became a veritable craze. Governed by elaborate rules and calling for great skill and wit, these *renga,* or "chain poems," were clearly derived from the classic thirty-one-syllable "short poem," alternating as they did the two basic components of the "short poem"— two 7-syllable lines and three lines of 5–7–5 syllables.

The most important literary development of the time was the Nō drama, which grew out of old and simple popular dramatic forms but was perfected into a highly literary, stylized type of drama at the court of Yoshimitsu. Nō featured a bare stage, a chorus, a limited number of actors who chanted their lines, and a stately dance by the main actor as the climax. The subject matter was usually popular Shinto or Buddhist beliefs, often exemplified through well-known incidents of history. Nō survives today in its classic form and continues to have a small circle of devotees.

The collapse of the *bakufu* and of all central power at the time of the Onin War (1467–1477) ushered in a century of rapid change in which Japan was in many ways made over politically and socially. Great changes in the whole nature of the warrior class and its economic foundations had actually been going on for a long time before the war broke out. Throughout the Kamakura period the *jito* had taken every opportunity to increase their income and power at the expense of the old proprietors of the *shoen* or local authorities who were not Kamakura vassals. The proprietors, in a desperate effort to hold on to as much of their income as possible, were often forced into various types of disadvantageous compromises. Among the commonest of these in the late Kamakura period were agreements to the equal division, between the proprietor and the *jito,* of the income from an estate. The endemic warfare of the half-century of the period of the Northern and Southern Courts gave warriors all over the country excuses to settle by arms their private quarrels with one another and to encroach further on the income and rights of the nonmilitary classes. Special military assessments of half the remaining income due the old proprietors became standardized in 1352 and 1368. This sort of erosion of the proprietory rights to the old estates and public lands continued throughout the Ashikaga period, until finally the Onin War and its aftermath of incessant fighting wiped out the last vestiges of the old system.

As the estates and public lands disappeared, the economic support of the warriors changed from *shiki* income as *jito* to the total revenue from the tracts of land over which they now had undisputed control. If a warrior was strong enough, he held this land with his own power; but in most cases he held it as a fief from some stronger warrior, to whom he owed in return his services as a vassal. Thus by the end of the fifteenth century the whole land had become completely feudalized.

Another great change in the warrior class had come from a gradual shift in military technology. Massed footsoldiers armed with pikes had become the chief force in battle, in place of the individual mounted knight, who now served more as a captain. This shift blurred the class lines between aristocratic fighting men and peasants. In the old days, only the rich few could afford the expensive accoutrements of battle, but now any sturdy peasant could become a pikeman. Armies grew much larger, and the lower classes could on occasion challenge the military domination of the upper classes.

The slow elimination of the *shoen* and the income from them all but wiped out the old imperial court and the aristocracy in Kyoto. The imperial family and a greatly shrunken court nobility suffered severe impoverishment, surviving on dues as patrons of the guilds in the capital area and later on the largess of leading military figures. The vestigial existence that the old imperial government still had was due primarily to the semireligious aura of the emperors and the continuing belief that only they could be the legitimate source of political authority.

The *shugo* system had never been very effective in controlling the provinces. Normally the area of theoretical authority of a *shugo* far exceeded his powers of control. Though responsible for one or several provinces, their own lands tended to be scattered and rarely constituted more than a small fraction of the total area of any of their assigned provinces. Some of the lesser warrior families in these provinces, known as *kokujin,* or "provincials," might be their vassals, but others were unattached military men who built up their own independent territories or formed leagues of small military families. The complete breakdown of central authority in the Onin War gave the "provincials" a chance to make a bid for more power. The next century in Japanese history is known as the period of the Warring States, again a name taken from an era in Chinese history, and was characterized by what the Japanese have called *gekokujo*—"the lower defeats the upper." Vassals overthrew their lords, and hitherto obscure "provincials" emerged as powerful new lords. Most of the *shugo* houses were replaced during this century by a new set of feudal leaders in control of smaller but much more consolidated domains.

These new feudal lords came to be known as *daimyo*. Though their domains might be quite small, all the warriors in them were clearly their vassals. The confusion of the European feudal system, in which men often held fiefs from more than one lord, was never tolerated in Japan. The daimyo domains and other feudal holdings had also become consolidated through the development of the custom of unitary inheritance by a single heir—a system comparable to primogeniture, though not quite the same because the heir was not necessarily the eldest son. A daimyo's vassals were enfiefed by him with their own lands or, as increasingly became the case, were simply salaried soldiers and administrators gathered around his headquarters, which was usually a centrally located castle. All the other people, peasant and merchant alike, were similarly under the daimyo's control, the merchants supplying him with materiel and transport for war and the peasants paying taxes to him or his vassals and providing extra footsoldiers when needed. "House codes" often spelled out the organization and laws of a domain. To the Europeans, who appeared in Japan in the middle of the sixteenth century, the daimyo appeared to be petty kings.

The daimyo, though fearing no higher authority, whether imperial or shogunal, were almost constantly at war with one another and at times had to deal with the military power of the lower classes. The southern commercial half of Kyoto fell under the control of the local merchants, and Sakai, now the southern part of the city of Osaka but at the time the chief entrepôt for trade on the Inland Sea and with China, became essentially an autonomous town. Peasant groups, particularly in the area around the capital, often marshaled military power to assert their rights. Political organizations of the common people were known as *ikki*, which in time came to mean "popular uprisings." Such disturbances became increasingly common in the fifteenth century, and they often forced the *bakufu* to issue *tokusei,* or "virtuous government" edicts, canceling the debts not just of the warriors, as in Kamakura times, but of all people.

Political groupings of the common people frequently centered around the temples and congregations of the popular faith sects. In Kyoto, Nichiren groups were particularly strong, but in other regions Shinshu predominated. It was known at the time as the Ikko, or "Single Minded," sect, and one hears a great deal of *Ikko-ikki,* or uprisings of its adherents. This sect even won military predominance in the province of Kaga north of Kyoto in 1488 and was recognized as the undisputed ruler of this province for several decades after 1531. The Shinshu sect also built a strong castle headquarters in the emerging port town of Osaka.

The rise of the footsoldier and of popular miltiary power posed a threat to feudal rule and typified the remarkably dynamic development of Japan at this time. Even though the Ashikaga period was an era of great political confusion and almost constant warfare, it witnessed extraordinary cultural innovation, institutional development, and economic growth. It saw the disappearance of all but the vestiges of the old imperial system and the emergence of a completely feudal society, comparable to that of high feudalism in Europe, though considerably better organized. The Japanese, who only a few centuries earlier had been a backward people on the edge of the civilized world, had grown to the point where they were able to compete on terms of equality with the Chinese and also with the Europeans, whom they were about to encounter.

6

THE REESTABLISHMENT
OF NATIONAL UNITY

The vigorous Japan of the first half of the sixteenth century still showed no signs of re-creating an effective central government, but the foundations for a new form of political unity had been laid. These foundations consisted of the daimyo domains, into which almost all of Japan was now divided. They varied greatly in size, but tended to be compact, well-defined political units. National unity could be achieved simply by establishing some form of association or accepted leadership among them. Naturally many of the stronger daimyo began to aspire to the creation of just this sort of unity by winning control over the rest.

The tendency was for stronger daimyo to reduce their weaker neighbors to vassalage or swallow them up completely. This process was probably hastened in the second half of the sixteenth century by the introduction of firearms from Europe. The first Europeans to reach Japan were Portuguese traders who landed on Tanegashima, an island off the southern tip of Kyushu, apparently in 1543. The Japanese at once took note of their guns, which were matchlock muskets, and began to imitate their manufacture and even improve on their technology. The use of guns soon became more prevalent in Japan than in contemporary Europe, and the winning side of a battle fought in 1575 had 10,000 matchlockmen in its force of 38,000, using them in serried

Consulate General of Japan

Central donjon of the Himeji castle near Kobe, the finest remaining example of a late sixteenth- or early seventeenth-century castle.

ranks to maintain a steady fire. The cannon introduced at the same time necessitated a new type of castle construction. In place of the many small hilltop castles that had characterized the preceding age, the Japanese began to build great fortresses made up of concentric circles of earth-banked stone walls surrounded by broad moats. Though the white-walled wooden structures that surmounted these walls were more decorative than defensive, the castle fortresses themselves were quite impervious to the firepower of the day.

With the aid of this improved military technology, the stronger and abler daimyo subdued their rivals at an even faster pace. The result was the relatively rapid reunification of Japan in the late sixteenth century. The process was achieved by three successive leaders, each building on the work of his predecessor. The first of these was Oda Nobunaga, a daimyo from a region east of Kyoto, who in 1568 seized the capital, ostensibly on behalf of a contender for the position of Ashikaga shogun, though his deposing of this man five years later brought a formal end to the Ashikaga *bakufu*. Meanwhile, Nobunaga had started to win control over the whole central region. He laid waste the Enryakuji, the great monastic headquarters of the Tendai sect on Mt. Hiei above the capital, and slaughtered its warrior monks; he destroyed the military power of the popular faith sects in the region, seizing the castle headquarters of the Shinshu sect in Osaka after a ten-year war; he forced most of the daimyo of central Japan to recognize him as overlord; and he abolished toll barriers and restrictions on markets in the areas under his control.

Nobunaga's career was cut short in 1582 when he was killed by a treacherous vassal, but his work of reunification was continued by his greatest general, Hideyoshi, a man of peasant origin who had risen from the ranks and only later in life assumed the aristocratic-sounding family name of Toyotomi. In 1587 Hideyoshi forced the submission of the great Shimazu domain of Satsuma in southern Kyushu and thereby won control over all western Japan. Three years later, after he destroyed the chief daimyo realm in the Kanto area, all of eastern and northern Japan submitted to him. After centuries of warfare and ineffectual central government, Japan once again had become a politically united nation.

Hideyoshi, recognizing that by tradition the post of shogun was open only to men of Minamoto descent, did not take that title for himself. But, claiming a shadowy Fujiwara ancestry, he did assume high court posts, including that of chancellor. In fact, he is known to history as the *taiko*, a term for a retired chancellor. Basing himself in Kyoto and the restored Shinshu castle at Osaka, he set about ruling the whole nation and putting order into its political structure. He started a great cadastral survey of the land in 1582 and on the basis of it assigned fiefs and duties to his vassals, moving them about quite freely. He standardized the currency and tried to monopolize foreign trade by insisting that ships could sail abroad only with his documents of authorization. In an effort to put an end to the warfare and popular uprisings that had characterized Japan for centuries, he decreed in 1588 the confiscation of all swords from the peasants, and in 1591 he issued orders that all warriors, peasants, and merchants must remain in their current occupations and positions.

After such a long period of warfare, Japan was naturally overflowing with military men, and it was possibly in order to lessen the dangers of this situation that Hideyoshi turned the interests of the military class to foreign campaigns, though his motives, of course, may simply have been those of the many men before him who had longed for more worlds to conquer. In any case, he embarked in 1592 on the conquest of the world, meaning for him China. He dispatched an army of about 150,000 men, which quickly overran Korea but was checked by Chinese forces near Korea's northern border and by Korean "turtle ships,'' probably the world's first armored vessels, which disrupted his lines of supply. In 1597 Hideyoshi renewed the attack, but the whole expedition was withdrawn when he died the next year.

Hideyoshi left only an infant heir under the protection of his five chief vassals, whom he had formed into a council, but the strongest of these men soon took power in his own name. This was Tokugawa Ieyasu, who had first achieved prominence as an ally of Nobunaga, protecting his eastern flank, and later, after Hideyoshi's subjugation of the Kanto in 1590, had been given by Hideyoshi a huge fief in that region. Here at Edo, the modern Tokyo, he had built a great castle headquarters, the central portion of which forms the contemporary imperial palace grounds. Ieyasu won his mastery over the country in a decisive battle in 1600 at Sekigahara, in a low pass between the capital area and the regions to the east, and he legitimized his position by taking the title of shogun in 1603. He made sure of his hold on the country in campaigns in 1614 and 1615 against the great Osaka castle, where the last adherents of the cause of Hideyoshi's heir were annihilated. Ieyasu, unlike his two predecessors, managed to stabilize the political situation and was able to pass his rule on to his heirs, who continued to occupy the position of shogun for more than two and a half centuries. The age from 1600 until 1867, therefore, is known either as the Tokugawa period or, from their capital, as the Edo period.

The system of rule that Ieyasu and his first two successors perfected in the first half of the seventeenth century was based on the daimyo domains that had grown up during the preceding century and on the methods of central control over them and the whole nation that Nobunaga and Hideyoshi had been developing. It was thus basically feudal in structure, but it represented a highly organized and stable stage of feudalism, unlike anything Europe ever witnessed. In fact, in terms of organization, efficiency, and order, it was, if anything, ahead of the contemporary kingdoms of Europe, at least until the late eighteenth century. This sort of highly organized, very stable, and relatively centralized feudalism is so at variance with the experience of Europe or even earlier feudal Japan that historians are unsure as to what it should be called, but it is probably best regarded as a stage of late feudalism that was unique to Japan and would have been impossible to maintain in any less isolated country.

Although in complete control of the country, the early Tokugawa shogun did not push ahead to an untried centralization of government of the type we know today, but instead made use of the thoroughly familiar daimyo system in order to bring quick stability to the land. The shogun reserved for themselves a huge realm consisting of about a quarter of the agricultural land of the country, located largely around their Kanto headquarters in Edo and the old capital region around Kyoto, but including also all the major Japanese cities, ports, and mines. The other three-quarters of the land was divided among theoretically autonomous daimyo, numbering 265 at the end of the Tokugawa period, and made up of three categories. First came the "related" daimyo, consisting of cadet branches of the Tokugawa family, including the three large domains of Mito, Nagoya, and Wakayama, which flanked the shogunal realm. Next came a relatively large number of *fudai*, or "hereditary" daimyo, who had been Ieyasu's vassals before 1600 and held relatively small fiefs, largely in the more central parts of Japan. Finally there were the *tozama*, or "outer" daimyo, who had been Ieyasu's allies or in some cases enemies at the battle of Sekigahara in 1600 and held for the most part relatively large fiefs at the western and northern ends of the islands, far from the strategically important central part of the country.

The domains of the daimyo varied greatly in size. They were based on the national cadastral surveys Hideyoshi had carried out and were ranked in terms of their rice production measured in *koku*, the equivalent of 4.96 bushels. The lowest yield that would qualify a man for the rank of daimyo was 10,000 *koku*, and the largest "outer" lord had a domain of 1,022,700 *koku*. Collectively, the more than 26 million *koku* yield of Japan was divided so that the shogun's realm and the domains of his "hereditary" vassals received slightly more than a quarter each, considerably more than a third went to the "outer" daimyo, and the remainder of about one-eighth was held by the "related" daimyo. Thus the Tokugawa coalition of shogun, "related" houses, and "hereditary" daimyo held well over half the agricultural land and virtually all the central and most strategic regions.

The Edo government, or *bakufu*, not only supervised directly the cities and the quarter of the land that constituted the shogun's realm, but also served as a supervisory government for the whole nation. In the fashion already pioneered by the Hojo of Kamakura, though in much more complex and highly developed form, it consisted of a series of councils; a number of two-man or four-man administrative posts, such as regional deputies and commissioners in charge of the various cities, financial matters, the control of religious institutions, and the like; a few intendants to supervise the shogunal lands; and a mass of petty clerical positions and military guard units. The top two councils, known as the "elders" and the "junior elders," which were in charge, respectively, of national affairs and matters relating to the shogunal realm, were made up of a few selected "hereditary" daimyo, who served as chairmen in monthly rotation. The lesser administrative posts, clerkships, and military guard groups were filled with minor direct vassals, or retainers, of the shogun. These were divided into two categories—almost 5,000 "standard bearers" (*hatamoto*) of relatively high rank and income and some 18,000 "honorable house men," who at the lower levels were footsoldiers with only subsistence salaries. The "related" houses, though providing shogunal heirs when the main line died out, did not normally participate in the Edo government, and the "outside" daimyo were strictly excluded from it.

As time passed, the majority of the shogun, coming to the post by heredity as they did, proved to be ineffectual leaders and gradually sank to a largely symbolic role, but the *bakufu* was a relatively efficient bureaucracy that could function even without shogunal leadership. The various posts in the government were open only to men of specific hereditary ranks, but since there were always many more eligible at each level than the posts available, it was possible to choose the more able ones for actual service, particularly in the higher positions. Men of outstanding ability, especially if they attracted the shogun's attention, might on occasion be raised in rank and income, thus qualifying them for higher posts. The availability of many candidates for most of the posts of importance gave rise in time to contending reformist and conservative cliques vying for power by winning the shogun's backing.

The general principles of the Tokugawa government and its control over the domains were spelled out in a code called Laws for the Military Houses, issued in 1615 and again in revised form in 1635. The domains, which later came to be known as *han*, were organized in

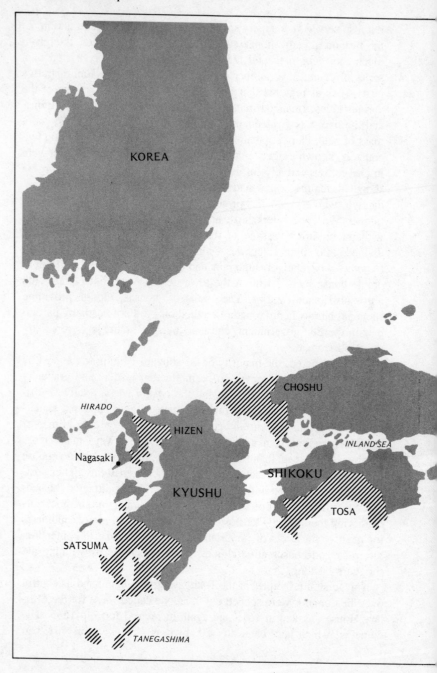

KOREA

CHOSHU

HIRADO

HIZEN

Nagasaki

INLAND SEA

SHIKOKU

KYUSHU

TOSA

SATSUMA

TANEGASHIMA

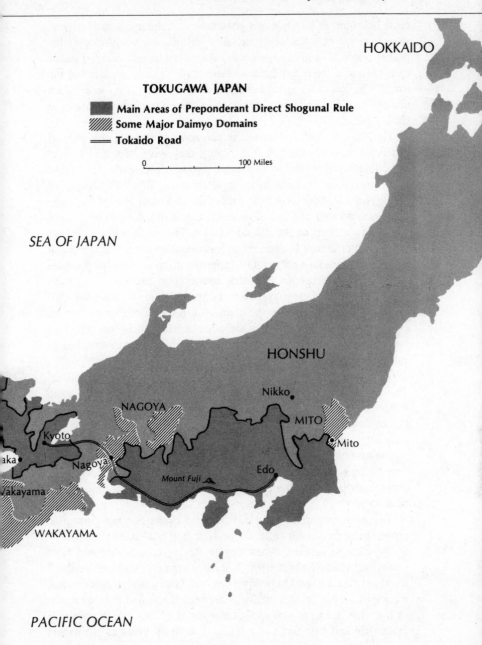

HOKKAIDO

TOKUGAWA JAPAN
- Main Areas of Preponderant Direct Shogunal Rule
- Some Major Daimyo Domains
- Tokaido Road

0   100 Miles

SEA OF JAPAN

HONSHU

Nikko

NAGOYA

MITO

Kyoto

Mito

aka

Nagoya

WAKAYAMA

Edo

Mount Fuji

Wakayama

WAKAYAMA

PACIFIC OCEAN

close imitation of the shogun's government. A daimyo's band of vassals consisted of a few chief vassals with subfiefs, who made up his higher councils, and lesser vassals, who were largely salaried rather than enfiefed, lived around his castle headquarters, and staffed the lower echelons of his government and made up his guard forces. Each domain had its own laws, but they were shaped to conform closely to those of Edo.

The daimyo were in theory autonomous in running the internal affairs of their domains, but in reality they were kept under strict surveillance and control by the central government and often treated as little more than its local officials. During the first half-century of Tokugawa rule there were 281 cases of daimyo being moved from one domain to another and 213 of the confiscation of a domain because of the lack of an heir or for alleged misrule. Though in later years both types of interference became much less frequent, the Edo government insisted throughout on its right to approve of all daimyo inheritances and marriages, restricted the castle construction and size of the military forces of the daimyo, prohibited direct relations between the various domains, and called on the daimyo for heavy contributions for the construction of its own castles and other public works. Naturally Edo considered all the armed forces of the domains as being subject to its call at any time.

The arbitrary moving about of the daimyo weakened their hold on the loyalty of the peasants they ruled but at the same time strengthened their control over their vassals and retainers. These military men had to move with their daimyo and, uprooted from their native soil, where their ancestors had once controlled both land and peasants, they were forced to rely entirely on their bonds to their daimyo. In the process, they became close-knit groups that presaged the business and other groupings that are such a predominant feature of contemporary Japanese society.

The most important way in which the domains were controlled proved to be the *sankin kotai*, or the system of "alternate attendance" of the daimyo in Edo. According to this system, which had been perfected by the 1630s, a daimyo spent alternate years in residence at the shogunal court and in his own domain. Great daimyo processions, especially on the Tokaido highway between Kyoto and Edo, were one of the more frequent and spectacular sights of the age. A daimyo's chief wife and heir had to be left in Edo at all times as permanent hostages. The *sankin kotai* system not only put a heavy financial burden on the daimyo by forcing them to maintain one or more large residences in Edo and make the costly annual trips there and back, but also tended to turn them and their families into Edo courtiers, somewhat out of touch with the people of their own domains.

In addition to controlling the whole military class in this way, the *bakufu* exercised strict supervision over the nonfeudal classes throughout the shogun's realm, which included the major ports of Osaka and Nagasaki and the old capital of Kyoto. It allotted a minuscule 187,000 *koku*, less than a tenth of 1 percent of the agricultural production of the land, to the support of the imperial court and its ancient noble families and only 600,000 *koku* to the maintenance of religious establishments, showing how far these once-great institutions had fallen in income and power. Desiring to stabilize social conditions, it strengthened the sharp lines that Hideyoshi had started to draw between occupational groups.

To support his effort to stabilize the country, Ieyasu found the theories of the great twelfth-century Chinese Neo-Confucian scholar Chu Hsi (Shushi in Japanese) to be of use, and he and his successors made a sort of Tokugawa orthodoxy of Chu Hsi's teachings. According to Confucian theory, society was divided into four classes: the scholar-rulers, or warrior-rulers in the case of Japan; the peasants, who were the prime producers of wealth; the artisans, who were the secondary producers; and merchants, whose function was seen as being basically parasitic, thus putting them at the bottom of society. This strongly agrarian bias naturally fitted the attitudes of the warrior class, which, having developed as a landowning aristocracy, was oriented toward agricultural production and land taxes rather than trade.

While little was done to enforce the divisions among the three lower classes, the lines between them and the top warrior-ruler class were made very sharp. This top class was a relatively large one, consisting of about 7 percent of the total population, larger by far than that in any feudal land in Europe. It is known in Japan by the generic term of *bushi*, "military families," but in the West usually by the more specific name of *samurai*, or "retainers." This top class was theoretically cut off from intermarrying with the lower classes. With the exception of the enfiefed members of its higher ranks, it had relatively little contact of any sort with the rest of the population, because it was congregated largely in Edo or at the castle headquarters of the daimyo.

It was distinguished from the lower classes by its right to bear family surnames, its special dress, and the two swords that men wore at all times as their badge of samurai status.

The unsettled conditions and the increasing military and political power of the common people in the century preceding the reunification of Japan had given promise of a more fluid society than the Tokugawa system turned out to be. The reassertion of firm control by a warrior class through an essentially feudal pattern of government has been seen by some historians as an unfortunate and anachronistic reversion to feudalism. But seen in another light, it was merely the standardization and perfection of known techniques of rule, which in a relatively short period of time produced for the Japanese a stable and carefully organized form of government, in many ways more efficient than the emerging nation-states of Europe. In any case, the Tokugawa system brought peace to Japan and proved capable of functioning with reasonable efficiency until the middle of the nineteenth century.

The maintenance of the political and social divisions and local autonomies of the Tokugawa system probably would have proved impossible if Japan had not reestablished relative isolation from outside pressures during this period. At first, this isolation was not the conscious policy of any Japanese ruler but resulted somewhat accidentally from the experience the Japanese had in their first contacts with Europeans and the Christian religion. Portuguese traders, who, because of their superior ships and seamanship, were coming to be important carriers of trade in Asian waters, continued to come to Japan after their first discovery of the islands in 1543, and by 1549 the newly founded Jesuit order started missionary work there. One of the great founders of the Jesuit order, St. Francis Xavier, was active in Japan from 1549 to 1551. He was followed by other able missionaries, many of whom were enthusiastic about the Japanese because of their responsiveness to Christianity and the fact that the Japanese feudal ethos made them much more understandable and admirable than other Asian peoples in the eyes of Europeans, who themselves were just emerging from their own long feudal experience.

To the Japanese, Christianity at first seemed to be a variant of the popular faith sects of Buddhism, and some Kyushu daimyo, noticing that the Portuguese traders tended to go where the Jesuit priests were welcome, embraced the new religion and ordered their subjects to follow suit. The port of Nagasaki, which was in time to become the chief contact point with the outside world, was founded by one of these lords in 1571 to attract the Portuguese trade. The Christian missionaries were also well received in the capital area, where Nobunaga saw them as allies in his fight to destroy the power of the Buddhist sects. For a while there was quite a craze for Portuguese things, and artists painted many scenes depicting the great ships, outlandish costumes, and somber black-robed priests of these *namban*, or "southern barbarians," who had approached Japan from the south. It has been estimated that by around 1580 there were some 150,000 Christians in Japan and perhaps twice that number in the early seventeenth century, which would be a larger percentage of the total population of Japan than is Christian today.

The missionaries' intolerance of other religions, however, resulted in strong resistance to them by the Buddhist clergy, and Hideyoshi,

A decorative screen showing "Southern Barbarians" landing in Japan.

Kobe Municipal Art Gallery

after reuniting the country, began to look on Christianity as possibly subversive to unified rule. The Japanese were not unaware of the Spanish political conquest that had accompanied the introduction of Christianity to the Philippines, and some of them began to fear that Christian loyalties directed toward a distant papacy could undermine a feudal system based on purely local loyalties. The Spanish began to come to Japan from the Philippines in 1592, bringing with them Franciscan friars, who quarreled with the Portuguese-dominated Jesuits. The Protestant Dutch in 1609 and English in 1613, who had no thought of proselytizing and were quick to criticize the Catholic Portuguese and Spaniards, also set up trading stations on Hirado, an island off the northwest coast of Kyushu, showing that trade with the Europeans could exist without tolerating their religion.

Even before the arrival of the Protestant Europeans, Hideyoshi officially banned Christianity in 1587 and in 1597 suddenly began to enforce this edict by crucifying nine missionaries and seventeen of their converts. At first Ieyasu was more tolerant. But in 1606 he began issuing anti-Christian edicts, and he started a full persecution in 1612, culminating in large-scale executions two years later. From then on the missionaries were methodically driven out and native Christians forced into apostasy or martyrdom. Suspects were made to trample on a Christian icon, known as a *fumie* or "treading picture." The Catholic church officially recognizes more than 3,000 martyrs in Japan, fewer than 70 of whom were Europeans. The final destruction of Christianity in Japan came with the defeat and annihilation in 1637–1638 of upward of 20,000 Christian peasants who, desperate over religious persecution and economic oppression, had broken out in revolt, basing themselves on an old castle at Shimabara in Kyushu. Christianity lingered on until the second half of the nineteenth century only in clandestine form in a few isolated Kyushu communities.

The suppression of Christianity soon led to the virtual isolation of Japan from the outside world. European traders were limited to Nagasaki and Hirado in 1616. In 1623 the English voluntarily closed their trading post as unprofitable. The Spanish were expelled the next year, to be followed in 1639 by the Portuguese. This left only the Dutch, who were confined in virtual imprisonment on the small island of Deshima in the harbor of Nagasaki. More important, in an effort to keep the virus of Christianity out of Japan, all Japanese were prohibited in 1636 from leaving Japan or from returning to Japan if already abroad, and ships large enough to sail to foreign countries were banned. As a result, sizable colonies of Japanese in Southeast Asia, who for a century had played a large role there as traders, pirates, and mercenaries, were left to wither away, and Japanese contact with the outside world was reduced to a strictly controlled trickle. Chinese traders and the Dutch could still come under careful restrictions to Nagasaki, and contacts with Korea continued through Tsushima and with China through the Ryukyu Islands. In the case of the Ryukyu Islands, which are inhabited by a branch of the Japanese people, the southern Kyushu domain of Satsuma had conquered the islands in 1609, making their kings vassals of the Shimazu daimyo of Satsuma but permitting them to continue trade contacts with China in the guise of tributary relations.

Japan, thus, was not completely cut off from the rest of the world, but it was isolated enough to remove all foreign pressures on the political and economic system. Japan slowly dropped out of the consciousness of the Europeans and began to lag technologically behind the now rapidly developing West. This situation, together with the reassertion of power at this time by a warrior class through a feudal type of political organization, has given rise to the concept that the Tokugawa period was a time of stagnation, but this was far from being the case. Peace and order brought rapid economic growth and a great increase in population. Japan was also large and diverse enough and had sufficient contact with the outside world to continue a rapid and even brilliant cultural development.

7

THE TRANSFORMATION OF THE LATE FEUDAL SYSTEM

The Tokugawa were supremely successful in achieving the political stability they sought. Between the mid-seventeenth and mid-nineteenth centuries they maintained conditions of absolute peace, internal as well as external, which is a record unmatched over a comparable period of time by any other large nation. No foreign war, revolution, uprising, or coup d'état in any way threatened their rule. People became accustomed to living peacefully according to accepted law and custom. The brawling, bellicose Japanese people of the sixteenth century gradually changed into an extremely orderly, even docile people. They learned to live together in their cramped islands with relatively few outward signs of friction. Nowhere in the world was proper decorum more rigorously observed by all classes, and nowhere else was physical violence less in evidence in everyday life. The peace and order of the land was broken only by occasional and sporadic outbursts of man and nature—great fires in Edo, destructive earthquakes, the last great eruption in 1707 of the now-extinct volcano of Fuji, an occasional outbreak by impoverished city dwellers (the worst was in Osaka in 1837), scattered riots by still more impoverished peasants demanding relief from crushing taxes or unjust officials—but nothing on a national scale and nothing that could shake the existing political or social order.

Perhaps the best idea of the carefully guarded political tranquillity of the time can be gained from the story of the only political incident that stirred the nation, at least emotionally, during these two hundred years and became a favorite literary and dramatic theme. This was the incident of the Forty-seven Ronin, which took place between 1701 and 1703. A minor daimyo was so grievously insulted by an important official of the shogun's court that in a rage he drew his sword and wounded his tormentor. To have drawn his sword within the castle grounds of Edo was an offense punishable by death, and the Edo authorities ordered the unlucky man to commit suicide and confiscated his domain. His feudal retainers lost their status as full-fledged samurai and became *ronin,* which was a term for a masterless samurai who had lost his normal place in society.

Forty-seven of these *ronin* vowed to take vengeance upon the lord who had caused their master's downfall, but realizing that the government would be watching for just such a move on their part, they decided first to lull its suspicions. They bided their time for two years, while their leader took up a life of debauchery to indicate that nothing was to be feared from him. Then, on a snowy winter night, they assembled in Edo, broke into the residence of their lord's old enemy, and avenged themselves by taking his head. By this act they of course flouted the authority of the *bakufu,* but their self-sacrificing loyalty to their master made them at once national heroes. After much debate, the government finally permitted them to atone for their crime by the honorable death of *seppuku.*

Tranquillity and order do not necessarily put an end to change. In fact, they can encourage peaceful evolution. The reunification of the land and then complete peace, which lasted from 1638 until the 1860s, naturally brought growth, and growth inevitably produced change. The outward political structure of the Tokugawa system was virtually the same in the mid-nineteenth century as it had been two centuries earlier. And yet, behind this unchanged façade, Japan altered a great deal internally. By late Tokugawa times, Japan was a far different country from what it had been at the beginning of the seventeenth century.

For one thing, a great increase in productivity had taken place. All the domains were naturally eager to expand the agricultural lands on which their wealth depended. This they did by the reclamation of swamps and other wastelands, which was particularly possible in the more peripheral, less densely inhabited areas. Agricultural technology also made steady progress, and by the late eighteenth century an extensive literature on improved farming techniques was being written. While the official production figures for domains tended to remain static after the middle of the seventeenth century, agricultural yields in many domains came in fact to far exceed these figures.

A steady improvement of technology and the consequent increase in production also took place in other economic fields, and trade grew by leaps and bounds, especially in the first century of Tokugawa rule. There were two main reasons for this rapid growth of trade. One was that all the major cities and much of the most advanced central part of the country were in the shogun's realm, which thus constituted a large free-trade zone. The merchants of this area, as the shogun's direct subjects, also enjoyed the *bakufu*'s protection in their dealings with the domains. The other reason was that the system of "alternate attendance" required all the domains to maintain costly establishments in Edo and pay for the expensive annual trips of the daimyo and their retinues to and from the shogun's capital. To obtain the necessary funds, no domain, however large, could maintain an isolated, self-supporting economy, as was their natural inclination, but had to produce excess rice or other specialized crops or manufactures for sale on the national market. The chief consuming areas were the great cities in the shogun's domain, such as Kyoto and Osaka, each of which had upward of 300,000 people, and Edo, which by the early eighteenth century had a population of at least a million and may have been the largest city in the world at that time.

Thus although Japan was politically divided in a feudal manner, it was economically united and developed the economic institutions appropriate to a unified economy. Most of the domains in western Japan maintained economic agencies in Osaka, which became the major entrepôt for trade in that part of the country, while Kyoto reestablished its position as the center of production for fine handicrafts. The economy became thoroughly monetized. Both the shogun's realm and some daimyo domains issued paper money, and paper credits of all sorts came into common use. Rice exchanges, with daily fluctuating quotations, developed at Edo and Osaka. People became accustomed to paying fixed prices in stores rather than haggling over each item, as was the rule everywhere else in the world until comparatively recent times. Toward the end of the period, landless peasants and other marginal groups worked increasingly for wages, rather than remaining in feudal subordination to some patron. All in all, the economy became far more commercialized and sophisticated than one would expect in a politically feudal land.

Though merchants were theoretically the lowest of the four classes, they came to play roles of great importance in the domains as well as in the shogun's realm by cooperating closely with the political authorities. Starting as brewers of *sake,* the Japanese rice wine, or as money-lenders or dealers in dry goods, many of the merchants of the shogun's cities built up extremely prosperous enterprises with branches in several cities. A good example is the house of Mitsui, which, starting in the early seventeenth century, survived the drastic changes at the end of Tokugawa rule to become one of the largest economic empires the world has ever seen. The city merchants took the lead in the expansion of trade in the seventeenth century, but then their economic activities leveled off, as Japan began to reach the limits of economic growth possible in an isolated country at its level of technological development. In the late eighteenth and first half of the nineteenth centuries, however, there was a new burst of commercial growth, this time led by rural entrepreneurs, who processed and sold the products of local agriculture, such as silk, indigo, and *miso,* or fermented bean paste.

During the seventeenth century, which was the period of most rapid economic development, the population more or less kept pace, almost doubling by the end of the century to close to 30 million, which was far in excess of any European country at that time. Thereafter, while improving technology and increasing levels of trade showed continuing economic growth, the population remained stable, producing what must have been an overall rise in standards of living, and thus defying the Malthusian law that population will always outstrip production. We have in modern times become accustomed to constantly rising living standards through a combination of the discovery of new lands to exploit, as happened in early modern times in Europe, rapidly improving technology, and more recently birth control, but Japan's case seems to be unique for an isolated premodern nation growing only slowly in technology.

What may explain this unusual situation is the Japanese system of inheritance through adoption. In most other countries, large numbers of children were necessary to ensure that at least one male heir would survive to continue the family line and provide the parents with security in their old age. In Japan, a daughter's husband, a relative's son, or some entirely unrelated person could serve through adoption as a perfectly satisfactory heir to the family farm or business or to the hereditary status and stipend of a member of the samurai class. Thus families could safely be kept small, even by infanticide if necessary, as happened among the poorer peasants. In any case, the Japanese population remained nearly static for a century and a half while production rose, and the Japanese probably became more affluent in per capita terms than any other Asian people. A sign of this can be seen in the rate of literacy, which in the first half of the nineteenth century may have risen as high as 35 percent, a figure quite comparable to that of Western countries at the time.

High literacy rates, to say nothing of economic growth, clearly indicated that society as a whole was far different from what it had been in medieval times. The change was probably greatest for the samurai, who had been transformed from rural, landowning warriors into peaceful city residents. Except for a few high-ranking retainers, who still held fiefs, the bulk of the samurai had been gathered into the shogun's capital or those of the daimyo. Castle towns grew up around every daimyo headquarters, becoming the foundations for the bulk of the middle-sized cities and prefectural capitals of today. Constituting about 7 percent of the total population, the samurai alone made up a considerable urban population, which was doubled by about an equal number of merchants and other commoners who gathered in these capital cities to perform necessary economic services. Japan, despite its feudal government, had thus become a rather highly urbanized land for that period of history, with some 10 to 15 percent of its total population living in towns and cities.

An even greater change for the samurai was their gradual transformation from a professional feudal warrior class into salaried civil bureaucrats and petty functionaries. They continued to prize highly their two swords and their warrior traditions, making a virtual fetish of swordsmanship and the concept of feudal loyalty, but in fact they earned their living basically as wielders of the writing brush rather than the sword. After 1638 they never again had a chance to practice their military skills in battle, and the use of guns, the chief weapon of the late sixteenth century, all but atrophied. Instead, samurai found education and the arts of civil administration of far more real value than military prowess. Though many remained simple guardsmen and a sort of reserve police force, by the eighteenth century an illiterate warrior samurai was a rarity, and most large domains eventually founded schools for the advanced education of their samurai in Confucian texts written in classical Chinese.

The status of the samurai class changed greatly during the Tokugawa period in still another way. At the beginning of the period the wealth of the nation was overwhelmingly agricultural and was in large part channeled through heavy taxation of the peasantry to the shogun and daimyo and through them to their salaried samurai. As the commercial economy grew, however, the samurai class, wedded to its feudal reliance on agriculture, received a diminishing proportion of the nation's wealth. Since standards of consumption were rising and city life became increasingly expensive, both the domains and their samurai fell heavily into debt to merchant moneylenders. This indebtedness of the top class to the theoretically lowest class was galling but was never corrected. The obvious solution—an adequate system of taxing trade—was never hit upon. Instead, various other schemes were tried, but without substantial success. The domains created monopolies to draw off the profits of certain particularly lucrative types of production, and the central government imposed fees on monopolistic associations of merchants. Sumptuary laws were repeatedly issued, and the salaries of the samurai were reduced to aid the finances of the domains. At times debts were canceled, and occasionally concerted efforts were made to stop or turn back the clock of economic change. The most notable efforts of this sort came in the 1720s and 1730s, again in the 1790s, and for a final time in the 1840s. The economic decline of the *bakufu,* the domains, and their samurai, however, continued unabated.

The reverse side of samurai decline, of course, was merchant prosperity. The *chonin,* or "townsmen," as they were called, naturally had to pay strict deference to the samurai class and abide by the government's rather harsh regulations, but they grew steadily in prosperity, managed their own internal affairs in the various villagelike units into which the commercial parts of the cities were divided, and developed a vigorous culture of their own in the larger cities. There were, of course, great differences in wealth between the different categories of townspeople, but the more affluent among them became thoroughly literate and quite cultured. The upper strata, which commonly worked closely with the government as its economic agents, were often given semi-samurai status, bearing family names and sometimes even wearing swords.

The bulk of the population remained in the countryside. But even for the peasants, life was changing. Villages had earlier replaced the *shoen* as the chief units of rural organization, and the draining of the samurai class from the land into Edo and the domain capitals and the establishing of sharp class lines between the peasantry and warriors, which had accompanied the reunification of the country, left these peasant villages in a far more autonomous position than ever before. The feudal authorities insisted on a strict enforcement of their laws through village headmen, whose selection they approved, and they held the villagers mutually accountable for each other's actions, but the peasants, in fact, were left quite free to handle their internal affairs. A village assembly, made up of representatives of all the land-owning families and in some cases tenant farmers as well, was the chief decision-making body. The villagers themselves selected the headman, always from among the top-ranking families in the village, to serve as the government's agent and their liaison with the authorities. Each village had its own codes and customary practices, which it enforced by such measures as ostracism, considered to be the most severe punishment.

The villages were, of course, heavily taxed by the *bakufu* and domains. The tax rate was extraordinarily high, being originally around 40 or 50 percent. It should be remembered, however, that this tax yield supported not just the government but the whole samurai class, the top 7 percent of society. Moreover, strange though it may seem, agricultural taxes were not substantially increased after the first half of the seventeenth century, despite the substantial growth in production. This situation obviously left a larger share of what was produced to the peasantry. A quarter or more of the villagers tended to be tenant farmers or dependents of the richer farmers, who were often relatively affluent. These richer peasant families were themselves often of proud lineage, having been warriors in medieval times but having decided to stay with their lands rather than move to the daimyo's headquarters at the time of national unification. Coming from such a background, they too bore family names and sometimes had the right to wear swords. They were usually literate, and the village commonly maintained a so-called temple school, so named because it was housed in a local Buddhist temple, in order to teach the rudiments of education to some of the village children.

This organization of rural Japan during the Tokugawa period had several important consequences. It provided a stable, well-ordered society in a countryside almost denuded of the ruling class. It produced the well-to-do peasant entrepreneurs who in late Tokugawa times increasingly concentrated on specialized cash crops and became the most dynamic commercial force of that period. It provided a class of sturdy, educated peasants who, after the collapse of Tokugawa rule, became the backbone of middle-level leadership and the emerging middle class in modern Japan. It left postfeudal Japan with no residue of estates owned by the old feudal aristocracy, like those that were prevalent in European countries until recent times. It also produced a growing class of tenant farmers, who, while providing the urban workers of modern days, also left a legacy of mounting social problems.

Despite the numerical preponderance of the peasantry and the political supremacy of the samurai class, it was the urban merchants who were in many ways the leaders in Tokugawa culture, and therefore it is not surprising to find the arts and literature of the time more the expression of their tastes than those of the other classes. The cities dominated Tokugawa culture, and in the cities the amusement quarters were the centers of social life. Here came the tired businessman and the "slumming" samurai for the free social contact with women denied them by the patterns of a society that confined women of breeding to their homes. This was the background for the development in more modern times of the *geisha,* the professional female entertainer, carefully trained in the arts of singing, dancing, and amusing conversation.

To a surprising degree, the art and literature of the time revolved around the amusement quarters. Artists of the Tokugawa period loved to portray the streets of these quarters and the famous beauties who lived there. The great seventeenth-century novelist Saikaku made the demimonde the usual subject of his amusing and somewhat risqué

Woodblock print of the amusement quarters in Edo.

novels. Thanks to the greatly increased use of printing in the
Tokugawa period, the novels of Saikaku and the works of other popular writers had a great vogue with city dwellers.

The drama of the age, like the novel, reflected the tastes of the city
merchants. A puppet theater developed in the seventeenth century
and, closely parallel to it, a new dramatic form known as Kabuki.
Both are still alive today. Kabuki stressed realism of action and of
setting. It utilized the revolving stage with great success, and the set-
tings it developed were in many respects superior to those of the West.
In sharp contrast to the slow-moving and sedate Nō drama of the
Ashikaga period, Kabuki maintained a high degree of emotional tension and dealt freely with melodrama and violence. The greatest of the
Tokugawa dramatists, Chikamatsu (1653–1724), drew both from
great historical themes and the social drama of contemporary city life,
such as double suicides of blighted lovers.

The most popular poetic form of the Tokugawa period, the *haiku,*
was also well suited to the wit and sophistication of an urban population, though it displayed more of the Zen spirit than characterized the
city bourgeoisie and was, in any case, a natural outgrowth of the
classical ''short poem.'' The haiku was even briefer—a reduction
from thirty-one syllables to a mere seventeen—but, in the hands of a
master like the seventeenth-century poet-monk Basho, it could be a

superbly clever creation, conjuring up a whole scene and its emotional overtones in a simple phrase or two.

The major artistic trends of Ashikaga times continued into the Tokugawa, but the great unifiers of the late sixteenth and early seventeenth centuries also showed a love of grandeur and display quite unlike that of earlier times. Major efforts were made to erect and decorate sumptuous palaces. Gorgeous decorative screens and panels, with brightly colored scenes and designs laid on backgrounds of gold leaf, were typical of the time. The expansive spirit of the age is well illustrated by the greatly increased scale of landscape gardening and by the elaborateness of architecture. This Baroque age of Japanese architecture is exemplified by the temple-mausoleums of the early Tokugawa shogun erected in a beautiful forest and mountain setting at Nikko, north of Edo. It is interesting that at this same time the very austere architecture and refined gardens of the detached imperial estate of Katsura near Kyoto were being created in the spirit of the Zen art of the preceding period.

While the major schools of Ashikaga painting were still patronized by the ruling class, a new popular art grew up in the cities in Tokugawa times. It was called *ukiyo-e,* or "pictures of the floating world," a Buddhist term for the transience of human life, which came simply to imply up-to-date stylishness. The development of woodblock printing, in which a number of differently colored wood blocks would be printed over one another to form a multicolored print, made it possible to reproduce many copies of colored *ukiyo-e* pictures and to sell them at reasonable prices. The subject matter was at first famous

Decorative iris screen by Ogata Korin (1658–1716).

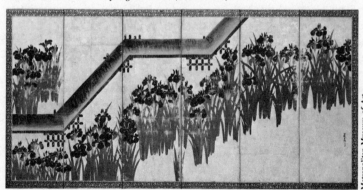

Metropolitan Museum of Art,
Louise E. McBurney Gift Fund, 1953

actors and well-known courtesans and other beautiful women, sometimes with erotic touches, but later beautiful or famous scenes—the
precursors of the picture postcard—became popular. This was the
world's first art for the masses, and it reached a glorious culmination
in the early nineteenth century in the landscape prints of two great
masters, Hokusai and Hiroshige. The woodblock prints of these popular though not much respected artists were the first form of Japanese
art to be highly esteemed in the West.

The increased industrial output of the Tokugawa period resulted in
great advances in the industrial arts. The making of fine pottery and
beautiful porcelain ware, at first under the guidance of Korean potters
brought back by Hideyoshi's armies, became a great industry with
high artistic standards. Gorgeous silk brocades were produced by the
expanding textile industry, and lacquerware of great decorative beauty
was made in quantity. In the industrial arts as well as in decorative
screens and panels for buildings, the Japanese showed great skill in
using elements from nature basically as designs verging on the abstract. This form of Japanese esthetics, called Rimpa from the name of
its greatest figure, Ogata Korin (1658–1716), has proved to have great
appeal in the contemporary West.

In the realm of thought, the *bakufu,* and most domains in imitation
of it, embraced the Neo-Confucian doctrines of Chu Hsi, which
stressed the moral basis of political authority and the need for absolute
loyalty. The more theoretical and removed from the realities of the
time the inherited warrior code became, the more rigidly the samurai
adhered to it and to Confucianism, developing an idealized combination of Confucianism and feudal ethics that came to be known as
bushido, or "the way of the warrior."

This Confucian orthodoxy and outmoded feudal ethics were intellectually stultifying, but many thinkers drew on other strands of Chinese thought to create a lively intellectual ferment. Some tried to get
away from Chu Hsi to earlier Confucian concepts or a more practical
interpretation of Confucian doctrines. Many showed a deep and very
pragmatic concern with the obvious economic problems of the day.
Some were influenced by the Chinese philosopher Wang Yang-ming
(1472–1529, known as Oyomei in Japan), who emphasized the individual's intuitive moral sense and the need to combine thought and
action. Such concepts, of course, could be subversive, and it is interesting to note that many of the leaders of the movement that overthrew

the Tokugawa in the nineteenth century had in fact been influenced by Wang Yang-ming's teachings.

Another aspect of Tokugawa thought was the rise of national self-consciousness and an eventual revival of interest in the imperial line. The Tokugawa was undoubtedly the most Confucian age in Japanese history, but Confucianism brought with it a stress on history, and this led to a looking back into Japan's past. There was a revival of history writing, which naturally called attention to the imperial rule of antiquity. A rising interest in ancient Japanese literature was another source for a renewed attention to the past. In the late eighteenth century Motoori Norinaga produced a great exegesis on Japan's first history, the *Kojiki* of 712, and his followers, in a movement called *kokugaku*, or "national learning," went on to espouse a great reverence for the emperors and even a belief that they had the right to rule.

Later Tokugawa thought was also enlivened by influences from the West. An earlier ban on all books from the Occident was lifted in 1720 for writings not containing Christian doctrines. This permitted a small group of scholars, centered around the Dutch in Nagasaki, to begin to study the scientific advances of the West. Working laboriously through the Dutch language, from which their work came to be known as "Dutch learning," they concentrated on such obviously useful subjects as gunnery, medicine, smelting, cartography, and astronomy. Though few in number, they had, by the early nineteenth century, built up a considerable body of knowledge about the contemporary West and its science and had imbibed some ideas that were inevitably subversive to Tokugawa rule. Other influences from the West can be found in the realism and the Occidental sense of perspective seen in the work of some Japanese artists of the time.

In all these various ways, the Tokugawa period was a time of slow but great change, when the economic, social, and intellectual foundations for modern Japan were established. The Japanese had had a chance to work over and perfect their own cultural heritage. They were stimulated by new influences from China and to a lesser extent from the West. Despite their relative isolation from the rest of the world and the stability of their feudal political system, the economy and society did not stagnate but showed signs of steady growth and constant ferment.

As economic, social, and even cultural conditions differed increasingly from the rather rigid political patterns established in the first half of the seventeenth century, strains and stresses also developed in society. The *bakufu* and domains for the most part fell into serious financial straits. The sharp lines between the classes were becoming increasingly blurred, as impoverished samurai married daughters of affluent merchant families in order to salvage their finances and ambitious merchants and even peasants found ways to win samurai status. Lower samurai of ability became outspokenly dissatisfied with a system in which positions in government were largely determined by birth and there was little opportunity for advancement through merit. At a higher intellectual level, ideas subversive to Tokugawa rule or even to the whole feudal system had emerged from historical studies or foreign influences and were harbored by some daring thinkers.

Among the commoners, the richer and better educated peasants had managed to shift a disproportionately large share of the tax burden to their poorer fellow villagers, accentuating the differences in wealth. During the second half of the Tokugawa period, there was a steady increase in the number and severity of uprisings by both peasants and city dwellers, probably reflecting an increasing maldistribution of wealth, a breakdown of the paternalistic feudal relationships that had earlier given more security to the poor, and a general rise in economic expectations. One sign of the malaise among the lower classes was the development of new popular religious sects, drawing largely on Shinto concepts and founded commonly by women. There were even occasional outbursts of a sort of millenarian religious excitement.

All these signs of change during the Tokugawa period have encouraged Japanese historians to label it the "modern" or "early modern" period, in keeping with the terminology used for European history. Japan indeed was probably a more self-conscious and self-contained national unit during most of this time than any of the countries of Europe and was more thoroughly bureaucratized. In many other features, too, it paralleled changes taking place in the West. But it was largely deficient in the belief in progress, the scientific method, the worldwide contacts of the West, and the beginnings of industrialization, which were starting to transform Europe. Though there were indeed great changes in Japan, the country's social and political system remained mired in feudalism.

However great the changes in Japan during the Tokugawa period and however many the parallels with the West, they were as nothing compared to those that were to follow the collapse of the Tokugawa in the middle of the nineteenth century. Japanese history falls quite clearly into a premodern period preceding this great change and a modern period that followed it. The Tokugawa system was showing many signs of erosion, but up until the mid-nineteenth century there was no hint of imminent collapse, such as had destroyed the Kamakura and Ashikaga *bakufu*. As late as 1850 a basic restructuring of the existing system or even a major challenge to it was almost unimaginable, despite the growing discrepancies between theory and reality. But the situation suddenly changed in the 1850s. The West, now vastly more powerful than it had been when driven away by the Japanese in the seventeenth century, was beginning once again to press upon the country. In less than two decades the whole Tokugawa system was swept away, clearing the ground for the building of a new Japan, which is the fully modernized, industrialized land we know today.

PART TWO

MODERNIZING
JAPAN

8

THE TRANSITION TO A
MODERN STATE

When Japan had closed its doors to the Europeans in the first half of
the seventeenth century, it had stood abreast of the Occident technologically, but by the nineteenth century rapid scientific progress and
the beginning of the industrial revolution had made the countries of the
West incomparably stronger in military and economic power. After
their expulsion from Japan, the Europeans had for a while all but
forgotten this distant island nation, but now their own steadily expanding economic interests brought them close once again to Japan's
shores. Observant Japanese were not unaware of European colonial
expansion and especially the military disasters and national humiliation the British inflicted on great China itself in 1839 to 1842 and
again, together with the French, in 1856 to 1858.

In the last years of the eighteenth century, the Russians, who had
slowly pushed their way across the vast expanse of Siberia and
reached the Pacific, began to attempt to establish contact with the
Japanese, and Russian and Japanese expeditions would sometimes
encounter each other in the islands north of Japan. The British, who by
this time had supplanted the Portuguese and Dutch as the chief traders
in eastern waters, found their commercial interests growing rapidly in
China and were beginning to look toward the Japanese islands that lay
beyond.

It was the Americans, however, who were the most interested in Japan, since their whaling vessels were active off its coasts and their clipper ships, bound for the Canton trade, sailed past its shores. Japanese ports where American vessels could take refuge or replenish their water supplies were particularly attractive to them, and as steamships came into use the need for coaling stations in Japan, the other side of the long Pacific crossing, added a new urgency to the availability of such ports. All the Western nations were also concerned about the treatment of sailors shipwrecked on Japan's shores. Japanese law decreed death for all intruders, and even though this was not normally enforced, Western castaways who eventually got out of Japan by way of Nagasaki usually had tales of extreme hardships to recount.

In the first half of the nineteenth century the Americans, British, and Russians repeatedly sent expeditions to Japan in efforts to persuade the Japanese to open their ports to foreign ships, and the Dutch urged the Tokugawa to accede to these demands. But Edo stood firm on its old policy. A few students of "Dutch learning" bravely advocated the opening of Japan, but the vast majority of the people, long accustomed to isolation from the rest of the world, were bitterly opposed to allowing foreigners into their land.

The American government eventually decided to try to force the doors open. For this purpose, it dispatched under Commodore Matthew C. Perry a fair-sized fleet that steamed in July 1853 into what is now called Tokyo Bay. After delivering a letter from the president of the United States demanding the opening of trade relations, Perry withdrew to Okinawa for the winter, with the promise that he would return early the next year to receive a reply. Edo was thrown into consternation over this sudden crisis, and the remaining decade and a half of Tokugawa rule, known as the *bakumatsu,* or the "end of the *bakufu,*" was a period of great unrest. The Japanese were appalled at the size and guns of the American "black ships," as they called them, and they were amazed by the steam-powered vessels that moved up the bay against the wind. They realized that their own antiquated shore batteries were almost useless against them and that Edo and the coastal shipping which provisioned it lay defenseless.

The government split into two factions—conservatives who advocated resistance to the foreigners and realists who saw that Japan could do nothing but bow to the American demands. In their own indecision, the Edo authorities did a most unusual thing. For the first time in over six centuries of military rule, the shogun's government asked the opin-

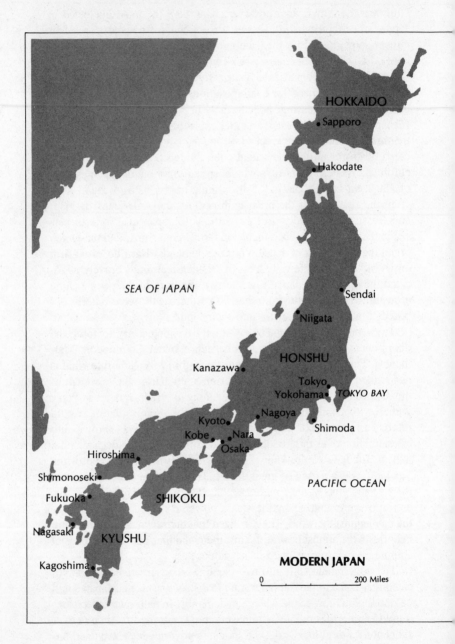

SEA OF JAPAN

HOKKAIDO

Sapporo

Hakodate

Sendai

Niigata

HONSHU

Kanazawa

Tokyo

Yokohama *TOKYO BAY*

Nagoya

Kyoto

Nara

Kobe

Osaka

Shimoda

Hiroshima

PACIFIC OCEAN

Shimonoseki

Fukuoka

SHIKOKU

Nagasaki

KYUSHU

Kagoshima

MODERN JAPAN

0   200 Miles

ion of the emperor on an important problem of state. It also invited counsel from the daimyo. Conservative Kyoto and many of the daimyo, most of whom were safely removed from the immediate threat, were of course strongly in favor of repelling the foreigners.

The Edo government was indeed caught on the horns of a dilemma when Perry's fleet returned to Tokyo Bay in February 1854. The emperor's court and the nation as a whole demanded a policy that the Tokugawa were quite incapable of carrying out. Under the threatening guns of the American ships, Edo had no choice but to sign a treaty with the United States, opening two ports to American ships and permitting a certain amount of closely regulated trade. The two ports were Shimoda, at the end of a peninsula near Edo, and Hakodate in Hokkaido, both insignificant ports located in relatively remote places, but adequate for the provisioning of American ships. An American consul was also permitted to reside at Shimoda, and it was stipulated that any new concession granted other Western countries would automatically apply to the United States as well, a provision taken from the "unequal treaty" system then being forced on China.

Once the door had been opened a crack, there was no closing it. Within two years Edo had been forced to sign similar treaties with the British, Russians, and Dutch. The Russian treaty added Nagasaki to the open ports and included another element of the Chinese "unequal treaty" system—extraterritoriality, or the right of Western residents in Japan to be tried by their own consular courts under their own national laws. In 1858 Townsend Harris, the first American consul, negotiated a full commercial treaty, which went into effect in 1860. Harris used as his chief argument the threat of the British navy, which was far larger than the American and, he declared, would be used more ruthlessly. The commercial treaty opened six ports to relatively free trade and won permission for the permanent residence of Americans in the great cities of Edo and Osaka.

The British, Russians, Dutch, and French once again followed the American lead and added in 1866 limitations, commonly of 5 percent, on the tariffs Japan would be allowed to impose on foreign imports. This was another key element of the "unequal treaty" system. Foreign merchants were particularly attracted to the newly opened deepwater ports of Yokohama near Edo and Kobe across the bay from Osaka, both of which were in time to develop into great cities. British and French soldiers followed the Western traders to protect them from diehard samurai opponents to their presence. To observers of the time,

The Granger Collection

American engraving of the White House reception given by President Buchanan in 1860 for the Tokugawa Embassy. The embassy was in Washington to ratify the Harris treaty of commerce.

Japan must have seemed well on the road to the semicolonial status into which China was already falling.

All Japan was thrown into turmoil by the sudden collapse of the policy of isolation. The differing rates between gold and silver in Japan and the rest of the world produced for a while a serious drain of gold. Textile markets were disrupted by cheap machine-made foreign imports. But, far worse, the credibility of the Edo government had been shattered by its inability to defend Japan and its meek acceptance of foreign policies that most politically conscious Japanese bitterly opposed. Edo had again consulted the daimyo before signing the commercial treaty with Harris in 1858, drawing as before largely negative reactions. There was no choice, however, but to go ahead with the treaties, and under the strong leadership of the chief "hereditary" daimyo, Ii Naosuke, the *bakufu* attempted to crush opposition by forcing the imperial court to give its assent and placing leading opposition daimyo under house arrest.

The nation, however, seethed with discontent and unrest over the national humiliation to which Edo had bowed. Unruly samurai, declaring themselves *ronin,* or "masterless samurai," attacked Westerners, killing Harris's secretary in 1859 and burning down the British legation in Edo in 1863. Another group, largely from Mito, one of the major "related" Tokugawa domains, waylaid Ii Naosuke in 1860 at a gate to the Edo castle and assassinated him. Still more flocked around the emperor's court in Kyoto, seeing in the emperor a symbol for united resistance to Tokugawa policies, and raised the double battle cry of *sonno,* "honor the emperor," and *joi,* "expel the barbarians." After Ii's death, Edo's control over the country rapidly disintegrated. Even the system of "alternate attendance" at Edo was abandoned in 1862, and the shogun humbly proceeded to Kyoto for consultations when summoned by the imperial court.

In some domains, extremist samurai gained control over the local administrations and attempted to use the power of their domains to influence national policies. At first they advocated various schemes to bring the imperial court and the *bakufu* closer together for greater national unity, but gradually their movements became openly revolutionary against the Tokugawa. Two leading but rival domains in these efforts were Choshu in the extreme western end of Honshu and Satsuma in southern Kyushu. Both were among the largest domains, had cherished anti-Edo feelings since their forced submission to the Tokugawa in 1600, had relatively large samurai populations because of the reduction in their geographic size at that time, were still quite cohesive feudal units because of their relatively remote geographic positions, and happened to be financially solvent and therefore could afford to purchase new Western arms.

The *bakufu* desperately but belatedly attempted to strengthen itself, dispatching missions abroad, introducing Western military technol-

ogy, and attempting to reform its administration and economic position. However, Choshu, Satsuma, and a few other domains were also
beginning to reform their military establishments. Though violently
antiforeign, Satsuma and Choshu had learned through bitter experience that the Westerners could not be driven away by a militarily
backward Japan. A British fleet destroyed the Satsuma capital of
Kagoshima in 1863 in retaliation for the assassination of an Englishman near Yokohama the year before. In 1863 American and French
ships and in 1864 a whole allied fleet demolished the Choshu forts
near Shimonoseki at the western end of the Inland Sea because these
forts had been firing on Western vessels in response to an order from
the imperial court, then under Choshu influence. Satsuma at once
proceeded to build up a modern navy with British assistance, and
Choshu speeded up the modernization of its forces, experimenting
with mixed rifle brigades made up of both samurai and peasants.

In 1863 the extremist Choshu forces were driven out of Kyoto in
the first actual fighting in Japan for two and a quarter centuries, and
the next year the *bakufu* still had the strength to marshal an army that
forced Choshu to submit temporarily to its policies. A second expedition in 1866 against renewed Choshu resistance failed miserably, however. Meanwhile Choshu and Satsuma had secretly joined forces and,
with the aid of some other domains, notably Tosa in Shikoku, and a
few radical court nobles, this revolutionary coalition seized control of
the imperial court late in 1867 (or on January 3, 1868, according to the
Western calendar).

The shogun had himself come from the "related" Mito domain,
which for a long time had been a hotbed of pro-imperialist sentiment.
Perhaps because of this background, he refused to put up a determined
fight for Tokugawa supremacy, though some forces loyal to the *bakufu*
did battle in his behalf outside Kyoto and then later within a part of
Edo and in some domains to the north, while the new Tokugawa navy
held out for another year in Hokkaido. On the whole, however, the
coalition of Satsuma, Choshu, and their allies, using control over the
person of the emperor as their justification, took over the whole country with surprising ease and remarkably little bloodshed. The
Tokugawa *bakufu,* which had seemed firmly established a mere two
decades earlier, had become so flabby with age and so hopelessly
outdated both administratively and ideologically during two centuries
of slow change that, when finally challenged by a few determined
opponents, it collapsed suddenly and completely.

Most of the domains and the great bulk of the Japanese people passively watched, irresolute, unconcerned, or financially paralyzed, while a small group of able young samurai from western Japan, mostly from the lower ranks of that class, together with a handful of court nobles who never before had been involved in political power, seized control of the remains of the central government. Edo had for so long been the real political capital of Japan that the new leaders made it their own headquarters. In the autumn of 1868 it was renamed Tokyo, or "eastern capital," and the emperor and his court were moved to the great Edo castle the next spring. The new government was supported by the military power of Satsuma, Choshu, and their allies—only a small minority of the hereditary warrior class of Japan—but had as its chief financial base the land tax from the huge shogunal realm, which it appropriated largely for itself. It also resorted to forced loans from rich merchants, as the shogun and daimyo had done when in need.

To create an effective new administration on the ruins of the discredited and bankrupt *bakufu,* however, was no easy task. The chief assets of the new leaders were their control of the imperial symbol of political legitimacy, the armies of the few domains they personally controlled, and the political paralysis that gripped the other domains and the shogun's realm. The new leaders had already learned that trying to "expel the barbarians" was an objective they would have to abandon, at least for the present. They soon signaled this change in attitude by having the emperor receive the representatives of the foreign powers in audience in the spring of 1868. The other slogan of the revolution, *sonno,* or "honor the emperor," remained central to their cause, however, since it was the only justification for their rule. They built their regime around the emperor, doing everything in his name, even though he was only fourteen years old at the time. In 1868 they changed the name of the "year period" to Meiji, meaning "Enlightened Rule," a name posthumously given to the emperor when he died in 1912, and the whole revolution and the tremendous changes that followed came to be known as the Meiji Restoration.

In theory the movement "restored" the imperial rule of antiquity, but nothing of the kind actually took place. While paying utmost deference to the emperor, the group of young samurai and court nobles who were in actual control ruled in a collegial manner, as had become customary in Japan, and they took their models for innovation not from ancient Japan but from the contemporary West. They did revive ancient court titles and the names of old institutions, but the resurrection of such names did not signify their restoration as functioning institutions. The real changes they made were the abandonment of the feudal structure of Tokugawa society and government and the piecemeal adoption of Western institutions of modern centralized rule.

All these changes were made under the motto of *fukoku kyohei*, "a rich country and strong military," because it was clear that until Japan was militarily powerful on the basis of its own economic strength, it could not expect to "expel the barbarians," even in the modified sense of winning military and economic security from the West and diplomatic equality with it. The whole tenor of the effort was expressed in a Five Articles Oath (also called the Charter Oath), which the new leaders had the emperor issue on April 8, 1868. In it he promised that "evil customs of the past shall be broken off," careers shall be opened to all people equally, and "knowledge shall be sought throughout the world."

In traditional Japanese style, the chief posts in the new government were given to high court nobles and the daimyo of the domains who had cooperated in the overthrow of the Tokugawa, but these men were mainly figureheads. Below them were the real leaders—the samurai and younger court nobles who had actually carried out the revolution. The main figure among them until his death in 1883 was the court noble Iwakura Tomomi, the oldest of the group at forty-three. The rest were mostly young samurai, among whom Kido Takayoshi of Choshu and Okubo Toshimichi and Saigo Takamori of Satsuma were the most prominent. For the most part these men occupied posts as councilors and as vice ministers in the new ministries that were being formed. Falling back on the old Japanese technique of collective leadership, they made their important decisions through consultation and consensus, whatever the formal structure of government might be. Not once did any of them attempt to acquire dictatorial power for himself, quite unlike most of the revolutions that have occurred in modernizing countries in more recent times.

It was clear that something more than a coalition of a few domains was needed to produce a unified and powerful nation capable of staving off the Western menace and maintaining order in a land smoldering with resentment at the presence of foreigners and the seizure of power by a group of men who were representative of only a small part of the country. The new government had no difficulty in taking over the shogun's realm and dividing it into centrally controlled prefectures, a system well known from Japan's own past, but the real tasks were to gain control over the domains, which constituted three-fourths of the country, and to eliminate the class divisions that stood in the way of modernizing the government, the economy, and, most important, the military.

The new leaders began by persuading the daimyo of Satsuma, Choshu, Tosa, and Hizen, a domain in northern Kyushu, to symbolically restore their territories to the emperor on March 5, 1869, and receive them back as lands over which they were now considered to be governors, with one-tenth of their former domain revenues as personal incomes. Most of the other domains quickly followed suit for fear of being discriminated against, and the remainder were forced to accept the new system. Then quite suddenly, on August 29, 1871, the new government abolished all the domains, putting them under centrally appointed governors and paying off the daimyo fairly generously with government bonds; these, of course, would have no value unless the new regime survived. The domains were so demoralized that they put up no concerted opposition, and the daimyo, accustomed to being little more than figureheads, meekly complied. Their bonds became an important source of future banking capital, but they themselves faded away for the most part into genteel and affluent obscurity.

The abolition of the domains, most of which had been well-established political units for several centuries, was achieved with surprising ease, but depriving the samurai of their feudal privileges was a more difficult and dangerous undertaking. They formed a wide stratum of society that monopolized military and political power and enjoyed the privileges of hereditary, even if often niggardly, salaries. In 1871 the government lifted all class restrictions on roles in society and decreed legal equality for everyone, including the semi-outcast elements, once known as *eta* but now usually called *burakumin,* who constituted about 2 percent of the population. Then, early in 1873, the government carried out what was in the Japanese context perhaps its most revolutionary reform, decreeing universal conscription and hence putting an end to the concept of a privileged military class. The point was emphasized in 1876 when the samurai were denied the right to wear their swords, which were their badge of class distinction.

Largely under the leadership of Yamagata Aritomo of Choshu, a new army of peasant conscripts was built up, at first on the French model and later on the Prussian, and the Prussian innovation of a general staff was adopted by the new army in 1878. Because of Yamagata's leadership, officers from Choshu were to dominate the army through World War I. To back the army up in maintaining domestic order, an efficient police force was also created. Meanwhile, Satsuma had taken the lead in building a modern navy on the British model, and men from Satsuma remained at its head until well into the twentieth century.

The samurai's loss of his cherished position as an aristocratic warrior-administrator was accompanied by the loss of his privileged economic status. Hereditary stipends, inadequate though most of them were, had been cut in half in the reform of 1869, and finally in 1876 the government forced those samurai who had not already done so to commute their remaining stipends into lump-sum payments of still further reduced value. Even then the payments to samurai and daimyo constituted an extremely heavy financial burden on the new government. Completely cutting off the feudal aristocracy would have been cheaper in the short run, but perhaps this relatively generous treatment is one reason why modern Japan had no continuing problem with the *ancien régime,* as did France.

There were, of course, strong reactions to these drastic reforms. Because of their traditions of leadership and education, men of samurai origin virtually monopolized all the important posts in the new government, while others made for themselves new careers in business and intellectual pursuits. But the bulk of the samurai had neither the talents nor the flexibility to adjust to the new conditions, and they sank into obscure poverty. So large a privileged class could not be disinherited without some turmoil. Irreconcilable conservatives among the samurai often defied the new government in its first decade of rule. Significantly, these troubles occurred largely in the same western domains from which the new leaders had come. Perhaps the authority of these men seemed less valid in areas where their relatively lowly origins were well remembered. The final and most serious of the samurai revolts came in 1877 in Satsuma itself. There some 40,000 discontented conservatives rallied around Saigo, who had withdrawn from the government in dudgeon four years earlier. In bloody fighting, the government's new conscript army managed to crush the rebels, proving to the diehards that the old order had indeed passed.

Within ten years of coming to power, the new government had thus cleared away the antiquated Tokugawa political and social system and had achieved unchallenged control over the country. But the development of modern political institutions, a new social order, and a new economic system to support modern military power was a much slower and more difficult undertaking.

The pragmatic new leaders adopted piecemeal elements of Western political organization, trying them out cautiously to see how they would work in Japan. The finance ministry became the core of the government, since it determined the use of funds. A banking system was created, at first along decentralized American lines and later on the basis of the centralized banking system of Belgium. The currency was made uniform, and in 1871 the *yen* was adopted as the unit of value. In order to make budgeting possible, the land tax, the chief source of revenue, which had been paid in percentages of yield, was shifted to a fixed money tax in 1873, and the payers of this tax were recognized as the outright owners of the land. This measure clearly gave the land to the peasantry, but the fixed money tax as well as military conscription were at first unpopular with the peasants, who broke out in sporadic but localized riots. Another more lasting result of the new tax system was the foreclosure of mortgages in bad years, raising the proportion of tenant-operated land from around 25 percent to 45 percent by the end of the century.

There was an urgent need to develop communications and industry as well as a strong military if Japan was to fend off the Western powers and the deluge of foreign manufacturers, against which the tariffs fixed by treaty gave little protection. The new government laid telegraph lines throughout the nation to facilitate communication and control and, in 1871, created a postal system. It improved ports and made a start on railroads in 1872 with a line between Tokyo and its port of Yokohama, a distance of 19 miles. It initiated an ambitious program of development in the northern frontier island of Hokkaido, which was still occupied largely by Ainu subsisting on hunting and fishing. It developed a modern munitions industry so that Japan could be independent of imported Western weapons. It also developed mines and built pilot plants in various industries.

The *bakufu* and some of the daimyo domains had already experimented with strategic industries such as munitions and shipbuilding on a small scale, and also with some consumer industries, such as cotton spinning and weaving. The new government expanded these efforts. It built pilot plants that led the way in the mechanization of silk reeling and the industrialization of cotton spinning, cotton weaving, the making of bricks and glass, and a number of other light industries. Some leaders hoped that jobs in the new factories might help alleviate the economic distress of unemployed samurai. Most of these industrial efforts, however, lost money because of the new government's lack of experience and the initial small scale of the operations.

The new leaders clearly realized that to succeed in all these efforts, Japan would have to learn a great deal about the technology, institutions, and ideas of the West and would also have to develop an educated public capable of supporting a modernized economy and society. The first decades of the Meiji period were essentially a time of learning from the West and adopting those elements of Western civilization the Japanese felt would be of use to them. It was a period comparable only to the era over a thousand years earlier when Japan had imported Chinese civilization, but this time the process of learning from abroad was more rapid and systematic. Students, including even a few girls, were carefully chosen on the basis of their capabilities and sent to study in countries selected with equal care. The Japanese intended to learn from each Western country that in which it particularly excelled. For example, they sent students to England to study the navy and merchant marine, to Germany for the army and medicine, to France for local government and law, and to the United States for business methods. The world was one vast schoolroom for them, but they themselves chose what and where they would learn and how they would use this knowledge to change life in Japan.

A few Japanese, including some of the leaders in the new government, had gone abroad even before 1868, and some of the other leaders went after 1868 for observation and study. From 1871 to 1873, Iwakura himself led a delegation consisting of about half of the top leaders, who first went to the United States and then to Europe. The mission was not successful in its primary objective—persuading the foreign powers to modify the "unequal treaties" forced on the Tokugawa regime—but it did gain a clearer idea of the West and what would have to be done to win security and eventual equality.

At first the new government was heavily dependent on hired Western experts, but these could be attracted only by salaries high even by Western standards, because Japan was not considered an attractive place to live. Hundreds of missionaries, mostly from America, provided free instruction in the English language and numerous other fields. Although the old ban on Christianity was not officially dropped until 1873, American Protestant missionaries had entered Japan as early as 1859, and they founded many pioneer schools. While the missionaries continued to teach gratis, the government replaced as quickly as possible its expensive foreign experts and teachers with Japanese trained by these experts or by students who had returned from abroad. Before the end of the century, foreigners in the government or in government schools had become a rarity, except in the field of Western languages.

Translations of Western works and books written by Japanese about the West were also important sources of information on the Occident. The greatest popularizer of Western lore was Fukuzawa Yukichi, who traveled to the West several times, starting with a *bakufu* mission in 1860, wrote immensely popular books, such as *Seiyo jijo* (*Conditions in the Occident*), and founded a school that in time grew into Keio University, one of Japan's two most prestigious private institutions of higher learning. During the 1870s and early 1880s, there was a virtual craze for almost everything Western, which was expressed in the slogan *bummei kaika,* "civilization and enlightenment."

The new leaders had recognized from the start that an extensive system of popular education was necessary for a modern state. By as early as 1871 they had created a ministry of education, which embarked at once on an ambitious program of universal education for girls as well as boys. Eventually compulsory education was extended to six years, though it took time to train the necessary teachers and develop the necessary facilities. Not until 1907 were all children actually going to school. Beyond the elementary level, the government developed a complex system of secondary and advanced schools, largely for boys, culminating in Tokyo University (founded in 1877) and later other so-called imperial universities, which were to produce the leadership elite.

The educational system, unlike those of the West, was thus almost entirely created *de novo,* and except for some missionary institutions and private universities that did not compare with the imperial universities in prestige, it was almost entirely in government hands. Thus it was free of the aristocratic aura and religious domination of many Western educational systems of the time and was, in fact, far more rationalized, secular, and state-oriented. Education was regarded primarily as a tool of government needed to train obedient and reliable citizens in the various skills required by a modern state. It was narrowly tailored to meet the national needs foreseen by the leaders: a literate working and military force, a broad group of technicians, and a small elite of leaders.

Within a generation or two, this highly rational system changed Japanese society from one in which prestige and function were largely determined by birth to one in which both were determined almost entirely by education. Thus Japan, still an essentially feudal society in the middle of the nineteenth century, had become much more egalitarian than England by the early twentieth century. A less happy result of central government control of education was its use for indoctrination. Education on the lower levels became increasingly a means for teaching the people what to think rather than how to think. The heavy burden of rote memory work imposed by the writing system may have heightened this tendency. In any case, Japan has the dubious distinction of having pioneered in the modern totalitarian technique of consciously inculcating national obedience and uniformity through a standardized and closely controlled educational system.

All the great reforms and innovations of its first decade of rule put a heavy strain on the new government's finances. Creating a modern army and navy was vastly expensive. Hiring foreign experts, sending students abroad, and establishing a nationwide educational system required much money. So also did the efforts to develop the island of Hokkaido, new communication facilities, new industries, and mining. The government was saddled with the debts and indemnity payments to foreign powers incurred by the Tokugawa *bakufu*. The liquidation of the old order through payments to the daimyo and samurai and the heavy outlays for suppressing the Satsuma rebellion of 1877 proved a tremendous financial drain. Unlike countries modernizing in more recent times, Japan found no outside financial or technological aid on which it could depend. In view of the predatory nature of Western imperialism, the Japanese were understandably fearful of foreign loans and used them only very sparingly. Loans, in any case, were obtainable only at high interest rates, because Japan seemed a poor risk to the West. In other words, Japan had to lift itself economically by its own bootstraps.

An accident of history had benefited Japan during the 1860s, its first decade of foreign trade. A silk blight in Europe had created a strong demand for Japanese silk and silkworm eggs. The enterprising peasants of the chief silk-producing areas in the mountains of central Japan rose to the challenge, and as a result Japan developed a favorable balance of trade with the West for a while. In the 1870s, as the artificial stimulus of the European silk blight faded, peasant entrepreneurs, following the government's lead, adopted the relatively simple process of reeling silk by mechanical power. They thus produced a more uniform silk thread, superior to that of other Asian countries. In time, this small innovation gave Japan the lion's share of the silk market in the West, and silk was to remain its largest export until well into the twentieth century.

A booming silk trade brought prosperity to some rural areas, and most people were benefited by the inflation that hit the country in the late 1870s, reducing the actual cost of the fixed money tax. This permitted substantial investments in agriculture, which, together with the improvement of transport facilities, the elimination of feudal barriers to trade, and the spread throughout the country of the superior agricultural technologies already developed in the more advanced areas, led to a considerable increase in agriculture production over the next few decades.

The government itself, however, faced financial collapse by the late 1870s. Its paper currency depreciated seriously, setting off a dangerous inflation that, while benefiting the taxpaying peasants, reduced the real tax income of the government and threatened its stability. Strong financial measures, which were obviously called for, were undertaken by Matsukata Masayoshi, one of the samurai leaders from Satsuma, who was appointed finance minister in 1881 and remained in this post for almost two decades. Matsukata carried through a program of stern retrenchment. He slashed the budget and sold off to private interests the government enterprises in Hokkaido and most of the government's plants in nonstrategic industries. The effort succeeded, and the government got back on a sound financial footing within a few years.

Matsukata's policies naturally caused serious hardships for the people, though the government was now strong enough to quell any resistance. These policies also had the accidental effect of concentrating much of Japan's nascent industrial resources in the hands of the few persons able to buy them from the government. Since few people had enough money to purchase factories, which in any case were still losing money, the payments received were far lower than the original outlays had been, and in this sense the factories were bargains for the buyers. In terms of the reduced capital costs, many of the factories soon began to bring in profits. In part this may have been the result of more flexible and energetic private management, but it was basically a sign that the Japanese had built up enough skill and experience to begin to overcome the initial difficulties of industrialization. The first substantial success was in cotton spinning in the mid-1880s, and this was followed by surges in one industrial field after another. Japan was well on its way to industrialization by the end of the century, but in part because of Matsukata's reforms, the financial benefits of this development became concentrated in the hands of a relatively small group of private businessmen, some of whom became the great financial magnates the Japanese came to call the *zaibatsu,* ''the financial clique.''

The industrialists and businessmen of Meiji Japan were not, as one might imagine, simply the descendants of the great urban merchants of Tokugawa days. Most of these proved unable to adapt to the new age. They were too tied to traditional industries and old-fashioned ways of doing business. Only a few, like the house of Mitsui established in the seventeenth century, became an important element in the new economy. Some of the new businessmen came from among the aggressive rural entrepreneurs who had appeared in the later part of the Tokugawa period. For example, after winning samurai status in the closing years of the *bakufu,* Shibusawa Eiichi, who came from a prosperous peasant business family in the environs of Edo, left government service in the early 1870s to become a leader in the cotton spinning industry, in banking, and in a host of other fields. Others among the new businessmen were persons of obscure origin—talented adventurers who seized the opportunities offered in a time of rapid change. The bulk of the new business community, however, came from the samurai class. Such men took advantage of their greater educational attainments and their connections with samurai in government to forge ahead in the business world. Some of them had had experience as business agents

Woodblock showing the celebration of the electrification of the Ginza avenue in downtown Tokyo.

for their daimyo. This was the case for Iwasaki Yataro of Tosa, who, starting in the field of shipping, built up his firm of Mitsubishi until it became second only to Mitsui.

By the mid-1880s it was clear that Japan had succeeded in making the perilous transition from a feudally organized premodern society to a modern nation. It was strong enough to be safe from further Western encroachments; it was politically stable at home; and it was becoming economically secure from Western domination and even competitive abroad in some fields, such as cotton thread. The magnitude of the achievement was not generally recognized at the time, when the ultimate outcome still seemed far from certain, but now that Japan is indisputably one of the leading industrialized nations of the world and we have seen how hard comparable transitions have proved to be for most other premodern societies, the Meiji transformation stands out as an extraordinary and perhaps unique story.

Japan's success is by no means easy to explain. Simply giving labels drawn from Western history is of little help and can be very misleading. To call the Meiji Restoration a bourgeois revolution is more confusing than helpful. The rich urban merchants provided loans to both sides in the struggle, but stood timidly aside in the contest between elements of the ruling feudal class. After the contest was decided, they were in large part replaced by a new business community drawn mostly from the samurai class. To compare Japan's transition to the triumph of absolutism in early modern Europe is even more inaccurate, since the Tokugawa system was already more absolutist than most of the kingdoms of early modern Europe, and the Meiji reforms led to liberalizing trends. To call the Restoration a counterrevolution is equally misleading. It is true that peasant and urban unrest rose to a crescendo in the decades immediately before and after 1868, but popular uprisings, except for the reactionary samurai revolts, which failed, were not aimed at changing the political system, only at correcting specific grievances over unduly heavy taxes or maladministration.

No European precedents are very useful in explaining the causes or effects of the Meiji revolution. It was clearly forced on a peaceful, stable Japan by the threat of foreign domination. It was carried out largely by able young men drawn almost exclusively from the lower ranks of the dominant samurai class. It succeeded because of a number of characteristics the Japanese possessed, the relative importance of which is not easily measured. They shared some of these characteristics with their neighbors and others with the peoples of the West, but probably no other people had exactly their particular mix of traits. To sum up, the Meiji Restoration cannot be pigeonholed in some neat compartment of historical theory. Certainly what happened during these decades would not have transpired just at that time in Japanese history without the pressures from the West, but neither would these pressures have produced the results they did without the specific historical experience and qualities of the Japanese people.

It is difficult to determine what aspects of premodern Japan were significant in shaping modern Japan and what their relative importance may have been. Certainly one significant factor was the natural isolation of an island nation, which, strengthened by more than two centuries of artificially enforced isolation, helped make the Japanese a very homogeneous people, extremely conscious of their own identity and distinctiveness. They lacked important ethnic minorities and religious cleavages, which have been the bane of many modernizing countries. In addition, they had a sense of nationalism not unlike that of contemporary European nations, but largely lacking in most non-Western lands at that time. Though maintaining feudal autonomies and bitterly divided over policies toward the West, no Japanese for a moment thought of supporting some foreign power against his own countrymen.

Why nationalism should have appeared so early and developed so fully in Japan, long before it became important in other Asian lands, is an interesting question. A sense of national identity seems to have been stirred as early as the first great period of cultural borrowing from China, probably inspired by a feeling of inferiority—the sharp contrast between a small and backward Japan and an incomparably larger, older, and more advanced China. One is reminded of the early nationalism of North Europe, which may have resulted from a similar inferiority complex toward the older and more developed cultures of the lands of the Mediterranean. This early awareness of the superiority of China had also produced a clear realization of the possibility of learning from abroad. Cultural imports to Japan had come by sea and had therefore been clearly identifiable. The Japanese, unlike most other peoples, East or West, had long been aware that much of their civilization had come from abroad. Therefore, unlike the Chinese and other non-Western peoples, they had no difficulty in realizing in the nineteenth century that there was much that not only could but must be learned from the West.

Japan's more than two centuries of enforced isolation had also made possible an equally long period of absolute peace and order, during which the Japanese had developed an extremely advanced and complex economy and society, high levels of education, an extraordinary degree of national economic and intellectual unity, and high standards of political efficiency. It was by no means a backward nation and lagged appreciably behind the West only in technology. In group coordination and skills in cooperation, it probably was well ahead of most Western lands. Long experience with orderly and peaceful legal processes probably account for the relative lack of violence accompanying the great changes that took place in the 1860s and 1870s.

The Japanese, like the other peoples of East Asia, had a strong work ethic and a deeply ingrained drive for education, characteristics not widely shared among most currently modernizing nations. But unlike the other peoples of East Asia, who had centrally unified monarchies, they had a basically feudal political structure and, during their long period of peace, had developed an economic, social, and intellectual system that no longer fitted this political structure very well. The top feudal class was seriously in debt to the theoretically lowest merchant class. Ambitious samurai of low rank hungered for a political system that recognized ability and achievement over birth. Secure in their feudal niches, merchants and peasants enjoyed broad autonomies in running their own town or village affairs and often developed into vigorous entrepreneurs. Japanese society was riddled with inconsistencies and, unlike the monolithically solid social and political systems of China and Korea, was ripe for change. It required no prolonged period of destructive blows from the outside before it collapsed, making way for new institutions.

When Western pressures forced a change, Japan had one other advantage over most other non-Western countries—a native justification for revolution. While other modernizing nations have usually had to find such a justification in some little-understood foreign ideology, such as republicanism and democracy or, in more recent times, in socialism and communism, Japan found it in the "restoration" of the imperial rule of antiquity. Bogus though it may have been, imperial rule was a revolutionary cause that was understandable and attractive to most Japanese.

One final important factor in the success of the Meiji Restoration may have been that its leaders were able to move slowly and pragmatically, as they saw fit. There was no established ideology they had to measure up to or any pressures of great expectation among their people or on the part of foreigners. Until Japan itself had accomplished modernization, no one believed that it was possible for a non-Western country to do so. The leaders were left free to take things in logical sequence, concentrating on fundamentals first and more difficult but less essential steps later. They established law and order, developed communications, concentrated on primary education before putting broad emphasis on higher education, and nurtured agricultural growth and the development of simple industries before attempting the more difficult and costly stages of industrialization. They could also be pragmatically experimental, quickly abandoning false starts and trying new ones until they found one that succeeded.

Unfortunately, the Japanese experience has been either ignored or misread by most later modernizing nations. Though lacking many of the advantages the Japanese had when they started modernizing, these other countries have expected to achieve industrialization and democracy or communism overnight. They have often started building at the top rather than the bottom, emphasizing universities over primary and secondary education, steel mills and jet airlines over agriculture and simple industries. They have attempted to create sophisticated democratic or socialist institutions before their own people had gained the knowledge and experience to operate either. They have sought to play a role on the world stage before they had put their own countries in order. It is probably for such reasons that Japan still stands alone as the one major non-Western nation to have made the full transition to a modernized society and economy with relatively little turmoil and extraordinary success.

9

CONSTITUTIONAL GOVERNMENT AND EMPIRE

The story of Japan's great transition from feudal rule to modern centralized government in the second half of the nineteenth century is usually told from the point of view of the small but talented leadership that guided this transformation. There is, however, another side to the story. The daring but pragmatic steps the leaders took to unify the country, reorganize its social and political system, and modernize its economy were, of course, necessary to the success of the whole venture, as was also their capacity to work together and not break up in fighting over personal power. But none of what they attempted would have really succeeded if it had not been matched by a vigorous response on the part of the Japanese people as a whole. This was as necessary for the Meiji ''miracle,'' as we might well call it, as the achievements of the leaders. Without it, well-meaning efforts at reform from the top down would probably have sunk into a quagmire of confusion, indifference, and stagnation.

It was basically the peasants who, on their own, aggressively took advantage of the silk blight in Europe and the possibility of producing a better quality of silk through mechanized silk reeling, and took control of the burgeoning market for silk abroad. It was the peasants, too, who seized the opportunities offered by the new conditions to expand agricultural production. Ambitious young men from all classes, wishing to learn English, modern science, and Western business methods, flocked to missionary schools, giving them their early importance in modern Japanese education. Other young men rushed to other private institutions, like Keio, which also had been set up before the government's own educational program could get under way. The government, of course, had to create the necessary financial institutions, develop suitable economic conditions, and lead the way in pilot industries, but without the enthusiastic self-generated efforts of thousands of private Japanese, this government initiative would have produced few results. A motley crew of daring entrepreneurs, drawn mainly from the samurai class but including many peasants and some urban merchants, took advantage of Matsukata's reforms to make Japanese industry pay its own way and become internationally competitive. Without this popular response, the government's efforts at economic modernization and industrialization would have proved to be nothing but an empty shell.

It is not surprising that private citizens such as these who took such an active role in the country's economy should begin to demand a role in its political life. The concepts of political rights and democracy had never existed in feudal Japan, but the autonomies of the feudal system had, in reality, given rights of a sort to all groups within their own specific niches of activity. The large samurai class in particular had enjoyed a place in local political leadership, and ambitious men from this class, stimulated by Japan's rapidly changing conditions and the flood of new ideas pouring in from the West, soon began to demand a share in the new government. The leaders in power were few in number and drawn overwhelmingly from Satsuma, Choshu, and a handful of other domains of western Japan. The bulk of the samurai and other outsiders came from the shogun's former realm or from domains that had played no part in the so-called Restoration. Many of them deeply resented or even despised the men from Satsuma and Choshu who were in political control, and it was not unnatural for them to begin to assert their own rights to a share in leadership, arguing in terms of constitutional government and parliamentary democracy that appeared to be so successful in the West.

The government leaders, too, were far from satisfied with the situation as it existed. By brilliant improvisation, they successfully weathered the first two perilous decades of the new regime, but they were still far from achieving their real objectives: winning full legal equality with the West by ending the "unequal treaties" and establishing a stable, smoothly running system at home that would be accepted by everyone without question and would therefore continue automatically after they themselves were gone. Japan remained in constant flux, and the Westerners still regarded it as semibarbarous. The leaders longed for the kind of stable order they themselves had been born into and for full recognition from the West as part of the civilized world.

Even the leaders felt that these objectives might best be achieved through a constitution of the Western type, including some sort of assembly to represent the people. Adopting such Western institutions, they felt, would win them the respect of the West, which was necessary if Japan was to be accepted as an equal. In addition, these institutions appeared from the Western experience to have inherent elements of strength, capable of creating firm bonds between the people and their government. From the start the leaders had also clearly realized it would be necessary to give a greater role in the government to the large numbers of samurai who were accustomed to having some political authority but were now totally excluded from the ruling group. Thus some form of a constitution together with a national assembly seemed to them, too, the best way to achieve a number of desirable objectives.

Concern about the samurai had induced the leaders to include in the Five Articles Oath of 1868 the statement that "deliberative assemblies shall be widely established and all matters decided by public discussion." This was not a promise of democracy, of which they knew very little at that time, but an attempt to reassure the samurai class as a whole that it would not be excluded from the new regime. Early attempts, however, to create assemblies for public discussion failed miserably, because there was no understanding of the working of such institutions. By the 1880s the leadership group, instead of growing, had shrunk to a small and well-defined oligarchy, which later came to be known as the *genro*, or "elder statesmen."

The government had continued to make promises to create an assembly and had made attempts at writing a constitution. In the meantime, however, some of the samurai outsiders had tried to take things into their own hands. In 1873 the leadership group had split over a proposal to send an expedition to Korea, ostensibly to retaliate for that nation's insulting attitude toward the new Japanese government but in reality to help restore the morale of the collapsing samurai class through a military campaign. Iwakura and other moderates, who had just visited the West and seen its frightening strength, overruled the proposal, but some of the chief members of the losing group, including Saigo and Itagaki Taisuke of Tosa, who, like Saigo, had been one of the main military leaders in the Meiji revolution, then withdrew from the government.

Saigo went back to Satsuma, where he eventually met his end as the leader of the great samurai rebellion of 1877, but Itagaki, returning to Tosa, organized a group of followers into an incipient political party to agitate for better treatment of the samurai and for popular participation in government. His following was at first largely limited to Tosa samurai, but soon he was joined by others, including well-to-do peasants and urban merchants, concerned with what was done with the taxes they paid. Intellectuals, inspired by Rousseau and British liberal thought, also joined the group, giving it a somewhat radical tinge, and it became known as "the freedom and people's rights movement" (*jiyu-minken-undo*).

By the 1880s the original top leaders of the Restoration were gone. Saigo had been killed in 1877, and Kido died the same year. Okubo, who had emerged as the strongest leader, was assassinated by a die-hard conservative in 1878 in revenge for Saigo's death, and Iwakura followed, though by natural causes, in 1883. This left control to a new and slightly younger group from among the leaders. Prominent among them were Ito Hirobumi of Choshu, Okuma Shigenobu of Hizen, who had taken the lead in many of the economic and administrative reforms, Yamagata of Choshu, the builder of the new army, and Matsukata of Satsuma, who had led in tax reforms and the restoration of fiscal stability.

In 1879 the leaders had the emperor request each of them for their personal views on plans for a constitution. Okuma, who was quite iconoclastic by Japanese standards and something of an outsider in the government group, being from neither Satsuma nor Choshu, presented in 1881 a radical proposal for the immediate adoption of the full British parliamentary system. The others were shocked and regarded Okuma's act as a dangerous play for popular support and increased personal influence. They decided to drop him from the government and countered his move by agreeing on a slow and cautious approach to constitutional government; in the emperor's name, they issued a promise that a constitution would be adopted by 1890. Okuma, on leaving the government, followed Itagaki's example by founding a political party in 1882. In the same year he also started a school to train political leaders, which grew into Waseda University, joining Keio as one of Japan's two most prestigious private universities. Thus by the early 1880s there were two popular parties demanding a share in political leadership.

Ito took the lead within the government in drawing up the new constitution. As early as 1881 certain basic principles of a strongly conservative nature had been agreed upon, and Ito then led a study mission to observe the working of the various constitutions of Europe, visiting both England and France but concentrating on relatively conservative Germany and Austria. The greater authority of the monarchs and the limited powers of the parliaments in these two lands seemed to him to better fit conditions in Japan than the political systems of England and the other more liberal countries.

This choice of conservative German and Austrian models for the constitution coincided with a swing in the mid-1880s away from a craze for all things Western and back toward traditional Japanese values. This was the first of the swings of the pendulum that have characterized Japanese attitudes toward the West during the past century and a half and are also found in the reactions of other non-Western countries that are attempting to modernize themselves. In such swings, a period of avid borrowing from the West is followed by a reaction against it, before a new swing toward Western influence begins again. In Japan's backward swing of the 1880s, certain unnecessary aspects of Western civilization were abandoned, such as ballroom dancing, which the Japanese leadership had been valiantly attempting to adopt. Philosophic justification for the reversion to older concepts was expressed in a document called the Imperial Rescript on Education, which was issued in 1890, the very year the new constitution went into effect. The rescript had little to say about education but extolled traditional Confucian and Japanese virtues, becoming in time a sort of revered manifesto of Japanese conservatism.

The actual drafting of the constitution did not take place until just before the promised date of 1890 and was undertaken with infinite care; German scholars were consulted so that the document would be philosophically respectable in Western eyes while still being applicable to Japanese social and political conditions. To be sure of its practicability, Ito and his colleagues first experimented with elements that were to become part of the new system. The central concern of the oligarchs was to protect the emperor's prerogatives, because these gave them their own authority and justification for rule. Ito also saw the emperor as a spiritual force taking the place of Christianity, which he felt lay behind the constitutions of the European states. In the constitution, the emperor was described as "sacred and inviolable," and full sovereignty and all powers were placed in his hands, at least in theory. The throne was also surrounded with institutions to bolster its strength, such as a privy council of undefined powers, created in 1888. In order to have a House of Peers to balance a popular assembly, as in the traditional British parliamentary pattern, a peerage was created in 1884. It was made up from the old court aristocracy, the former daimyo, and the new leaders themselves, who eventually promoted their most prominent members to the top ranks of prince and marquis.

In 1885 a modern cabinet system was adopted to exercise central executive control, though it was not specifically mentioned in the constitution so that the elected assembly could not, in the future, force the whole cabinet to resign as a group. Ito became the first prime minister, and the rest of the cabinet was virtually a roster of the oligarchs. For the next decade and a half the oligarchs shuffled the posts around among themselves and their leading protégés, and until 1898 they strictly followed the custom of alternating the prime ministership between men from Choshu and Satsuma.

In 1885 a very advanced civil service system was also adopted, based on the German model. At first, graduates from Tokyo University automatically qualified for the bureaucracy, but soon an excess of candidates made it necessary to add qualifying examinations. These were later opened to all university graduates, though Tokyo University graduates still predominate in the higher civil service today. Both the cabinet and civil service systems as established in 1885 have continued to operate without basic change ever since.

The constitution contained a section on the rights of the people, including most of the civil rights then generally accepted in the more advanced Western nations, but these rights were carefully circumscribed by phrases such as "within the limits of the law." The great innovation of the constitution, of course, was the popular national assembly it created, and great care went into planning for it. Voting and assemblies were first experimented with on the local level, with very limited electorates and powers for these bodies. Prefectural assemblies were first tried in 1879, then village, town, and city ward assemblies in 1880, and finally city assemblies in 1888.

On the basis of this experience, a national House of Representatives was created through the constitution, with an electorate limited to adult males paying at least 15 yen in direct taxes and with powers confined to the passage of laws and the budget. The voting qualifications restricted voters to 1.26 percent of the population, which represented about 6 percent of Japanese families—about the same proportion of the population as the samurai class had been, but made up largely of landowning peasants instead. The naturally very conservative House of Peers enjoyed equal powers with the House of Representatives, further limiting its role. The bicameral legislature formed by these two houses was called the Diet in English, perhaps to make it seem less like the British Parliament. The oligarchs took care to reserve all executive powers for themselves as the self-selected ministers of the emperor, and they accepted the advice of German political scientists that the crucial pursestrings of budgetary control be kept out of the hands of the Diet by a provision in the constitution that if the Diet refused to vote an acceptable new budget, the previous year's budget would continue in effect.

The constitution was promulgated as a gift from the emperor to his people on February 11, 1889, and the first Diet was elected and convened in 1890, on the schedule promised nine years earlier. The constitution has usually been regarded by later historians as having been so conservative that it doomed democracy in Japan to failure from the start. Western commentators of the time, however, felt that the Japanese were trying to move too fast in changing their political system and usually counseled a slower pace. The real wonder is not why the oligarchs did not create a more liberal system, but why they shared as much power as they did with the elected representatives of the people. One reason, of course, was the continual pressure from the parties founded by Itagaki and Okuma and a rising public opinion in favor of representative government, though the oligarchy was now so strong that it could quite safely have created a more restrictive constitutional system than it did. Another reason was the conviction of at least some of the oligarchs that, as in the democracies of the West, a constitution and national assembly would strengthen Japan by winning greater support for the government from the people and would avoid revolutionary pressures by allowing opposition sentiments the fairly harmless escape valve of parliamentary debate. Perhaps most important, however, was the hope of impressing the West with Japan's progress toward "civilization."

This last reason was by no means unfounded. The successful inauguration of constitutional government, together with a complete remodeling of the legal system in accordance with Western practices, did induce the British to agree in 1894 to give up their extraterritorial privileges by 1899, when the new legal system was to go fully into effect, and the other powers quickly followed suit. All that then remained to remove the "unequal treaties" was to win back full control over Japanese tariffs, which was accomplished by 1911. At last Japan stood on terms of full legal equality with the West.

Whatever the new constitutional system did for Japan's image abroad, it proved far less satisfactory to the oligarchs themselves, differing greatly from their expectations. They had failed to realize that the great social and economic changes they had initiated were just beginning to take hold as the first post-Restoration generation was coming to the fore. Their vision in the 1880s of what a stable and permanent political system for Japan should be was rapidly being undermined by the swift economic, social, and intellectual developments they had themselves sponsored. Industrialization was advancing rapidly, and business enterprises were growing tremendously in size, profitability, and influence; the lives of the people were changing under these new conditions, and Japan was becoming rapidly more urbanized; education was becoming truly universal at last; higher education was expanding rapidly, as the government founded new universities, by then called imperial universities, and as many private institutions, which were to grow into huge universities, were organized to teach the new legal system; new concepts kept pouring in from the West, and intellectual life was burgeoning and becoming more diverse; mass public opinion was becoming a significant force; and this public opinion was being fed by rapidly growing newspapers and magazines, founded largely by political outsiders who, as critics of the government, gave a basically antigovernment tone to the press that is still detectable today.

Under these conditions the constitution worked much less smoothly than the leaders had hoped it would. In addition, they had made some serious miscalculations. The House of Representatives proved to be no tame debating society, much less a claque to muster popular support for the government. The political parties had gained electoral skills and parliamentary experience through the local assemblies, and the men elected to the first and all subsequent lower houses proved to be overwhelmingly opposed to the oligarchy, which they dubbed the Satsuma-Choshu (or Satcho) clique. The opposition representatives in the lower house quickly coalesced into two major parties, the Liberals (Jiyuto), who were Itagaki's followers, and the Progressives (Kaishinto), who supported Okuma. Realizing that control of the budget was their one clear avenue to a share in political power, they zeroed in on it, slashing it severely in 1890, and it took a great deal of political maneuvering on the oligarchs' part to limit the cuts to 8 percent.

The next year Matsukata, who was then the prime minister, dissolved the Diet, making do with the previous year's budget. In the election that followed in 1892, the government made use of every means of intimidation, coercion, and bribery open to it through its control of the police and local governors. This proved to be the most corrupt and violent election in Japanese history, but the government still failed to win a majority. Clearly the oligarchs had given away more power than they had intended. The German political theorists had been wrong, because their trump card—continuing last year's budget—was not adequate in a rapidly growing economy. The oligarchs were forced to make compromises with the Diet, and thus the politicians had a foot firmly in the doorway to power.

Appalled by this situation, some of the more conservative oligarchs suggested scrapping the constitution entirely, but this was not easy to do. It had been sanctified as a gift from the emperor, and its early failure would have made the country lose face before the West, indicating that Japan was indeed not yet a "civilized" land. Ito, the constitution's chief author, was particularly determined to make it work. As prime minister for a second time in 1893, he managed to get the budget passed through clever political maneuvering, dissolved the Diet again in 1894, and in 1895 found that the government was supported by the Diet because of popular patriotic enthusiasm over the war then in progress against China. He also managed to work out a sort of compromise by giving Itagaki the powerful post of home minister, in charge of the police and local government, in return for the support of his party. Matsukata followed suit, when he returned as prime minister in 1896, by obtaining the support of Okuma's party in return for making Okuma foreign minister.

The parties, however, kept raising the price for cooperation. When the Liberals demanded four cabinet seats from Ito in his third round as prime minister in 1898, he balked, and the oligarchs, treating Itagaki and Okuma as merely wayward members of their own group, asked them to try their hands at organizing a cabinet. The resulting experiment was a dismal failure, lasting only three months. The two leaders and their party followings were jealous of each other, and the bureaucracy and military proved uncooperative.

Yamagata then took over for a second turn as prime minister, determined to attempt to readjust the system to make it work better. In order to keep the cabinet "transcendent," that is, above politics, as the original intention had been, he strengthened the police laws and controls over political activity. To make the military doubly secure from political interference, he established in 1899 the rule that army and navy ministers must be generals or admirals on active service and therefore under military control. To protect the bureaucracy from political influence, he made all ranks up through the level of vice-ministers open only to professional bureaucrats who had entered through the examinations for the bureaucracy. To make it more difficult for big parties to develop, he introduced an electoral system of large electoral districts with up to thirteen Diet seats each, but with each voter having only one vote. This made candidates of any major party run against other members of their own party and was expected to open the way for the election of more government supporters in a roughly proportional representation system. To get his reforms enacted into law, however, he had to make some concessions to the politicians. These included an increase in Diet seats, the adoption of the secret ballot, and the lowering of the tax qualification for voting to 10 yen, which almost doubled the electorate.

But the struggle between the cabinet and the Diet continued, and Ito, back as prime minister for the fourth time, was finally permitted by the other oligarchs to do what he had long advocated—to form his own political party. In 1900, combining his bureaucratic following with the political line stemming from Itagaki, he formed the Seiyukai, which was to be the major political party for the next few decades and was to act as the supporter of the cabinet for most of that time. By 1901, however, Ito, now party president as well as prime minister, had wearied of the constant bickering of day-to-day politics, and none of the other oligarchs, averaging around sixty years in age by this time, was willing to take up the heavy burden of the prime ministership, which none of them ever assumed again. Although they remained very influential and continued to exercise the emperor's theoretical prerogative of selecting the prime minister, they withdrew into the background somewhat, becoming, indeed, the *genro*, or "elder statesmen."

When Ito resigned in 1901, Yamagata's protégé, General Katsura Taro of Choshu, was selected to succeed him; when he resigned at the end of 1905, he was followed by Ito's protégé and successor as president of the Seiyukai, Prince Saionji Kimmochi of the old court aristocracy, who had imbibed a considerable number of liberal ideas from a long sojourn as a student in France and England. Katsura and Saionji alternated in office until 1912, with the Seiyukai participating fully in the cabinet under Saionji and on the whole supporting it under Katsura. Japan's parliamentary experiment was clearly succeeding and had reached a balance of forces that gave more than a decade of relative tranquillity to the political scene. It was not working quite in accordance with Ito's original plan, but at least it had survived its perilous infant years. For the first time, a parliamentary body in a non-Western country was becoming an established and meaningful part of the political process. In fact, it was showing signs of following the same line of evolutionary development taken by the mother of parliaments in London, though many ups and downs still lay ahead.

During the years that Japan was making this start in its own particular form of constitutional government and was winning legal equality with the West, it also was becoming a major military power and was establishing its own small empire. In those days, no conflict was seen between what we now would consider contrasting trends toward liberalism and conservatism. After all, England and France were not only leading democracies but the greatest empires of the time. Japan's military power and empire were built in clear imitation of such countries, with the purpose of giving it greater security from the West and prestige among the world powers.

Japan has often been described as a traditionally imperialistic nation, but this is far from accurate. Japanese pirates had harassed neighboring countries from the fourteenth to the sixteenth centuries, and Hideyoshi had overrun Korea from 1592 to 1598, but otherwise the Japanese had kept much to themselves. The proposed expedition against Korea that had split the ruling group in 1873 had been designed as a welfare measure for the impoverished samurai class and in any case was never attempted. As a compromise, however, a small expedition had been sent to Taiwan in 1874 to punish a few aborigines for killing some mariners from the Ryukyu Islands. China's payment of an indemnity to Japan because of this incident established, according to Western law, that the Ryukyu Islands were legally part of Japan and not a tributary state of China. They had in fact become a subfief of Satsuma in 1609, and their inhabitants were linguistically and culturally a close variant of the Japanese people, although, under their own kings and tributary to China, their international status had hitherto been ambiguous. Now they were fully incorporated into Japan and made the prefecture of Okinawa in 1879.

Japan settled its northern frontiers in the islands north of Hokkaido by a treaty with Russia in 1875, exchanging Japanese claims to the large island of Sakhalin for Russian claims to the Kuril Islands. The next year Japan became the first country to establish modern treaty relations with Korea, employing the same techniques of naval power Perry had used to force the Tokugawa shogunate to open its doors to the West. Thereafter Japan exercised increasing political influence in the peninsula and began to regard it as a strategic area in terms of security. As China still considered Korea to be its tributary state, rivalry for control over the peninsula began to arise between Japan and China, with reformist elements in Korea looking to Japan for support and conservatives opposing Japanese penetration. In 1885 China and Japan agreed to withdraw their respective military forces from Korea and notify the other if they were to be sent back in. A rebellion of a conservative religious group in 1894 did bring the armies of both countries back into Korea, and this soon led to war between them.

To the amazement of the West, the now thoroughly modernized forces of the small island nation easily triumphed over the Chinese

S I B E R I A

OUTER
MONGOLIA

MANCHURIA

Amur R.

SAKHALIN

KURIL ISLANDS

INNER MONGOLIA

Vladivostok

SEA OF JAPAN

JAPAN

•Peking

LIAOTUNG PEN.

KOREA

CHINA

Weihaiwei

SHANTUNG

•Tsingtao

Nanking•

Hankow•   •Shanghai

Yangtse R.

EAST CHINA SEA

BONIN
ISLANDS

RYUKYU ISLANDS

•OKINAWA

PACIFIC OCEAN

FUKIEN

Canton•

TAIWAN

PESCADORES ISLANDS

Hong Kong

THE JAPANESE EMPIRE

Extent of Japanese Empire

Manchurian Railway Lines

0   300 Miles

SOUTH CHINA SEA

PHILIPPINE ISLANDS

giant. The Japanese swept through Korea and into Manchuria, destroyed the Chinese fleet, and occupied the port of Weihaiwei in North China. The Treaty of Shimonoseki, agreed to on April 17, 1895, brought an end to the Sino-Japanese War. In it, China ceded to Japan the island province of Taiwan, the nearby Pescadores Islands, and the tip of the Liaotung Peninsula in southern Manchuria, paid a large indemnity, accepted the full independence of Korea, and accorded the Japanese the same unequal diplomatic and commercial privileges the Westerners had extorted from China.

In an age of rampant imperialism, the Westerners, far from condemning the Japanese for their aggressions, applauded them as being apt pupils. They went on to teach the Japanese how ruthless the game of imperialism could be and how unwilling Westerners were to accept other races as full equals. Russia, France, and Germany banded together to force Japan to return the Liaotung Peninsula to China, since Russia had its eyes on the ice-free ports of this area. Three years later these same powers cynically seized new slices of China, the Russians taking the Liaotung Peninsula for themselves. Even Britain followed suit by taking Weihaiwei, the port the Japanese had occupied in North China.

The Japanese swallowed this humiliation, but they began to foresee an inevitable clash with Russia, which was already dominant in Manchuria and was extending its influence into Korea. Not wishing to face a coalition of European powers again, the Japanese sought a Western ally. This they found in Britain, which was not averse to seeing its Russian rival embroiled in war in East Asia and was eager to share the growing burden of world naval supremacy in distant areas. The resulting Anglo-Japanese Alliance of 1902, which guaranteed that Russia would not be joined by other Western nations in a war with Japan, was the first entirely equal military pact between a Western and non-Western nation.

The stage was now set for a showdown with Russia. Choosing their time in February 1904, the Japanese set a new pattern of modern warfare by first crippling Russian naval strength in East Asia and then declaring war. Russia was far stronger than Japan, but had the disadvantage of having to fight the war at the end of a single-track railway several thousand miles long. Its military operations were further hampered by revolutionary movements at home. The Japanese were consistently victorious, bottling up the Russians in the Liaotung Peninsula ports, which fell after costly assaults, and driving their other armies northward through Manchuria. Russia sent its European fleet from the Baltic Sea around Africa to the Pacific, but the entire Japanese navy waylaid and annihilated it in the straits between Japan and Korea. Although Russia was being soundly trounced, Japan was so exhausted that it welcomed the peace arranged by President Theodore Roosevelt, who greatly admired Japanese efficiency and pluck. A treaty signed in Portsmouth, New Hampshire, terminated the Russo-Japanese War on September 5, 1905. In it Russia acknowledged Japan's paramount interests in Korea, transferred to Japan its lease of the Liaotung Peninsula and the railways it had built in southern Manchuria, and ceded the southern half of Sakhalin in lieu of an indemnity. Japan, the military ally of Great Britain, the victor over Russia, and the possessor of an expanding colonial empire, was becoming a true world power.

Relieved of Chinese and Russian competition in Korea, Japan quietly annexed the whole of the peninsula in 1910, without the slightest protest from any Western power. Even at that late date, it was generally accepted in the West that strong and advanced nations had the right to rule over weaker and more backward lands for the good of the colonies as well as for the benefit of the colonial masters. In Korea, as earlier in Taiwan, Japan embarked on an ambitious program of economic development and exploitation, which brought railways, school systems, factories, and other outward aspects of the modern world to these lands. The Koreans and Taiwanese, however, were subjected to the repressive rule of an efficient but sometimes ruthless colonial administration and an omnipresent and often brutal police force. Particularly in Korea, where annexation had come later and had encountered the proud traditions of a homogeneous people who had had their own centralized, Chinese-type bureaucratic state for more than a thousand years, Japanese colonial rule proved extremely oppressive and was deeply hated.

In 1914 World War I gave Japan another chance to expand, this time with little risk or effort. As the ally of Britain, it soon declared war on Germany. Little interested in what happened in Europe, Japan happily proceeded to pick up German colonies in the East, taking Tsingtao on the Chinese coast and all the German interests in the surrounding province of Shantung, and seizing the German islands in the North Pacific—the Marianas, Carolines, and Marshalls—which were later assigned to Japan in the form of a mandate by the Versailles peace treaty. With the eyes of the rest of the world turned toward Europe, Japan also found this a good time to win more concessions from China and, in 1915, presented it with the so-called Twenty-one Demands. Although the Chinese succeeded in resisting the most sweeping of these, which would have turned their country into a virtual protectorate, Japan did win broad new economic rights in Manchuria, Shantung, and the coastal province of Fukien opposite Taiwan.

Thus, only fifty years after the Restoration, Japan in 1918 emerged from World War I as Britain's chief rival for domination in China. It went to the peace conference at Versailles as one of the Big Five among the victors, an accepted world power. The Meiji leaders, who had set out in 1868 to create a Japan that would be militarily secure from the West and fully equal to it, had, within the lifetimes of their more long-lived members, done exactly that. Few generations of political leaders anywhere have proved so fully successful in attaining their goals.

10

ECONOMIC AND
POLITICAL GROWTH

Japan's development as a military power was not just matched by its
great economic advances but was, in large part, based on them. Starting with the boom in cotton spinning in the 1880s, Japan succeeded in
the light industries in one new field after another. The Sino-Japanese
War with its indemnity and even the exhausting Russo-Japanese War
proved to be strong stimulants to the economy. World War I was even
more of a boon, because it cost Japan little but gave it the markets of
Asia cut off from the factories of Europe by the war. Japanese businessmen took full advantage of this opportunity to make deep inroads
into rich markets previously monopolized by Europeans.

As the first non-Western land to adopt the industrial and commercial techniques of the West on a significant scale, Japan found itself in
a unique position. Western technology and cheap Oriental labor made
an excellent combination for low-priced production. The rest of Asia
had cheap labor but as yet lacked technical skills; Europe and North
America had high technology and far greater natural resources than
Japan, but also much higher standards of living and therefore correspondingly higher wages. This discrepancy between Oriental and Occidental standards of living and the lag in the industrialization of other
non-Western lands gave the new Japanese industries and commercial
enterprises an exceptional chance for rapid growth. Producing for its

own relatively poor citizenry and for the even poorer populations of the rest of Asia, Japanese industry became particularly oriented toward cheap and sometimes shoddy consumer goods. Textiles accounted for more than half of factory employment at the end of the nineteenth century and predominated in the export trade. Heavy industries such as steel and shipbuilding were developed to some extent, but largely for strategic reasons. It was not until the 1930s that the Japanese could begin to compete with the much more industrially experienced Western nations in these fields.

Japan found itself provided with an ample and competent supply of labor. The poorer classes were already familiar with working for wages, and Japan's relatively advanced traditional industries had made them skilled workers. Modern education made them even more valuable. The population, responding to modern medicine and transport facilities, doubled to 60 million within a little over a half-century after the Meiji Restoration, and rural Japan, already saturated with people in the Tokugawa period, became a seemingly inexhaustible reservoir for cheap urban labor.

The contrast with the United States was sharp. There the mechanization of farming released workers for urban labor, but at the same time greatly increased the scale and prosperity of agriculture. This pattern was possible only where land was abundant and labor scarce. In Japan there was a minimum of land and an abundance of labor. Since there was little unused land, except in Hokkaido, and the average size of a farm in the other islands was only 2.5 acres, the increased rural population had to drain off to the cities. But the new industries could not grow fast enough to absorb it all; thus rural areas remained saturated with people, and city wages remained inexorably tied to the inevitably low living standards of Japanese agriculture. Farm girls between the termination of their schooling and marriage in their twenties became the bulk of the workers in textile mills. Herded into dormitories, they provided a cheap but docile and efficient working force. Younger sons, forced to migrate to the cities, became in time a more permanent urban working class; but tied as they were to their rural backgrounds, and returning to their old homes for subsistence in hard times, they were at first little more than an urbanized peasantry.

Japan's great industrial success thus did not bring a rapid rise in living standards for the lower classes. Population growth was too great, and the drag of a dense, impoverished peasantry too strong. All classes did benefit from cheaper and better manufactured goods, such as inexpensive cotton cloth, rubber-soled footwear, rubber boots, and bicycles, and they also benefited from modern services, such as public schooling, improved medicine, electric lighting, and cheap and convenient railway service. The rapid descent of Japan's numerous though small rivers was fully exploited to bring electric power to all corners of the land. Municipal water and gas systems and streetcar networks were developed in cities. But there was little improvement in such basics as food and housing.

Another reason why the masses failed to share fully in Japan's tremendous growth was that the government, like those of the West at that time, was concerned more with national power than the equalization of wealth. It permitted and even encouraged the heavy concentration of private wealth in the hands of a few individuals. One reason for this situation was Matsukata's economic policies in the 1880s, which had given a relatively small group the chance to get hold of most of the more promising new industries. A more important reason was the continuing government policy of channeling business and financial aid to those they regarded as best able to build the economic sinews Japan needed. Since these were often men with whom the government leaders were closely connected by previous background or marriage, much of this favoritism would be judged scandalous by contemporary standards. For example, Iwasaki got his start in building up the Mitsubishi interests through ships and funds provided by the government in connection with the Taiwan campaign of 1874 and the Satsuma rebellion of 1877. But scandalous or not, such collusion between government and private business interests did help to produce rapid economic growth.

This situation resulted in a relationship of cooperation and trust between government and big business, which stood in sharp contrast to the American tradition of suspicion and hostility between the two. Japanese businessmen readily accepted guidance and control from the government—this, after all, had also been the situation in Tokugawa times. Now guidance and control took modern forms, such as mergers and cartels sponsored or encouraged by the government. The Mitsui and Mitsubishi shipping interests, for example, merged in 1885 to form a single strong Japanese shipping enterprise more capable of competing with Western shipping lines. Similarly, the cotton spinners, in order to strengthen their hand in buying cotton on the world market, formed a strong cartel in the 1890s under Shibusawa's leadership. The net result of such mergers and cartels was that the Japanese showed more conscious effort and greater skill in shaping the national economy than had as yet been shown anywhere in the West.

Under these conditions, the individual economic enterprises grew to be huge and powerful. Mitsui, Mitsubishi, Sumitomo, and Yasuda were the four largest and set the pattern for the unique Japanese institution of the *zaibatsu* combines, or conglomerates as they might be called today. Commonly there was a central, family-owned "holding company," which, through large blocks of shares, controlled major industrial and commercial firms, which in turn controlled lesser affiliates. A zaibatsu combine was not concentrated in a single field, as were the great business enterprises of the West at that time, but was spread throughout the whole of the modern sector of the economy. Combines usually centered around great banking institutions, but they were also likely to include manufacturing, mining, shipping, and foreign trade. This last was in the hands of a general trading company (*sogo shosha*), a purely Japanese innovation. The trading companies developed great networks of foreign contacts and gathered information in order to sell and purchase a wide variety of goods abroad and perform various other services connected with foreign trade, which most individual firms would not have had the facilities to perform for themselves.

The structure of a zaibatsu combine was not unlike that of the Tokugawa *bakufu*, with its fiefs and subfiefs. There were feudal overtones in the personal relation within the combines as well. Loyalty was strong, since young businessmen joined a combine for life and rose by moving among its various units. A system of interlocking directors further strengthened solidarity. The system of lifelong careers within a single economic enterprise also began to extend in the early decades of the twentieth century to the central core of skilled workers, who were seen as a valuable commodity. They too came to enjoy lifetime job security, and their loyalty to the firm was further ensured by wage scales that increased with length of service. This pattern of job security and salaries determined by seniority for both management and labor came in time to be one of the most distinctive features of Japanese business enterprises as compared with those of the West.

The great wealth and broad base of the combines enabled them to finance promising new fields in the economy and thus increase their share in its fast-growing industrial sectors. It gave Japan the concentration of risk capital needed for long-range investments in risky new fields. The zaibatsu families, apparently influenced by Confucian and

UPI/Bettmann Newsphotos

Downtown Tokyo before the 1923 earthquake.

feudal Japanese values, proved to be conspicuous underconsumers. Unlike the wealthy in some developing lands, they did not go in for yachts, foreign bank accounts, and villas abroad, but assiduously plowed back their profits into expanding their economic empires. The common people, largely through post office savings accounts, also showed a comparable propensity for saving that has continued to the present day.

Despite their acceptance of government guidance and leadership, the zaibatsu developed great rivalries with one another, and the competition between Mitsui and Mitsubishi came to be legendary. The zaibatsu also became increasingly influential in politics. Because of their size, the government had to pay attention to their views, and the political parties began to look upon them as their major means of financial support. In the 1880s, even before there was a Diet, the parties were accusing each other of being the pawns of Mitsui or Mitsubishi, and it was commonly believed that the political line from which the Seiyukai grew was tied to Mitsui, while the other major political line was popularly associated with Mitsubishi.

The basic role of the zaibatsu in Japanese history has been a highly debated subject. One view is that their drive for international trade caused Japan's modern imperialism, but this interpretation seems exaggerated. On the whole they preferred peaceful trade abroad and lower taxes at home. Their great size made them unwieldy and therefore economically inefficient in some ways. Quite clearly their concentration of private wealth proved unhealthy for the nation's social and political development. At the same time, their ability to undertake long-range investments in order to open up promising new economic fields and their heavy reinvestment of capital in economic expansion undoubtedly helped account for Japan's extraordinarily rapid industrial growth.

Japan's rapid economic, political, and military rise was accompanied by great social and intellectual changes that occurred in a much more confused and uneven way. Between 1890 and the 1920s the percentage of the population in cities and towns rose from slightly over 10 percent to close to 50 percent. Such changes involved basic shifts in life styles and in attitudes. A fully literate citizenry was emerging, and higher education increased almost tenfold between 1900 and 1940. A strong, self-confident business community was developing, as well as a huge new urban class characterized by the well-educated white collar worker, who came to be called the "salary man" (*sarari-man*) and became in time the basic Japanese self-image.

A second post-Restoration generation was appearing, purely the product of the new education and lacking entirely the old background, with its shared feudal and Confucian values. The original Meiji leaders, coming from a uniform and stable background, had never doubted their own Japaneseness or the primary national goals of security from the West and equality with it. But these goals had been achieved, and the new generation, with its more varied experiences, was not agreed on what the new goals for Japan should be. They were torn between the Japanese environment in which they lived and their education, which was largely focused on the West and its technology. They were subject to diverse and often conflicting intellectual influences. Their more specialized training led individuals to different careers and contrasting points of view. They were less sure than their predecessors just who they were and what Japan's role in the world should be— questions that have bothered the Japanese periodically ever since.

The early popularizers of Western ideas and institutions, such as Fukuzawa, had spread concepts of English utilitarianism, Social Darwinism, and the philosophy of Rousseau. Some of the able young samurai, largely from the parts of the country that had had no share in the Meiji revolution and the political leadership it produced, eagerly embraced Protestant Christianity as a substitute for discredited Confucianism. They created a strong native church that, together with the missionary educational institutions, gave Christianity far more intellectual influence in Japan than one would have expected from the number of its adherents, which never exceeded 1 percent of the population in modern times. Uchimura Kanzo, a Christian stalwart whose "No Church movement" consisted of an unstructured group of Christian intellectuals who rejected the sectarian divisions of Western Christianity, became a nationally prominent advocate of pacifism and helped establish Christian values as a liberal alternative to the official government ideology. In particular, Christianity emphasized the Western concept of individualism, which ran counter to the Japanese tendency to subordinate the individual to family and group solidarity. Christians also led the way in fostering higher education for women and in various efforts at social welfare work.

In sharp contrast with these Christian influences, the swing back toward Japanese values in the 1880s produced new ultraconservative trends of thought, and the standard philosophy of the government higher schools and universities came to be based on Hegel and the German type of idealism. Socialist thought also began to creep into Japan. At first it came largely through some Christians who, returned from study in the United States, took the lead around the turn of the century in trying to start labor unions and a Socialist party, which was immediately suppressed. A Christian revived the labor movement in 1912 and another tried to create tenant unions in the 1920s. Throughout, however, there had also been non-Christian socialists and anarchists, and following the Russian Revolution of 1917, Marxist influences became predominant in both the labor and socialist movements, though an identifiable Christian element survived until well past World War II.

In a now fully literate society, the vigorous mass media became the center of public opinion, which was by now broad and strong enough to influence national policy. This could first be detected in the strong popular demand for revision of the "unequal treaties," which swept Japan in the decade before 1894 and made the negotiations for ending the treaties all the more difficult for the government. Mass public opinion was even clearer in the vast outpouring of patriotic fervor during the wars with China in 1894–1895 and with Russia in 1904–1905. At the close of the Russo-Japanese War, public feeling erupted in violent riots against the government, which the people, unaware of Japan's near collapse, believed had betrayed the country by not obtaining an indemnity from Russia. Again in 1918, serious rioting broke out all over the country against the high price of rice. Clearly public opinion had become a force to be reckoned with.

The speed of Japan's transformation produced a ferment of intellectual activity, but also considerable confusion and even alienation. This was first seen clearly in literature. Literary activity in the early Meiji period had been largely concerned with the translation of Western books and the popularization and adaptation of Western ideas. But, as a more purely native Japanese literature revived around the turn of the century, it showed clear signs of alienation. Caught between the trends of rapid modernization inspired by the West and the traditional, more collective values of Japanese life, the new writers turned inward, away from society and toward their own individual psychological concerns. The greatest of the early writers, Natsume Soseki, who as a professor of English literature at Tokyo University had obviously been greatly influenced by the West, explored the psychological problems of his countrymen with keen perception and often with humor. Others showed a more pessimistic strain. The intensely personal "I novel," as the Japanese call it, which often focuses on highly individualistic, eccentric, or even bizarre psychological problems, became common and is still characteristic of much of Japanese writing even today.

With the economy, society, and intellectual life all changing rapidly, it is not surprising that the balance among political forces that had given Japan relative political stability between 1900 and 1912 gave way to a period of comparatively rapid political change. The shift started in 1912 with a dispute between the army and the cabinet over the military budget, but behind this incident lay more basic factors.

The death of the Meiji emperor in the summer of 1912 and the accession of his son, whose "year period" was named Taisho, gave rise to a general feeling that an era had ended and a new one begun.

This mood was heightened by the new emperor's mental incompetence and, therefore, his clear inability to exercise the powers theoretically reserved for him by the constitution. The fading away of the *genro* also contributed to a feeling of change. If the oligarchs had still been in power the crisis of 1912 could not have occurred, but by then they were indeed merely "elder statesmen," still making the final decision on who the prime minister would be, but by no means in full control of the whole government.

The situation revealed a major weakness of the 1889 constitution—the assumption that an alter ego would exercise the emperor's powers for him. Perhaps Ito had expected the oligarchy to be self-perpetuating or that some other organ, such as the privy council, would grow to take its place. But neither happened, and the Japanese government began to break up into a series of semiautonomous but balancing elite groups—the high court officials around the throne; the civil bureaucracy, itself divided into a number of quarreling ministries; the military, divided between the mutually jealous army and navy; the Diet, with its contending parties; and behind the parties, big business and the general public. The *genro* were something of a unifying force, but they were beginning to disappear from the scene. Ito, after serving as resident general in Korea before its annexation, was assassinated in Manchuria by a Korean patriot in 1909. Most of the others died between 1900 and 1916 and the last two, Yamagata and Matsukata, in 1922 and 1924.

The crisis of 1912 started late that autumn when the army, dissatisfied with the budget Saionji, the prime minister, had assigned it, withdrew the army minister from the cabinet, as had been made possible by Yamagata's 1899 reform, thus forcing the cabinet to resign, since it could not operate without an army minister. As usual, General Katsura was called in to replace Saionji, but the Seiyukai, furious with the army, refused to cooperate with this former army leader. Katsura had the emperor instruct Saionji to request the Seiyukai's cooperation, but it paid no attention. Katsura then tried to organize a second political party for support, but the attempt came too late, though the party itself was to become the Seiyukai's chief rival under a series of changing names, the best known being the Minseito, or Popular Government party, which was adopted in 1927. There was a great public outcry called the "movement to preserve constitutional government." Ironically, what the public was attempting to "preserve" was a cabinet responsible to a parliamentary majority, exactly the system the framers of the constitution had been determined to avoid by having "transcendental" cabinets that would be above politics.

The crisis, known as the "Taisho political change," indicated that it was no longer possible to rule without majority support in the Diet. It also showed the futility of an imperial appeal to the politicians, and none was ever attempted again. More ominously, it revealed that the military could act on its own by making use of its constitutional prerogative—subordination only to an inactive emperor. To correct this situation, the 1899 ruling that army and navy ministers must be on active service was changed in 1913, but without avail because no prime minister ever dared challenge the autonomy of the armed services by taking advantage of this change.

The crisis subsided early in 1913, when an admiral of Satsuma origin was chosen as a sort of compromise prime minister and formed a cabinet that included six members from the Seiyukai, thus ensuring its support. When this cabinet resigned the following year over a scandal involving the purchase of naval vessels from Germany, it was succeeded by one headed by Okuma, the old oligarch turned politician, who had the support of the party Katsura had formed to oppose the Seiyukai.

Though Okuma himself had been a major political figure ever since the 1870s, a real change of leadership was taking place. The strong man of his cabinet was the foreign minister, Kato Takaaki. A product of the new age, Kato had gone through the new educational system and had become a successful foreign ministry bureaucrat and, in 1914, the president of the anti-Seiyukai party. Now, as foreign minister in 1915, he paid no attention to the *genro* when deciding to make the Twenty-one Demands on China. In 1914 Saionji was succeeded as president of the Seiyukai by Hara Kei, like Kato, a new type of leader. Descended from a very high samurai family of a domain in northern Honshu, Hara, as an outsider to the old Satsuma-Choshu clique, had battled his way to the top, first as a newspaperman critical of the government and then as a Seiyukai politician who had been the strong man behind Saionji all along. He was an astute politician skilled in pork-barrel politics, who used his usual cabinet post as home minister to reward electoral districts that voted Seiyukai with the plums of government spending and to win the cooperation of bureaucrats with promotions. He had no compunction about frustrating army wishes for strategic, broad-gauge trunk railway lines, using the railway budget for more politically advantageous small branch lines instead. Feeling himself an outsider, he refused to be rewarded with a title of nobility. Thus the two strong leaders of the two main political parties were both entirely products of the new age.

When the Okuma cabinet resigned in 1916, Yamagata tried to return to the old system of "transcendental" cabinets under one of his protégé generals from Choshu, but the experiment proved a failure; the cabinet, faced with the rice riots over the high price of this staple food, resigned in 1918. Bowing to the inevitable, Yamagata finally accepted a real politician as prime minister. He chose the wily and ingratiating Hara over Kato, who Yamagata thought was arrogant, disrespectful, and Anglophile. With the formation of Hara's party cabinet in September 1918, the politicians' small share of power through partial budgetary control in 1890 had expanded to full control of the cabinet. In slightly less than three decades, Japan seemed to have traveled the whole way from the creation of a feeble national assembly to responsible parliamentary government, a process that had taken centuries in England.

Hara had led the fight for parliamentary supremacy, but he was scarcely a liberal by modern standards. He refrained from carrying out the now-insistent popular demand for universal male suffrage. Instead, he compromised with a further reduction of the tax requirements for voting to 3 yen in 1919, which increased the franchise to about a quarter of the male heads of families. He also abandoned Yamagata's large electoral district system for one-seat constituencies of the Anglo-American type, through which major parties could operate more easily.

Hara proved a skillful leader and, if he had enjoyed a prolonged period of power, might have profoundly affected the later course of Japanese history. But unfortunately he was assassinated by a demented youth in November 1921, and his Seiyukai successor, Takahashi Korekiyo, proved much less competent and resigned within seven months. Starting in 1922 there was a two-year return to successive nonparty prime ministers, two admirals and a bureaucratic protégé of Yamagata, but none of their cabinets met with much success. The first of these cabinets, although it lasted the longest, was actually dominated by the Seiyukai; the other two lasted only four and five months each. When the last of the three cabinets saw its supporters hopelessly outvoted in the election of May 1924, it resigned, and Japan returned to party cabinets, with Kato finally having his chance as prime minister. Since all the original oligarchs were now dead, the choice this time was made by Saionji who, because of his descent from the ancient court aristocracy and his own long service as prime minister, had been added to the group. He was to remain the "last *genro*" until his death in 1940.

Kato's government dropped all tax qualifications for voting in 1925, thus achieving universal manhood suffrage at last. Britain itself had not accomplished this until 1867, and it was no mean achievement for Japan, less than sixty years after the abandonment of a feudal system of government and only thirty-five years after the establishment of its first national assembly. In this same reform, a "middle size electoral district system," a compromise between Yamagata's "large" and Hara's "small" systems, was adopted. According to the new system, three to five seats were assigned to each electoral district, but the individual voter had only a single vote. The result was a reasonably close approximation to proportional representation. This system and many of the election regulations instituted at this time are still in force today. In 1926 another political reform, this time in the field of local government, loosened central government control over local politics somewhat. The counties, which had been the lowest level of direct central government control, were abolished, and municipal mayors were chosen by the locally elected assemblies.

Unfortunately, Kato died in 1926 and was succeeded by a less competent lieutenant. In 1927 the cabinet passed back into the hands of the Seiyukai, by now under the presidency of General Tanaka Giichi, who after heading the army had switched to parliamentary politics as the way to supreme political power. Two years later the cabinet returned to the hands of the other party, by then called the Minseito, but from 1931 to 1932 it was once again controlled by the Seiyukai.

The years from 1913 to 1932, which saw the rapid rise of parliamentary power and then the leadership of party cabinets, have been called the period of "Taisho democracy." This term is not limited to political matters, but includes the broad range of liberalizing tendencies and the swing of the pendulum back to enthusiastic borrowing from the West that characterized these years. Behind these trends lay the great expansion of the Japanese economy, which peaked during World War I, and the enthusiasm for liberal Western concepts that swept Japan when the outcome of the war proved to be the triumph of Britain, France, and the United States, the major Western democracies, and the downfall of the more autocratic nations—Germany, Russia, and the Austro-Hungarian Empire.

There was a general loosening of old social patterns during this period, at least in urban areas. A great worldwide influenza epidemic in 1918 together with the great Kanto earthquake and fire of September 1, 1923, helped accelerate the rate of social change. This cataclysm, which destroyed half of Tokyo and most of Yokohama and took approximately 130,000 lives, helped sweep away old ways and cleared the ground, literally, for new cities and, figuratively, for a new society.

Downtown Tokyo became a city of wide thoroughfares and steel and reinforced concrete buildings, with sections resembling the cities of Europe and America more than those of Asia. The Marunouchi district around Tokyo's main railway station became the pride of the nation and a symbol of the new Japan. Other cities followed Tokyo's lead. Modern office buildings, school buildings, large movie houses,

Destruction in Tokyo resulting from the great Kanto earthquake and fire of September 1, 1923.

UPI

great stadiums, and sprawling railway stations became the typical architecture of urban Japan. The morning newspaper, long daily commuting by train and streetcar between home and office, and the quick break for lunch came to typify a new urban life style.

Family solidarity, paternal authority, and male dominance remained salient features of Japanese society, but increasingly the younger generation in the cities joined the worldwide revolt of youth and began to question time-honored social customs. College students embraced the freer social concepts of the West, and there was a growing demand on the part of youth to be allowed to have marriages of love rather than marriages arranged by families through go-betweens. Women office workers became a feature of the new social system, and many middle-class Japanese men began to treat their wives almost as social equals. The women of Japan slowly began to free themselves from their traditional position as domestic drudges.

The mass culture of the modern West was also manifested in Japan. As in the United States, the symbol of the twenties was the "flapper," called by the Japanese the *moga*, a contraction of the English words "modern girl." Moving pictures, made either in Hollywood or in Japan on Hollywood patterns, had a tremendous vogue, and American jazz and Western social dancing became popular with the more sophisticated. A growing taste for Western music was evident in the organization of symphony orchestras and in the huge audiences that gathered to hear visiting Western musicians. Taxi-dance halls appeared; all-girl musical review troupes rivaled the popularity of the movies; Western and Chinese restaurants became numerous; and there was a mushroom growth of so-called cafés, where gramophones ground out American jazz and emancipated young men enjoyed the company of pretty young waitresses of doubtful morals.

The Japanese threw themselves into Western sports with enthusiasm. Tennis was already extremely popular, but now they concentrated on track and field sports as well, with a view to making a better showing at the Olympic Games, and they actually came to dominate the Olympic swimming events in the 1930s. Golf links were built for the rich, while young people took up skiing. Baseball, however, was the great national sport, and university and high-school baseball games drew crowds comparable to those attending major college football and big league baseball games in the United States.

Great changes were occurring not just in life styles but intellectually as well. Thousands of books poured from the presses, and the literature of the whole world became available in cheap translated editions. Great Tokyo and Osaka newspapers came to have circulations in the millions. Higher education expanded rapidly. In 1918 some private colleges were granted university status, and by 1935 there were forty-five imperial and private universities. The first women's college was founded in 1901, and it was followed by others, turning out a thin stream of educated women. In scholarship and the sciences, Japanese began to produce work that drew international attention. On the basis of a broadly expanded mastery of modern technology, business firms began to enter a great number of new and more advanced fields, establishing the roots of many industries that were to flourish greatly after World War II. Meanwhile the zaibatsu combines expanded enormously, and the patterns of industrial organization that were to prove very advantageous to Japan after the war were gradually developed and refined. In all ways urban Japan was changing and in doing so was drawing ever further away in thought and habits from the rural parts of the country.

On the surface, it may have seemed that Japan, already having managed the transition from a feudal state to a modern, centralized nation, was now succeeding in making the even more difficult passage from an authoritarian society to a modern, liberal mass democracy. But this proved not to be the case. Beneath the surface much remained unchanged, and the modern attitudes and ways of life were largely limited to the cities. There were also many unsolved problems, some of which were coming to a head.

The return of the Europeans to the markets of Asia after World War I compounded the difficulties of adjusting Japan's overexpanded wartime economy to postwar conditions. Japanese economic growth in the 1920s was the slowest of any decade from the 1880s to World War II. Agriculture did poorly, since no significant new technological advances were made, and Japanese farmers had to compete with the low-wage production of Japan's new empire in Taiwan and Korea. As the decade progressed, conditions worsened: Bank failures swept the country in 1927, and in 1929 the worldwide depression hit, cutting deeply into foreign trade. Between 1925 and 1931 the prices for rice, Japan's chief agricultural product, and for silk, its chief export, plummeted by over 50 percent. People in sections of rural Japan faced starvation, and cases of desperate farm families selling their daughters into prostitution were highly publicized by the press. The whole economy was in a state of crisis.

Another economic problem had also reached serious proportions by the 1920s. This was what the Japanese have called the "dual economy," which was a deep division between the highly productive modern industries on the one hand and agriculture and the traditional, low-productivity handicraft industries and services on the other. The people of rural Japan, half the population, were in the lower section, left far behind by the industrial progress of the cities and resentful of their own declining relative position. The appearance of a "dual economy" has characterized rapidly industrializing countries everywhere, but in Japan this problem was particularly severe because of the speed of the nation's economic growth. The situation was at its worst during the period following World War I.

Still another economic as well as social problem was that, as the Japanese economy developed, the old ties between employers and employees became less personal, leading to greater friction. Tenant farmers, for example, began to show serious signs of discontent. Although tenancy had been limited to the 45 percent level it had reached by the beginning of the twentieth century, there was a sharp increase in tenant–landlord disputes in the 1920s and some organization of tenants into unions. Urban labor, which was beginning to free itself from its agrarian background, was also becoming restive. More than 300,000 workers were involved in labor disputes in 1919 alone, and by the end of the twenties a like number had become organized into unions. Early in the century, a few small starts at social and labor legislation had been made to meet the changing conditions of an industrializing society and these were somewhat expanded in the 1920s, but as in the case of the Western democracies, the effort lagged badly behind the needs.

To many Japanese the country's growing dependence on foreign sources of raw materials and markets seemed to be its most serious economic problem. Industrialization and a rapid increase in population had made the entirely self-sufficient Japan of only sixty years earlier into a country dependent on outside sources of iron ore, cotton, wool, and a great many other essential industrial materials, and therefore equally dependent on foreign markets for Japanese exports to pay for these imports. The problem of security was shifting from the military to the economic field. This could already be seen in the heavy emphasis on economic issues in the Twenty-one Demands imposed on China in 1915 and in the eagerness with which Japan took over the German interests in Shantung in China and fished for advantages in the roiled waters of the Russian Revolution. In 1918 it sent a force of 72,000 men to Vladivostok in Siberia in a joint expedition with a much smaller American force, ostensibly for the purpose of bolstering an eastern front against Germany.

Imperial expansion for the sake of military security had slowly merged with expansion for the sake of raw materials and markets, but at the end of World War I a profound change took place that made the two objectives somewhat contradictory. A sense of nationalism had been growing for some time in China. After an emotional student outburst in Peking on May 4, 1919, further imperialistic expansion there began to run into the higher costs of boycotts and determined Chinese opposition. This situation became all the more marked when in the mid-1920s the Chinese Nationalists under Chiang Kai-shek swept northward from Canton and effectively unified much of the country for the first time in several decades. President Woodrow Wilson of the United States, through his Fourteen Points, the Versailles Peace Conference, and the founding of the League of Nations, had championed the concept that strong nations should no longer victimize weak ones through imperialistic conquest, and since the European powers were exhausted by war and satiated by earlier imperial expansion, they felt compelled to accept Wilson's doctrines.

Japan was faced with a choice between seeking to meet its economic needs through continued imperial expansion, against rising nationalistic opposition and mounting world disapproval, or allowing its economic security to depend on open world trade and international trust. It was Hara's government that first clearly faced this choice, and it opted for peaceful trade. The decision was in tune with the spirit of the time and the interests of Japanese big business, which stood behind the parties and wished to avoid the double costs of expensive armaments and Chinese trade boycotts. But it was a decision complicated by what had become a naval race among the world's three major sea powers—Britain, the United States, and Japan. To limit the buildup of naval armaments, the United States called a conference of the major world powers in Washington in the winter of 1921–1922. By the time it met, Hara had been assassinated, but the policies Japan followed were his. It agreed to accept a ratio in battleships, the core of the navies of that day, of three for Japan's one-ocean navy to five each for America's and Britain's fleets. In return, Japan obtained American guarantees that bases would not be built west of Hawaii and British guarantees of the same east of Singapore. Japan also agreed to restore by steps the province of Shantung to China, the first voluntary withdrawal of any of the foreign powers from Chinese territory. In 1922 it withdrew its vastly unpopular military expedition from Siberia as well. Between 1919 and 1926 the Japanese actually cut the percentage of their gross national product that went for military purposes by over half.

Although all these decisions had had wide popular and government support when they were made, many Japanese began to doubt their wisdom when the world economy turned sour at the end of the 1920s and major sections of the Japanese economy deteriorated or stagnated. Japan, they felt, had been duped by the nations of the West. The Western powers, having won vast territories in the past, were now content to call a halt to empire building, leaving Japan with too small an empire to maintain its industrial machine in an age of rising trade barriers and shrinking world trade.

Following World War I the party governments faced a series of difficult problems that overburdened their strength. For one thing, parliamentary supremacy was still far from secure. Japan had no long tradition of democratic rule behind it to help its democratic institutions weather such stormy times. The highly conservative House of Peers, unlike the British House of Lords, still had equal powers with the House of Representatives. The privy council and the high court officialdom could still speak for an emperor whose authority, as described in the constitution, appeared almost unlimited. The prime minister did not automatically achieve his position because he was the leader of the majority party in the lower house, as in Britain, but was selected by Saionji, and only then was an election usually held in which he won the necessary majority. There was no deep emotional commitment to democratic principles on the part of most Japanese, and many of them viewed with distaste the open clash of private interests in elections and in the parliamentary process, preferring the older ideal of a harmonious, unified society, governed through consensus by loyal servants of the ruler. In particular, the great financial influence of the zaibatsu and other business groups over the politicians seemed morally unacceptable to people still attuned to Tokugawa prejudices against the merchant class.

In a sense, the "dual structure" of the economy was paralleled by an even more dangerous "dual structure" of society, divided between better educated and largely urban people, who on the whole were in sympathy with the current trends, and less educated and mostly rural people, who were bewildered or repelled by the conditions of the times and looked back nostalgically to older values. Rural Japan remained a vast reservoir of traditional ways and attitudes. As the 1920s progressed, these older attitudes were strengthened by the beginning of another swing of the pendulum away from Western models and back toward those of traditional Japan.

One ominous sign was the lack of wide intellectual support or solid philosophical underpinnings for parliamentary rule. There was a sense of malaise among intellectuals and a groping for concepts more satisfying than the open conflict of interests in a democratic system. Minobe Tatsukichi, a professor at Tokyo University, attempted to bridge the gap between the theoretical powers of the emperor and the reality of parliamentary rule by describing the emperor as the highest "organ" of the state. Although this so-called organ theory was accepted as orthodox at the highest intellectual levels, it had no popular appeal, and at the lower levels, at the military schools, and even among some professors at Tokyo and other universities, the sacrosanct, autocratic powers of the throne continued to be emphasized. A dangerous "dual structure" in political thought was thus also appearing.

Parliamentary supremacy was also undercut by the wave of Marxist ideology that reached Japan in the wake of the Russian Revolution. There had been some socialist and even anarchist thought in Japan since the beginning of the century, but after World War I leftist doctrines became much more widespread and attracted a relatively large proportion of the best minds. Socialism seemed to be a more comprehensive and orderly substitute for traditional Confucianism than parliamentary democracy. Yoshino Sakuzo, a popular Christian professor at Tokyo University during World War I, had advocated most democratic causes but retained an elitist suspicion of mass rule. Many of his disciples turned to Marxism, seeking to be its elitist vanguard. They and similar groups at other great universities, such as Kyoto and Waseda, became the intellectual core of the Marxist movement after graduation, founding leftist parties and trying with occasional success to enlist the support of the working classes. A Communist party was founded in 1922 but was driven underground almost at once. Other so-called proletarian parties, though constantly dividing in sectarian disputes, managed to remain within the law and in 1928, in the first election after the adoption of universal manhood suffrage, elected eight representatives to the Diet.

The older parliamentary parties, having just won their battle for political leadership with the old establishment, showed no desire to share power with these new forces of the Left. Ironically, in 1925, the very year that the vote was extended to all men, the Diet passed a strengthened Peace Preservation Law, which made it a crime to advocate a change in the basic political system or the abolition of private property. This curtailment of free speech and political activity was scarcely propitious at a time when reactionary forces of the Right were beginning to reassert themselves. It showed how weak the ideological support for democracy still was.

Historians have emphasized the shortcomings and failures of the period of "Taisho democracy." This is natural because of what was soon to follow—the collapse of democracy and the tragedy of World War II. But Japan's failures at this time were not really worse than those of the West. Even countries like Britain and the United States handled the problems of the interwar decades poorly, while Italy turned almost at once to fascism, and Germany was taken over by Hitler's Nazi regime in the early 1930s. In fact, the failure of democracy in the West encouraged many Japanese to look upon fascism as the wave of the future. Seen in longer perspective, however, the positive aspects of the period of "Taisho democracy" stand out as probably more significant than the negative ones. It was the political and social ideas of this period that were to reemerge after Japan's defeat in World War II as the solid foundation for the democratic Japan of today, and the industrial advances of the period underlay Japan's postwar economic "miracle."

11

THE RISE OF MILITARISM

The rather sudden shift from the liberalizing trends of "Taisho democracy" during the twenties to the imperial expansion, militarism, and ultranationalism of the thirties has often dominated the discussions of modern Japanese historians. To many observers, it has seemed that naturally authoritarian and militaristic characteristics of the Japanese people finally reemerged after a period of apparently successful but actually superficial "Westernization." To support such views, some cite the seven centuries of rule by a feudal military class, which had come to an end only a few decades earlier, the importance the Meiji leaders placed on creating a strong military, the oligarchic nature of their rule, and the decidedly authoritarian core they tried to give to their constitution of 1889.

Other factors, however, argue against this interpretation. For more than two centuries during the period of late feudalism under the Tokugawa, Japanese society had been extraordinarily peaceful, orderly, bureaucratic, and nonmilitary. The emphasis on military power had been forced on Meiji Japan by the predatory nature of Western imperialism in the nineteenth century. At the same time there was the spontaneous demand by large numbers of Japanese for greater freedom and a share in political rule, which produced a basically parliamentary government by the 1920s. Finally, no major people since World War II have shown themselves to be more confirmed pacifists than the Japanese. Japan, like most other lands, was authoritarian in the past, and like any country with a feudal background it had a broad streak of militarism. But on the whole the Japanese have not shown any special propensity for militarism and authoritarianism that distinguishes them from the people of other nations.

One might compare what happened in Japan in the twenties and thirties with developments in Italy and Germany during this same period, although there were almost as many differences as similarities. All three nations were characterized by unsatisfactory domestic conditions arising from severe economic problems, deep cleavages in life styles and ways of thought among different sections of the population, and national dissatisfaction with their international position as "have not" countries. But Japan's specific transition to militarism and authoritarianism was quite different from the road taken by Italy and Germany.

In Japan there was no charismatic leader, no clear-cut Fascist or Nazi type of philosophy, no mass party to support the leader, and little suppression of the opposition by force. The change was made strictly within the ambiguities of the 1889 constitution by a series of small adjustments among the various forces that constituted the political balance of power. In the twenties the Diet, with the backing of big business interests and public opinion, was beginning to take the leading role over the court officialdom, the bureaucracy, and the military. By the end of the 1930s it was the military, aided by foreign wars and heavy indoctrination of the people, that had clearly taken the driver's seat. In many ways Japan, like Italy and Germany, was moving toward totalitarianism, which, whether of the Right or Left, might be defined as authoritarian rule over a modern educated people through the government's attempt to control their lives and thought completely. The Japanese government, however, remained much more pluralistic and far less harsh in the control it exercised than did the rightist and leftist totalitarian states of Europe.

There was a long background to the return to authoritarianism and the upsurge of militarism and ultranationalism that swept Japan in the thirties. Until recently, authoritarian rule had been taken for granted; seven centuries of feudalism had made rule by military men seem natural; and the way Japan had been forced open by the West against its will naturally spawned a strong nationalistic and militaristic reaction. During the Meiji period there had already been signs of what was later to be called ultranationalism. At first it had been part of the general protest movement of outsiders against the government, most spectacularly manifested in the samurai uprisings of the 1870s. Slowly, however, this ultranationalism became a separate movement, stressing support for revolutionary movements against Western domination in other Asian lands and subsequently championing the expanding empire of Japan as the best way to stop the West's subjugation and perversion of the East.

At first, the leadership in the pan-Asian movement came from activists from western Japan who, being closest to the continent, were perhaps more conscious of the problems in other Asian countries than were other Japanese. An organization called the Genyosha was founded in Fukuoka in northern Kyushu in 1881, and in 1901 this spawned another organization called the Kokuryukai. This name has been dramatically translated as the Black Dragon Society, but it was actually based on the Chinese name for the Amur River and signified that Japan's natural strategic frontiers were on this northern boundary of Manchuria.

The imperialistic pressure groups became increasingly involved in reactionary political causes at home, and the whole movement became larger and more influential after World War I. Certain conservative bureaucrats of high standing founded more intellectually respectable nationalistic societies, and several popular propagandists appeared. These men, for the most part, looked back to the authoritarian and agrarian traditions of the past, and like the Meiji leaders before them drew the cloak of imperial sanctity around their own ideas. They claimed that what they advocated was the true *kokutai*, or ''national polity,'' and asserted that they represented the real ''imperial will.'' While both terms had long been in use, it was at this time that they became widely popularized.

The ultranationalists drew encouragement from the successes of the Italian Fascists and later the German Nazis, and they commonly looked for leadership to the army and navy, which were strictly modern institutions based on Western models. Nevertheless, the ultranationalists were fundamentally anti-Western, at least on a selective basis, being firmly against the democratic, individualistic, and capitalistic aspects of the West. They saw party politicians as the venal lackeys of selfish moneyed interests, epitomized by the zaibatsu, which was used as a term of opprobrium, and they regarded the current social trends of the cities as the utter corruption of beautiful traditional Japanese ways. Naturally there was a strongly sympathetic response to such ideas among rural Japanese and others who were in the lower half of the "dual structure" of the economy and society. For them, with their lesser educations, the nationalistic indoctrination of the modern school system proved more important than the new horizons education had opened for others. Most families had remained internally authoritarian; there was still an easy acceptance of hierarchy; elitist assumptions were strong on the part of leaders of all sorts; and the old Confucian ideals of social harmony and conformity still had a much greater appeal than the individualism of the West and the admitted clash of interests of parliamentary government.

Such traditional attitudes strengthened in the late 1920s as Japan's economic problems worsened and the pendulum once again swung away from imitation of the West. These trends also took on strongly racist overtones, as Japanese came to feel that, despite Japan's status as one of the great world powers, Westerners were still not willing to accept them as full equals on racial grounds. At the Versailles Peace Conference in 1919 Japan had argued for the inclusion of a clause on "racial equality," but this had been blocked by the United States and Britain because there was strong opposition in America, Canada, and Australia to Oriental immigration. Moreover, throughout the Occident there had been for decades much racist talk of the "yellow peril." In the United States, Orientals had been declared ineligible for naturalization on racial grounds, and California and other western states denied them the right to own land. California went so far as to put Japanese children, like Chinese children before them, into segregated schools. To ease the strains of this situation, Japan and the United States had in 1908 worked out a Gentlemen's Agreement that virtually ended Japanese immigration. Despite this, Congress passed an Exclusion Act in 1924 that applied specifically to Japanese as aliens ineligible for citizenship. This was deeply resented by all Japanese as a gratuitous insult. Though really a part of American rather than Japanese history, it is worth noting that anti-Oriental racism in the United States was to reach its peak in the early days of World War II, when the whole Japanese population of the West Coast, loyal, native-born *nisei* citizens and their inoffensive, elderly, immigrant parents alike, were driven out of their farms and homes and herded into virtual concentration camps. Not until 1988 were some amends made by the payment of a paltry $20,000 to each of the surviving internees of the camps.

The organized ultranationalist movement remained relatively small in Japan and never proved politically dominant, as it did in Italy and

Germany. It was principally significant for helping stimulate a much broader but more inchoate reaction against the liberal trends of the twenties. It was natural for this reaction to center around the army and navy, which despite their modern origins seemed to symbolize the old values. The military officers were no Junker class, and the samurai coloring of early Meiji days had largely been lost. By the 1920s military leaders, like most of the other elites, were the product of a specialized education and career and not distinguished by birth. Nonetheless, Japanese found it easy to believe that army and navy officers, as servants of the state, were more honest and dependable—or, as they put it, more ''sincere''—than rich industrialists and self-seeking politicians. The military officers themselves, segregated from other Japanese by education at a relatively early age and deeply indoctrinated in a proud tradition, believed this fully. Naturally they tended toward conservative views and were particularly concerned that the abandonment of imperial expansion in the twenties would ultimately undermine Japan's security.

In some ways, the peasantry had a special affinity for the military. Though the descendants of peasants who for almost three centuries had been denied swords or other arms and had been treated with disdain by the samurai class, they were soon induced by the new mass education to take pride in Japan's military exploits and to glory in the ideal of military service to the emperor and, if necessary, death in his name on the battlefield. Constituting the great bulk of the conscripts, they often found service in the armed forces their one exciting release from an otherwise boring life of farm labor, and the reservist organizations of military men who had completed their terms of active service were important forces in the life of rural Japan. The military officers, for their part, worrying that the rural depression of the late twenties was undermining the health of the peasantry on whom they relied for manpower, were seriously concerned about economic conditions in the countryside. There was thus a genuine resonance in emotional attitudes between the military and the peasantry.

Some historians have suggested that if the party governments had been wiser and had won the confidence of the people to a greater extent, the militaristic reaction of the thirties might have been avoided. In particular, it has been argued that if the new parties of the Left had been given greater freedom, the tragedy of militarism might have been averted. But this seems doubtful. The older parties continued to win overwhelming majorities in elections right through the thirties, at the very time when real power was slipping from their grasp. Perhaps if the twenties had been more favorable economically and party government had had the chance to function for a couple of decades of relative calm and prosperity, democratic precedents might have strengthened sufficiently to bear the weight of more difficult times, but this was not what happened. Parliamentary government had only a decade of troubled supremacy before it was forced to shoulder what proved to be unbearable problems.

In the late 1920s there were many reasons for discontent and anxiety, but, as in the 1850s and 1860s, it was foreign issues that proved crucial. Throughout the decade, the civil government basically followed a policy of accommodation to Chinese nationalism and conciliation toward the views of Britain and the United States. Much has been made of the contrast between the relatively liberal policies of the cabinets of the Minseito line from 1924 to 1927 and 1929 to 1931, in which the foreign minister was Shidehara Kijuro, and the "hard line" toward China of General Tanaka as Seiyukai prime minister from 1927 to 1929, but the difference between the two was more a matter of style and nuance. Both parties clung tenaciously to Japan's established position but sought to avoid open confrontation.

As the decade progressed, however, there was growing discontent, particularly in the military. Japan, it was felt, was being bottled up by hostile forces that would keep it a second-class nation permanently. Japanese were denied the right to emigrate to the attractive open lands of North America and Australia; their exports were meeting growing restrictions abroad; they had been persuaded to give up trying to win a greater empire in China and were even having trouble holding on to the rights they had already won, as Chinese nationalist fervor swept northward into Japan's special bailiwick of Manchuria. Meanwhile, Japan's dependence on foreign sources of raw materials and food increased steadily as population and industry both grew.

The nation, it seemed to many, faced a serious population crisis that could only be solved by military expansion. The leadership at home appeared weak and irresolute, while national will and public morals were degenerating. The time for drastic action was at hand;

Japan must reverse course and seize an adequate empire, more comparable to those of the Western powers in order to support its burgeoning population and industry. History was to prove such thinking wrong. The wars it produced were disastrous, and Japan after World War II, unencumbered by any empire, has become a far more prosperous and successful country than ever before. But in the late twenties and thirties militaristic concepts seemed like common sense to many Japanese.

The army and navy were most concerned with foreign policy and thanks to Yamagata had retained a large degree of autonomy from the civil government, enabling them to act on their own. The army had shown signs of independence in 1912, but the first clear indication of just how willing it was to act on its own came in 1928. In May Japanese army units temporarily blocked the northward advance of the Chinese Nationalist armies in Shantung, and in June young officers of the Kwantung Army, the Japanese military force in Manchuria, blew up a train to get rid of the local warlord and Japanese puppet, Chang Tso-lin, whom they considered insufficiently cooperative. The new emperor, Hirohito, who after five years as prince regent for his incompetent father had succeeded to the throne late in 1926. He had come to maturity at the height of postwar liberalism and had studied briefly in England in 1921. He was outraged at the unauthorized killing of Chang Tso-lin and demanded of his prime minister, General Tanaka, that the responsible officers be disciplined. The army refused Tanaka's request, claiming that such discipline would hurt army prestige and that, according to the constitution, the civil government had no authority over the army, which came under the "supreme command" of the emperor alone.

This incident was very revealing in three ways. As far as is known, this was the first important political action a Japanese emperor had initiated in modern times, and it failed. Also, the army successfully defied the civil government, even though the prime minister was a man who had recently been in charge of the army. And the crisis, which helped commit Japan to a more intransigent stand in Manchuria, had been precipitated by middle-grade officers in the field, who received the support of their sympathetic seniors on the grounds that the man on the spot had to be given wide discretionary powers.

It is doubtful that this insubordinate action would have occurred if the mood of the nation and particularly the military had not changed considerably from what it had been only a short time earlier. This shift in mood was again revealed in the 1930 London Naval Conference, which was a follow-up to the earlier Washington disarmament conference. The limitations on naval construction were extended to include a ratio for heavy cruisers of 10:10:7 among Britain, the United States, and Japan. The agreement was not accepted in Japan without violent protest and the almost fatal shooting of the Minseito prime minister by a fanatic. In 1935 a third naval conference, again held in London, ended in complete failure.

The full turn of the tide came in 1931 with another case of "direct action" by some middle-grade officers in Manchuria, but on a larger scale than in 1928. On the night of September 18, they blew up a small section of the South Manchurian Railway, which Japan owned. Claiming that this had been sabotage, they used this pretext to overrun all Manchuria in a series of rapid military moves. Obviously they could not have done this without tacit approval by elements of the high command in Tokyo, and the whole of the army closed ranks behind them. The emperor and the leaders of the civil government tried to keep the "incident" under control, but found themselves helpless. The navy, jealous of the army's glory, stirred up a fight with the Chinese in Shanghai late in January 1932, but its landing party was unable to finish the job and had to be rescued by three army divisions. The army separated Manchuria from China, making it a puppet state, and in September 1932 Japan recognized this as the nation of Manchukuo, under the last Manchu emperor of China, who had abdicated the throne as an infant in 1912.

In January 1932 the United States enunciated a policy of "nonrecognition" of Japanese conquests, which it held to thereafter. The League of Nations sent a commission of inquiry to Manchuria, which brought in a report condemning Japan. But when the League adopted this report in March 1933, Japan simply withdrew, thus contributing to the League's rapid decline. In 1933 and 1934, undeterred by foreign criticism, the Japanese army continued a series of smaller "incidents" that established its control over the eastern part of Inner Mongolia and areas in North China around Peking.

The so-called Manchurian Incident created a war psychology in Japan. The populace was swept by a nationalistic euphoria over the spectacularly easy conquest of Manchuria, an area far larger than Japan itself, with a population of 30 million hard-working Chinese. The army became committed to an expansionist policy on the continent, from which it could not back down without great loss of face and

UPI

Japanese troops entering Harbin in northern Manchuria in February 1932.

of power in Japan itself. The "incident" also made clear what had been merely hinted at in the murder of Chang Tso-lin in 1928: The emperor and the civil government could not control the army. In fact, it was the army that was establishing Japanese foreign policy through *faits accomplis*, and all the civil government could do was serve as an unhappy apologist for this policy before the world. A sort of dual government was emerging, with the military holding the upper hand so far as foreign policy was concerned.

The military is commonly spoken of in the singular, but it was itself a complex, pluralistic aggregate of individuals and factions. The army generals were divided between the modernizers, who sought to build a more fully mechanized force, and those who emphasized the "spiritual power" of the emperor's army as the true source of its strength. The latter element, which came to be known as the "imperial way faction" (*kodoha*), enthusiastically supported such acts as the assassination of Chang Tso-lin and the Manchurian Incident. The modernizers, though not at all averse to military expansion, were more aware of the needs for greater mechanization in the face of growing Soviet military power and were less approving of middle-rank officers whose adventurous "direct action" verged on insubordination. This group, later called the "control faction" (*toseiha*), felt the need for more discipline and contended bitterly with the "imperial way faction" for control of the army.

Another division in the military existed between the army and navy, which had always been jealous of each other. The navy, patterned on the British navy and more open to the influence of world opinion because of its higher technology and greater international contacts, tended to be more cautious than the army. It was concerned about the sources of fuel for its ships, which at the time was oil largely from the West Coast of the United States and from Indonesia, then known as the Dutch East Indies. The navy was primarily interested in a strategy directed southward toward Indonesian oil and the bases of Anglo-American naval power, while the army thought in terms of a northern strategy aimed at expansion on the nearby continent and against Soviet land power.

Another cleavage in the military had developed between the older, more conservative officers and the more thoroughly indoctrinated younger officers, who were eager for daring action as well as promotions, but saw themselves blocked in both by their elders. Protected by the "imperial way" firebrands among their superiors, junior officers in the field frequently bullied their more cautious commanders into taking "direct action," while staff officers in military councils in Tokyo put more subtle pressure on their superiors. By the early 1930s the so-called younger officers problem had reached serious proportions. A small extremist element among the younger officers was beginning to adopt terrorist tactics at home by reverting to the sort of political assassinations that had been common during the last troubled years of the Tokugawa. For the most part these men were young zealots who had become disciples of one or another of the popular ultranationalist propagandists. Younger officers of this type plotted in the spring of 1931 a "Showa Restoration," named for the year period of Hirohito's reign. This and a second plot that autumn were quashed by the military authorities, but in February 1932 young officer extremists did succeed in assassinating the finance minister who had just left office and a leading Mitsui executive, and on May 15 (in the so-called 5–15 Incident), they assassinated the Seiyukai prime minister, Inukai Tsuyoshi, who was probably the most democratic person to have attained that post and had been specifically chosen by Saionji the previous December in order to control the Manchurian Incident. Similar assassination plots were nipped in the bud in 1933 and 1934, but in 1935 a lieutenant colonel cut down one of the three chief generals of the army in his office in an outburst of factional violence.

The army's direct actions in Manchuria had brought a reversal of Japan's foreign policy, and this was soon followed by a shift in the balance of power within the civil government at home. The shift was a direct outgrowth of three related factors—the increased influence of the military as the controller of foreign policy, the changed public mood produced by military success abroad, and the terrorist activities of some of the younger officers. Although the military did not officially condone the acts of the young zealots, it used them to put pressure on the civil government. In their trials the culprits were allowed to expound their own views at length and to condemn their victims, with the result that the trials seemed to be aimed more at the victims than at their murderers. The public proved extraordinarily tolerant of these deeds of violence, tending to admire openly the "pure" motives of the young assassins and condoning crimes they saw as mitigated by the "corruption" of those who had been killed.

Some civil leaders thought of bringing the army under control through the budget, but the majority felt this would be too dangerous, possibly sparking a military coup d'état. Under these circumstances, Saionji concluded that it was time to return to "national unity" cabinets, a new version of the old "transcendental" concept. Since the navy was considered less controversial and more moderate than the army, he selected Admiral Saito Makoto, known as the most "liberal" of the Japanese governor-generals of Korea, as successor to Inukai in 1932. Saito still had seven party politicians in his cabinet, and Admiral Okada Keisuke, who succeeded him in 1934, appointed five. But Okada also included several of the so-called revisionist bureaucrats, who supported the army's new foreign policies. He also took the supervision of Manchurian affairs from the foreign ministry and put it under the army ministry, and he opened civil service posts to military officers, starting what turned out to be a growing penetration of the civil government by the army and navy.

Another big turning point in domestic politics was precipitated by the February 26 Incident (or 2–26 Incident) of 1936. A group of young extremist officers used elements of the First Division in Tokyo to try to sweep away all the top government leaders of whom they disapproved. They succeeded in killing the current finance minister and former prime minister, Takahashi; the Lord Privy Seal, who was the former prime minister, Admiral Saito; and one of the three top generals of the army; but they only wounded the Grand Chamberlain, Admiral Suzuki Kantaro; while Saionji and the current prime minister, Admiral Okada, managed to escape, the latter because his brother-in-law happened to resemble him and was killed instead through mistaken identity. This "incident" was the biggest military challenge to the government since the Satsuma rebellion of 1877. The "control faction" of the army, by then in control, saw that it had to crack down on this sort of insubordination, and it firmly suppressed the incipient coup d'état and dealt severely with the leaders. This was made possible because the emperor was determined that such acts be punished and because the navy decided to back the more conservative army forces, marshaling its power in their support. Discipline was restored to the army, and there was no further violent factional fighting or rank insubordination by younger officers. But from the army's point of view, there was no longer any need for that sort of "direct action" either. By then the military had achieved control over the civil government as well as over Japan's foreign policy.

Following the February 26 Incident, Hirota Koki, one of the revisionist bureaucrats from the foreign ministry, supplanted Okada as prime minister. Although he retained four party men in his cabinet, it had a decidedly more conservative cast than the preceding cabinet, and he cooperated in the further penetration of the civil government by the military. He also restored Yamagata's old ruling that only generals and admirals on active duty could head the service ministries. In February 1937 Hirota was followed by General Hayashi Senjuro, who for the first time had no party men in his government. The parties had thus lost any foothold in the cabinet. But the two main parties still could win elections. Five months after the outbreak of the Manchurian Incident, they had won between them 447 out of the 466 seats in the lower house. Six days before the February 26 Incident of 1936, they were able to win 379 seats, and in April 1937 they carried 354 seats. In the 1936 election the Minseito actually won a clear plurality with the slogan "What shall it be? Parliamentary government or Fascism?" The new leftist movement was also doing well at the polls. The Social Mass party (Shakai Taishuto), which was an amalgamation of the more moderate leftists who were willing to work through parliamentary methods, won 18 seats in 1936 and doubled its showing to 37 the next year.

But despite overwhelming majorities in the Diet and occasional daring speeches by some Diet members, the parties had lost virtually all political power. The public, while voting for them, emotionally supported the army's foreign policies and the belief that the "crisis" required cabinets of "national unity." The parties, in an effort to hold on to whatever political power they could, had employed the same strategy of pragmatic compromise they had used to come to power—but now the process worked in reverse. Each successive compromise left them with diminished influence.

The powerful civil bureaucrats, divided among mutually jealous ministries, fought to maintain their various prerogatives but failed to take concerted action to block military domination, and their revisionist members jumped on the army bandwagon. Only some of the high court officials around the emperor stubbornly held out in favor of the old Meiji interpretation of national unity. In January 1937 Saionji attempted to arrange the selection as prime minister of a former general who had cooperated well with the parties in the twenties and was willing to be his own army minister, but in the face of determined army opposition the attempt failed. In June 1937, after the resignation of General Hayashi, Saionji again sought to create a truly "transcendental" cabinet by selecting his own protégé from the old aristocracy, Prince Konoe Fumimaro, as prime minister. Konoe, however, turned out to be a weak and ambivalent man, and the outbreak of war with China only a month after he took office robbed him of any chance to rein in the military. On the contrary, he permitted the formation in October 1937 of a Cabinet Planning Office, staffed in large part by military officers, which usurped the power of financial coordination from the ministry of finance, thus giving control of the very heart of the civil government to the military. Saionji, aware of his own great age, created a body of "senior statesmen," consisting of former top admirals and generals and retired prime ministers, and theoretically this group took over his duties when he died in 1940 at the age of ninety-one. But by then the military was firmly in control of the government.

After the outbreak of the war with China in July 1937, a so-called Imperial Headquarters (*Dai hon'ei*) was set up between the army and navy to direct the war, and it became the place where the truly important national decisions were made. Liaison Conferences between it and members of the cabinet became the medium for passing the decisions of the military on to the civil government, which in a sense had come to be merely in charge of managing the home front in behalf of the military. Particularly important decisions were ratified by so-called Imperial Conferences, in which military decisions were presented to the military and civil leaders assembled in the presence of a silent emperor. Finally, in the face of imminent war with the United States, this dual but imbalanced structure of government was reunified. On October 18, 1941, General Tojo Hideki, the army minister, became at the same time the prime minister and for a while the home minister in charge of local government. Thus the military's control over the whole government became completely clear.

As the military leaders took control step by step and a war psychology increasingly permeated the country, Japan took on some of the totalitarian coloring of the Fascists and Nazis of Europe, though in considerably more muted shades. The army and navy had no love for industrial capitalism, and many officers tended toward the national socialist thinking of contemporary Europe. The zaibatsu leaders and most other businessmen, on the other hand, looked with alarm at the adventurist policies of the military abroad and their soaring budgets at home. But neither side proved doctrinaire in its attitudes, and a sort of marriage of convenience ensued.

There was less economic change than one might have expected. Despite its supposed concern for the peasantry, the army did little or nothing directly to alleviate rural conditions. The twenties and thirties saw the continued development of the economy from light industry to heavy industry and chemical production. This happened to fit in well with military needs for expanding arms production. War also demanded increased budgets through deficit financing, bringing Japan quite early to a sort of Keynesian solution to the economic depression then gripping the world. The result was another burst of industrial expansion. While the older zaibatsu firms were wedded to traditional international trading patterns and the earlier kinds of industry, new entrepreneurs eagerly developed the fields of chemical production and heavy industry.

At first the army had been determined to exploit the economy of its new Manchurian empire on its own, but when it found itself lacking the skills for this, it encouraged the participation of these "new zaibatsu" in the development of this continental empire. Much has been made of the supposedly pro-militarist stance of the "new zaibatsu" as opposed to the older ones, but the real distinction between them was not so much their political attitudes as the types of industrial activity on which they concentrated. The army for its part, while theoretically despising businessmen and favoring some sort of national socialism, did almost nothing to nationalize the economy. It sought instead to mold the existing forms of business and industry into a self-sufficient, industrially strong "national defense state" and to achieve "total mobilization," which, rather than national socialism, were the catchwords used to describe its economic goals. Under wartime conditions and attitudes, Japanese industrialization pushed ahead as fast as it could, channeled by the military leaders toward strategic objectives, but not constrained by political and social theories.

Changes that were much greater and more clearly totalitarian took place in the areas of personal freedom and thought. The Peace Preservation Law of 1925 had made it a crime to advocate the overthrow of the "national polity" or the abolition of private property, and after 1931 laws such as this were enforced with new vigor, at home by the "special" police, often called the "thought control" police, and throughout the empire by the infamous military police, the *kempeitai*. Hundreds of leftist political and labor leaders, intellectuals, and university students were thrown into prison and forced to recant their "dangerous thoughts." Professors were dismissed for their theories. Minobe, whose "organ theory" had been generally accepted by sophisticated Japanese in the twenties, was now accused of *lèse majesté*. In 1935 he was dismissed not only from his university post but from his appointive seat in the House of Peers, and his writings were banned. This sort of official McCarthyism on the part of the government was outdone by volunteer McCarthyism perpetrated by ultranationalist enthusiasts, whose tactics of harassment and intimidation proved very effective in silencing most dissent in what was still a relatively tightly knit and conformist society.

The other side of the coin was indoctrination. The Japanese government had engaged in this from the start of its program of modernization, but now the effort was stepped up and spread not just through the schools but also through the mass media. Textbooks were repeatedly revised to bring them in line with the spirit of the time. There was, however, no *Mein Kampf* of Japanese totalitarianism. An effort was made to produce a national philosophy, resulting in a book called *Kokutai no hongi* (*Fundamentals of National Polity*), but this was a strange amalgam of outmoded ideas. It stressed the ancient mythology and the superiority of Japan to other countries because of the uniqueness of its unbroken imperial line. There was a great deal of material about the "imperial will," but also much about the Confucian virtues of harmony, loyalty, and filial piety as well as Japan's own medieval "way of the warrior." It was deeply anti-Western and even more specifically aimed against individualism, which was alleged to be responsible for all the Western vices from democracy to communism. But there was little to give guidance to the movement.

The *Kokutai no hongi* was characteristic of much of the thought of the time, which increased in emotional intensity but not in intellectual content. Its positive ideas were at best vague. It fell back largely on undefined terms like "Japanese spirit," "national polity," and assorted slogans, such as one dug out of ancient Chinese philosophy and thought to mean "the whole world under one roof" (*hakko ichiu*). Conveniently, this could be interpreted as innocuously referring to the natural bond between all peoples or more menacingly to worldwide Japanese domination. The thought of the time was somewhat more explicit in what it condemned: greedy capitalists, corrupt politicians, individualism, internationalism, and a menacing but at the same time effete West. These were all lumped together in obloquy, each helping to discredit the others through their common Western background in a sort of institutional guilt by association. All Westerners were looked upon with suspicion, and by the late thirties children sometimes shouted the English word "spy" at any Westerner encountered on the street.

These political and intellectual trends had their effects on society. Anything considered "un-Japanese" was condemned, though the term proved as slippery to define as "un-American." Ballroom dancing was frowned upon as an immoral Western custom, but no one dreamed of abandoning Western military technology. Baseball remained popular, but golf was criticized as a Western luxury sport. A not very successful effort was made to stem the flood of English words into Japanese conversation and writing. Street and railway signs were remade with the Romanized equivalents of place names omitted. Students, labor unions, and newspapers were curbed with increasing rigorousness. And women, while encouraged to come out of the home and fill the work-force needs of a wartime economy, were at the same time told to be nothing more than the obedient wives and dutiful mothers of Japanese tradition.

The trends toward a totalitarian society were unmistakable, but unlike Germany and Italy, no organized mass totalitarian movement emerged. In 1940 Konoe, back as prime minister for a second time, did paste together a large number of organizations into an "Imperial Rule Assistance Association" (*Taisei yokusankai*), but as its ponderous name suggests, it had no life. All the parties were forced to dissolve and enter its parliamentary branch, but even in the wartime election of April 1942, candidates with its official blessing could garner no more than 64 percent of the votes, the rest going to stubborn holdouts. Something closer to a mass organization was created during the war by reviving the traditional Tokugawa system of neighborhood associations (*tonarigumi*) to supervise rationing, spread information, and ensure absolute conformity.

What ideology the reaction of the thirties did have was directed back in history toward the ancient imperial mystique and the virtues of Tokugawa times, but of course there was no turning back to a premodern society or even to Meiji times. What had emerged was a far cry from the social solidarity of earlier days or the natural unity of ideals and objectives of the Meiji leaders. The latter, if they had survived to see it, would have been appalled by the artificial unity forced on a now very diverse society by a military dictatorship, itself divided between a largely autonomous army and navy controlling a supine civil government, disregarding the expressed wishes of the emperor, and embarked on a perilous course of adventure abroad.

The parallels were more with the emerging totalitarian states of Europe, particularly those of the Right, than with anything in Japan's past. As an at least partially modernized country, with an educated populace and a pluralistic society, Japan could scarcely reestablish the old unity and harmony of a simpler, more static age. Nor could there be a traditional and generally accepted autocracy. Educated men inevitably had their own ideas, and they would demand a share in decisions, or else the government had to control them very carefully, limiting not only what they did but what they said and wrote. As in the modernized West, the premodern types of autocracy were no longer viable; totalitarianism had become the only real alternative to democracy. Modernization, moreover, had brought the means to transform premodern autocracy into modern totalitarianism: mass education, mass media, modernized police and military power, and a great centralization of both economic and political controls.

There were great differences, however, between the Japanese experience in totalitarianism and those of the Italians and Germans. The Japanese people, being closer to an authoritarian past, may have been more docile and easily led, while the opponents of the new trends were not well enough entrenched in their liberal ways and ideologies to put up much resistance. In any case, there was no revolutionary change, no sudden, wrenching break with the past, and no liquidation of large numbers of opponents. The changes came in small steps, none seemingly definitive in itself. Japanese totalitarianism thus appeared less harsh and more moderate—and in any case it was a truncated experience that never developed into a fully totalitarian system. Most surprising, it was achieved within the framework of the 1889 constitution. This helps account for the survival of much from the dream of the Meiji oligarchs as well as from the parliamentary system that had evolved out of it.

The constitution indeed proved to be a flexible and ambiguous document. It had accommodated the development of a fair facsimile of the British parliamentary system and then a military dictatorship with totalitarian leanings. This was its virtue in the twenties and its fatal flaw in the thirties. The theory of imperial rule without the reality had left an essentially headless system. It had never really been clear who was in charge—who would choose the prime minister or the other high officials around the emperor who acted in his name. This situation had raised no problems at first because a well-entrenched group of oligarchs occupied these posts and made the decisions; but when they disappeared, no one person or group clearly took their place. The twenties had produced one answer to the problem, the thirties an entirely different solution.

12

WORLD WAR II

World War II, which was in reality the first true "world war," actually started with the outbreak of Japan's conflict with China in 1937, not with the European war of 1939 or the American joining of both wars in 1941. The foreign policy of the Japanese military was based on one seriously mistaken assumption. While giving full rein to Japanese chauvinism, it assumed that Japan's neighbors would not only welcome Japan as a deliverer from Western oppression but would content themselves with docile subordination to Japanese leadership. Nationalism, however, was swelling rapidly, especially in China, and the realities of colonial rule in Korea and Manchuria made the Japanese no more attractive as masters than Europeans or Americans. As Japan's empire grew, so did the Chinese determination to resist. Japan's rise to power in East Asia and its drive for empire had come too late in world history for the same easy success that imperialistic adventures had had in the nineteenth century.

The war with China, which the Japanese euphemistically called the "China Incident," was neither planned in Tokyo nor engineered by insubordinate officers in the field. On the night of July 7, 1937, fighting broke out accidentally between Chinese and Japanese troops on maneuvers near Peking. The Japanese military command in North China tried to settle the trouble locally, but the Chinese government, tired of many such local settlements, which had always been at China's expense, and bolstered by a far more nationally aroused citizenry than had supported it in 1931, demanded a basic settlement. The Tokyo government, now dominated by the military, followed suit by demanding its own version of a "basic settlement." During this impasse, Chinese planes attempted to bomb Japanese warships in the river at Shanghai on August 14, but hit the city instead. A major land battle around Shanghai ensued, while the fighting in the north continued to spread.

The Japanese government decided that the only answer to such Chinese intransigence was a quick knockout blow. It mounted a major military effort, with the army sweeping south and west from its bases in North China. Meanwhile, in heavy fighting, the crack divisions of Chiang Kai-shek's army were finally defeated around Shanghai, and in December the invaders pressed on to capture Nanking, the capital, where Japanese soldiers indulged in an orgy of rape and pillage. But the Chinese continued to fight, and the Japanese doggedly pushed on, seeking the elusive knockout blow. By the autumn of 1938 Hankow in the center of the country and Canton in the far south were captured and most of Inner Mongolia and North China were overrun. The Japanese controlled all the largest cities, all the major ports, the bulk of the railway lines, and most of the more productive and heavily populated parts of the country. But the Nationalist government continued to fight from its provisional capital at Chungking in mountain-girt West China, while a troublesome guerrilla resistance developed around the Chinese Communist center of Yenan in the northwest.

The Japanese set up a puppet regime in North China, and in March 1940 they persuaded Wang Ching-wei, once a major leader among the Nationalists, to head a new, subservient national government in Nanking. But the Chinese masses accorded it nothing more than sullen acquiescence, and the military resistance continued. There seemed to be no end to the war. Chinese nationalism would not bow, and even the great Japanese war machine could not break it. Japan, frustrated by guerrilla tactics in a backward country, thus became the first of the modern military powers to find itself sinking into what was later called the quagmire of Asian nationalism.

The situation was made worse for the Japanese and better for the Chinese by the growing storm clouds of war throughout the world. While the Japanese navy had long regarded the United States as its chief potential enemy, the army expected to fight mainly with the Soviet Union. For this latter reason, Tokyo entered into an Anti-Comintern Pact with Nazi Germany in November 1936, which Italy joined the next year. In the summer of 1938 a large-scale, twelve-day battle did take place with the Soviets on the eastern border of Manchukuo, and beginning the next spring there was a still larger five-month battle on its western frontiers. The Japanese, defeated in both contests, saw that they needed to mechanize their forces a great deal more.

The outbreak of the war in Europe in the summer of 1939 seemed at first a godsend to the Japanese. It helped draw world attention away from East Asia, as had happened in World War I to Japan's economic and military benefit. The collapse of France permitted the Japanese in September 1940 to extend military control over northern Vietnam, or French Indochina as Vietnam, Cambodia, and Laos were then known, in order to block the railway line from there into southwest China. At the same time, they were emboldened to form a full Tripartite Alliance with Germany and Italy in an effort to discourage American interference. In July 1941 they extended military control over the rest of Indochina to secure its potential naval bases. Japan's New Order in East Asia, which had been announced in November 1938 as embracing Japan, China, and Manchukuo, was expanded to accommodate Japan's dream of hegemony over the whole of East Asia. The concept was cloaked by a euphemism—the "Greater East Asia Co-Prosperity Sphere"—and eventually found administrative expression in 1942 in a Greater East Asia Ministry.

The Japanese government failed to realize that the war in Europe and Japan's Tripartite Alliance with Germany and Italy would arouse the American government and people to the potential danger of a world in which a hostile Germany held sway over Western Europe and a hostile Japan over East Asia. Washington had hitherto limited itself to a policy of verbal protests and the doctrine of nonrecognition of the results of Japanese aggression. Now it began to take more substantive countermeasures while building up its own military strength. In July 1939, just before the European war broke out, the American government denounced its commercial treaty with Japan, thus freeing its hand for further economic moves. In July 1940 it adopted a policy of licensing scrap iron and oil shipments to Japan in order to cut down on the flow of these materials, which were essential to the Japanese war machine, and when Japan seized southern Vietnam in July 1941, Washington, together with the British and the Dutch, adopted a total oil embargo.

Japan was now caught on the horns of a dilemma. Both the army and navy were dependent on imported oil and had only about a two-year supply on hand. Victory in China must come soon, or the armed forces would grind to a halt. Japan had to act quickly and decisively. Two choices were open. One was to bring an end to the war in China by generous concessions, withdraw the Japanese troops as the United States demanded, and settle back to profit economically from the war in Europe, as it had done during World War I with such splendid results. This was clearly the course of economic self-interest. With the factory power of Europe temporarily cut off from Asia and threatened with destruction, Japan could take another great step forward in establishing an economic empire in Asia without the attendant costs of conquest, if it could but disentangle itself from the war in China.

But economic self-interest was not to carry the day. To the military, withdrawal from China seemed a national loss of face that could not be tolerated. It would have been interpreted by the Japanese public as an open admission that the military's program of economic security through conquest had failed, and the inevitable public disapproval would have endangered the military's hold on the government. The United States, moreover, was unrealistically insistent that no settlement could be discussed until Japan had relinquished the fruits of its aggressions since 1931. Japan would have to yield first and discover what the terms were later.

The alternative was to sail south, break the tightening economic blockade by seizing the resources of Southeast Asia, particularly the oil of the Dutch East Indies—that is, Indonesia—and thus achieve at one great stroke the much-vaunted Greater East Asia Co-Prosperity Sphere. In preparation for such a move, Tokyo had secured its rear by signing a neutrality pact with the Soviet Union in April 1941. The Japanese had been terribly embarrassed when their German allies, who had a similar agreement with the Soviets, invaded Russia in June, but early Nazi successes seemed to put the Soviets even further out of the picture. The one great danger in the policy of southern conquest was the war that it would undoubtedly precipitate not just with Britain and the Netherlands, which had little military strength in East Asia and were desperately fighting to survive in Europe, but with the United States, which was an incomparably bigger economic power than Japan. But so long as Germany remained undefeated, the United

States, it was felt, would not dare to concentrate much of its military might in the Pacific. Germany would be the first line of Japan's defense. If it won, Japan was safe. If it lost, the Germans would at least have fought a rear-guard action in Japan's behalf by tiring their mutual enemies and giving Japan time to bring China to its knees and to build an invulnerable economic and military empire, protected by the vast expanses of the Pacific and Indian oceans and containing enormous natural resources and hundreds of millions of industrious people.

Japan faced an agonizing, fateful decision. As the result of small initial wagers in 1931 and 1937, it had now been forced into the position of either ignominiously withdrawing from the game and losing what had already been won, or else making a win-all, lose-all play. Konoe and other civilians in the government desperately tried to find some compromise with Washington but ran into a rigidly moralistic American stance. The emperor made his disapproval of the war policy clear. But to the military, in the summer and autumn of 1941, the chances for success seemed good, and with victory would come the creation of the most populous and perhaps the richest empire the world had ever seen. The Japanese military miscalculated not so much on military, geographic, or economic factors as on the human equation. They counted heavily on their own moral superiority, the much-vaunted "Japanese spirit," and the supposed degeneracy and pacifism of the Western democracies, particularly America, which they believed to be corrupted by too much luxury. They were convinced that Americans did not have the will to fight a long war, especially if early Japanese successes showed how great the costs would be.

Repeating the strategy used against Russia in 1904, the Japanese started the war with a brilliantly successful surprise attack on the American naval base at Pearl Harbor in Hawaii at dawn on Sunday, December 7, 1941. They crippled the American navy with this single, sharp blow, virtually eliminating its battleship fleet. However, they missed the aircraft carriers, which were to prove far more important weapons in the ensuing war. The attack on Pearl Harbor cleared the way for an easy conquest of Southeast Asia and the islands north of Australia. It was indeed an unqualified military success for Japan, but it was also a psychological blunder. It united an outraged American people, who had been bitterly divided over the question of participating in the wars in Europe and Asia. The Americans took up arms, grimly determined to crush both Japan and Germany.

Japanese planes sank Britain's two major naval vessels in East Asia off Malaya early in the war, and the Japanese then invaded Singapore from the land and captured this great bastion of the British Empire on February 15. By March 1942 the Dutch East Indies were for the most part under their control. Resistance by the combined American and Filipino forces ended in the Philippines in May, and that same month the conquest of Burma was largely completed. Meanwhile Thailand, the only independent nation in the area, had bowed to prevailing military winds and joined Japan as a passive ally.

The United States, however, threw itself into rebuilding its naval strength and dispatched what forces it could to the Pacific to try to hold the line against Japan. In May American and Australian naval units fought the Japanese to a draw in the Coral Sea northeast of Australia, and the next month the American navy, aided by having broken the Japanese naval communication code, administered a sharp defeat to a Japanese fleet preparing to seize Midway Island west of Hawaii. In September a Japanese effort to cross the island of New Guinea to its south coast was stopped, and in a bitter jungle campaign between August and February, the Americans turned the Japanese back at Guadalcanal northeast of Australia. Japanese forces had thus reached the limit of their conquests within the first year of the war, but it was a long time before the Americans could make serious inroads into the vast empire they had seized.

Japan had entered the war with the United States after four years of war with China, and its economy was already in high gear with its resources fully mobilized. The great conquests in Southeast Asia and the Pacific put a heavy strain on it. Now the United States, with twice the population and more than ten times the economic power of Japan, started to build up overwhelming superiority. The "Japanese spirit" did indeed prove strong, and Japan's forces fought ferociously and often to the last man, but bit by bit they were outclassed on land, on the sea, and in the air. American submarines and aerial mines laid in harbors cut slowly but deeply into Japanese shipping, until by the end of 1944 the overseas armies and garrisons were virtually isolated and could be picked off by the Americans one at a time. The drastic decline in shipping tonnage also reduced the flow of raw materials to

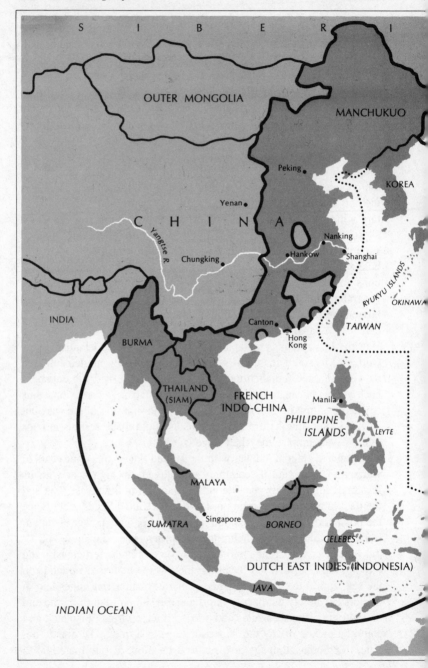

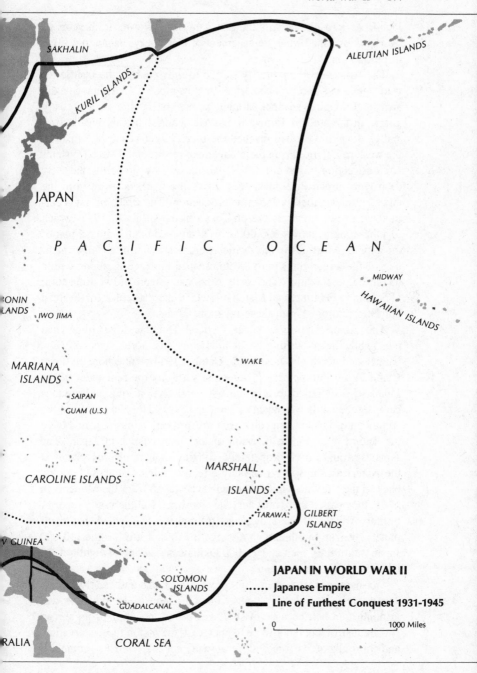

SAKHALIN

ALEUTIAN ISLANDS

KURIL ISLANDS

JAPAN

PACIFIC   OCEAN

MIDWAY

ONIN
LANDS   IWO JIMA

HAWAIIAN ISLANDS

WAKE

MARIANA
ISLANDS

SAIPAN

GUAM (U.S.)

MARSHALL
ISLANDS

CAROLINE ISLANDS

TARAWA   GILBERT
ISLANDS

V GUINEA

JAPAN IN WORLD WAR II

SOLOMON
ISLANDS

...... Japanese Empire

GUADALCANAL

Line of Furthest Conquest 1931-1945

0   1000 Miles

RALIA   CORAL SEA

Japan. As a result, Japan's industry, already suffering from years of overwork and inadequate replacement of machinery, began to decline in production.

The Americans had already started to move across the Pacific toward Japan in a two-pronged drive. In November 1943 the navy began an island-hopping advance straight across the Pacific with a costly attack on the atoll of Tarawa in the Marshall Islands in mid-Pacific, and by June 1944 it had reached the much larger island of Saipan in the western Pacific. From there American planes could start a systematic destruction of the cities of Japan, largely by firebomb raids. By destroying urban dwellings, they drove the workers away from the cities, further crippling Japanese production. The firebomb raids culminated in two great attacks on Tokyo in the spring of 1945, which together took well over 100,000 lives and wiped out the greater part of the capital. Most of the other cities were dealt with in a similar manner; of the larger cities only Kyoto escaped destruction, along with a handful of lesser cities. The costly American seizure of Iwo Jima north of Saipan in February and March of 1945 secured a refuge for disabled bombers returning from these raids on Japan.

The American army, under General Douglas MacArthur, had meanwhile been pushing westward along the north coast of New Guinea and nearby islands, and in October 1944 went ashore on Leyte Island in the Philippines. A desperate sortie by the remainder of the Japanese fleet failed to turn the tide, and after a long and arduous campaign, Manila was taken in February 1945. The two prongs of the American offensive then converged in April on Okinawa, slated to be the staging area for an invasion of the main islands of Japan. The Japanese fought back desperately, flinging their remaining planes at the American ships in remarkably effective suicide attacks. Looking back to the "divine wind" that had saved Japan from the Mongols in 1281, they called these attackers the *kamikaze*. But the vastly superior military weight of the Americans triumphed: The island was completely overrun by June, with a staggering loss of life—some 110,000 Japanese military men and 75,000 Okinawans, about an eighth of the island's civilian population.

Germany had surrendered on May 8, and Japan had clearly lost the war as well. Its cities lay largely in ruins; industrial production was grinding to a halt because of shortages of raw materials from abroad and an insufficient labor force to operate it; the nation faced starvation; and the bulk of its forces were abroad, cut off from the homeland because of lack of transportation. But there was no serious breakdown in civilian morale. The people stoically faced starvation and the mounting war disasters. They appeared resigned to fighting to the end. Moreover, it seemed doubtful to anyone that the Japanese army and navy would ever surrender.

Some high civilian leaders around the emperor, however, had seen the hopelessness of Japan's position as early as 1944 and had started to maneuver toward ending the war. In July of that year General Tojo had been persuaded to pass the prime ministership on to another more moderate general, and a few days after the invasion of Okinawa, the latter was replaced by the aged Admiral Suzuki, who had almost died at the hands of the extremists in the February 26 Incident in 1936. In June the emperor, seizing the initiative, called on the Supreme Council in Tokyo to find a way to end the war, and it attempted to persuade the Soviet Union to mediate. The United States had repeatedly spoken in terms of "unconditional surrender" for Japan as well as Germany, but together with Britain and China, it issued the so-called Potsdam Proclamation on July 26, in which the conditions for Japan's "unconditional surrender" were wisely elaborated. Japan was to be stripped of its empire and occupied until it had remade itself into a peaceful demilitarized nation, but it would retain its national identity, and the people would be free to decide themselves on their future form of government.

The Japanese government probably assumed that it had until mid-autumn to work out a surrender, because the Americans were unlikely to attempt an invasion of the home islands before the typhoon season had ended. But the Americans, uncertain that the Japanese military would ever yield, dropped on Japan on August 6 and 9 two atom bombs they had long been constructing. The bombs wiped out the two large cities of Hiroshima and Nagasaki, killing close to 200,000 people and ushering in the horrors of the nuclear age. The world would never be the same again. In historical retrospect the argument can be made that the first bomb dropped on Hiroshima was necessary to convince the Japanese military that Japan must surrender and also to contribute to the subsequent worldwide realization of the terrible realities of nuclear warfare. But no such justification can be made for the second bomb.

Meanwhile the Soviet Union had invaded Manchuria on August 8 and found the vaunted Kwantung Army of the Japanese little more than a hollow shell. At the Yalta Conference in February, Joseph

American soldier looking at the building above which the atomic bomb exploded over Hiroshima on August 6, 1945.

Stalin had promised his allies to enter the war against Japan within three months of Germany's surrender, and he was eager to enter the fray before it ended in order to have a say in the postwar settlement with Japan.

In the midst of all these disasters, the leaders around the emperor remained deeply concerned about the old concept of "imperial rule." On August 10 they accepted the terms of the Potsdam Proclamation, but only on the understanding that it did not prejudice the emperor's position as a "sovereign ruler." The American reply to this condition was ambiguous, and the Supreme Council split three to three over it. The emperor then made the decision to surrender, the first important political decision a Japanese emperor had been called upon to make since ancient times, and he himself broadcast the surrender announcement to his people on August 14. The war was over. An imperial prince was made prime minister to help ensure the acceptance of the decision by the military. Everywhere the army and navy accepted Tokyo's decision and did not continue to fight on their own, as many

A member of the Japanese surrender delegation signing the document on board the American battleship Missouri *on September 2, 1945. MacArthur stands in front of the microphones at the right, backed by representatives of the allied armies and navies.*

foreign observers had feared they would. On September 2 Japan formally surrendered to General MacArthur on board the battleship *Missouri* in Tokyo Bay.

PART THREE

POSTWAR
JAPAN

13

THE AMERICAN
OCCUPATION

In the late summer of 1945 Japan lay in ruins. Some 3 million of its people had died in the war, a third of them civilians; 40 percent of the aggregate area of the cities had been destroyed, and urban population had dropped by over 50 percent; industry was at a standstill; even agriculture, short of equipment, fertilizer, and workers, had declined. The people had poured all their energies into war, blindly trusting their leaders and confident that the "Japanese spirit" would prevail. Now they were physically and spiritually exhausted. Many were homeless and half-starved, and all were bewildered and mentally numbed. The "divine wind" had failed. For the first time in history, Japan was a conquered nation. The Japanese faced the prospect with trepidation, but as the emperor had put it, they had no choice but to "bear the unbearable."

The period that followed, however, has turned out to be the most glorious in Japan's long history. No one could have imagined such an outcome. It makes the labeling of the whole period simply as "postwar" seem somewhat incongruous. The term did apply fully for a few years, but ever since Japan regained its independence in 1952 people have repeatedly announced that some event or development marked the real end of the postwar period. Meanwhile, however, a new meaning has crept into the term, altering its original reference simply to

World War II. The Japanese people ever since 1945 have been strongly antimilitarist and thoroughly pacifistic. Postwar in this broader sense may well apply to Japan for the remainder of its history, because it is doubtful that the nation could survive the type of war mankind can now wage.

This does not change the fact that the seven years of American occupation and tutelage from 1945 to 1952 clearly constituted a postwar period in every sense of the term. It was also a unique experience not just for Japan but in world history. Never before had one advanced nation attempted to correct from within the presumed imperfections of another advanced nation. And never before had the military occupation of one world power by another been so satisfactory to the victors and tolerable to the vanquished. There was, of course, much to complain about on both sides, but the occupation proved to be an unprecedented international success for the United States and a far less unpleasant experience than the Japanese had anticipated. In fact, in retrospect it came to be seen as a crucial time of rebirth for Japan, comparable only to the Meiji Restoration.

The Japanese and Americans share the credit for this extraordinary outcome. The Americans, far from proving the vengeful, cruel conquerors the Japanese had expected, were basically friendly and benevolent, throwing themselves with enthusiasm into the task of reforming Japan. Fear of the American conquerors soon turned into hope that they would lead Japan to a better day. The Japanese, for their part, turned out to be not at all the fanatical fighters the Americans had come to know on the battlefield, proving instead to be a docile, disciplined, cooperative people at home. When the emperor and his top leaders surrendered, the American army of occupation became the unchallenged locus of authority, and the Japanese people and government, including the army and navy, obeyed it without question.

Perhaps American conquerors were easier to accept than any others because of the long influence of American teachers and missionaries in Japan and the great admiration of many Japanese for the United States, despite all the wartime propaganda and because of, rather than despite, the overwhelming victory of the American forces. There could be no doubt that the Japanese leaders had forced the nation into a disastrous blind alley. Many Japanese felt that since the militarism and authoritarianism of the past had led to catastrophe, then the democracy the Americans extolled, or else the socialism or communism of other Western lands, all of which their recent leaders had condemned, must

be right. The pendulum swung abruptly back toward enthusiastic acceptance of Western influences and away from traditional Japanese
values. The terms "nationalism" and "patriotism" became virtually
taboo.

The complete failure of the military's foreign policy and the terrible
suffering of the war years made most Japanese turn away in revulsion
from military leadership and any form of militarism. They longed for
lasting peace and rapidly shifted their self-image; they no longer saw
themselves as a warrior race but became the most passionate of pacifists. The people were horrified to learn that, far from being welcomed
as the deliverers of Asia from Western oppression, they were bitterly
hated throughout China, Korea, and the Philippines and thoroughly
disliked in other Asian lands. Japanese soldiers, who had left home as
heroes, were spat upon by resentful city crowds as they returned dispirited from overseas. Most Japanese, feeling that they had been duped
by their leaders, were free of any personal sense of guilt and eager for
change.

Even hard-headed leaders, though resentful of American domination and doubtful of some American reforms, realized that open resistance was useless and that only through cooperation could they hope to
influence the policies of the occupation and help bring it to an early
end. They could also see that the military's solution to Japan's great
economic problem stood entirely discredited. In the postwar world
Japan, with its narrow geographic and economic base, could not hope
to be a military competitor with the new superpowers, the United
States and the Soviet Union. Clearly, Japan could not conquer and
hold its own economic empire. If the destitute, overcrowded country
was ever to reestablish a viable economy, it would have to be through
trade in an internationally open and peaceful world. Even former military expansionists rapidly turned into sincere internationalists. The
result of all these changes in attitude was a remarkable degree of
cooperation with the Americans and considerable respect and even
goodwill between victor and vanquished.

The physical, social, and spiritual disruption brought by the war
and by defeat had cleared the ground for a new beginning. Japan lay
wide open to new influences, and the Americans, with supreme self-
confidence, rushed in to fill the vacuum. They brought a massive
flood of new attitudes and institutions, comparable only to the Western
impact in the mid-nineteenth century, but this time much more sudden
and pervasive.

Emperor Hirohito calling on General MacArthur at the American Embassy Residence in October 1945.

General MacArthur had been designated Supreme Commander for the Allied Powers, or SCAP for short. Pronounced "scap," this term was soon applied to the occupation as a whole. MacArthur was a good choice from the point of view of domestic American politics. As the viceroy of a Democratic administration and the hero of the Republican opposition, he enjoyed the confidence of both sides and thus prevented occupation policies from being embroiled in American politics, as happened with China policy. He was also a good choice from the

Japanese point of view. He was undoubtedly a forceful and able leader, and his messianic pose and turn of phrase gave inspiration to the Japanese at a time when they desperately needed it.

The occupation MacArthur headed, though termed Allied, was entirely American, with the exception of some Australian soldiers and an occasional non-American in the headquarters staff. The Soviet Union refused to put troops under MacArthur's command, and Chiang Kaishek was too busy trying to win back North China from the Communists to participate. Subsequently, through an agreement announced at Moscow on December 27, 1945, two international bodies were set up to supervise the occupation. The Far Eastern Commission in Washington, made up of the eleven (later thirteen) countries that had fought in the war against Japan, was to determine major policies. The Allied Council for Japan in Tokyo, made up of the four major powers, the United States, the Soviet Union, Britain, and China, was to advise MacArthur in the field. Neither institution was to prove meaningful. The Allied Council became simply a forum for angry debate between the Soviet and American representatives before their embarrassed colleagues from China and the British Commonwealth. Since the United States had the right to a veto in the deliberations of the Far Eastern Commission and the right to take steps unilaterally in Japan pending the Commission's decisions, that body could in effect do nothing more than approve American policies, which MacArthur in any case was already carrying out.

The Americans, realizing the impossibility of directly administering a nation as complex and as culturally and linguistically alien as Japan, decided to rule through the Japanese government. They inundated the nation with American and Australian troops for a short time to demonstrate the futility of opposition, but concentrated on developing a large occupation bureaucracy in Tokyo to supervise the Japanese government, with relatively small teams maintained in the prefectures to check on the results. The occupation bureaucracy, entirely military in composition at first, gradually became civilian in large part, but retained a basically military structure until the end.

Perhaps the chief reason for the lasting success of the occupation's reforms was that the American government had given careful thought to postwar Japan while the war was still in progress. In striking contrast to its failure to prepare for postwar problems and responsibilities in Korea and the rest of East Asia, the United States trained large numbers of military men in the Japanese language and the problems of controlling Japan, while a small group of experts at the Department of State, in cooperation with other branches of the government, gave careful thought to what reforms should be attempted in postwar Japan. Because of this preparation, the United States was ready at the end of the war for the hasty drafting of the Potsdam Proclamation and the much more extensive United States Initial Post Surrender Policy for Japan. This was an extraordinarily broadminded and far-seeing document, which served as the basic guide for the crucial early stages of the occupation. The American policy was stern but constructive. It was based on the realization that a program of revenge and retribution would breed lasting hatred and unrest and that only through enlightened reform was Japan likely to change from a disturber to a supporter of world peace. The wisest of the American decisions was that, instead of attempting to transplant American democratic institutions to Japan, reforms were to be based on the past democratic achievements of the Japanese, particularly their partial development of a British type of parliamentary government during the period of "Taisho democracy."

The first few months of the occupation were essentially a period of organization and of ground-clearing for the reforms the Americans intended to carry out. The first objective was negative—demilitarizing Japan. The surrender had, of course, brought a speedy end to Japanese control not only over their recent conquests but over Korea and Taiwan as well, and a start was made on repatriating all Japanese from overseas. Over 6 million soldiers and civilians were gathered up and dumped back in Japan by the end of 1947, leaving only a few hundred thousand still in Soviet prison camps in Siberia. The army and navy ministries were converted into the First and Second Demobilization Ministries, which oversaw the speedy demobilization of the military forces and then went out of existence themselves. All munitions industries were closed down, and the occupation embarked on an ambitious program of making available, as reparations to the countries Japan had despoiled, all of Japan's industrial capacity in excess of its bare living needs. But this proved to be unrealistic. The victors could not agree on the division of the spoils; worn-out Japanese industrial equipment was not worth transporting to other countries, to whose economic needs and capacities it was not necessarily adapted; and it was soon discovered that Japan had no excess industrial capacity, but itself faced a grim fight for economic survival.

On the political side, organizations deemed ultranationalistic or militaristic were disbanded; repressive laws were annulled; Communists and other political prisoners were freed; and the special tie between the Shinto religion and the state was dissolved. As a result of this last measure, many of the great historic shrines, thrown back on their own inadequate economic resources, fell into serious financial difficulties. Large numbers of military men accused of atrocities were brought to trial as war criminals and speedily handled on the spot, either in Japan or abroad, and twenty-five former government leaders were tried by an international tribunal in Tokyo for crimes against peace, in the same manner as the Nazi leaders at Nuremberg. There had been, however, no clear-cut leadership group or plot in Japan. By the time the judgments were finally handed down late in 1948 and seven men hanged, including Tojo and one civilian, the former prime minister Hirota (Konoe had "escaped" by committing suicide), the attitude of the Japanese public toward these discredited old men had turned from anger to pity.

A more significant move was the so-called purge. All those felt to be in any way responsible for Japanese conquests abroad were banned from government service and from any position of substantial influence in society. All former military officers and military police were placed in this category, together with most of those who had occupied high positions in overseas regimes or the top posts in the civil government at home, all politicians who had accepted sponsorship by Konoe's Imperial Rule Assistance Association, and some leading businessmen. Purge proceedings were extended to teachers and, combined with the desperate economic plight of this group, resulted in many resignations from schools. Roughly 200,000 persons were involved in the purge, and many others were driven out of office or positions of influence by its threat. The purge can be criticized because it was based on categories, not on individual actions, and thus undermined the democratic concept of individual rights. Still, it did sweep away much of the old leadership, at least temporarily, and made room for new, even if not necessarily better, men.

More important than these negative actions were the occupation's constructive moves toward creating a more democratic political system, on the reasonable assumption that a democratic Japan was more likely to support peace than an autocratic country. The political reforms centered around the writing of a new constitution. When the Japanese government came up in February 1946 with what MacArthur felt to be unsatisfactory proposals for constitutional reform, he had his own staff quickly draft an entirely new document, originally in English. After only slight modifications by the Japanese cabinet, this was presented to the Diet as the emperor's amendment to the 1889 constitution, was passed by this body with only slight alterations, and went into effect on May 3, 1947.

The new constitution made two basic changes in Japan's political structure. One brought the theory of the emperor's position into line with reality by transferring his "sovereignty" to the Japanese people and by making it absolutely clear that he was merely "the symbol of the State and of the unity of the people" and had no political powers whatsoever. On January 1, 1946, the emperor himself had prepared the way by announcing to his people that he was in no sense "divine"—which, of course, he had never been considered to be as "divinity" is understood in the West. The treatment of the emperor was the most controversial aspect of the occupation reforms, especially abroad, where many people wished to see him tried and punished as a war criminal. To have done so, however, would have been quite unjust in view of his actual lack of power and his personal antiwar attitudes. It also might have produced, sooner or later, a dangerous reaction in Japan. This was the chief reason why MacArthur and the American army refused to countenance such action. Instead, during this period of massive change the imperial institution was deflated through the constitution—and subsequently in Japanese minds—to a status comparable to the constitutional monarchy of England. This approach to the problem proved to be a safe and lasting solution.

The other major change in the constitution was its unequivocal establishment of the British parliamentary system. The constitution made explicit the supremacy of the House of Representatives, which remained in form essentially the same as it had been in the twenties, and it abolished all competing centers of political power, such as the military, the privy council, and the House of Peers. The high court officials and the bureaucracy were made clearly subordinate to the prime minister, who was elected by the House of Representatives from among the members of the Diet. The House of Peers was replaced by a purely elective House of Councillors, half of which was chosen every three years for a six-year term, two-fifths by the country as a whole and the other three-fifths by prefecture-wide constituencies. The powers of the upper house were subordinate to those of the House of Representatives. On the choice of the prime minister, the budget, and the ratification of treaties, the decision of the lower house prevailed, and on other matters a two-thirds vote of the lower house could override the upper. Amendments to the constitution, however, required a two-thirds vote in both houses.

The new constitution devoted no less than thirty-one articles to "fundamental human rights," which were described as "eternal and inviolate." All people were to be "respected as individuals," labor was specifically given the right to "organize and act and bargain collectively," and all discrimination by sex, age, or in any other way was banned. Thus women were guaranteed the vote and were specifically given equal rights in marriage.

Another significant feature of the constitution was the creation of a Supreme Court to supervise an independent judiciary and exercise powers of judicial review on the constitutionality of legislation, in the American manner. Judicial review of legislation, however, was an unfamiliar concept to the Japanese and in a sense was inconsistent with the British system of parliamentary supremacy. In a sort of compromise between the two systems, the Supreme Court has been rather chary in passing judgment on actions by the Diet, but has vigilantly ensured that administrative rulings do not impinge on the human rights guaranteed by the constitution.

The most interesting provision of the constitution was the "Renunciation of War," as its second chapter (Article 9) is entitled. This was well fitted to both the American aim to disarm Japan permanently and the Japanese revulsion against militarism that had swept the land. The country "forever" renounced war and the maintenance of "land, sea, and air forces, as well as other war potential."

The occupation buttressed its constitutional changes with a flood of supporting legislation and lesser reforms. One area of such reform was local government, which seemed important to the Americans, accustomed as they were to the various autonomies of a widely spread out nation. They broke up the infamous home ministry, which had controlled both local government and the police, and its rump organization was demoted to the Autonomy Agency, though later it was again raised to the status of a ministry. Prefectural and municipal assemblies were already elected and mayors were selected by the municipal assemblies, but now all chief local authorities, including prefectural governors, were made elected officials by the constitution. Control over the police and education was transferred from the central government to the prefectures and municipalities, and local governments were given greatly increased powers of taxation and legislation. On the whole, however, this atomization of authority did not work well in a country as geographically small, densely populated, and homogeneous as Japan. From the start local governments exercised less authority than expected, and control over the police and education later gravitated in large part back into the hands of the central government. Only long after the occupation was over, when problems of local pollution and overcrowding became serious, did local governments develop some of the importance the occupation authorities had envisioned for them.

The desirability of democratizing the Japanese political system in order to make it less military may have been obvious enough, but it is more surprising that the Americans realized that Japan needed a thoroughgoing economic and social transformation in order to strengthen the foundation for these democratic reforms. The American record at home and abroad does not usually make one associate the United States with economic and social revolution. The wartime planners, however, had come to realize that a more equitable division of wealth, power, and opportunity would help create a more stable and peaceful society in Japan. The usual justification for the somewhat uncharacteristic American revolutionary zeal in Japan was that Japanese society was so thoroughly evil that only drastic measures could correct it. This justification was in part the result of ignorance and in part the product of Marxist interpretations, which prevailed at this time in the United States with regard to Japan and lasted until swept away by the Cold War then developing between the United States and the Soviet Union. But however wrong the diagnosis, the medicine proved efficacious. MacArthur turned out to be the most radical, one might even say unconsciously socialistic, leader the United States ever produced, and also one of the most successful. But of course revolutionary change is easier to effect through arbitrary military power in someone else's country than through democratic means at home.

One of the few specific reforms called for in the Initial Post Surrender Policy for Japan was the dissolution of the zaibatsu combines, which were singled out on the questionable Marxist reasoning that great concentrations of commercial and industrial wealth were the root source of Japanese militarism and imperialist expansion. The central holding companies of the zaibatsu were dissolved, the zaibatsu families and their high executives were purged, the bulk of their assets were taken over by the government for future disposal, and the wealth of the individual members of the zaibatsu families was all but eliminated, first by wartime destruction and then by a capital levy that ran up to 90 percent. Steeply graduated income and inheritance taxes were also imposed, making the future accumulation of great wealth much more difficult than in the past. As a consequence, the Mitsui and other zaibatsu families were reduced to modest affluence and political irrelevance, and Japan today has one of the most even distributions of wealth of any country in the world.

The zaibatsu combines were dissolved into their various component companies, and at first it was planned to further break up more than 300 of these in an operation reminiscent of "trust-busting" efforts in the United States. This program, however, proved both difficult and inadvisable in the face of continuing economic stagnation in Japan and by 1949 was scaled down to affect less than a score of companies. Because of the failure to break up most of the component corporations in the zaibatsu combines, it is frequently asserted that the zaibatsu system has been restored in Japan. This is quite incorrect. Old names, such as Mitsui, Mitsubishi, and Sumitomo, were retained or later revived, and the former corporate members of old combines have established informal, somewhat clublike relations with one another. Natural growth and mergers have made many of the giant corporations comparable to those of the United States. But the integration of Japan's postwar business and industry is quite different from the prewar system, with the old zaibatsu groupings playing only a peripheral role and the zaibatsu families none at all. Former member companies of zaibatsu combines may have a closer relationship with one another than with other companies, but far more important are the associations of firms in certain lines of enterprise, such as steel, electric power, or banking, and the overarching Federation of Economic Organizations, or Keidanren, which was founded in 1946 and grew to be a major guiding force in the development of big business and the whole Japanese economy.

Paralleling zaibatsu deconcentration was the effort to develop the political consciousness and power of industrial labor and the peasantry. Labor legislation was revised to conform to the most advanced concepts of Europe and the United States, and veteran Japanese labor leaders from the twenties, with the active encouragement of the occupation, built up a rapidly burgeoning and often violently assertive labor movement. By 1949 more than 6.5 million workers had joined labor unions. From the start, the movement differed from that of the United States in that the communists controlled a large share of the unions for a while and a high percentage of the organized workers were government employees—teachers, white collar workers in government offices, or laborers in the national railways or in other nationalized industries. As a result, the occupation authorities soon discovered, to their distress, that organized labor often showed less interest in bargaining with management than in political agitation, which seemed to them a more direct way to affect government wage scales or achieve communist goals.

The most sweeping and successful of all the occupation reforms was aimed at improving the lot of tenant farmers and awakening their political consciousness. This was the land reform program, which appears to have been one of the few major reforms MacArthur sponsored primarily on his own authority, though with considerable assistance from Japanese specialists. Started late, it was largely carried out between 1947 and 1949. Tenant-operated land, which had remained at about 45 percent since early in the century, was reduced to less than 10 percent by banning all absentee landowners and permitting the ownership of only a small amount of agricultural land beyond the area cultivated by a farm family itself. Generous credit terms and a runaway inflation made it easy for the tenant cultivators to acquire the land and reduced the recompense to the former owners to only a penny on the dollar in real terms. However socially salutary the results may have been, this was the kind of reform that could never have been carried out through democratic procedures; external power was necessary. It left the average Japanese farm a mere 2.5 acres in size, which in later, more prosperous times was a serious handicap, but it established a stable, egalitarian, and satisfied farming population, determined to retain its rights in the new democratic age.

The occupation authorities also carried out a wide range of social and educational reforms in order to strengthen respect for the individual and the equality of all citizens, as called for in the constitution. The peerage was abolished and, with the exception of the emperor and his immediate family, all titles were dropped. Women, who had already been pushed into more independent economic roles during the war years, were now given full legal equality with men in every way and began to gain greater social equality. The authority of the family head over other adult members and over branch families, a survival from the feudal past, was eliminated.

From the start elementary education had been egalitarian, but now an effort was made to reduce the elitist flavor of the higher levels of schooling and to shift the emphasis throughout from rote memory work and indoctrination to thinking for oneself as a member of a democratic society. Textbooks were entirely revised to eliminate militaristic and nationalistic propaganda, and the old courses on ethics, which were thought to have inculcated these doctrines, were banned in favor of new courses in the social sciences. There was no great difficulty in extending compulsory education from six to nine years, because even before the war most children had sought some education beyond the required six years. The standing of schools at each level was equalized, at least in theory, so that the next level of education would be open to all those who had completed the preceding one. In addition, the levels beyond the initial six years of primary school were made to conform to those then customary in America: the three-year junior high school, three-year senior high school, and four-year college, or university as it is always called in Japan. In the process, most of the old five-year middle schools added another year to include both junior and senior high schools, while the various types of three-year higher schools, by dropping their lowest year, adding two higher years, and then combining with other higher schools, became multi-faculty universities, equaling the old prewar universities in name if not in reality or prestige.

Tremendous confusion was caused by the shift from what the Japanese called the 6–5–3–3 school system, referring to the number of years at each level, to the American 6–3–3–4 system. The sudden jump in the number of universities and the great increase in students attending the higher levels of education, together with the elimination of one year at the top of the system, also resulted in a substantial lowering of university standards. All this was deeply resented by many Japanese. On the other hand, the new system did widen educational opportunities beyond the elementary level, and the new emphases, particularly in the lower grades, produced in time what almost seemed a new breed of young Japanese—more direct, casual, and undisciplined than their prewar predecessors, but at the same time more independent, spontaneous, and lively.

Japanese intellectuals have always drawn a sharp distinction between the early reforming years of the occupation, of which they in general approved, and the occupation's later years, when a 180-degree turn to conservative and even reactionary policies was thought to have occurred. It is true that during 1947 and 1948 there was a general shift in the spirit and emphasis of the occupation. By that time most major reforms had been completed or else were well under way. The focus of interest began to shift from reform to economic recovery, as the success of the reforms now seemed less doubtful than the economic viability of Japan itself. In 1946 industrial production had dropped to a seventh of what it had been in 1941, and even agricultural production was down to three-fifths. Meanwhile the population, under the impact of the return of 6 million Japanese from abroad and the postwar baby boom resulting from the reunion of long-separated families, had soared to around 80 million. It seemed doubtful that adequate sustenance for that many people could ever be found on so narrow a geographic base. The sweeping reform programs had forced the government to live beyond its means, contributing to a rampant inflation of more than a hundredfold, while the possibility of further reforms made it difficult to stabilize the economy and start its reconstruction.

Japan had suffered considerably more from the war than any of the other major combatants and had recovered appreciably less. The Japanese were living at a bare subsistence level, and at that on American largess—a dole of close to half a billion dollars a year. In the long run, democracy or political stability of any sort would be impossible without economic stability. Political and social reforms, however desirable in themselves, had little chance for eventual success without a sound economic foundation.

Outside of Japan, the world situation also contributed to the change in the spirit of the occupation. At the end of the war Japan had been a defeated, isolated nation facing a united, triumphant world. There seemed ample time for reform, and its economic progress seemed to be a matter of concern for the Japanese alone. But the unity of the outside world had withered in the chill winds of the Cold War. By the autumn of 1948 it was clear that the Communists were winning the civil war in China. Much of the rest of Asia was in chaos. There was obviously no united world, but a growing division into what seemed at the time to be two hostile camps, with Japan standing on the border between them both geographically and politically. MacArthur and his staff still concentrated on reforming Japan, but in Washington Japan was seen as a potential battlefield in the Cold War and, because of its once considerable industrial power, possibly an important factor in the worldwide contest.

Economic recovery thus became a major objective in itself, and reforms that seemed to conflict with it were modified or dropped. It was at this time that the effort to break up the larger industrial firms was scaled down and the attempt to distribute Japan's supposed excess industrial facilities as reparations was abandoned. On the basis of the recommendations made in April 1949 by the Dodge Mission, which was headed by a Detroit banker of that name, the Japanese government embarked on a program of severe fiscal austerity. It managed to stabilize the yen at 360 to one American dollar, as opposed to the prewar ratio of about 3 to 1. Labor union activities that might endanger production were restricted. As early as February 1, 1947, the occupation had stopped a proposed general strike, and in July 1948 it prohibited strikes by civil servants and government employees—a policy that became a major source of political controversy for a long time. Japanese industrialists took advantage of the retrenchment enforced by the recommendations of the Dodge Mission to carry out a so-called Red purge of troublesome leftist activists from their payrolls.

The forces of the Left in Japanese society, which had at first enthusiastically welcomed the occupation reforms as helping to achieve their own objectives, now felt betrayed by the Americans. More conservative Japanese, while disapproving of many of the reforms, began to look upon the Americans as allies in stemming leftist pressures within Japan. Both sides, however, were becoming tired of the occupation. The despair and confusion of the early postwar years were wearing off, and most Japanese had come to realize that not all that was distinctively Japanese was bad and not all that the Americans were attempting was wise. They became increasingly irritated with the arrogant self-assurance of the Americans and resentful of the privileges and luxuries the Americans had provided for themselves, often at the expense and inconvenience of the impoverished Japanese. Resentment of this sort was inevitable in such a situation, and though it was surprisingly slow to develop, it became an increasingly important factor.

The occupation, too, had lost much of its earlier élan. The youthful and somewhat undisciplined draftees who had taken the place of the original war veterans in the army of occupation could not command the respect of the Japanese public. The civilian employees and professional military officers on routine assignments who succeeded to the posts of many of the original staff officers, while conscientious and devoted workers for the most part, could not recapture the full enthusiasm of those they replaced. Also, the military organization of the occupation was increasingly getting in the way of the reforms it was trying to achieve. There was, after all, a basic contradiction between the absolute authority of an external military force and the development of democratic institutions, and this became clearer with each passing year. The time to end the occupation had obviously come. Its very nature and the opposition it was starting to stir up against itself were beginning to militate against the success of the reforms it had initiated. There was a definite limit to what could be accomplished by foreign dictate.

In 1947 Washington had begun efforts to end the occupation through a peace treaty, but in a divided world this was not easy to do. The Soviet Union blocked all attempts to hold a peace conference by insisting that the peace settlement should be decided solely by the great powers and that the Soviet Union must have a veto in such decisions. The resulting impasse prolonged the occupation for several years. Eventually the United States decided to proceed without Soviet participation if the Soviet Union would not change its stand. In April 1950 John Foster Dulles, later secretary of state, was put in charge of preparing a peace treaty, and in September the United States announced its intention. Dulles started bilateral negotiations with the various countries involved and in this way worked out the text of the peace treaty in advance of the peace conference.

The occupation was obviously entering a new and final phase. The terms of its liquidation were already being drafted, and Japanese and Americans alike looked forward to the imminent restoration of Japanese sovereignty. Earlier plans for the peace treaty had envisaged certain formal Allied controls over Japan lasting for many years. The long delay in the treaty, however, had made such controls undesirable. Japan was to be restored to full sovereignty and would soon be in a position to revise the postwar reforms as it saw fit. The remaining days of the occupation provided a transition period in which the Japanese could resume responsibility for their own affairs and start the inevitable process of adapting and revising the work of the occupation.

This transfer of authority was accelerated by two external developments. One was the invasion of South Korea by the Communist regime of North Korea on June 25, 1950, and the heavy involvement of the United States in the war that resulted. The attention of the American authorities in Japan and of the government in Washington became focused primarily on military developments in Korea rather than on reforms in Japan. At the same time, the Korean war brought a sharp increase in American purchases of goods and services in Japan, markedly improving the economic situation there. Thus Japanese self-confidence and economic strength both grew just when American interest in domestic Japanese affairs declined.

Then, as a by-product of the Korean war, MacArthur was dismissed on April 11, 1951. At first the Japanese were shocked and apprehensive lest this meant a sudden change in American policy toward Japan. When they saw this was not the case, they were not only greatly relieved, but they also began to look upon the dismissal as a valuable object lesson in democracy. For all the American preaching about democracy during the earlier occupation years, the Japanese were still deeply impressed to see that a single message from the American civil government could in actuality end the authority of a great military pro-consul, who to them had seemed all-powerful. MacArthur's unintentional last lesson in democracy for the Japanese was by no means his least.

Since MacArthur's role had been unique, his successor as SCAP and as military commander in the area could not really take his place in Japan. Wisely, he made no attempt to do so but instead encouraged the Japanese to assume leadership with only a minimum of direction from the occupation authorities. The transition from occupation to independence was now fully under way. Already the Japanese were being allowed to resume normal relations with the outside world. The process of revision had started and was most clearly seen in the growing numbers of persons and groups removed from the purge classification. When the peace treaty was signed in San Francisco on September

8, 1951, it was only one incident in the process of transition—a clarification of the rules for the formal transfer of authority, which finally took place when the treaty went into effect on April 28, 1952.

Forty-eight nations signed the peace treaty with Japan, but its two giant neighbors, the People's Republic of China and the Soviet Union, did not. The latter, to everyone's surprise, had come to San Francisco but only to refuse to join in the treaty. Since the United States recognized the Nationalist Chinese government, now on Taiwan, while several of the signatory nations recognized the People's Republic in control of the Chinese mainland, it had proved impossible to decide which Chinese government should be invited to San Francisco. The next most populous country, India, had also abstained from the conference, largely as a protest against the exclusion of China. Subsequently, however, both India and Nationalist China signed treaties of peace with Japan.

The peace treaty stated that Japan acquiesced to the dismemberment of its empire, which had already taken place in conformity with the Potsdam Proclamation and the terms of surrender. Korea once again had become an independent though tragically divided nation. Taiwan and the Pescadores Islands had reverted to China and then had become the sole remaining refuge of the Chinese Nationalists. The North Pacific Islands, which the Japanese had held under a mandate from the League of Nations, had been formally transferred to the United States in 1947 as a trusteeship territory under the United Nations. The Soviet Union, in accordance with the Yalta Agreement of February 1945, had occupied Southern Sakhalin and the Kuril Islands north of Hokkaido. Similarly, the United States had occupied the Ryukyu and Bonin islands and administered them as areas separate from Japan. In the peace treaty Japan renounced its claims to all these territories. The treaty thus confirmed Japan's limitation to the four main islands of Honshu, Kyushu, Shikoku, and Hokkaido and the smaller islands that adjoined them. The treaty, however, did not specify to what countries some of the areas Japan had given up would ultimately be assigned. Nor did it resolve certain other basic problems. For example, reparations, although mentioned, were not discussed in detail and hence were left in an uncertain state.

Because imports still exceeded exports, the Japanese economy remained dependent on American aid even after the treaty went into effect, and no sharp line can be drawn between the occupation and postoccupation periods in the economic field. Japan also remained heavily dependent on the United States in the field of defense. The shift of most American ground forces to Korea following the outbreak of the war there had led to the establishment of a National Police Reserve, a sort of embryonic army of 75,000 men, to replace the American soldiers. Although, for a country of Japan's size, this was only a tiny military force, the people as a whole remained violently opposed to any substantial rearmament. Because American bases in Japan were essential for the defense of South Korea, which was serving as a military buffer for Japan, the only solution to Japan's defense problems seemed to be a bilateral security pact with the United States. This was signed on the same day as the peace treaty and provided for the continuation of American bases and forces in Japan.

Japan had regained formal independence, but it could by no means stand fully alone. Its economic future seemed precarious. It was surrounded by turmoil throughout East Asia and by the hostility of the peoples it had ravaged. American military bases and forces remained in the land. And yet to the Japanese people, the prospects looked far more hopeful than had seemed possible in the early postwar years. Americans, too, could look back with satisfaction on the occupation. More had been achieved in reforming Japan than had been expected; United States policy toward Japan had proved to be by far the most successful aspect of its postwar activities in Asia.

14

NATIONAL SURVIVAL

Americans tend to give themselves credit for the postwar transformation of Japan, and certainly American occupation policy did help set the course, but other factors were even more important in determining what happened. Without the Japanese people's capacity for hard work and cooperation, their universal literacy, their high levels of government efficiency, their great organizational skills and industrial know-how, and their considerable experience with the democratic institutions of elections and parliamentary government, the American reforms would probably have foundered in a sea of confusion. If the Japanese had not turned their backs emphatically on militarism and authoritarian rule themselves, American efforts at reform might well have ended in complete frustration.

Naturally, the occupation did rule out certain possibilities for Japan while favoring others. A division between American and Soviet rule, or occupation policies limited to revenge, or confused in objectives and weak in execution, would have produced far less happy results. The supreme self-confidence of MacArthur and his almost unlimited powers as an external *force majeur* speeded up reforms that would have taken much more time or would not have been made at all if the Japanese had had to carry them out on their own in the confused conditions of postwar Japan. So the American occupation did help determine the direction of the reforms and the speed at which they progressed. At the same time, they succeeded, fundamentally, because American hopes for Japan's future were in line with what the Japanese themselves wished, and because the Japanese people possessed the qualities that enabled them to reach these goals.

Much of what the occupation brought to Japan would probably have been achieved in the long run in any case, though perhaps more slowly and uncertainly. American misconceptions about the unmitigated evils of Japanese society made occupation efforts desirably vigorous and even radical, but their success ultimately depended on the nature of Japanese society and the substantial foundation for democracy and liberalism the Japanese themselves had already established. Unfortunately, the Americans assumed that their achievements in Japan were entirely of their own making. So they subsequently sought to do the same elsewhere in the world, where they lacked the powers they had enjoyed in Japan and where the local people did not have the desires, experience, or skills of the Japanese. The results usually were disastrous.

At first, after the sudden end of the war in August 1945, the Japanese were an exhausted, dispirited, and bewildered people; but they fell back on their fatalistic acceptance of adversity and, determined to rebuild their nation, put their faith in dogged hard work. Long accustomed to restoring their country after the natural devastations of typhoons and earthquakes, they embraced this task with undaunted resolve. A scum of shacks began to cover the burned-out wastes of the cities, and in time these were replaced with progressively sturdier buildings. Efforts were made to restore destroyed industries with makeshift new ones, utilizing the wreckage of the war as raw materials.

Japan's farms, despite lack of fertilizer and new investment, had maintained themselves better than the factories, but it had been a long time since domestic agriculture, even under the best of circumstances, had been able to feed Japan's rapidly expanding population. Naturally it was the city dwellers who suffered most. Their caloric intake fell to the semistarvation level of 1,500 calories. Those whose homes had not been burned out made exhausting trips to the countryside to seek food from the farmers in exchange for their remaining family possessions. This peeling off of successive layers of their goods they wryly called an "onion existence." Others attempted to supplement their diet with pathetic crops grown on whatever scrap of land they could find—an unused roadway or the burned-out site of their former home. Runaway inflation further plagued the wage- or salary-earner. Most Japanese were completely absorbed in just trying to stay alive.

These conditions drastically reversed relative economic status between rural and city people. In the countryside, the peasants still had their old homes and produced ample food for themselves. But urban residents had in large part been burned out of their homes, and had seen their means of livelihood destroyed. Many were kept alive only by American food shipments, often of unfamiliar and, to Japanese, unappetizing substitutes for their normal rice diet. Only the black market prospered in the cities—but it was dominated by gangsters and Koreans. The latter had been brought to Japan during the war to work in the mines and factories vacated by Japanese draftees, and after Japan's defeat some 600,000 of them elected to stay on in Japan. Until November 1945 the occupation accorded them a special status as semivictors, and they, with their deep resentment of Japan, regarded themselves as above its laws. No city dweller could live without recourse to the black market. This was not only costly but psychologically damaging to the Japanese, with their punctiliousness about observing both law and custom. The squalor and dirtiness of postwar Japan was also damaging to a people who tended to be meticulously neat and clean.

After a decade and a half of military domination, war, and crushing defeat, Japan was an intellectually confused and politically divided nation. It had been through a series of great shocks that had left deep wounds in the Japanese psyche. All the old values had been cast into doubt, and new ones were bitterly disputed in a rapidly changing situation. The objectives of the American occupation forces were sometimes obscure to the Japanese and in any case were beyond their control. There were some things, however, on which most Japanese were agreed. One was the largely unspoken realization that economic recovery must take precedence over all other concerns. The nation was completely bankrupt and unable to support itself. It was viewed with hatred and contempt by most of the outside world. Great deprivation and heroic effort were needed to get Japan back on its feet.

Another point on which most Japanese were agreed was that Japan must never again become involved in war. There was a deep longing for peace and a passionate outburst of pacifistic sentiment, which still remains strong. It seemed self-evident that the militarists had been tragically wrong and that Japan could never solve its economic problems by war. It seemed imperative that it maintain a neutral position outside the conflicts that embroiled other countries. As the only people who had ever suffered nuclear attack, the Japanese showed particular sensitivity to nuclear weapons. They were adamantly opposed to introducing such weapons into Japan, even for defense purposes, and passionately protested their development and testing by other nations, particularly the United States. The renunciation of war in the new constitution had overwhelming support. Even after Japan had regained its independence and eventually its economic strength, the Japanese preferred to maintain a "low posture" in international affairs, speaking softly and carrying no stick at all. Realizing the deep animosities their wartime conquests had stirred in neighboring lands, they held back from assuming leadership even in those countries that needed their help and could have profited from their guidance.

The Japanese also shared a general loss of confidence in their country, an attitude that faded only slowly. This lack of national self-esteem was manifested in the avoidance of all nationalistic expressions, verbal or visual. Even the Japanese flag was used sparingly, and the national anthem was played so seldom that children who years later heard it over television at the opening of the professional *sumo* wrestling bouts thought of it as the "sumo song." Anything international was automatically viewed with favor, anything strictly national with a certain degree of suspicion. For a long time the Japanese tended to seriously underrate themselves. In part this was because, with unconscious snobbery, they compared themselves not with other non-Western countries but only with the most advanced countries of Western Europe and North America.

Still another attitude on which Japanese generally agreed was that authoritarian rule of any sort must be avoided if catastrophes such as those caused by the militarists were to be prevented. Democracy was an ideal on which all could unite, and it was the announced objective of the Americans. But when it came to defining democracy, deep differences of opinion and bitter distrust became evident. Was Japan's new system to follow the American pattern of political democracy combined with a relatively free economy, or the more socialistic democratic patterns of some Western European countries, or the so-called democracy of the "dictatorship of the proletariat" in communist lands?

The division of opinion on these points was varied and confused. Differences by age group are common in most fast-changing societies, but they were especially pronounced in Japan, where the time of "Taisho democracy," the period of military domination and war, and the postwar era contrasted sharply with one another. The gulf between people of different professions was also broad—certainly broader than in the more fluid society of the United States. The government official or big businessman lived in a different world from the so-called intellectual, or *interi,* a term of pride in Japan that was used for a wide variety of people, particularly university professors, writers, and the like, but also included almost anyone who had received a higher education but was not a businessman or government official. Businessmen and government officials were largely the products of the same universities as the intellectuals and had received the same Germanic sort of theoretical, idealistic education, but their professions forced them to become more pragmatic than the intellectuals, who tended to cling to their bookish theories, unsullied by any compromise with sordid reality. Such differences are not unknown in the West, but on the whole the gap was much greater in Japan than in the United States.

A similar intellectual gap existed between residents of rural and small-town Japan and city intellectuals and their younger cohorts in the universities. Rural and small-town Japan, the traditional stronghold of the old political parties, had its own well-established patterns of pragmatic democratic politics based on personal association, patronage, and other local considerations—a pattern not unlike that of much of the United States. City intellectuals tended to reject all this as "feudalistic," insisting on their own more theoretical concepts of democracy, socialism, or communism.

Industrial labor, proud of its new organizational strength and determined to share in political power, deeply distrusted management and the whole prewar establishment. In the early postwar years, when business remained moribund and there was little in the way of profits to fight over, organized labor made a determined bid to take direct control of industry. It constantly went out on strikes, sometimes seized plants and ran them itself, and frequently held public parades and demonstrations. Even when the economy began to come back to life and bargaining over wages and working conditions became the focus

UPI

Confrontation between labor unionists and the police during the annual "spring struggle" over wages in 1958.

of attention, labor expressed its continuing militancy by applying the term "spring struggle" to its annual bargaining sessions with management preceding the start of the new fiscal year in April.

The first few months after the war were a time of great political uncertainty and confusion. Official American policy, as enunciated in the Initial Post Surrender Policy for Japan, would have permitted a popular revolution to unseat the emperor and the old government but did not encourage one. Despite MacArthur's unauthorized drafting of a constitution and other high-handed acts, the Americans had promised that Japan was to have a government "supported by the freely expressed will of the Japanese people." There was no sign of a revolution, however. Instead, the citizenry gradually sorted itself out into two mutually hostile groups, which came to be known as the "conservative camp" and the "reformist" or "progressive camp."

The "conservatives" were essentially the remnants of the prewar establishment. Deprived of the army and navy and with the high court officials bereft of power and the bureaucracy clearly subordinate to Diet control, this side consisted primarily of the two traditional major parties, their business supporters, and the bulk of rural and small-town voters. Though the two traditional major parties had been the "liberals" of earlier days, winning power for the Diet from the older establishment and then reluctantly yielding it to the military, in the new political spectrum they were the "conservatives." There was only a tiny and politically insignificant fringe of old-fashioned nationalists and militarists further to their right.

The "progressives" were those who deeply distrusted all surviving elements of the prewar establishment and leaned instead toward socialist or communist ideas. Intellectuals had suffered most from "thought control." Labor felt it had been cruelly exploited. City people in general, both white collar workers and manual laborers, living under worse conditions than rural Japanese and suffering more from the disruption of the economy, were eager for a complete break with the past. Such people viewed any remnants of the old controlling groups as dangerous links to the past, threatening a return to the bad old days. The conservatives for their part considered many of the progressives to be impractical idealists and easy dupes for dangerous revolutionaries who, they felt, would like to discard the good of old Japan along with the bad and destroy the nation's identity. The depth of the hostility and bitterness between the two sides can only be understood in terms of the very real fears the one side had that the other would set back the clock to prewar days and the equally real fears of the other side that their opponents would obliterate what they considered to be the true Japan. Although neither fear proved valid, they were wholly genuine and were expressed with undisguised animosity.

One reason for this unfortunate cleavage of opinion was that the Americans, despite their many admirable reforms, had not explained their whole program in clear philosophic terms. Because they themselves took democracy so much for granted, they did not put much effort into expressing it in words. The Japanese, particularly the intellectuals, with their background in the all-embracing Confucian philosophy of Tokugawa times and, more recently, in German idealism, wished something more philosophically coherent than what the Americans seemed to offer. It may have been just as well that a basically military occupation did not try to formulate a great guiding philosophy, but nonetheless the Japanese were left to interpret the American reforms for themselves. For most small-town and rural people, this meant their interpretation was based on how the reforms affected their private lives, and the reaction was overwhelmingly favorable. For intellectuals and many other urban groups, it was largely based on the theories they already knew, and these were largely Marxist.

Marxist doctrines, which had appealed to university students and other intellectuals at the end of World War I, had continued to spread despite the militaristic reaction of the thirties. Conservative thought at that time was retreating behind the mystical concept of the "imperial will," and liberal, democratic thinkers found themselves caught between this obscurantist doctrine and the emerging reality of totalitarian controls. In any case, they never developed a coherent philosophy, and their adherents in the parties, following their usual practice of pragmatic compromise, discredited themselves by temporizing with the military. Only the extreme Left had resisted compromise and had thereby preserved its doctrines intact as an appealing alternative to military dictatorship. When the militarists and emperor-centered conservatives went down in ignominious defeat, the Japanese public assumed that their socialist and communist critics had been right. The American occupation left the intellectual field open to them, and they came to dominate the magazines, newspapers, university faculties, and student bodies. Nikkyoso, the powerful union of primary and secondary school teachers, came largely under the control of the extreme Left. Though the reforms of the occupation and the Japanese institutions these helped to produce were grounded in a liberal, democratic tradition, Japanese thought took on a heavily Marxist flavor.

Japanese Marxism remained much truer in doctrine to the classical Marxism of the nineteenth century than did most postwar derivatives in the rest of the industrialized world, whether in communist, socialist, or so-called capitalist countries. Classical Marxism assumed that, following "feudalism," there would be a stage of "capitalism," which was Marx's analysis of the early period of industrialism in the West. This would be followed by "socialism," which was his utopian view of the future. Since capitalism, he claimed, bred imperialism and thus caused war, all international unrest could be laid at its door. That this interpretation failed to explain the unfolding facts of twentieth-century history, particularly in Japan itself, did not seem to lessen the theory's popularity. Nor did the generally infertile soil for Marxism in Japan, where a very homogeneous society, a fully open educational system, and the economic equalization resulting from the occupation reforms made Japanese feel little sense of "class," which is absolutely essential to the whole Marxist interpretation.

Ironically, there were deeply ingrained prejudices in Japan against the major so-called socialist countries—the Soviet Union and China—and in favor of the principal so-called capitalist areas—North America and Western Europe. The Japanese feared the Russians more than any other people, and they thought of the Chinese more with condescension and guilt than with real respect. By contrast, there was much admiration for the United States and the democracies of Western Europe. Most Japanese realized how tremendously important friendly relations with the United States were to Japan, and there was also an amazingly strong grassroots respect and affection for America, expressed in the most sincere of all ways—wholesale imitation.

The conflict between the conservatives and progressives took shape only slowly. The occupation was all-powerful and gave stability to what would otherwise have been a very confused situation. Progressives were enthusiastic about the American reforms, and conservatives, who were in control of the Japanese government, approved of many of them and realized the necessity of complying with the others. But, after the so-called reverse course in occupation policies started in 1947 and subsequently authority was increasingly restored to the Japanese government, the political confrontation between Left and Right became clearer and more heated. It also became deeply embroiled with attitudes toward the United States. The progressives increasingly viewed the Americans as enemies, while to the conservatives they came to appear more and more as allies. Almost every political dispute took on anti- and pro-American overtones, and Japanese leftists came to debate with utter seriousness whether it was "American imperialism" or "Japanese monopoly capitalism," a term used rather loosely to embrace all big business, that was the chief enemy of the Japanese people.

Such attitudes clearly aggravated the "American hangup," which naturally characterized Japan, as it did so many other countries in the early postwar years when American power so dominated the world. Japan had been almost completely destroyed by Americans and was then occupied and run by them for a number of years. The American presence in Japan was so overwhelming that almost anything someone disliked could be attributed to the United States, and fears that Japan might lose its national identity could reasonably be blamed on pernicious "Americanization." All Occidentals in Japan were assumed to be Americans, unless there was clear proof to the contrary, and children quite simply called all of them Americans rather than *gaijin,* or "outsiders," the usual somewhat pejorative postwar term for Westerners. With Americans and their policies so much on Japanese minds, an already deep cleavage within Japanese politics was further exacerbated by a dangerous divergence of views on relations with the United States, which came to be the focus of most political conflict.

Despite the years of military domination and war, it soon became obvious that many political trends of the twenties had survived reasonably unchanged. Soon after the surrender, all the prewar parties sprang back to life, reemerging from the dead shell of the Imperial Rule Assistance Association. In early November 1945, only two months after the start of the occupation, the Minseito was reborn as the Progressive party (Shinpoto) and chose as its president Shidehara, the liberal foreign minister of the twenties. On October 9 Shidehara had become prime minister in place of the imperial prince chosen to ensure the surrender of the armed forces. The Seiyukai reappeared under its nineteenth-century name of Liberal party (Jiyuto). The former Social Mass party made a fresh start under the less ambiguous name of Socialist party (Shakaito). Even the Communist party (Kyosanto), which had not been a legal entity since 1924, was reborn on December 1. It was organized by old leaders who had been freed from prison and were soon joined by other old leaders returning to Japan after long periods of refuge with the Chinese Communists.

Despite the revival of the old parties, however, the political situation was quite confused, as was revealed by the first postwar election on April 10, 1946. More than a third of the vote for members of the lower house of the Diet went to independents and some sixty minor new parties. Still, the traditional parties did quite well. The Socialists almost doubled their 1937 share of the vote from 9.1 to 17.8 percent. The Communists, despite great publicity, won only 3.8 percent. The remaining 43 percent went to the Liberals and Progressives, far less than their combined 71 percent in 1937, but still an impressive demonstration of political continuity. This was all the more remarkable since most of their former Dietmen had been purged as members of the Imperial Rule Assistance Association. The Liberal party won a plurality in the House of Representatives, with 140 of the 466 seats. Since its reconstitution its leader had been an old politician, Hatoyama

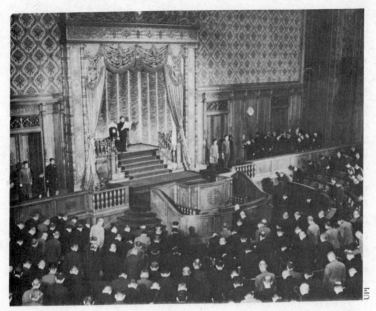

The emperor opening the Diet with a brief message on November 27, 1945.

Ichiro, but the occupation purged him on the eve of the election. His successor, Yoshida Shigeru, a former foreign ministry bureaucrat and ambassador to London who had escaped the purge because of a clearly antiwar stand, became prime minister on May 22 and served in this post for seven of the next eight and a half years.

Yoshida typified certain characteristics of the politics of the times. He was one of many former bureaucrats who, seeing the new locus of political power, joined the parties and ran for election to the Diet. Such former bureaucrats were often the cream of the Japanese educational system and had had broad experience in governmental matters. As a result, they often dominated the conservative parties, and they occupied the prime ministership for all but three of the first twenty-seven postwar years. Yoshida's position illustrated the Japanese government's peculiar status as executor of the policies of the American occupation. The most important function of his government was to deal with the Americans and try to influence them. To accomplish this task, a good knowledge of English was useful, and it is no accident that Shidehara, Yoshida, and Ashida Hitoshi, another one of the four prime ministers under the occupation, were all products of the foreign ministry. The government's peculiar relationship with the occupation also meant that Yoshida, even when backed by only a minority in the Diet, could with occupation support run things in a more heavy-handed manner than proved feasible after the occupation ended. He was the only strong political leader to emerge in postwar Japan and was given by his countrymen the English sobriquet of "one-man" Yoshida.

In April 1947 a series of elections was held to prepare for the inauguration of the new constitution the next month. The prewar tendency to avoid party labels in local elections reasserted itself, and virtually two-thirds of the forty-six prefectural governors, more than two-thirds of the city mayors, and nine-tenths of the town and village mayors were elected as independents. Even in the first election for the House of Councillors, close to half the members elected were also independents. At the same time, the overwhelming majority of all these independents were clearly conservatives, close to the policies of the traditional parties in their political views and often intimately allied with them. What had been the emerging mainstream of Japanese politics in the twenties had, after a decade and a half of violent disruption, asserted itself once again, almost as strong as ever.

The second postwar general election for the lower house on April 25, 1947, revealed a considerable shakedown of the political situation. One new political group, the Cooperative party (Kyodoto), won 7 percent of the vote, but the other minor parties and independents dropped to a mere 11 percent of the total. The Communist vote stayed almost constant, and the remaining 78 percent was divided almost equally among the three major parties, the Socialists, the Liberals, and the Democrats (Minshuto), as the Progressive party had renamed itself.

The election also illustrated another significant point. In prewar elections the party in power, being able to distribute rewards, usually gained seats. The Liberals, though ostensibly "in power," were not in a position to provide such rewards under the occupation, and they had to accept criticism directed against occupation policies. They lost 9 seats, and the Socialists, though a hairline below the Liberals in popular votes, emerged as the plurality party with 143 seats. On May 24 they formed a coalition cabinet with the Democratic and the Cooperative parties, under the leadership of the veteran Christian Socialist, Katayama Tetsu.

The Socialist-led government was a strange amalgam of diverse forces, and the Socialists in any case were in no position to carry out a socialistic policy. Indeed, it was they who were now vulnerable to criticism directed against occupation policies. Old prewar divisions within the Socialist movement reasserted themselves, and Katayama, in the face of a revolt of the left wing of his own party, resigned and was succeeded on March 10, 1948, by the former diplomat Ashida, the head of the Democratic party, as the leader of a coalition cabinet made up of the same three parties. This second coalition had an even less happy history; Ashida was forced to resign only seven months later by the defection of the Socialists, amid widespread charges of corruption.

Yoshida returned as prime minister on October 15, 1948, again with only minority support in the Diet, but he dissolved the lower house and held a general election on January 23, 1949. The Democratic, Socialist, and Cooperative parties were all seriously discredited in the eyes of the public as having been the instruments of the occupation in the two preceding cabinets, and as a result their popular vote fell drastically. On the other hand, the Communists more than doubled their vote to 9.7 percent, and the Liberals, with about 44 percent of the vote, won 264 seats, the first one-party majority in the postwar Diet. Yoshida and his cabinet of Liberals vigorously continued on through the rest of the occupation period and thus headed the Japanese government in power at the time the peace treaty went into effect.

The peace treaty came none too soon. In the course of 1951 the purge had been lifted on many categories and was completely abandoned when the peace treaty went into effect on April 28, 1952, but the increasing irritation of the Japanese public with American domination showed itself a few days later on May Day, the great leftist holiday, when there was widespread rioting and damage to American property. With Japan finally out from under the occupation, the time had come for new elections, which Yoshida held on October 1, 1952. His Liberals increased their popular support a little, though poorer distribution of the vote resulted in a loss of seats to 240, still a clear majority.

The Progressives, as they once again were called, had absorbed the Cooperative party after the last election and showed some recovery from their 1949 electoral disaster, but the parties of the Left were in serious trouble. During the summer of 1949 the Communists had been discredited by several acts of violence generally attributed to them. Ever since the war, the Japanese public has reacted sharply against any violence that took human lives. The Communists fell into even worse difficulties after Moscow openly censured them in January 1950 for their realistic but soft line, according to which they even tolerated the imperial institution and called for a "lovable Communist party." The subsequent return to hard-line attitudes and activities lost them support and led to a suppression of their newspaper and a purge of their leaders by the occupation. For the most part the Communist leaders went underground, and the decline of the party became evident when it won only 2.6 percent of the vote and not a single seat in 1952. Many voters who had deserted the Socialists for the Communists in 1949 returned at this time to the Socialist column.

The Socialists, however, had their problems too. Ideological divisions revived from prewar days had helped wreck the Katayama cabinet, and disagreement over the peace treaty produced a complete split of the party into left- and right-wing factions in October 1951, with the left wing refusing to support the peace treaty because of the exclusion of the Soviet Union and the People's Republic of China. The two wings of the party entered the 1952 election with separate slates, and though together they won 21 percent of the vote and 111 seats, with the right wing in a slight lead over its rival, they undoubtedly did less well than if they had been unified.

Behind the split in the Socialist party was an equally sharp division among the labor unions. Since these provided the bulk of the grassroots organization for the party, about half its Diet membership, and a large part of its vote, they exercised a disproportionately large influence on party decisions. From the early days of the occupation there had been violent struggles between the Communists and Socialists for control of the labor movement. The Communists, better organized and disciplined, were skillful at winning control over unions, but there were repeated rank-and-file "anti-Communist" or "democratization" movements that brought most unions back under Socialist leadership.

Even the Socialist-controlled unions, however, began to divide into two types. Those of blue collar workers in private industry increasingly emphasized strikes and bargaining aimed at increasing their own wages, while unions of white collar workers and government employees remained focused on direct political action against the government and on global issues. Unions mostly of this second type formed a national federation called Sohyo, which had started in 1950 as an "anti-Communist" movement, and this became the main labor group supporting the left wing of the Socialist party. A considerably smaller grouping, made up largely of the more moderate, economically oriented, blue collar unions, became the chief support of the right wing. In 1954 it took the name Zenro, which was changed to Domei in the early sixties. Some unions remained under Communist control, and many others chose to be independent of national organizations or joined a loose grouping of "neutrals," but the two most politically significant labor federations were Sohyo, with about 4.5 million members, and Domei, which was close to half that size.

The conservative parties, too, though in firm political control, had their problems of unity. They had always been basically clubs of Diet members grouped together for more effective action in the legislature, but the grassroots organizations of the parties themselves were weak, as the overwhelming success of independents in local elections indicated. The real foundations for the conservative parties consisted of the personal local power bases (*jiban*) of the individual Dietmen and their personal support organizations (*koenkai*), which they increasingly developed on a broader geographic scale after the war. The essential ingredient for both types of organization was the support of local politicians and interest groups, which centered around local rather than national issues. The conservative parliamentarian was thus more the product of his own local political connections, as in the United States, than the product of a centrally controlled national party, as in England. This independence of the Dietman from the national party was heightened by the peculiar electoral system adopted in 1925, in which three to five persons were elected from a single electoral district, thus putting candidates from the same party into more serious electoral competition with one another than with candidates from other parties. A Dietman's chief political rivals in elections were other members of his own party, just as they were his chief rivals, when the party was in power, for appointment to such high government posts as cabinet ministers, committee chairmen in the Diet, or strategic positions in the national party organization.

Such a situation might have led to a highly undisciplined party vote in the Diet, as in the American Congress. That it did not illustrates, perhaps, the greater Japanese tendency toward cooperation and the survival of premodern patterns of interpersonal relations. The average conservative Dietman attached himself to some leading politician in his party, who could help channel him funds for elections and win him a high position in the central government, in return for his support of the leader's bid for the party presidency. The result was that the conservative parties were not cohesive ideological groupings but rather congeries of factions divided not by policy issues but by personal loyalties. These factions could easily switch sides between the two conservative parties, accounting in part for their rise and fall in votes and Diet seats. This was precisely the way the traditional parties had operated before the war, and the revival of this system was another clear sign of political continuity.

Yoshida's Liberal party had faced a particularly severe factional division because he, a former bureaucrat, had achieved the leadership of the party only because Hatoyama and the other older party leaders had been purged. Released from the purge by the end of the occupation, these men tried to reclaim their old positions. When Yoshida refused to yield, Hatoyama and his following split off from the party in March 1953. Yoshida, now lacking a parliamentary majority, dissolved the Diet and held an election on April 19. His wing of the Liberal party won 39 percent of the vote and obtained 199 seats, well short of a majority but far ahead of the Progressive party and the divided Socialists, and he continued precariously on in power for another year and a half.

Hatoyama returned to the attack in the autumn of 1954. In November he joined the Progressives and reorganized them under their alternate name of Democrats. Meanwhile, another veteran politician threatened to desert Yoshida, who finally relinquished his weakening grasp on the prime ministership in December 1954, passing it on to Hatoyama. To consolidate his position, Hatoyama held elections on February 27, 1955. The Liberals declined sharply (26.6 percent of the vote), and the Democrats emerged as the plurality party with 36.6 percent of the vote and 185 seats, confirming Hatoyama's hold on political leadership.

In this election the combined vote of the conservative parties showed an overall decline and that of the opposition rose. This seems to have been mostly the result of changing demographic conditions, particularly the rapid shift of the population from the countryside to the cities and rising educational standards. Over the next two decades the conservatives lost an average of about 1 percent of the vote per year and the so-called progressive camp gained correspondingly. The conservatives saw the need to unite their two parties if they were to maintain control of the government. The Socialists could see even more clearly that, unless they were reunited, they could never achieve their goal of becoming the majority party. On October 13, 1955, the two wings of the party joined together again, and on November 15 the two conservative parties combined under the joint name of the Liberal Democratic party, usually abbreviated to Jiminto in Japanese and to LDP in English.

The unification of the two major political groupings created virtually the two-party system that Japan had been leaning toward in the 1920s, but it also made the conflict between the conservative and progressive "camps" all the sharper. One of the major reasons the conservatives came together was to muster sufficient strength to revise some of the occupation reforms. All the purges had been dropped with the end of the occupation, and now the chief objective was to revise the constitution because of its clearly foreign origin and its strange-sounding verbiage. In particular, the conservatives wished to get rid of the unrealistic Article 9, which renounced war and all armaments, and to restore theoretical "sovereignty" to the emperor. The opposition forces, however, fought desperately against any changes in the constitution, even though they might be merely stylistic or theoretical, because they feared that the slightest alteration might open the door to more substantive changes. Thus, curiously, the progressives, though strongly anti-American, had become the chief defenders of the constitution MacArthur had forced on Japan. As it happened, the conservatives were unable to revise the text of the constitution, because by 1955 they lacked the two-thirds majority needed in the two houses of the Diet to make amendments. As their majority continued to decline in later years, their hope for constitutional reform became progressively less feasible and gradually faded away as a practical political issue.

The conservatives, while unable to amend the constitution, did carry out some lesser reforms of the system, though only against determined and sometimes violent opposition by the progressives. One such reform, made in 1954, was a partial recentralization of the police into prefectural police systems under the coordination and guidance of a National Police Agency. Though bitterly opposed by the progressives, who feared this would lead to the reconstruction of centralized police controls of the prewar type, the new system worked much more efficiently than the municipal system introduced by the occupation. The progressives prevented the formal restoration of certain police powers by law, but the public granted these powers to the police in effect through their increasing cooperation and trust, and the postwar Japanese police system evolved into one of the most efficient and respected police systems in the world.

Another reform effected by the conservatives was a reconsolidation of certain educational controls. Elected prefectural and municipal school boards, which had generally been very unpopular, were changed in 1956 to appointed local boards, and more authority for the supervision of textbooks and curriculums was returned to the education ministry. The radical teachers union fought all these changes bitterly, as well as the reintroduction of the course on ethics in 1958 and of national student evaluation systems over the next several years, which it was feared would make possible political control of the teachers. The battle between the teachers union and the ministry of education has continued ever since, with only slowly declining hostility between the two, but there has been virtually no use of education for reactionary indoctrination, nor has the running fight between the union and the ministry impaired the high quality of elementary and secondary school education.

The problem of Japanese rearmament was also solved at least temporarily by a slowly shifting reinterpretation of the meaning of Article 9. The National Police Reserve of 75,000 men, created in 1950 to replace the American soldiers sent to Korea, was expanded in August 1952 to a National Safety Force, including a small naval component, and then in 1954 was further expanded into Land, Sea, and Air Self-Defense Forces, under a Self-Defense Agency. Though limited to 250,000 men, the Self-Defense Forces, known for short as the Jieitai in Japanese and the SDF in English, were an embryonic military. They were kept under strict civilian control and carefully eschewed anything remotely bordering on politics, stressing instead internal public disaster services and other noncontroversial tasks. Still, they embodied a reinterpretation of Article 9, permitting Japan the right of self-defense.

The parties of the Left quite naturally opposed this reinterpretation of the constitution as well as the 1952 security treaty with the United States and the continuation of American military bases in Japan. They argued that all three steps contravened the spirit of the constitution and threatened to embroil Japan in what they considered to be America's adventuristic and imperialistic foreign policy. The three issues together formed the white-hot center of postoccupation political controversy. Popular feeling was so strong that the conservatives were forced to act and speak with great caution on such matters. They found that they could not raise the status of the Defense Agency to a ministry, as they had planned, and they were forced to accept a tacit limit of 1 percent of gross national product (GNP) for the military budget.

The conservative governments of the early postoccupation years did not merely concentrate on negative efforts to undo aspects of the original American reforms, but made serious efforts to restore Japan to world society. They were aided in this by the quickening pace of economic recovery. At first the conditions of dire want and demoralization following the surrender improved only very slowly. As late as 1950 per capita income had climbed back to only $132, even then an extremely low level for an industrialized nation. But then economic recovery began to pick up speed. The reforms recommended by the Dodge Mission in the spring of 1949 helped balance the budget, check the inflationary spiral, and eliminate the black market, thus creating a stable foundation for further growth. The outbreak of the Korean war in 1950 produced a big American demand for Japanese goods and services, and a sudden spurt in the whole economy resulted. Once started in motion, Japanese industry rolled ahead with increasing speed, until by the mid-fifties both national production and per capita income had returned to the prewar heights of the mid-thirties. Able to export industrial goods again, Japan could now start to settle its reparation debts, left undetermined by the peace treaty. It did this by reparation agreements in the form of Japanese goods, which incidentally created markets for future exports that further stimulated the economy.

At the time of the peace treaty the United States had insisted that Japan sign a treaty with the Nationalist Republic of China on Taiwan in conformity with the American position on the two Chinas. Both Chinas, however, decided to forego reparations from Japan in view of the huge Japanese investments in their territories that had already been taken over. Japan made its first reparations settlement in 1954 with

Burma, and during the next five years settlements with the Philippines, Indonesia, and South Vietnam followed. The last and most important settlement, however, did not come until 1965, when a "normalization" agreement was finally signed with South Korea.

Hatoyama was determined to settle matters with the Soviet Union as well, in order to lessen the danger of being associated only with the American side in the Cold War and to remove the Soviet veto of Japanese membership in the United Nations. But this was not easy because there were real bones of contention between the two countries, and Japanese resentment against the Russians ran high. For one thing, large numbers of war prisoners had never returned from Siberia and had to be considered the victims of conditions in Soviet prison camps. Another problem was that, while in the peace treaty Japan had renounced its claims to the Kuril Islands, the Japanese insisted that Shikotan and the Habomais, which were small islands the Soviets had seized, were actually part of Hokkaido and that the two southernmost Kurils, Kunashiri and Etorofu, were indisputably Japanese by all rights of discovery and development and should therefore be returned. These claims were met by an uncompromising Soviet stand on territorial matters that made a full peace treaty impossible. But Hatoyama was able to achieve a "normalization" of relations with the Soviet Union in October 1956, and as a consequence, Japan finally won acceptance into the United Nations two months later. In the meantime, Japan had become a member of the GATT, or the General Agreement on Tariffs and Trade, in 1955. Thus bit by bit it was resuming its normal position in the world as an independent nation.

The decade following Japan's surrender in 1945 had been a confused and difficult one, but Japan had survived the trauma. There had been no revolutionary upheavals or breakdown of society. Japanese desires for change and American zeal for reform had blended successfully to create political and social trends that, if one overlooked the intervening two decades of turmoil and suffering, were virtual extensions of the more democratic and liberal tendencies of the twenties. Despite the distasteful foreign authorship of the constitution, parliamentary democracy had been firmly established, life was settling down again, and Japan was becoming an extraordinarily egalitarian and classless society. The economy was coming back to life, and Japan was showing signs of becoming an economically viable nation once again. It was also being allowed back into international society, though as a timid and meek member, longing to be able to put its faith in the goodwill of other nations and in the ideal of universal peace embodied in the United Nations.

The general patterns had also been set for Japan's domestic and international development over the following few decades. The Japanese, whether they wished it or not, were closely linked with the United States in defense, trade, and culture, leaving relations with China and the Soviet Union less than satisfactory. The conservative inheritors of the liberal parties of prewar days had firm control of the Diet, though the Socialists hoped that they could in time replace them as the majority party. Deep cleavages existed between the conservative and progressive forces, which continued to view each other with profound suspicion and animosity. The constant political warfare between the two sides tended to focus on the controversial relationship with the United States. Japan remained a relatively poor land and its people politically divided. But at least the nation had come through what had probably been the greatest crisis in its history in surprisingly good shape.

15

THE FIRST POSTWAR FLOWERING

Japan in the mid-1950s was still economically fragile and in a state bordering on political turmoil. Long years of foreign military rule and a constitution dictated by the conquerors seemed almost to guarantee a dangerous reaction someday. And yet beneath the surface, profound and constructive changes had taken place. A functioning democratic political system was becoming well established, society was settling down into new molds, and the country was actually beginning to show signs of prosperity. The work ethic of the Japanese, their well-established tradition of fine workmanship, their high levels of education and technical skills, their old habits of domestic peace and social order, their special genius for cooperation between business and government and between management and labor, their advanced skills in business enterprises, and, above all, their implacable determination to overcome past disasters and present handicaps had given them unmatched capabilities for economic growth and institutional development.

Once the change in occupation economic policy and the outbreak of the Korean war in 1950 had set the economy in motion, it steadily picked up speed, soaring in the mid-fifties past the prewar peak established almost twenty years earlier and then maintaining a rate of growth for the next two decades of almost 10 percent a year in real terms—that is, after discounting inflation. This was a speed of economic expansion no major country had ever approached before. By the mid-fifties the Japanese were facetiously referring to the "Jimmu boom," meaning the greatest economic boom since the mythical founding of the nation by the emperor Jimmu in 660 B.C. Before long the rest of the world was also taking note and speaking of the "Japanese miracle." But it was, of course, no miracle. It was the springing back, under favorable conditions, of a war-ravaged but industrially advanced country, a far different matter from the first steps of industrialization in an underdeveloped land. Much the same phenomenon was occurring in Germany. The Japanese were merely continuing the industrial growth that had tentatively started in the 1860s, had shown its first signs of success in the 1880s, had been gradually picking up its pace since then, and was now surging ahead all the faster because of the setbacks of the war years.

The special relationship with the United States and certain other unusual factors contributed to the speed of Japan's recovery. For example, Japan's military burdens were largely borne by the Americans. Even after the Self-Defense Forces had been established, they absorbed only about 1 percent of Japan's GNP, as compared to the more usual 3 to 5 percent for most other large countries or 10 to 20 percent for some. More important, the United States opened its own vast markets to Japan and encouraged its allies and friends to do the same. Thus Japan became the full beneficiary of the postwar American effort to build a peaceful world of open trade for all.

Another factor was America's willingness to share its technology and financial resources with Japan in order to help get the nation back on its feet. Wrecked or worn-out Japanese machinery was replaced by the latest equipment, and new technology developed in the West since 1937, when the war started to cut Japan off from industrial advances abroad, was introduced through hundreds of patents and affiliations between American and Japanese firms. All this know-how was provided by the United States and other Western countries at what now seem ridiculously low prices, because no one at that time could imagine that the Japanese would ever become serious industrial competitors again. The Japanese thus saved on expensive research and development costs, though they frequently improved on the technology they acquired at these bargain prices by making relatively inexpensive though ingenious modifications that made the Japanese product more attractive than its original Western model. A large flow of American credit to capital-hungry Japan also helped immensely. The Japanese wisely saw to it that this was mostly in the form of bank loans, so that foreigners would not buy up their still very feeble reborn industries.

A fortuitous revolution in energy sources also greatly helped Japan to restore its industries. Cheap oil, largely from the Persian Gulf and transported at declining costs by mammoth Japanese tankers, began to overshadow limited hydroelectric power and relatively costly Japanese coal, giving promise of what then seemed unlimited cheap energy. New Japanese factories were located by the sea to exploit this cheap foreign oil and to reduce the transport costs of bulk imports and exports. These new water-level factories, fitted out with the latest machinery and technology, soon began to be formidable competitors to older Western factories, often less advantageously placed or as well equipped.

Still another factor in Japan's industrial recovery was the skillful government guidance MacArthur's occupation had bequeathed Japan. Though dedicated to "economic deconcentration" in the private sector, the occupation itself was the most unchallengeable and effectively centralized government Japan had ever seen. Faced with the desperate economic conditions of the early postwar years, it encouraged centralized planning for the economy, which gave the Japanese government a greater capacity to guide industry than most other countries have ever had, including those that boast a fully planned economy. Through tax incentives, judicious credit allocations, control over the importation of technology, and the encouragement of mergers and cartel arrangements, the government helped steer Japanese industry into the most promising fields for growth and away from the dying ones. In the 1950s such basic fields as steel, electric power, shipbuilding, and the chemical industries were emphasized. These were all fields in which Japan had already gotten a good start during the twenties and thirties.

Close supervision of tradesmen during Tokugawa times and the encouragement of industry by the Meiji leaders had attuned Japanese businessmen to the concept of economic leadership by the government. Added to this long tradition was the efficient, highly professional bureaucracy, which was an elite corps drawn from the best universities and at the time was at the height of its prestige and power thanks to the legacy of the occupation. It was in a good position to exercise economic leadership. The bureaucrats, of course, came under the ultimate control of the politicians, but many politicians were of bureaucratic origin themselves and had been classmates of the bureaucrats and top business magnates at the same high schools and universities. Thus the three groups formed a cozy cluster of old friends well suited to cooperating with each other. The frequent description of leadership at the time as being a triumvirate of bureaucrats, politicians, and big businessmen was not far from the mark.

The key agency for steering the economy was the Ministry of International Trade and Industry, commonly known as "infamous" MITI in the West, where it acquired an almost magical reputation. MITI and the other organs of government developed a very efficient system in which leadership was exercised not so much by clearly articulated laws as by the control of available capital, incredibly complex red tape, and what was called "administrative guidance," which amounted to veiled threats and promises. It was MITI's task to see to it that the most advanced technology was acquired from abroad on the most favorable terms by those Japanese companies best able to exploit it, but at the same time to ensure that there would be two or more rival private firms in each field to provide the efficiency that competition bred. In this way Japan had the advantage of careful government planning for the overall economy—the macroeconomy—while maintaining efficiency through competing firms in the microeconomy. The result may have been the most successful blend anywhere in the world of the planned economy of the communist system and the free economy of classical capitalism. The system may have been necessary at the time to provide Japan's war-ravaged industries sufficient protection to get back on their feet. Westerners found it hard to fathom and came to call it "Japan, Inc." The term is still sometimes used, though the system of protectionist controls has been greatly relaxed in the meantime.

Another factor in Japan's economic growth was the general consensus that economic recovery must come first. This was put into practical application through the ability of the Japanese to forego present consumption in favor of saving and reinvestment. A thoroughly destroyed Japan, of course, needed foreign capital, but it also was able to generate a surprising amount of investment from its own economy. For more than a century, the Japanese have proved to be the world's most assiduous savers, regardless of the political or social system under which they were living. Even in the relative poverty of postwar Japan, they were able to set aside more of their income as savings than any other modern people and to reinvest it in growth.

The structure of postwar Japanese industry was also a help to growth. With the elimination of the zaibatsu families and most private wealth, the old corporations fell into the hands of their professional managers, who basically ran them on banking capital, which represented the nation's financial credit and the savings of the people at large. In other words, the managers did not have to answer to stockholders concerned with quarterly profits and instead could plan their strategy in terms of long-range growth. In a sense Japan inadvertently entered into a postcapitalistic stage of nationalized industrial development. The unsettled times also opened the doors to a number of innovative entrepreneurs, and they, in typically Japanese style, were bent on rapid expansion of their industries rather than personal consumption.

Despite the political strife between labor and management, the internal organization of industry also aided industrial growth. Early in the twentieth century, businessmen had discovered that well-trained workers were a valuable asset and had started to work out a system of retaining them through guaranteed career-long employment, numerous fringe benefits, paternalistic interest in their general welfare, and perhaps most important, wages that rose with seniority. This system, which also applied to management, became prevalent among all the large industries after the war and greatly contributed to the development of a strongly loyal and efficient labor force. Certain of the sys-

Testing the brakes at a contemporary Toyota factory.

Toyota Motor Corporation

tem's overtones were reminiscent of earlier Japanese interpersonal relations, especially those of the intensely loyal samurai members of the
domains of Tokugawa times. But it was essentially an innovative Japanese response to the new problems of modern industrialized society.

This internal organization of industry did not mean that labor
unions were unimportant. They existed in large numbers and bar-
gained determinedly with management for the wages and rights of
workers. In a sense most of them were "company unions," since all
the workers in a single company belonged to its union, but the union
itself was independent of management control and worked strenuously
for the well-being of its members. At the same time, the last thing any
union wanted to do was harm the financial competitiveness of the
company on which it depended. Strikes, therefore, became essentially
symbolic, demonstrating the potential power of labor but not hurting
the company. Workers identified themselves with the company, taking
great pride in its prestige and products. They felt themselves to be
members of the team and required no outsiders to ensure quality control. Such attitudes accounted for the relatively conservative stance of
the Domei unions in private industry as compared with the more intransigent posture of the Sohyo unions, which, composed mostly of
government employees, had no worry about the competitive position
of their employer. The loyalty of the workers in private industry to the
firm and their concern for the firm's future combined with the high
educational standard of postwar Japan to give the country probably the
most efficient and hardest working industrial force in the world.

As Japan's industry recovered, it began to recapture its old markets
and find new ones, but not without difficulty. Its Asian neighbors still
nurtured deep resentments against Japan and fears of its economic
dominance, while in Europe discriminatory limitations were placed on
imports from Japan. Still, the reparation agreements helped open the
doors in Asia, and the excellence and modest price of Japanese products gradually won them markets everywhere. The first great successes in foreign trade were in textiles and the other light industries
that the Japanese had mastered long before the war, but then they
entered more advanced and complex fields, such as cameras, motorcy-

cles, shipbuilding, and electronics. These required a great deal of highly skilled labor, and the Japanese, with their combination of advanced industrial skills and relatively low wages, had an advantage over less skilled or more highly paid competitors. Bit by bit, Japan's worldwide image changed from that of a producer of cheap and shoddy goods to that of a producer of quality manufactures. Trade names like Nikon, Canon, Seiko, Sony, Panasonic (the brand name is "National" in Japan), Hitachi, Honda, Kawasaki, Yamaha, Toyota, and Datsun (now Nissan) became world famous.

Although Japanese industry showed the fastest rate of expansion, agriculture, too, grew rapidly in productivity. This was not the result of any increase of area, since this was impossible. Nor was it the result of land reform, because the prewar farmer, tenant and owner alike, had been as hardworking as was possible. What had happened was that a great new surge in technology and investment had taken place. There had been a decade of scientific advances in the world that the farmers of Japan had lost out on. There were new insecticides and improved chemical fertilizers, which the Japanese came to use lavishly, and new machinery, such as small motorized threshers. In time, miniature tractors, called by the Japanese "bean tractors," which were well adapted to their tiny fields, came into common use. The Japanese farmer, moreover, being relatively well off in the postwar years, had the capital to invest in these improvements. The net result was that by the mid-fifties bumper crops had become the rule, and the Japanese suddenly realized that this was due not just to unusually favorable weather conditions year after year but to the entirely new level of agricultural production that had been achieved.

For the first time in some decades, Japan became self-sufficient in rice. In part, however, this was the result of a decline in per capita rice consumption, as the Japanese ate more wheat, meat, dairy products, and other protein foods. This was a clear sign of increased prosperity. The richer diet, combined with a greater tendency to sit on chairs rather than on the floor, produced an extraordinary side effect on the Japanese physique. Children became markedly taller and heavier. Almost ludicrous differences in size between young Japanese and their parents and grandparents were produced as a result. A fat boy or girl, once a rarity, became a common sight.

Not all the economic growth was healthy. At first much of it went into a rash of pinball establishments—known as *pachinko* parlors—and other tawdry amusements. There was also a disconcerting tendency for the economy to "overheat" by going too fast, thus threatening a dangerous return to inflation and large balance of payments deficits. This happened in 1953, 1957, and again in 1961. Each time it proved necessary for the government to tighten credits and take other measures to slow the economy down. The very success of industry also revived the old problem of the dual economic structure. The farmers had become more productive, but not at all to the same extent as workers in the newer industries. A 2.5-acre farm remained far too small for affluent living. The relative economic status of the farmers could be maintained only by a disproportionate allocation of tax revenues to rural areas and by high price supports for rice. These were an economic drain on the rest of the economy but were generously maintained by the Liberal Democratic politicians, who realized that much of their electoral strength lay in the rural areas. Service workers and those in the old handicraft or less mechanized industries, which were less well organized politically, lagged behind. All the large industrial enterprises came to be surrounded by clusters of small feeder plants, where workers received lower wages and lacked the benefits of job security.

The most serious problem produced by rapid industrial growth was the imbalance of the economy between fine new industrial plants and inadequate public facilities and services. Little was done in social security, which was left largely to the individual, the family, or the company to provide, and there was a great shortage of public facilities, such as public buildings and parks. A relatively short period of industrial modernization together with terrible wartime destruction had left Japan a capital-poor country not just in the financial sense, but also in terms of basic capital improvements. Schools, hospitals, and other public buildings were substandard for a country like Japan. Sewage systems and some other modern facilities were largely lacking. The road system was still almost primitive. Traditional wooden architecture, which was more sensible than stone in a forested, earthquake-prone country but was easily destroyed by fire in peacetime as well as in war, left Japan without a backlog of more permanent structures surviving from earlier centuries, such as exist in Europe and many other regions. Worst of all, there was a woeful lack of adequate housing in the war-ravaged cities.

Part of the problem, of course, was the absence of sufficient space in a terribly overcrowded land. The more Japanese industry forged ahead, the worse conditions grew. The cities of Japan became hopelessly overcrowded; water and air became seriously polluted; water supplies in Tokyo fell to dangerously low levels at times; inadequate roadways became the scene of the world's worst traffic snarls; the death toll on streets and highways rose alarmingly; the superb rail network and vast urban commuting systems became absurdly over-crowded. Living space was incredibly restricted in tiny individual houses or in even smaller apartments in *danchi,* the clusters of four- to six-story walkup concrete apartment buildings that came to surround the large cities. Millions of workers were condemned to long hours of commuting every day by train, bus, and subway. An hour each way was considered short, and two hours was not at all unusual.

Naturally, the tremendous expansion of the Japanese economy in the fifties and sixties had a deep effect on society and people's attitudes. If the population had kept pace with economic growth there might have been less change, but the economy was going much too fast for this, and in any case, once the postwar baby boom had run its course, population growth slackened off to only about 1 percent a year, one of the lowest rates in the world. This was the result of liberal abortion laws, loosely applied, and a great enthusiasm for birth control, against which there was little religious or social resistance. It was vigorously advocated by both government and industry, but the chief motive power was probably the desire of most parents to see that their children were well educated in order to have a chance to succeed in life. This seemed more possible with two or at the most three children than with the traditional large family. A 1 percent rate of population increase subtracted very little from a 10 percent rate of economic growth, leaving much room for a general increase in wealth.

The destruction of the war and the upheavals of the occupation had themselves been enough to set off vast social changes, but these were accelerated by the breakneck economic pace and the unaccustomed affluence it began to produce. The disaster of defeat had discredited all traditional authority and values. The dispersal of population caused by imperial expansion and the wartime air raids and grinding poverty of the early postwar years had further disrupted traditional patterns of life. And then, when recovery did come, it brought with it a vast

Rick Smolan/Contact Press Images

Danchi *(developments) in the Tokyo suburbs.*

urbanization of the population, the blighting of mining areas as imported oil replaced domestic coal, changing patterns of personal relationships, and an accelerating pace of life as prosperity introduced an intense, almost frenetic, new tempo of activity.

In retrospect, it is surprising to see how firm the Japanese family remained and how many of the new social patterns were essentially continuations of those already well established in the twenties. The socially liberalizing trends of the period of "Taisho democracy," now free of the reactionary pressures of the thirties and the war years, reappeared with increased vigor. The prewar breakup of the typical family into the nuclear unit of the conjugal pair and their preadult children and the independence of women and younger people from the authority of the *pater familias* were greatly strengthened by the occupation reforms and the new conditions. There was also a veritable explosion of education, as most children went beyond the compulsory nine years to senior high school and often to a university, and anxious parents, eager to provide their children with the best educational opportunities, sent them to special cram schools, known as *juku,* for supplementary training, or hired individual tutors. Eventually, well over 90 percent of the children continued on through senior high school and more than a third through some form of higher education. While underfinancing and overcrowding left much to be desired of the universities, the twelve years of education up through high school were as academically demanding as anywhere in the world, and overall the Japanese probably became the most highly educated people in the world.

The decline of respect for governmental and familial authority made the sources of public information all the more important. The Japanese had long been a reading people, but with the new affluence there was a great increase in the publication of books and circulation of magazines. Monthly magazines had been important for decades, but now there was a flood of new weeklies, and newspapers became even bigger and more influential than ever. The three largest, *Asahi, Mainichi,* and *Yomiuri,* which were published and distributed throughout the nation, came to have morning circulations of 4 to 6 million and evening circulations only somewhat smaller. Middle-size national or regional papers exceeded the 1 million mark. Taken as a whole, the quality of the newspapers was excellent and their influence enormous, probably greater than in any other nation. During the fifties and sixties they were joined in importance by television, which became known not as TV or the "telly," but as *terebi* in Japan. Japanese television was divided into two government networks, one of them purely educational, and some five private networks, and the competition between them produced a diversity and balance between amusement and education as good as that of any country.

Nothing was more strikingly evident in the fifties and sixties than the rapid rate of urbanization. While every prefecture with a predominantly rural makeup lost population, all the cities grew fast, and the larger they were, the more rapid was the pace. In the sixties Tokyo passed the 8 million mark in population, becoming the largest municipality in the world. Yokohama and the large number of other satellite cities and towns added several million more to the Tokyo population node. All the major cities witnessed a feverish building boom of steel-boned structures in their downtown areas. In the case of Tokyo, major rail interchanges created four or five subsidiary "downtowns," each complete with its high-rise buildings, department stores, and amusement areas. Giant department stores, already well established before the war, developed into fabulous institutions, crowded with goods and people and offering such side attractions as art exhibits, a wide variety of restaurants, and children's amusement parks on the roofs.

In the fifties and on into the sixties, Japan was clearly producing its own version of modern mass society, not yet quite as affluent as that

UPI/Bettmann Newsphotos

A human sea meets the ocean on the Shonan beaches near Tokyo.

of the West, but perhaps for that very reason more lively. The long hundred-year race to catch up with the West, renewed with increased vigor after the setback of the war, was paying off. Japan was beginning to draw abreast of the leading countries of the world and was far outstripping the others. It was clearly becoming a tremendous success. The chief impression the cities of Japan gave was one of vitality, cheerfulness, and unbounding vigor. All the arts, both native and

Western, flourished exuberantly. Tokyo alone had some five fully professional symphony orchestras. It also offered an unsurpassed variety of cafés, each with its own musical specialty, and its restaurants were as varied as those of any city in the world. Intellectual life was more vigorous and prolific than ever before. Imaginative literature and films abounded. The pleasure districts of Tokyo, with their nightclubs, cabarets, bars, cafés, and fantastically variegated neon lights, became probably the biggest and gaudiest in the world.

Almost all Japanese homes, rural as well as urban, included a color television set. Virtually everyone had a good camera. Small washing machines and electric refrigerators became commonplace. Electric rice cookers and numerous other mechanical conveniences eased the life of the housewife, and many homes and apartments had electric air conditioners. Even the family car began to make its appearance, though with disastrous consequences for Japan's inadequate road system. The English word "leisure" became the catchword of the day, and everyone spoke of the "leisure boom." Professional baseball games, skiing resorts, and summer beaches were all inundated with people.

The dark mood of the early postwar years had been largely dispelled, and *akarui,* meaning "bright," became the favorite adjective to describe "life," "society," and almost anything else to which it could be logically affixed. Even rural Japan shared in the new life. A television set bringing its citified fare into the farm household, a motorcycle and later a small truck or family car, a party phone operated by the local agricultural cooperative—such things deeply affected the lives of those on the farms. The gulf between rural and urban Japan produced by an earlier stage of modernization began to close.

Many of these changes, of course, had their seamy side, as did the economic growth that had helped produce them. Generation gaps widened, as children raised under postwar conditions developed attitudes that conflicted with those of their parents, who deplored the casual manners, spendthrift ways, and lack of discipline of their children. Some of the ills of most industrialized, urban societies became more evident. A sense of alienation and confusion was felt by many people, adrift in the human sea of the modern city. Crime and juvenile delinquency seriously worried a people accustomed to strict obedience and strong family bonds. As the postwar black market faded, one began to hear of *yakuza,* the Japanese gangsters, who specialize in loan sharking, protection rackets, and strong-arm services for shady politicians and businessmen. It should be emphasized, however, that coping with such ills was minor when compared to the much more severe adjustments being made in the urban industrial societies of North America and Europe. By comparison, Japan was extremely orderly, amazingly free from crimes of violence, and, if anything, still too tightly structured socially, with its heavy educational pressures on youth, its career-long employment in large business, and its discouragement of lateral movements in jobs and of freer, more personalized styles of life.

Despite Japan's growing prosperity and social stability, political tensions remained severe throughout the fifties. Confrontation was more prevalent than the traditional Japanese spirit of compromise and consensus. Although the Socialists were confident that they would eventually come to power through a parliamentary majority, they were discouraged at the slow rate at which the conservative vote declined and theirs increased. The left wing of the party and the Communists to their left saw no reason to compromise with the conservatives and were eager to disrupt the rule of the Liberal Democrats, by force if necessary.

Life in Japanese cities, particularly Tokyo, was characterized by constant political demonstrations. In the new democratic Japan perhaps the most frequently heard word was *demo,* but ironically this stood for "demonstration" rather than "democracy." Confrontations in the streets were encouraged by the inflamed rhetoric of the press, which tended to lean to the left. Confrontation also spilled over into the halls of the Diet, where there was little cogent debate but countless efforts to disrupt parliamentary processes. On critical issues, the opposition forces would try to obstruct the holding of sessions by keeping the speaker in his office by force or to disrupt the procedures on the floor. Interpellations were designed to trap the responding officials into some unwise or poorly phrased statement, which could then be used to divert debate from the original issue. Roll call votes were requested as often as possible, and were slowed to a virtual standstill by the "ox walk," the snaillike pace the opposition Dietmen took as they walked up to the ballot boxes. The LDP retaliated by "ramming" through necessary legislation, sometimes by surprise sessions and votes. This led to outcries over the "tyranny of the majority." Constant trouble in the Diet forced the LDP to limit controversial bills to a few particularly crucial ones each session. The result was a considerable restraint of its powers despite its sizable parliamentary majority.

Affluence and stability at home and growing economic bonds with the United States abroad did not lessen the severity of the political division over the American relationship. The recovery of Japanese self-esteem made the presence of American troops and bases in Japan all the more galling. Dependence on the United States for some 30 percent of Japan's trade seemed to some to increase the danger that Japan would be swept up into America's "imperialistic" policies and prevented from developing its own socialistic society. For progressives, the American alliance, instead of offering security at very little financial cost, seemed more to threaten Japan's hoped-for peaceful neutrality.

Almost anything that some Japanese objected to in postwar Japan could be blamed at least in part on the United States. If even the French could decry "coca-colonization" and "Franglais," it is small wonder that many Japanese worried about the "Americanization" of their culture. There was, indeed, a huge influx of English words and American ways. It should be noted, however, that virtually all of this came at Japanese instigation, and that the English words greatly enriched the language. They were used in inventive new ways and provided a vast and useful vocabulary that was not only more international but also less cumbersome than words invented by combining polysyllabic Japanese stems, and more aurally understandable than terms derived from sound-alike Chinese words. Thus English terms had great vogue not just because they were stylish but because they were useful.

Concern over American domination of Japanese foreign policy was more valid. The Japanese government had elected to take a "low posture" internationally, attempting to remain out of sight, as it were, behind the diplomatic and military skirts of the United States. At the same time, however, Japan did its best to develop trade and amicable relations with all parts of the world, in so far as this was possible within the strictures of American foreign policy. De Gaulle is said to have spoken contemptuously of the Japanese prime minister as seeming like a transistor salesman. But the Japanese policy paid off, and the country was able to develop quite satisfactory economic relations with most lands, while avoiding the tensions of international politics and the costs of a large military establishment.

Japan, however, did encounter some problems with certain countries. Hatoyama, on becoming prime minister in 1954, made a special point of trying to work for an independent Japanese diplomatic position, concentrating on the "normalization" agreement with the Soviet Union finally made in 1956. This did clear the way for Japanese admission to the United Nations, but it did not lead to a massive Japanese exploitation of Siberian gas and oil resources, as was hoped for at various times. The problem was not American hostility to the scheme but rather the immensity and difficulties of the undertaking, distrust between the Japanese and the Soviets, the incompatibility of the two economic systems, and Japanese fears that the project might worsen relations with China.

China presented a special problem. Whatever the regime that ruled this vast continental mass might be, the Japanese people as a whole tended to look on China with romantic warmth as the source of their civilization—their Greece and Rome, as it were. This attitude was compounded by a sense of guilt over wartime misdeeds in China and by the lure of the hundreds of millions of potential customers next door—a lure repeatedly felt by much more distant Americans. Japanese businessmen, particularly those in the less prosperous fields, kept hoping that deft political maneuvering might somehow open these supposedly lush new pastures.

The Japanese government, eager for trade with any country, devised the slogan "the separation of politics and economics" to justify Japanese recognition of the Nationalists on Taiwan and trade with both Chinese regimes. Peking, however, was not very cooperative, since the Communists hoped to put pressure on Japanese politics by manipulating the Japanese desire for trade. Seizing on a minor incident, in which a rightist youth tore down a Chinese Communist flag in Nagasaki in May 1958, Peking cut off all trade with Japan, and it was some years before it was restored to significant levels. Nevertheless, most Japanese continued to hope for better relations with their great neighbor and were deeply dissatisfied with the existing situation, which they in general blamed on America's intransigent China policy. Socialist and Communist leaders beat a path to Peking, where some of them joined the Chinese authorities in public statements that "American imperialism" was the "common enemy" of the Chinese and Japanese people.

Such attitudes toward China, combined with growing leftist irritation and anxiety over the presence of American troops in Japan, sharpened tensions within Japan over relations with the United States. Occasional incidents involving American servicemen or the extension of airfield runways to accommodate larger planes—an issue of particular sensitivity in land-hungry Japan—could easily be stirred up by the press into major crises. American testing at the atoll of Bikini in the mid-Pacific resulted in an accidental nuclear fallout on a Japanese fishing vessel in March 1954, and the subsequent death of one crew member stirred vast resentment and, with absurd hyperbole, was linked with Hiroshima and Nagasaki as the third atomic bombing of humanity. Annual memorial meetings held at Hiroshima on August 6, the anniversary of the dropping of the first atom bomb, grew into mammoth protests against nuclear testing by the United States (the activities of the Soviet Union in this regard were largely overlooked) and were expanded into general attacks on Japan's ties with the United States.

By the late fifties the prewar politicians were mostly old men. In December 1956 Hatoyama had to resign the prime ministership because of ill health, and his successor, another prewar politician, had to do the same within two months. On February 25 he was followed by Kishi Nobusuke, an ex-bureaucrat who, as a former member of Tojo's wartime cabinet, epitomized what the progressives feared. When Kishi held a general election on May 22, 1958, however, the LDP won a clear majority of 57 percent of the popular vote and 287 seats in the lower house to 166 for the Socialists.

Because of Japan's economic recovery and the increased self-confidence as well as anti-American sentiments that accompanied it, both the Japanese and American governments felt it would be wise to revise the security treaty. The original pact had allowed the United States wide powers in using its bases in Japan for ''the maintenance of international peace and security in the Far East'' and ''the security of Japan.'' Its forces could also be employed, if requested by the Japanese government, ''to put down large-scale internal riots and disturbances in Japan.'' These features, together with the lack of any terminal date for the agreement, made the relationship seem semicolonial to some Japanese.

After protracted negotiations, a new Treaty of Mutual Security and Cooperation was signed on January 19, 1960. This agreement, together with its supplementary documents, made clear that the United States would consult with the Japanese government before using its bases in Japan directly for combat elsewhere in Asia, as had happened during the Korean war, or before introducing nuclear weapons into Japan. This meant in effect that the Japanese would have a veto over their use. There was also to be a limit of ten years on the treaty, after which either party could terminate it on one year's notice.

All references to the use of American troops in Japan were also omitted. In these various ways the new treaty was obviously better for Japan than the old one, and a large part of the right wing of the Socialists, adopting the name Democratic Socialist party, decided to support it. But the other Socialists and members of the opposition decided to fight it to the bitter end, because Japan shared in responsibility for the new treaty whereas the old one had been forced on the country before it had regained its independence.

Since the LDP held a solid majority in the Diet, the leftist challenge might have amounted to only one of the many turbulent but minor incidents in Japan's postwar relations with the Untied States had it not been for certain coincidental factors. On May 1, 1960, an American U-2 plane was downed deep in Soviet territory, and the Kremlin indignantly responded by calling off a planned summit meeting between President Dwight Eisenhower and Prime Minister Khrushchev, to the sharp disappointment of the Japanese public. Still more unfortunate were the circumstances surrounding the proposed visit of Eisenhower to Japan scheduled for June 19, 1960. Probably wishing to have the treaty ratified by that date, even if the House of Councillors failed to act, Kishi decided to hold a sudden surprise vote on ratification in the House of Representatives in the early morning hours of May 20. Since the Socialists had been trying every possible delaying tactic in the Diet, including boycotting sessions and demanding more time to debate the issue, both the opposition and the public decided that Kishi had "rammed through" the treaty by unconstitutional or at least "undemocratic" means. Even some of his own party deserted him. Two of the faction leaders, who were both eager to replace him as party president and prime minister, had not been consulted on the decision to hold the vote and as a consequence refused to support his action.

Although Kishi did succeed in clearing the chief legal hurdle to ratification on the night of May 19–20, he had aroused popular indignation to the point of explosion. To the antitreaty clamor was added an even louder din against Kishi himself and the visit of Eisenhower. Many sincere believers in democracy felt they must come out into the streets to oppose Kishi for what they saw as his "undemocratic" conduct in not permitting the opposition to air its views fully on an important controversial issue. And many people essentially friendly to the United States voiced opposition to the American president's visit, since it had become entangled in their minds with the debate over ratification and therefore seemed to constitute outside intervention. The powerful press was almost unanimous in its condemnation of Kishi.

The more radical groups led the attack, and large masses of the urban public responded. University students were in the forefront. The Zengakuren, an abbreviation for the National Federation of Student Self-government Associations, had been organized in 1948 and had soon become a politically active group. It was under firm Communist control until 1957 but subsequently became an autonomous movement

President Eisenhower's personal representative mobbed by protesters at Tokyo International Airport on June 10, 1960.

UPI

of even more radical bent, tending toward Trotskyism or anarchism. The Zengakuren activists now found their normally more apathetic fellow students ready to follow them by the thousands in riotous, snake-dancing demonstrations through the streets of Tokyo. Labor unions, long accustomed to mass demonstrations, mobilized their followings, and housewives, shopkeepers, university professors, and other usually passive groups joined in.

By June the crowds of protesters numbered in the hundreds of thousands, but they remained extraordinarily good-tempered and orderly compared to mobs in most other countries. Individual Americans could move about the streets without fear, little property was damaged, and injuries, usually occasioned by clashes between Zengakuren zealots and the police, were relatively few and largely superficial. Only one fatality occurred when, on the night of June 15, during the most massive and violent of the demonstrations, a female student from Tokyo University was trampled to death in the confusion. But the demonstrations were nonetheless effective in intimidating and paralyzing the government. On June 16, humiliated and fearful, it requested President Eisenhower to cancel his visit, and the American government readily complied.

During the rioting of May and June, it seemed that Japan and its democracy were tottering on the brink of chaos. But once the ratification of the treaty went automatically into effect on June 19, the vast disturbance subsided almost at once. It had served as a sort of catharsis for the frustrations of the progressives and the dissatisfactions of the city dwellers, but people in general reacted against the violence, and most of Japan had remained entirely calm. Even the newspapers engaged in some second thoughts about the turmoil they had helped stir up. Since their early development in the 1870s they had regarded themselves as outside critics of an all-powerful government, but now they began to realize that, by helping to create public opinion, they were as influential as the government and must use their power with responsibility.

More basically, the great economic growth of the fifties and the general stabilizing of society had made the outburst of 1960 somewhat anachronistic, and nothing quite like it ever occurred again. It was generally agreed, however, that Kishi must go, and Ikeda Hayato, an ex-bureaucrat from the influential finance ministry, was chosen to be his successor on July 19. Ikeda was a faction leader less to the right than Kishi, and he announced he would take a "low posture" in domestic politics, giving the opposition free rein for debate on controversial issues. His was to be the more typically Japanese strategy of compromise and consensus. Desiring to direct public attention away from the political conflicts of the past to the economic successes of the present, he announced, with considerable fanfare, a noncontroversial "income doubling plan" for the decade. This was more a prediction than a plan, and it actually fell short of reality: Japanese incomes doubled within seven years.

The general elections Ikeda held on November 20, 1960, showed that the uproar of the preceding spring had done the LDP no harm. It emerged with 57.5 percent of the vote, almost exactly the same figure as in 1958, and a small increase in the number of Diet seats to 296. The steady conservative undercurrent of Japanese politics was shown to be still flowing strong.

Ikeda's term in office was a period of hitherto unprecedented stability and goodwill, which continued after his resignation on November 9, 1964, shortly before his death from cancer. His own personality and policies were, of course, the major reason for this calm. He was a skilled leader and, unlike most of his successors, was a man of broad national and international vision. He was also aided by the inauguration of John Kennedy as president of the United States in January 1961. As elsewhere in the world, Kennedy enjoyed extraordinary popularity in Japan, especially among the young people and progressives who were most likely to be anti-American, thus softening opposition to the American relationship. The United States also made conscious efforts to redress the relationship with Japan as inherited from the occupation days by trying to establish a more equal partnership. For example, in November 1961 joint annual meetings of certain members of the two cabinets were begun, and much more careful attention was paid to Japanese sensitivities. In April 1964 the United States insisted, against European opposition, on the admission of Japan into the OECD, the Organization for Economic Cooperation and Development, making it the first non-Atlantic member of this significant grouping of the most advanced nations. Sensationally successful trips to Japan by Robert Kennedy, the president's brother, in January 1962 and again in January 1964, shortly after the president's assassination, also helped improve the American image in Japan.

The basic reason, however, for the quiet of the Ikeda years was the realization at last by the Japanese themselves that their country had fully restored itself and was doing far better than ever before. The economy continued to race ahead at breakneck speed, dazzling the Japanese as well as the rest of the world, and from this new affluence emerged a growing sense of self-esteem and contentment. GNP continued to grow at its phenomenal average rate of 10 percent per year in real terms, at times rising as high as 14 percent. Before the end of the decade, Japan's economy had become the third largest in the world, displacing West Germany's and trailing only those of the two admitted superpowers, the United States and the Soviet Union. Per capita incomes had soared well above $1,000. Japan, long a trade-deficit country, was developing a trade surplus. Its productive power was approaching four times that of all Africa and twice that of Latin America, and it was coming close to equaling all the rest of Asia combined. Living standards as measured in monetary terms were still only about half those of northwestern Europe and a quarter those of the United States, but they had shot past the levels of much of southern and Eastern Europe and were fast closing the gap with the most advanced nations.

This prosperity was largely the result of the tremendous expansion of industry. In some years Japan produced over half the world's shipping tonnage, and it reached third place in steel production, third place in motor vehicles, and second place in electronics. The growth was largely in heavy industry, chemicals, electronics, and sophisticated machinery. Textiles and the other light industries did not do as well, with newer competitors in Asia pushing into these fields just as Japan itself had more than fifty years before. In fact, Japanese businessmen began to transfer some of their more labor-intensive and technically less difficult manufacturing processes to affiliates they established in countries where wages were lower but industrial labor was reasonably efficient, such as South Korea, Taiwan, Hong Kong, and Singapore—all, incidentally, areas that shared with Japan the basic East Asian work ethic and emphasis on education. Even Japan's paucity of raw materials was an advantage in some ways. For example, the steel industry, lacking significant domestic supplies of iron ore or coking coal, could draw on the cheapest sources of supply throughout the world and benefit from plummeting transport costs as oil tankers and bulk carriers became behemoths in size. The result was that Japan's steel industry could bring together Australian or Indian iron ore with American coking coal and produce steel that could be sold in the

United States in competition with the products of aging and less well-placed American steel mills.

Industrial labor shared in the economic advance and, in contrast to earlier stages of industrialization, a shortage of labor developed. The vast pool of surplus rural population, which at one time had held back the development of a true urban labor force, was drying up. Factories and service industries still continued to use labor more lavishly than in the United States, and relatively early retirement ages meant that there was considerable slack in the labor market. But the supply of young new workers began to run short. Japanese employers competed eagerly for college and high-school graduates, bidding competitively for their services and signing them up long in advance of graduation. Japan, unlike the countries of Western Europe, did not make up for labor shortages by importing foreign "guest" workers. An insular abhorrence of large numbers of foreigners in their midst ruled out this solution and thus saved them from the problems such tactics later produced.

Labor shortages even benefited workers in the service areas and in less efficient factories, since workers could be retained in these fields only by higher wages. The dual structure of the economy thus started to disappear. Farmers in particular did better because of the drastic drop in rural population, the widespread use of farm machinery that made this possible, and generous price supports ensured by the LDP Dietmen they elected. Farm boys and girls, on completing their educations, deserted the countryside en masse, attracted by the glitter and excitement of the cities and the less arduous work in factories. In places 90 percent of graduating classes flowed to the cities, and some eldest sons who remained at home to take over the family farm had difficulty finding wives. Many farmers were drawn to higher-paying factory jobs in nearby towns or, if they lived in more remote areas, worked in the cities on a seasonal basis. Farming increasingly became an activity, as the Japanese put it, of "mummy, grandpa, and grandma." Agriculture, which had absorbed close to half the labor force as late as the end of World War II, now used little more than a tenth. The remaining Japanese farmers became quite affluent, at least by Asian standards. Many came to own cars and some could afford vacation trips, organized by their local cooperatives, to Hong Kong, Hawaii, or even Europe.

Rural affluence, however, also produced problems. The dearth of males in the off season in some rural areas raised social difficulties,

and long city sojourns for farmer husbands resulted in disruptive liai-
sons with city girls. The long-range problems were even more serious.
An agricultural system that was made basically inefficient by its minuscule size could not be supported forever by constantly raising rice
prices at the expense of city consumers. Farms of 2.5 acres, tiny
patches of agriculture in remote valleys, and terraced fields on steep
mountainsides hardly fitted the type of economy Japan was developing. In the long run, the only real solution to the agricultural problem
was to consolidate farms into much bigger units and abandon less
productive fields, but the process had as yet hardly begun.

Continued rapid industrial growth thus did not solve all Japan's
economic problems. Higher wages for workers who did not increase
their productivity inevitably led to a steady rise in prices, and the
speed of economic growth generated other inflationary pressures.
Tokyo real estate prices came to be matched only by those of midtown
Manhattan. Social services continued to lag markedly behind those of
the West. A beginning was made for a social welfare system similar to
that of most modern Western lands, but it was still relatively small.
The huge expansion of higher education that had taken place was
seriously underfinanced. The congestion in transportation at times
threatened to suffocate Japan with its own prosperity. Pollution of air
and water grew steadily worse. Urban housing remained extremely
cramped, city parks few, and roads unbelievably narrow and crowded.
Fine new prefectural offices, city halls, and "people's auditoriums"
were built in most cities, and in the larger ones the construction of
great office buildings went on apace. The withdrawal of the old earth-
quake-inspired limit on the height of buildings permitted skyscrapers
of forty or more stories to appear in Tokyo. But a large proportion of
the public buildings, such as hospitals and schools, were antiquated
and often dilapidated, and urban housing remained in distressingly
short supply.

On the whole, however, prosperity together with the passage of time
gradually freed the Japanese from many of the anxieties of the early
postwar period. Affluence undercut leftist predictions of economic
catastrophe, diverted popular attention from the promised panacea of

revolution to the enjoyment of immediate pleasures, and soothed strife between labor and management. Japan's worst postwar labor dispute, which occurred at the Miike coal mines in Kyushu, was settled on November 1, 1960, when the striking miners were forced to bow to the inevitable rationalization and cutback of coal mining because of the availability of cheap fuel oil from the Middle East. Unions discovered that there was much more to be gained from peaceful bargaining over wage increases, made possible by a burgeoning economy, than from demonstrating in the streets for remote and theoretical political objectives. As labor–management relations in the sixties became decidedly less turbulent, the annual "spring struggle" over wages became basically a series of lackluster parades and wage negotiations. May Day, labor's day for demonstrating solidarity, became a festive occasion to which workers brought the kiddies.

Japanese became decidedly more satisfied with their lives and more confident in their country. The national flag came more into evidence and the national anthem was heard more often. The word "patriotism" was still used only by extreme rightists, but "nationalism" as a concept became respectable. Since the old Japanese word for it had been discredited by past usage, the Japanese as usual borrowed from English and spoke of *nashonarizumu*. Opinion polls showed that between 80 and 90 percent of the people considered themselves middle class—hardly a basis for leftist revolutionary fervor. People might be distressed by the educational pressures put on their children to pass the examinations required for entrance into the more prestigious educational institutions, which led to positions in the higher bureaucracy and managerial jobs in the bigger firms, but they considered the system to be basically fair and open to talent. Culture in all forms prospered and proliferated, and in 1968 all Japanese were thrilled when Kawabata Yasunari was awarded the Nobel Prize in literature, the second man writing in a non-Western language to be so recognized. Japanese architects became world famous. Japanese scientists and scholars were winning recognition throughout the world. Countless international conventions were held in Japan.

Japanese took increasing pride in their country; they felt it good to be a Japanese. Conditions in the rest of Asia seemed pitiable by contrast, and even the West appeared a little stodgy and slow-moving. The floods of Japanese businessmen and tourists who roamed the world came home content to be back. It was intellectually stimulating for the graduate student to spend a year at an American university, but

Taurus Photos

Elevated highways in Tokyo.

unless he was in New York City or some other major center, he felt as if he had gone to "the sticks." No place seemed to hum with life and cultural activity quite like Tokyo. Not only had it become the biggest metropolis in the world; it had perhaps the highest concentration of university students, close to half of Japan's total of a million and a half.

Despite the continuing rash of street demonstrations, Japan showed far greater calm and stability and a much more vigorous cultural life than it had for more than a century. The nation was creating its own very satisfactory version of a lively, affluent twentieth-century life. The 1964 Tokyo Olympic Games gave the Japanese a chance to show the world their achievements, which they did with great pride and gusto, in what were generally recognized to be the finest Olympic Games held to date. To accommodate the games, the Japanese threw themselves into a frenzy of building fine new sport facilities, a greatly expanded subway network in Tokyo, fine new hotels, high-speed elevated roadways, the start of a nationwide system of high-speed highways, and a "New Mainline" railway, the Shinkansen, which averaged speeds of well over 100 miles an hour in a crowded but incredibly punctual schedule between Tokyo and Osaka. In 1970 a great International Exposition in Osaka provided the impetus for a corresponding upgrading of transportation facilities and public buildings in the Kansai, the great population and industrial node around Osaka, Kobe, and Kyoto, and Tokyo's one great rival region for national leadership.

Japan in the early and mid-sixties was characterized by relative political tranquillity, massive economic growth, vigorous intellectual and cultural activity, and general goodwill. The sturdy nation had survived the greatest trials of its long history to rise from the ashes of the war and within two decades had burst forth into a blossoming far more glorious than anything anyone could have imagined. But the story of a nation is no mere fairy tale, ending with "and so they lived happily ever after." Japan was to go on to even greater flowerings, but on the way an endless series of new problems kept springing up to plague its course.

16

THE PROBLEMS OF GROWTH

Japan's economic growth remained phenomenal throughout the sixties and into the early seventies; it was becoming a truly affluent country. There was a certain fragility to this affluence, however. Japan depended on imported energy, raw materials, and even food. It was correspondingly dependent on foreign markets to pay for these necessary imports. Its population, now past the 100 million mark, provided a huge national market—the foundation for its booming economy— but large-scale foreign trade was essential if this economy was to operate. The pattern of trade was not regional and therefore potentially controllable by Japan, but global and hence entirely beyond its abilities to regulate or defend.

Some weaknesses in the Japanese economy were alarming. The country was more than four-fifths dependent on foreign energy resources—basically oil, which came largely from the Persian Gulf, but also on coal from the United States and Australia, and liquified natural gas. All or virtually all of its iron ore, most other crucial ores and metals, cotton, wool, and about half of its lumber and wood pulp had to be imported, largely from North America, Australia, Southeast Asia, South America, and even Africa. Almost all of its wheat and feed grains and some of its meat came from the United States, Canada, and Australia, and most of its soybeans, needed for protein and for oil for human consumption, from the United States. Its major animal source of protein was fish, caught in the seven seas. The Japanese imported 20 percent of the food they ate and, counting feed grains, about half of the calories that were turned into food.

Though nearby Taiwan and South Korea were becoming important markets, Japan's largest market was the United States, which took about a third of Japanese exports in the early sixties and more than a third two decades later. Southeast Asia also loomed large, as did more distant areas, such as Europe and Latin America. Relatively little of Japan's trading area lay within 2,000 miles of Japan. Most of it was from 10,000 to 15,000 miles away. Japan's economy had become truly global. To have tried to subsist merely on trade with nearby areas, which its military leaders once thought could be shaped into an economic base for Japan as the Greater East Asia Co-Prosperity Sphere, would have spelled economic disaster for Japan as it existed in the sixties.

Despite these notable weaknesses in Japan's foreign trade position, world trading patterns seemed relatively stable, and the Japanese had only vague apprehensions about the future. Politically the nation also seemed more settled than it had during the first two postwar decades, though unperceived political as well as economic problems lay just ahead. The old political hostilities remained, but some of the fire had gone out of them. Japan was an obvious success, and life was essentially well ordered and placid.

Younger persons, perhaps because of the more liberal new education and certainly because they were less psychologically scarred by the past, approached problems in a more open-minded way than their elders had. Beginning with economics, Japanese scholarship started to free itself from its Marxist straitjacket. Young scholars led the way in developing less doctrinaire, more pragmatic lines of reasoning about internal politics and world affairs. They discussed problems of defense and international tension without embarrassment. The tone of the newspapers followed suit. The Self-Defense Forces, developed in the fifties despite the violent opposition of leftists, began to win general acceptance. Most Japanese remained proud that Japan had "renounced" war and were strongly opposed to "rearmament," but they came to feel that Japan had a right to self-defense and that the modest Self-Defense Forces were of appropriate size for this purpose.

The gradual erosion of the conservative vote continued, but meanwhile several things happened to undermine the opposition and give the LDP a continuing hold on the government. One was the rift in the Communist world in 1959 between the People's Republic of China and the Soviet Union, which threw the Japanese leftists into ideological disarray. The split, which had become obvious by the early sixties, embarrassed the Socialists and put great strains on the Communists, who swung back and forth between Moscow and Peking and ended up alienated from both. China's 1962 attack on India, a country considered admirable in leftist circles for its outspoken neutralism, caused further embarrassment, and China's development and testing of nuclear weapons from 1964 on proved even more divisive. Chinese nuclear fallout was brought over Japan by the prevailing winds; American nuclear tests had never had this result. Even before this, the whole antibomb movement, which had been an important "united front" activity in the fifties, had fallen apart. The Democratic Socialists deserted the annual August 6 ceremonies in Hiroshima, forming their own movement in 1961, and two years later the Socialist party, which felt that the Communist nuclear powers as well as the United States must be condemned, broke off from the Communists and founded a bitterly competing movement. The ultimate solution to this awkward situation was to let the annual ceremonies lose their domestic political coloration and become a generalized, popular antinuclear movement.

In the first years after Mao Tse-tung's triumph in China in 1949, it had seemed to many Japanese that the Chinese Communists might be charting a better road into the future than the one to which the American occupation had helped steer Japan. But by the early sixties, it had become clear that China's Great Leap Forward had been an economic disaster. The confusion caused by the Cultural Revolution in 1965 and the disorders of the Red Guards, which started in the late summer of 1966, were followed by a second economic decline that further weakened the image of the People's Republic as a world leader. With Red Guards reminding the Japanese of the excesses of their own "young officers" in the thirties and with Japanese living standards soaring more than ten times higher than those of China, it took a very doctrinaire person indeed to see the Chinese as providing a useful model for Japan.

An even more serious blow to the long-nurtured hope of the Socialists to replace the LDP as the majority party was the proliferation of opposition parties in the 1960s and the corresponding decline in the Socialists' share of the progressive vote. As mentioned previously, the greater part of the Socialist right wing, supported by the Domei unions (then known as Zenro), broke away in January 1960 to form the Democratic Socialist party. Its 8.7 percent of the popular vote in the election of November 1960 cut heavily into the support for the Socialists. The new party was deeply committed to parliamentary democracy, and the division between it and the more Marxist left wing of the party was to prove unsurmountable.

The remaining Socialists were further weakened by the serious ideological divisions that existed among them. Although the party retained the strong support of Sohyo, the largest of the labor federations, its leaders were becoming old and out of touch with changing conditions in Japan and the world. Although Japan was clearly dependent on trade with the United States and its allies, the Socialists remained wedded to a dream of close association with China and the Soviet Union, which had little foreign trade and were feuding bitterly with each other. The Socialists talked an anachronistic language of class struggle to an increasingly affluent population, which regarded itself as middle class. The doctrinaire leadership would swing the party to the left at party conventions, but candidates for election would have to swing back toward the center when they approached the voters. Bitter struggles for power developed among the left wing, the part of the right wing that had remained in the party, and a centrist group. In 1962 Eda Saburo of the right wing put forth his ''vision'' of the Socialist objectives as a combination of American prosperity, the Soviet Union's thoroughgoing social security system, British parliamentary democracy, and Japan's own ''peace constitution,'' but such a formulation of ideals was, of course, anathema to the Left. A seesaw battle for party control continued through the sixties and into the seventies between politicians who, while wearing the same socialist label, championed essentially irreconcilable points of view.

Meanwhile, another opposition party was growing, the only clearly new party in postwar Japanese politics. This was the Komeito (sometimes called the Clean Government party in English). It was an outgrowth of a new religious movement, the Soka Gakkai, meaning the Value Creating Association. Theologically an offshoot of Nichiren Buddhism, Soka Gakkai has been the most successful of the so-called new religions since the war. These new religions have been an important phenomenon in Japan for more than a century, but none of the earlier ones had as great success as Soka Gakkai, which quickly built up an ardent following of several million people. Its appeal, as with many of the other new religions, appears to be less religious than social. It seems to have been able to answer the need for a sense of group identity among many of the less educated and financially less successful residents of Japanese cities who, lacking the old village roots or membership in such large groupings as great industrial enterprises or labor unions, felt isolated in society. Soka Gakkai's simple doctrines of absolute faith and immediate worldly benefits are hardly distinctive in Japan, though its militant proselytizing techniques, which recall Nichiren's own intransigence in the thirteenth century, are unique. Its real reasons for success, however, probably lie in its firm leaders and their superb skills at organization and showmanship. Since Soka Gakkai membership is overwhelmingly urban and from the lower end of the economic scale, which is just where one would expect much of the Socialist vote to be concentrated, this development of a rival party was another blow to Socialist hopes. In fact, ever since the election of 1969 the Komeito has won close to 10 percent of the electorate and the Socialists only around 20 percent or less.

The Soka Gakkai ventured into the political fray only cautiously at first, and its actual political views long remained vague. Being opposed to the ruling LDP, it has tended to phrase its stand on international questions in terms borrowed from the Left. But behind this rhetoric the leaders of Soka Gakkai and Komeito appear to be essentially old-fashioned and conservative Japanese, more representative of the lower middle class than of radical intellectuals or militant labor groups. The Soka Gakkai first ran candidates for local election in 1955 and for the House of Councillors the next year, winning six seats then, fifteen in 1962, and twenty in 1965. In 1964 it organized the Komeito party as its political wing, and the new party won 5.4 percent of the popular vote in 1967 and 11 percent in 1969.

Another factor in the splitting up of the opposition vote was that the Sino-Soviet rift, instead of damaging the fortunes of the Japanese Communist party, benefited it by allowing the party to cast off subservience to foreign Communist movements and to stress its own independence and nationalism. The Japanese Communists broke with the Soviet Union in 1964 and with China in 1966. Tightly organized and well supported both financially and ideologically by a successful newspaper, *Akahata,* or "Red Flag," the Communist party rose to new heights of popularity under the strong leadership of Miyamoto Kenji, who had been chosen party chairman in 1958. It restored its popular vote to 4 percent in the election of November 1963, received almost 7 percent in December 1969, and earned 10.5 percent in December 1972. Like the Komeito, its chief source of strength lay in what had become a large urban protest vote, which preferred these fresher, more tightly organized parties to the Socialists for expressing their opposition to the ruling LDP.

The restoration of the Communists to a significant role, the appearance of Komeito, and the defection of the DSP all cut drastically into Socialist prospects. The opposition was now split four ways, and the Socialist vote was beginning to erode even more rapidly than that of the LDP. With a relatively old and ideologically inflexible leadership, it was hard to create a fresh image and attract new voters. Between 1958 and 1972 its share of the popular vote for the lower house fell 11 percent, compared to 9 percent for the LDP, proportionately a much greater loss for the Socialists in view of their smaller size. With voting strength down to only a fifth of the total, Socialist hopes of replacing the LDP as the majority party faded away.

Against a badly split opposition, the LDP became relatively stronger. When Ikeda was forced to resign in November 1964, Sato Eisaku, the blood brother of Kishi (whose name had been changed by his adoption into another family), became the new prime minister and managed to hold on to the post for over seven and a half years, the longest tenure in Japanese history. In place of a real two-party system, Japan had evolved what people came to call a "one and a half party system," with the LDP an apparently permanent majority, facing a divided and frustrated opposition. Sato's relationship with Kishi and the fact that his own faction was, next only to Kishi's, on the extreme right did not help his image with the public and he was never as popular as Ikeda, but the first years of his administration went quite smoothly.

In general, Sato continued Ikeda's policies. In 1965 he managed to bring to completion, after a decade of difficult negotiations, the "normalization" agreement with Korea. This was the last of the major reparation settlements and set the stage for rapid economic growth in South Korea, a tremendous surge in trade between the two countries, and large economic investments there by Japan. Sato also continued Ikeda's efforts to expand Japan's role in the rest of East Asia. It became the dominant trading partner of many Asian countries and an important provider of economic aid through reparations, small supplementary grants, and commercial investments, which greatly expanded Japanese exports. When the Asian Development Bank was set up in 1966, Japan equaled America's contribution of $200 million to its capital, the first time since the war that any country had matched the United States in a major undertaking of this sort. Trainees in Japan from other Asian countries passed the 1,000 mark annually, and Japan started a small "peace corps" type of operation, with over 300 volunteers in certain South Asian and African countries.

Sato held the first general elections under his leadership on January 29, 1967. This election showed that the LDP vote was continuing to erode, as was to be expected because of the declining numbers of farmers and the soaring of urban populations. Another factor, however, was a series of minor political scandals, dubbed the "black mists" of corruption by the opposition. This was the first time since its formation that the LDP failed to get a majority of the popular vote, winning less than 49 percent, as compared to almost 55 percent in 1963. However, because of the division of the opposition into four parties, the number of seats won by the LDP in the lower house continued to be a solid majority.

In the next two elections, in December 1969 and December 1972, five months after Sato had resigned, the percentage of popular votes for the LDP fell only slightly, and since the party could usually count on ten or more independents joining its ranks, its percentage of lower house seats remained at over 55. The conservative independents who regularly joined the party after each election were mostly rising younger politicians who, having failed to receive the party's nomination, still had the confidence to run against the designated candidates of the party and had won. With their aid, the LDP's control over the Diet remained quite firm.

The opposition parties became increasingly frustrated over their inability to win as much support among the younger voters as they had hoped to. They attributed this to the "my home-ism" of the younger generation, using these English words to describe the younger people's greater interest in their own personal lives and happiness than in the great social and political issues of the day.

Domestically Japan had become an extraordinarily stable country, exuding self-confidence, satisfaction, and optimism in its economy, its society, its culture, and to some extent even in its political life. But clouds were gathering outside of Japan. The most serious was the Vietnam war. Almost unnoticed by the American public, to say nothing of the Japanese, the United States had gradually become involved in military activities in the divided former French colony of Indochina. During 1965 this involvement became massive, and it grew into a large and terrible war over the next several years. Some Japanese had been critical of American intervention in Vietnam all along, but now most of the public became deeply concerned. To many it seemed that the old Marxist theory was proving right: The great "capitalist" power was showing its inevitable "imperialistic" tendencies and pressing mindlessly forward in a constantly expanding war that could spread to China, as the Korean war had, possibly involve the Soviet Union, and end up by drawing Japan in too. The security treaty with the United States, just as the leftists said, might lead to insecurity rather than peace.

Japanese quite rightly tended to equate the American entrapment in the quagmire of Vietnam with the fate of their own armies in China in the thirties. Battles might be won with superior weapons, but local nationalism would triumph in the long run. Also, American bombing reminded them of what they had suffered in World War II. Their sympathies were with the Vietnamese. The enterprising Japanese press and television networks provided their public with the same visual and verbal fare that shocked Americans, and the Japanese reacted with even greater revulsion. The image of the United States, which had been so favorable just a few years earlier when Kennedy was president, steadily worsened. Violent race and urban disorders in the United States, which were at least partially related to the Vietnam war, further damaged the reputation of the country. Accustomed to the extreme homogeneity of their own tight society, the Japanese were appalled by the problems of an ethnically diverse land. These they viewed more with sympathy or condescension than with condemnation. But many Japanese concluded that the United States was a weaker and less stable nation than they had thought, and they began to have doubts about the continuing value of American friendship and protection.

The rising sense of national pride made Japanese less tolerant of rigid American policies not only in the Vietnam war, but in other matters as well. Sato himself enunciated in 1971 three nuclear principles for Japan, which were not to produce, possess, or introduce any nuclear weapons. In particular the Japanese chafed at what they felt was American prevention of the establishment of normal relations between Japan and its great and historically revered neighbor, China. To Japanese, it seemed that Americans, safely across the Pacific and possessing their own natural resources, could ignore trade with China and maintain an attitude of unrelenting hostility, but that Japan could not take the same stand toward this fifth of humanity living, as it were, right next door. Before World War II China had seemed an area of vital economic importance to Japan, and even under changed postwar conditions it appeared to have great economic significance to Japan.

Actually the United States did not stand as much in the way of the development of Sino-Japanese relations as the Japanese public assumed. Although the Japanese government felt it prudent to follow official American attitudes toward China, by the late sixties a large amount of trade and cultural contacts had grown up between China and Japan on the basis of Japan's formula of "the separation of politics and economics," which Peking vociferously denounced. Japan had become China's largest trading partner by far, though trade between the two countries remained a relatively insignificant 2 to 3 percent of Japan's worldwide international commerce. Part of the Sino-Japanese trade, known as "memorandum trade," was carried out under a semiofficial agreement between the two countries, the rest through so-called friendly firms in Japan. In some cases these were dummy companies set up by big corporations that did not wish to risk endangering their relations with their American associates by trading with China openly. Japan had also developed more cultural contacts with China than had any other country, including even the communist nations.

Despite all these relations with the People's Republic, Japan's trade and other contacts with the Republic of China on Taiwan remained far more significant, as did its trade with South Korea. Both Taiwan and

South Korea were violently opposed to Peking, and their attitudes underlined American policies in inhibiting the Japanese government from following the inclination of most Japanese, who wanted to extend diplomatic recognition to Peking, as most of America's other chief allies had already done. Unhappiness over the lack of full relations with China joined with indignation and fear regarding the Vietnam war to create a rapidly growing anti-Americanism in Japan. This found ready targets in the American military bases in Japan and in the flow of men and materiel through them to the war in Vietnam. Demonstrations against American bases proliferated and became more violent. The mass media became increasingly shrill in its condemnation of the United States. The more prosperous and self-confident Japan became, the less tolerable was continued subservience to American foreign policy and the presence of American bases on Japanese soil.

Several other factors helped to make the late sixties a period of rising tensions with the United States. One was the realization that it was not far to June 23, 1970, the terminal date for the revised security treaty, after which it could be denounced by either side on one year's notice. Ever since their failure to block the treaty in 1960, all its opponents had aimed at 1970 as the time to break the relationship with the United States and throw the conservatives out of power. As the date drew near, political tensions mounted, and some groups consciously began preparing for the "crisis of 1970."

Another factor straining relations with the United States was rapidly rising concern over Okinawa. It is surprising that the separation in 1945 of Japan's 47th prefecture from the rest of the country and its continued rule by the American military had not stirred up a quicker reaction within Japan proper. But in the early postwar years the Japanese in the main islands were too demoralized and too concerned with their own economic recovery to worry much about Okinawa. The Okinawans themselves were at first somewhat ambivalent in their attitudes. They spoke a decided variant of Japanese, closer to the ancient language; they had had a partially separate history before the late nineteenth century, having had their own kings; and they resented the second-class status mainland Japanese had accorded them before the war and the fact that they had suffered more heavily than other Japanese during the conflict. But American military rule soon made them the most patriotic of all Japanese, and they began demanding their return to Japan long before the rest of the Japanese became much concerned over the issue.

In the peace treaty of 1952 Japan had promised to support American proposals that Okinawa be made a trust territory of the United States, but it had soon become evident that the United Nations would not grant such a trusteeship. Secretary of State Dulles then began to speak of Japan's "residual sovereignty" in the islands. The term came to be understood as a promise that Okinawa would be returned to Japan some day, when strategic conditions in East Asia permitted. But this remained a distant goal, and in the meantime most of the attention of the Okinawans remained focused on winning better economic treatment and more political autonomy.

In 1965, however, along with increased worries over the Vietnam war, there was a considerable rise of interest in Japan in the Okinawa *irridenta,* and within two years the clamor for "reversion" had become intense. In June 1968 the return to Japan of the small and lightly populated Bonin Islands, strung far out in the Pacific south of Japan, did nothing to alleviate the situation. It seemed intolerable to many Japanese that close to a million Japanese in Okinawa should be ruled by Americans in what amounted to the only colony in the world created since World War II. A comparable situation between the United States and its European allies was unthinkable, illustrating how unusual the Japanese psychology had been after the war, and also, perhaps, the racist attitudes Americans had brought with them to Asia. It became increasingly clear that a quick solution to the Okinawa problem was necessary.

Reversion was no simple matter, however. With the exception of the naval port of Yokosuka near Tokyo, the extensive bases in Okinawa were the most important American bases in all of East Asia, and while the Vietnam war was going on, there was great reluctance on the part of the American military to surrender full control over them. But political sentiment was such in Japan that the limitations of the 1960 security treaty would have to apply to these bases, as it did to the others, when Okinawa reverted to Japan. The Japanese called this the "mainland level" (*hondonami*) formula, and it meant no nuclear weapons and no "free use" of the bases for direct military action elsewhere without "prior consultation" with Japan—in other words, without Japanese consent.

The problem was finally solved in a communiqué issued by Prime Minister Sato and President Richard Nixon on November 21, 1969, which stated that Okinawa would soon be restored to Japan and that the limitations of the security treaty would thereafter be applied to the

American bases there too. Since this would put the use of the American bases in Okinawa for the defense of Taiwan and South Korea under a virtual Japanese veto, Sato sought to reassure the Americans by mentioning in the communiqué the importance Japan placed on "the security of the Republic of Korea" and the "peace and security of the Taiwan area." But most Japanese took great alarm at these statements, believing that they indicated a Japanese commitment to the defense of these areas and therefore signaled that the Japanese government was moving toward rearmament. The formal agreement for the return of Okinawa was signed in June 1970, and control over the islands finally reverted to Japan on May 15, 1972.

One basically extraneous matter that became related to the troubles over foreign policy in Japan in the late sixties was the worldwide student unrest, which reached its apogee in Japan as elsewhere in the world during these years. After 1960 the Zengakuren had splintered in a way typical of radical ideological movements. By the late sixties there were three main radical factions, each controlling the student movement in some universities or in certain faculties of universities, and all battling desperately with one another for supremacy. By this time the activists had come to wear brightly colored construction-worker helmets for purposes of protection and identification. They used square-cut wooden poles as their chief weapons and, on occasion, steel pipes and Molotov cocktails. Larger and better-disciplined student organizations were under the control of the Communists, the Socialists, and even the Soka Gakkai, but for the most part these remained out of the fray, though they were available for coordinated political action if the opportunity arose.

Student unrest derived from many sources, not simply from foreign policy. There was dissatisfaction with the universities themselves—their increasing tuition rates, inadequate student facilities, and general system of organization. There was also a great deal of criticism of the less desirable aspects of modern urban society that were becoming increasingly evident in an affluent Japan. Such attitudes prevailed throughout the industrialized world, but in some ways Japanese students were even more concerned with them than were their contempo-

Rioting students, with variously colored workers' helmets to distinguish different factions, meet a line of armored riot control police.

raries in the West. Japan had become a socially egalitarian country, but one of strict educational hierarchies. A person's future depended almost entirely on his or her education, and the pressure to get into the best universities, through extremely mechanical examinations, extended downward until Japanese children were subjected to the psychological stress of educational competition at the elementary school level. The university entrance examinations came to be known as the "examination hell." Those who failed to win entry to the university of their choice on their first try commonly tried again and again, becoming what were called *ronin*, the name given to the "masterless samurai" of the Tokugawa period.

Once accepted into a university, students found classes boring and graduation almost automatic in a very lax, large-scale, and impersonal system. Many devoted themselves more to political agitation, hobbies, or sports than to study. Enrollments had increased enormously, but this increase had not been met by a corresponding investment in higher education on the part of society. Many of the new government schools were inadequately equipped and staffed, and the private universities were simply overwhelmed. The war had wiped out what endowments they might have had, and the lack of tax benefits to donors and the absence of a tradition of this sort of giving meant that private universities were almost entirely dependent on tuition and on fees for entrance examinations. On this wholly inadequate financial base they tried to accommodate about 75 percent of the student population. (By way of contrast, only about 40 percent of the university students in the United States, and virtually none in Europe, were in private universities.) Not surprisingly, almost all private universities in Japan were hopelessly in debt. The quality of Japanese university education was further impaired by the Germanic tradition of putting research above teaching and by faculty control, which resulted in weak university administrations and powerful faculty interests that discouraged innovation in teaching methods and the development of new fields of study. All in all, university education was one of the areas of most obvious trouble in an otherwise highly successful and smoothly running society.

Student outbreaks mounted steadily in frequency and violence in the second half of the sixties, until by 1968 a large number of Japanese universities were in serious trouble. Buildings were seized and vandalized, university officers and professors were held prisoner and tried by kangaroo courts, and pitched battles were fought between rival student groups or with the police. Prestigious Tokyo University was partially inoperative for more than a year, and many other universities were forced to suspend normal activities for months at a time. The chief object of student animosity was the universities themselves, but the students also seized every opportunity to oppose the Vietnam war, American bases, and the whole relationship with the United States. Starting in November 1964, American nuclear-powered submarines on guard in the Pacific had been allowed to enter American bases in Japan for rest and recuperation for the crews, and the protest demonstrations these visits had at first sparked had gradually died away. But when, in January 1968, at the height of the Vietnam war, a nuclear-powered aircraft carrier, the *Enterprise*, was unwisely allowed to enter port, it produced an outburst reminiscent of those of the spring of 1960. Student extremists were delighted to serve once again as the vanguard in a great anti-American crusade.

The rising excitement in the late sixties over breaking the relationship with the United States, combined with the assumption that LDP control of the Diet was nearing its end, gave rise to a feeling that 1970 would see a great political explosion and a drastic shift of Japanese domestic and foreign policies, but nothing of the sort occurred. The November 1969 communiqué promising the return of Okinawa defused this issue before it could become part of the expected conflict over the renewal of the security treaty in 1970, and in any case the security treaty battle never materialized. Because the Japanese and American governments avoided any proposals for change, the treaty remained automatically in effect; hence there was nothing, such as Diet debates or ratification procedures, on which discontent could focus. Most important of all, the Vietnam war showed signs of coming to an end. This was clearly signaled by President Lyndon Johnson's decision in the spring of 1968 to put a limit on further increases of American troops in Vietnam and Nixon's start of a slow withdrawal the next year. Although the war was to drag on until the cease-fire of 1974 and the complete collapse of the South Vietnamese regime in 1975, anxieties over Vietnam were already diminishing in Japan by the beginning of the seventies, and the war gradually faded as a major issue.

At the same time, student unrest waned as a significant political force. The public, remembering prewar "thought control," had been extremely tolerant of student violence at first, and the universities, insistent on their long-established academic autonomy, had strongly opposed any police interference in university disorders. But gradually public opinion soured on the students. The probable turning point came on January 18–19, 1969, when the police finally laid seige to the main hall of Tokyo University, long held by students, and drove them out. On August 3 a bill was passed in the Diet that provided for the reduction of professorial salaries in long-disrupted universities and for eventual dissolution of the institutions if they could not put their houses in order. The result was a marked drop in serious disturbances.

Some student extremists remained active, but the bulk of their followers became interested in other things. The opposition parties, realizing that the public was disenchanted with student violence, took care to dissociate themselves from the remaining activists who, though reduced greatly in numbers, became all the more extreme and violent. Gradually they turned their attention away from the universities and even from the American defense relationship and focused instead on society as a whole. Divided into small sectarian groups, they turned to terrorism, including the hijacking of a jet on March 31, 1970; a murderous attack on passengers at the Tel Aviv airport in Israel on May

30, 1972; the bombing of the headquarters of Mitsubishi Heavy Industries in Tokyo in 1974; and numerous bloody clashes between rival
groups and executions of their own recalcitrant members. Student extremists of this sort had become irrelevant in Japanese politics, and
only occasionally could they find causes that brought them back into
touch with the mainstream. One such cause was the fight to prevent
the construction of Tokyo's new international airport at Narita, in
which they were joined by local farmers and environmental groups.
Starting in 1966, this controversy culminated in a violent fracas in
1971. The opening of the airport was successfully delayed until May
1978, with occasional violence continuing even after that.

Clearly, the "crisis of 1970" never materialized, but in its place a new
set of problems arose. Unlike the frictions that had peaked in the late
sixties, these were not inherited from the time of Japan's weakness
and the Cold War, but were more the problems of Japan's success and
of changing world conditions. American withdrawal from Vietnam
soothed Japanese fears of becoming involved in that war. But, together with the disorders of the late sixties in American society, it
raised doubts about the reliability of American defense commitments
to Japan. These were not allayed by the ambiguities of the so-called
Nixon Doctrine, first enunciated by the president at a press conference
on Guam Island on July 25, 1969. Nixon seemed to be calling on
America's allies to take greater responsibility for their own defense.
Henry Kissinger's concept that there was a five-sided balance of
power in the world, with Japan, Western Europe, and China joining
the two superpowers to make this configuration, was even more
alarming to a largely disarmed and strongly pacifist Japan. Constant
American grumbling about Japan's "free ride" in defense at America's expense was also not reassuring. It seemed possible that Americans, in their disillusionment over Vietnam, would withdraw into their
traditional isolationism, leaving a militarily weak Japan exposed and
isolated. The original problem in Japan's military relationship with the
United States was being inverted. The progressives' worries about
becoming involved in American imperialistic policies were being

overshadowed by the conservatives' fears that the American alliance could no longer be depended on.

This unease almost turned into panic on July 15, 1971, when the United States suddenly announced that Kissinger had been secretly negotiating with the Chinese in Peking and that Nixon would visit China the next year. Since the Japanese government had faithfully conformed with American policy on China, despite strong popular pressure for recognition of the People's Republic, and the United States had repeatedly assured the Japanese that it would closely coordinate its China policy with Tokyo, the July 15 announcement came as a thunderbolt and was promptly dubbed the "Nixon shock." Some Japanese feared that the United States, in acting with such callous disregard of past promises and the difficult position of the Japanese government, caught in the past between American intransigence and Japanese yearnings for relations with China, was signaling its decision to dump Japan as its chief ally in East Asia in favor of China.

This, of course, was not the case. The American-Chinese rapprochement was basically the result of mounting Chinese fears of the Soviet Union and declining worries about American aggression in Vietnam, paralleled by a gradual mellowing of American attitudes

Tanaka Kakuei campaigning in 1976 for reelection to the Diet in his native constituency in Niigata, on the west coast of Japan, two years after he had left office as prime minister.

UPI

toward China. It was exactly what the Japanese government had hoped would happen, but of course not in the way it did. When Nixon went to Peking in February 1972, he did not go so far as to recognize the People's Republic, but the Sino-American thaw did make it possible for Japan to go a step further than the United States, extending official recognition to Peking. Tanaka Kakuei, who had succeeded Sato as prime minister in July 1972, did this in a visit to Peking in September. Japan, however, continued its highly successful relations with Taiwan on an ostensibly informal and private basis, a pattern the United States itself was eventually to follow when it recognized the People's Republic in 1978. The Nixon shock had thus produced a situation that was fundamentally beneficial to the Japanese government and people, all but eliminating what had long been an area of serious political controversy in Japanese politics. But the thoughtless manner in which the United States had acted frightened the Japanese and left continuing worries about the value of American friendship and the reliability of its defense commitments. Japanese expectations that the United States, as the stronger member of the partnership—the elder brother as it were—would treat Japan with special consideration, or *amae* as the Japanese call it, had been shattered. The worries Nixon's action stirred up at this time were revived from time to time throughout the seventies by recurring American proposals for military withdrawal from South Korea, an area Japan looked upon as its vital first line of defense.

The Nixon shock had seriously damaged Japanese pride just at a time when economic affluence and revived self-esteem were making Japanese still more dissatisfied with the continuing inequality in their relationship with the United States and restive about Japan's position in the world community. The splendid Osaka International Exposition of 1970 and the successful hosting of the Winter Olympics at Sapporo in Hokkaido in 1972 contributed to national pride, and there was talk that Japan should be made a permanent member of the Security Council of the United Nations. But this was not enough. For more than a century Japanese had seen themselves as recent and still marginal members of an essentially Occidental family of nations, in which they might never achieve full equality. This Western orientation, and particularly the heavy infusion of American influence since the war, seemed to be pulling them away from their own cultural roots. A nationalistic reaction was only to be expected, and in the late sixties and early seventies there were increasing signs that one was beginning and that Japanese were turning back to certain more traditional attitudes.

Ikeda had spoken of an "autonomous" foreign policy, meaning a greater sense of Japan's making its own decisions in its relations with the United States and other countries. In the minds of some Japanese, this grew into a concept of an "independent" foreign policy that would be quite separate from that of the United States and might even involve an independent military stance. Stories and films about World War II became popular, particularly among the generation that had not experienced it. Mishima Yukio, a leading writer, became the open champion of a return to traditional values, including the militarism of the past. On November 25, 1970, he thrilled the Japanese and startled the world when, after haranguing members of the Self-Defense Forces, he committed suicide by performing *seppuku*. Most Japanese, for all their fascination with suicide, regarded his act as a bit of romantic idiocy. Pacifism and antimilitarism remained strong, and there was no sign of increasing what had become the traditional allotment of 1 percent of GNP to defense expenditures. As we have seen, Sato in 1971 officially formulated Japan's three nuclear principles: not to produce, possess, or introduce nuclear weapons into Japan. These principles and the 1 percent limit on defense were accepted by almost everyone and still have overwhelming popular support. But to people in other countries, especially to Japan's neighbors, Mishima's spectacular suicide seemed a menacing sign of the rebirth of Japanese militarism, and it did indeed symbolize a broader sense of malaise within Japan over its seeming subordination to the United States. To many persons both in Japan and abroad, it appeared that Japan and the United States were approaching a parting of the ways.

Other factors contributed to the apparently growing estrangement between Japan and the United States. A steady and rapid rise in Japanese exports to the United States and some other industrialized countries produced many new frictions, which were soon to mount to mammoth proportions. At the same time, Japan's underlying anxieties about its food supplies were also exacerbated by several developments. One was a trend among the maritime countries to claim wider strips of their coastal waters, sometimes up to 200 miles, thus cutting down drastically on fishing areas open to Japan.

In the summer of 1973 the United States delivered another "shock," which roused Japanese worries about its food supply and further undermined Japanese faith in American goodwill and reliability. Fearing that unusually heavy Soviet purchases of soybeans would create a shortage, the United States suddenly put an embargo on all soybean exports, overlooking the fact that American soybeans were a principal source of protein in the Japanese diet and that the highly profitable American soybean industry had been developed in large part to meet the Japanese market. The embargo was soon lifted as being unnecessary, and promises were made to Japan that it would not be repeated, but the Japanese were appalled by America's easy oversight of their country and its callous disregard of vital Japanese requirements.

The soybean incident proved to be merely a prelude to a far more serious trade crisis—the oil shock of 1973, which grew out of the Arab–Israeli war that year. In October the Arab countries and their allies placed an embargo on oil, which threatened the very life of Japan. Unlike the United States, Japan had scant domestic sources of energy, and it used imported oil not just for transportation and heating but for the bulk of energy to power its industry. By this time imported oil constituted roughly three-quarters of Japan's total energy supplies, and more than 80 percent of this came from the Persian Gulf. Fortunately for Japan, the embargo did not last long, but the bulk of the oil-exporting nations, calling themselves OPEC (the Organization of Petroleum Exporting Countries), formed a cartel that quadrupled prices. This was a harder body blow to Japan than to any other major industrialized power. While the United States could reasonably talk of energy self-sufficiency, the Japanese were forced to scramble wildly to secure oil supplies wherever and however they could. The world would never again seem economically as secure to them, and doubts increased about the long-range compatibility of Japanese and American interests.

The 1973 oil shock, of course, had strongly negative effects on the Japanese economy, as it did on all the industrialized nations. Other problems had already forced the government into deficit financing and the first adverse balance of trade in several years, but both conditions worsened sharply as a result of the oil crisis. The whole economy slowed down markedly, and Japan's GNP even contracted slightly (0.6 percent) in 1974 for the first time since the start of the postwar recovery. Inflation also soared, rising above 20 percent for a while, and shortages appeared in some consumer goods, notably toilet paper.

The Japanese, however, brought these conditions under control more quickly than did most of the other industrialized countries, even though they were not as severely injured as Japan. The rate of economic growth was restored to around 5 or 6 percent and, after a second oil shock sharply hiked prices in 1979, gradually leveled off at around 3 or 4 percent. Such growth rates were much lower than the 10 percent increases in the glory days of the Japanese "miracle," but they were on the whole appreciably higher than those of the other industrialized countries. Being based on an already huge economy, they added up to enormous annual increases in GNP.

There were several reasons why Japan was able to surmount the oil shocks so successfully. With typical Japanese skill in cooperation, workers, realizing the situation, agreed to reduce the rate of growth of their wages, and business firms accepted government advice to take distasteful measures. Most important, the government and business agreed on shifting their emphasis from labor-intensive industries that required large quantities of raw materials and energy, such as heavy industries and chemicals, to industries requiring less of these ingredients but demanding large inputs of technical skills instead. These enterprises they called the "knowledge industries." They not only cut down on imported raw materials and energy but moved the economy up a notch by increasing the use of advanced technology in so-called high-tech enterprises in place of the traditional smokestack industries. Japan also reduced the consumption of energy in such ways as emphasizing the production of high-mileage cars that used little gasoline and by recycling waste materials.

The spiraling inflation set off by the oil shocks proved to be the most difficult problem to get under control. A worldwide reduction in the use of oil and the catching up of other prices to those of oil eventually eliminated the pressures of the oil shocks themselves and created an oil glut, but not before a rapid increase in world prices had occurred. The rise in prices was particularly high in Japan, coming as it did on top of the inflationary tendencies of an already booming economy. Inflation rates were in time brought down from two digits to one and eventually to levels among the lowest in the world, but the cost of living kept rising. Land prices, because of the scarcity of usable land in Japan, led the way, rising to ridiculous heights. A National Land Agency established in 1974 proved largely ineffective. Because of astronomic housing costs, most urban Japanese lived crowded into minuscule apartments, and the cost of living in Tokyo during the seventies climbed steadily toward the top, until in the eighties the city finally achieved the dubious distinction of being the most expensive place to live in the world.

The slowdown of the rate of growth caused by the oil shocks, however, did have some benefits. It gave the Japanese a breathing spell in which to reflect on the ills their breakneck economic growth was bringing them. Such growth had produced not only terrible urban crowding but unparalleled pollution of both air and water. In some metropolitan areas the air had become so bad by the early sixties that some traffic police were forced to wear masks and oxygen stations were installed for pedestrians. Mt. Fuji, which once could be seen clearly from Tokyo during much of the year, was by then visible only under extraordinary weather conditions a few times a year. Rivers had become too filthy for fish, and some coastal waters were almost equally polluted. The consumption of mercury-contaminated fish caught near a chemical plant at Minamata in Kyushu produced the world-famous Minamata disease, and other pollution sicknesses became common. Worsening traffic conditions further lengthened the already long commuting woes of city dwellers. Urban housing remained pathetically inadequate, giving rise, in the late seventies, to a casual British comment that Japanese live in ''rabbit hutches,'' which deeply wounded Japanese pride. Big buildings threw permanent shadows over private houses and apartments, denying residents what they felt was their right to sunshine, so important for winter heating and laundry drying in Japan. ''Noise pollution,'' as the Japanese called it, from superhighways, high-speed trains, and jets plagued the lives of millions of people. They lumped all these inconveniences of modern urban living together as *kogai,* or ''public nuisances.''

There were also other more subtle problems. Hitherto Japan had done comparatively little in the field of social security, but the life span of the people had lengthened extraordinarily since the war, becoming among the highest in the world. This meant that much more money had to be devoted to the support of the retired and care for the aged. The great majority of older Japanese, some 80 percent, still lived with or near one of their children, but urban crowding made this impossible for an increasing proportion of the population. Another problem was that, in per capita terms, park and road space in cities was only a fraction of what it was in Western cities, and schools, hospitals, and many other public buildings were often relatively flimsy or dilapidated. Sewage facilities were particularly inadequate, being available to only about a fifth of urban dwellers. A massive redirection of Japanese efforts and resources was needed if the life of the average city dweller was to be improved and not deteriorate still further.

Local protests over pollution cases had occurred as far back as the 1890s, when strong opposition to the pollution of a whole river basin by the Ashio copper mines in central Honshu had finally produced some mild government corrections. But it was not until the 1960s that the nation as a whole began to become conscious of the problem, inspired in part by the rising concern among Americans over their own much less serious environmental problems. The Japanese woke up to the fact that they were literally choking themselves to death on their own industrial success. Further industrialization in the rapid and reckless manner of the past was likely to worsen rather than better their lives. Growth at any price was no longer a viable policy, and quality of life needed to be taken into consideration as much as the quantity of production.

Earlier popular movements, called *shimin undo,* or "citizens' movements," had usually been directed toward big national and international issues and had taken on strong political coloration, but now new kinds of *jumin undo,* or "residents' movements," grew up over these local issues. These sought to put pressure on local governments but tried at the same time to remain nonpartisan in politics. At first the LDP, with its strong connections to agriculture and big business, was less responsive to these movements than were the progressive parties. As late as 1972 Tanaka, on becoming prime minister, issued a much-publicized book called *The Remodeling of the Japanese Archipelago,* which was merely a plan to spread industrialization more evenly throughout the islands and had the effect of sending land prices rocketing. The greater responsiveness of the progressive parties to these local issues, together with the usual concentration of the opposition vote in the large cities, led to progressive victories in the late sixties in municipal and prefectural elections in the majority of the great metropolitan areas. Among the first signs of this new pattern was the capture of the Tokyo assembly by the opposition parties in 1965 and the election as governor of Tokyo in 1967 of Minobe Ryokichi, the son of the Minobe of "organ theory" fame in the 1930s and himself, too, a professor at Tokyo University of Education. By 1973 progressive mayors had been elected in all six of Japan's largest cities. The progressive mayors and governors who had come to dominate the local governments in most metropolitan areas were usually elected by coalitions of two or more of the progressive parties, but they commonly had the support of the "residents' movements" as well.

The sudden salience of these local "public nuisance" problems gave local government an importance it had never had before. For example, Yokohama pioneered in 1964 in pollution control agreements between local government and industry. These issues, however, were in time taken up by the national LDP too. A comprehensive social security system had been adopted as early as 1959 but was not adequately funded until 1965. Starting in 1966 the national government began to go into deficit financing to pay for the increased costs of the social security system and also began to extend health insurance coverage, particularly for the aged, who by 1973 were being given completely free medical care. An Environmental Agency was formed in 1971 to work on pollution problems, and in the next few years the budget of the Health and Welfare Ministry was greatly expanded.

After long years of generally unrewarding court cases, a breakthrough in pollution control was made between 1971 and 1973, when a series of major court cases clearly established the principle that the pollutor must pay for the damage caused. Japan quickly formulated and enforced emission and other pollution controls as stringent as those anywhere in the world, and in 1973 it also became the only country with a completely functioning system whereby factories and even private motorists were assessed to provide compensation for those whose health was injured by pollution. The results were amazing: The skies of Tokyo and other cities visibly cleared year by year, and water pollution lessened. Because of its terribly crowded cities, the problem of pollution remained relatively serious, but, in any case, efforts and investments had been shifted in a major way from singleminded industrial growth to social services and environmental controls that would improve the quality of life.

During the 1970s Japan absorbed the oil shocks with amazing resilience and handled the problems of pollution with extraordinary skill. The country clearly remained very strong and well organized economically, and in many ways a 3 to 6 percent rate of growth was healthier and easier to accommodate than the earlier "miraculous" speed of 10 percent. But politically Japan appeared to be weaker than it was economically. The LDP majority became paper thin and the opposition parties remained so fragmented as to be unable to take its place. Leadership within the LDP also became less firm, and none of Sato's immediate successors as prime minister approached the lengthy tenures earlier prime ministers had enjoyed, averaging less than two years each. But these were merely superficial problems. Although some people feared that Japan would collapse into political immobility, basic political stability actually increased greatly. Below the surface there was a growing consensus on the part of most of the public on what had formerly been matters of violent dispute, and the once bitterly contending parties were forced by their electoral supporters to take more cooperative stands toward one another. Political changes seemed less predictable than before, but the political process of decision making continued to operate with undiminished efficiency.

One of the reasons Sato had resigned as prime minister in July 1972 was because his long anti-Peking stand had made him unacceptable to the Chinese for the establishment of diplomatic relations. Tanaka Kakuei, who succeeded him, had a very different background. Unlike his predecessors of elite educational and usually bureaucratic origin, he lacked any university education at all, a most unusual condition for a Japanese political leader. He was, however, a brashly self-confident and vigorous self-made man, who had amassed considerable wealth in the construction business. People called him the "computerized bulldozer." A man of the people, he was widely popular, especially in his home constituency in Niigata on the west coast of Japan.

Tanaka successfully negotiated the diplomatic recognition of China in September 1972, but his position was somewhat shaken by a weak LDP showing in the House of Councillors election of July 7, 1974, when it won only 62 of 130 seats under contest and its majority in the house was reduced from 26 to 7. Two of the leading LDP faction leaders deserted his cabinet soon after the election, accusing him of too-lavish use of money in pursuing political power, and some leading business institutions dropped direct financial support of the LDP. The main blow to Tanaka, however, was the publication by a leading magazine, *Bungei Shunju*, in its November issue of an exposé inspired by Watergate reporting in the United States and alleging unethical activities in his use of political influence to amass his fortune and in his use of his fortune to influence politics.

Tanaka felt forced to resign, and after a standoff between his two strongest would-be successors, Fukuda Takeo and Ohira Masayoshi, a third faction leader, Miki Takeo, was selected as a compromise candidate, becoming prime minister on December 9, 1974. Miki was the ideal person for the time, because he fitted the role of ''Mr. Clean'' in LDP politics, represented the most liberal wing of the party, and was virtually the last active politician surviving from prewar days. Under his leadership, a new Political Funds Control Law was passed in 1975 to make parties and politicians more accountable for their political spending and to reduce the type of money manipulation alleged against Tanaka. The situation, however, remained basically unsatisfactory. Miki achieved virtually none of his real objectives. The regulations on electioneering, in some cases inherited from the election reforms of 1925, remained unrealistically restrictive, and politicians actually used far greater sums of money than the laws permitted. These contributions were donated by business firms (which is legal in Japan), trade unions, and other groups, and they were spent in large part through the politicians' *koenkai,* or personal support organizations, which masqueraded as cultural rather than political organizations.

In local elections in April 1975 Minobe was reelected governor of Tokyo, and progressives came to hold the governorships of three of the four most populous prefectures, but on the whole the local elections were a victory for the LDP and their allied independent conservatives. A new political upheaval, however, was brewing. At hearings at a Senate subcommittee in Washington in February 1976, it was revealed that the American Lockheed Corporation, in connection with sales of military aircraft to Japan the previous year, had passed several million dollars to certain Japanese politicians through a dubious right-wing activist and supposed power broker named Kodama Yoshio. The allegation stirred up great indignation among the Japanese people, who are very sensitive to issues of political corruption and financial scandals. Tanaka and other LDP politicians, as well as the great trading firm of Marubeni, were implicated. In March Kodama was indicted, and Tanaka was briefly arrested in July and formally indicted the following month. All this political excitement delayed for the first time the passage of the annual budget beyond the usual date of the end of March. In June Kono Yohei, the son of a former LDP leader, deserted the party with five colleagues to found the New Liberal Club, which sought to create a young and fresher image than that of the older party leaders, and in August Fukuda and Ohira, joined by 70 percent of the LDP Dietmen, called for Miki's resignation.

The coup de grace for Miki was the lower house election held on December 5, 1976. In large part because of the desertion of the New Liberal Club, which elected seventeen members on a little over 4 percent of the vote, the LDP share of the vote fell 7 percentage points from 48.86 to 41.78, and its seats declined to less than a majority for the first time, though a slim majority was soon restored by the usual joining of the party by a group of independents. Ironically, Tanaka and most of the other implicated politicians were reelected by their loyal home followings. In the face of this election defeat, Miki resigned and on December 24 was followed as prime minister by Fukuda, who as a former finance ministry bureaucrat was cast in the same mold as the earlier LDP leaders.

In the House of Councillors election of July 10, 1977, the LDP majority in the house slipped even further from seven to four, and control of nine out of the main fifteen committees in the house passed to the opposition. This together with the 41.78 percent vote for the LDP in the lower house election of 1976 marked the low point to date of the party's parliamentary strength. A substantial reshuffling of power in the Diet was widely expected at the time of the next election. Although no one assumed a take-over by the badly divided opposition parties, a breakup of the LDP seemed possible, and a larger role for the centrist opposition parties—the Democratic Socialists and the Komeito—seemed likely.

Japan had undergone many vicissitudes since 1965, and a stormy future seemed predictable. The vastly expanded size and complexity of the economy were producing difficult new problems. Japan had become economically so large that it was being forced out from the safe haven of its own isolated waters into the open seas of world turmoil, and it was encountering rougher going than it was accustomed to. Neither Japanese nor foreigners were at all sure of its ability to master the transition. The surrounding world was decidedly menacing; relations with the United States seemed much less stable and friendly than in earlier years; the financial costs of dealing with pollution and providing greater social benefits were huge; and the domestic political situation seemed downright shaky. For all its extraordinary achievements since the war, Japan's future appeared to be by no means secure.

17

THE ECONOMIC GIANT

Despite Japan's many problems, one thing was clear as it entered the 1980s: The country was a resounding economic success. Surprise at its ability to restore its shattered economy during the early postwar years had given place to a half-condescending admiration of the Japanese economic "miracle" and this in turn to a realization that the country was indeed becoming a major economic force. As it continued to grow rapidly through the eighties, it increasingly came to be regarded as an economic superpower—a veritable economic giant—comparable in its field of strength to the United States and Soviet Union as military giants, or China and India as giants in population.

But what did it mean to be an economic superpower? To Japanese it was a gratifying concept that made them more self-confident and sometimes a little arrogant. It made the United States and Japan's other allies expect from it a much greater contribution to world peace; it made the poorer nations count on it for more aid; and it made the Japanese themselves nervous about all these expectations and puzzled as to what their role in the world should be. Western commentators, joined by some Japanese, pointed out that in the past there had never been an economic great power that had not also been a major military and political power. Japan's position as an economic giant that maintained a low political profile and eschewed major military might, they argued, was an anomaly. But the thought that Japan would inevitably become a military superpower made the other world powers uneasy and frankly frightened its neighbors. Japan seemed to be creating through economic strength the Greater East Asia Co-Prosperity Sphere that it had failed to achieve by arms during the war. Such ideas breathed new life into the old controversy in Japan over the Self-Defense Forces and the military relationship with the United States. The decade of the eighties, while establishing Japan firmly as an economic superpower, left it and the world still uncertain about its future. More questions seemed to be raised than were answered.

Japan had not become an economic giant overnight but had achieved this status only through long, steady growth decade after decade. The magnitude of its trade disturbed old and familiar economic patterns and caused new frictions and anxieties. Whereas Japan's foreign trade after the war had at first been overwhelmingly with the United States, it grew to embrace virtually the whole world. By the early seventies Japan was the first or second largest trading partner of every nation, communist or capitalist, in East and Southeast Asia, in some cases accounting for about 40 percent of a country's total foreign trade. In the noncommunist countries Japanese goods flooded the stores, Japanese neon signs dominated the skylines of the cities, Japanese corporate affiliates sprang up like mushrooms, Japanese tourists marched in well-ordered ranks through the tourist attractions, and Japanese businessmen wandered everywhere. South Koreans feared that Japanese money was spreading corruption in their country and that Japanese economic imperialism might take the place of the old colonial domination; Thai students stirred up boycotts against Japanese goods; and Indonesians fulminated against the exploitation of their forests and other natural resources by unprincipled Japanese businessmen. Japanese grants in aid, loans, and investments were becoming crucial to the countries of the area, but there was a general feeling that Japan provided these on less favorable terms than did other advanced countries and that they were focused exclusively on Japanese rather than local interests. Communication with the Japanese was difficult because of their inadequate command of English, the usual language of contact. As fellow Asians, their strong clannish nature was resented more than the clannishness of Americans or Europeans.

The Japanese were aware of their poor image in neighboring lands and the many frictions produced by their dominant economic role. They realized that, as a leading economic power, they must learn to think of their impact on the less developed countries and not exclusively of their own economic needs. They understood that they must

An earnest Japanese tourist group having the mysteries of Notre Dame in Paris explained to it.

treat these poorer countries with greater generosity and be more careful about local sensitivities. But it was easier to comprehend such matters intellectually than to change the attitudes and habits of the average Japanese businessman. The size of the problem was shockingly underlined for the Japanese as early as January 1974, when Tanaka made a goodwill tour of Southeast Asia and encountered anti-Japanese demonstrations in almost every country, including massive rioting in Indonesia.

Japan's remarkable growth brought even more severe strains in its relations with the industrialized countries, particularly the United States. The GNP of Japan rose on average 10 percent per year until 1973, and after that, though proceeding at a slower pace, climbed at a considerably more rapid rate than in the United States and the other industrialized countries. Up until 1973 Japan doubled its GNP every seven years. This meant that a small and resource-poor country like Japan had to double its foreign trade every five years. The result was a rapid increase in Japan's share of world trade, largely at the expense of the West. Its share had been only 2 percent in 1960 but had risen to 9 percent by 1973. The larger the Japanese economy grew, the more disruptive was its rate of growth for the other industrialized countries. The pressures created by Japan's soaring industrial rise could be seen most clearly in the changing balance in international trade and payments. In the early postwar years Japan had run serious deficits, but in 1965 it began at times to enjoy favorable balances, and by the 1980s Japanese surpluses were huge.

The growth of Japan's balance of trade was so constant and massive that it completely unbalanced the trade between it and the other industrialized countries, particularly the United States, bringing down a storm of criticism on its head for endangering the whole system of world trade. The tremendous increase in Japan's exports was at first ascribed to the nation's low wages, but as the economy surged ahead and wages rose, it became clear that this was not the reason. Pay scales mounted rapidly and almost without interruption, until finally in 1988 the drastic fall in the value of the dollar pushed them above American wages, in monetary terms if not in buying power.

A more plausible explanation was that Japan's faster rise in exports was the result in large part of tariff and quota barriers created to protect its once-weak industries from the American economy, which had been overwhelmingly powerful in the early postwar years. At that time, quotas and high tariffs virtually excluded many American manufactured goods and limited American exports to Japan largely to goods that the Japanese themselves could not provide in adequate quantity, such as raw materials (coal, lumber, scrap iron, and cotton), foodstuffs (soybeans, wheat, and feed grains), and some complex machinery and scientific goods that the Japanese could not yet manufacture in sufficient supply. The Japanese, on the other hand, exported technically advanced manufactured goods to the United States and the rest of the West. It was a pattern like that between a metropolitan country and its colonies, with the United States playing the role of colony as the supplier of raw materials and Japan the role of colonizer by providing more advanced manufactured goods.

There had been good reason for this situation at first, but as Japan recovered industrially, it became less justifiable. Japanese manufactured goods began to inundate the American market. Whole areas of American industry were drowned out by a flood of Japanese imports, helping to create what was called the "rust belt" in the industrial Northeast. Japanese could no longer expect free economic access to the markets of the rest of the world while denying others access to theirs. American and European discontent with the situation mounted steadily, and there were constant demands for the Japanese to "liberalize'' their trade practices. The industrialized countries kept prodding Japan, which responded slowly and reluctantly, commonly opening up a field to Western imports only after Japanese production had become strong enough to keep out most foreign goods.

Even the Japanese eventually realized that these conditions could not be allowed to continue. They gradually got rid of their tariff barriers and quotas, other than those on farm products, which many Western countries also maintain. Japanese tariff limitations, in fact, became among the lowest in the OECD community of industrialized nations. But Japanese trade surpluses continued to skyrocket. The countries of the West then shifted to blaming this largely on "unfair" Japanese practices that created a playing field for trade they claimed was not level. They attributed the chief cause for this situation to close cooperation in Japan between government and industry, which Westerners labeled "Japan, Inc." The Japanese government, it was claimed, maintained hidden barriers against imports, consisting of a complex system of red tape and arcane and unreasonable regulations on foreign trade, enforced by MITI and other branches of the government.

This charge against Japan was in part true, though the Japanese were also correct in arguing that many of these regulations were merely long-established, routine economic practices. A more accurate description of the situation would have been to say that Japanese were accustomed to dealing with old and trusted associates to the exclusion of other companies, Japanese or foreign, and that they laid great store on personal relationships, which outside companies usually lacked.

The Japanese also pointed out that the problem of insufficient industrial imports into Japan was to be blamed in part on Americans and other Westerners for not trying as hard as Japanese did to sell abroad. Westerners usually failed to learn the Japanese language, to master Japanese marketing practices, or to produce goods specifically designed for sale in Japan. As Japanese liked to say, they themselves would not have gotten very far in developing markets in the United States if they had not learned the English language, how Americans did business, and what American preferences were. Westerners simply had been too lazy and arrogant in expecting that there would automatically be a demand for their goods in Japan even though the Japanese were capable of producing at comparable prices goods of equal or superior quality, fitted to their own specific needs. Why should Japanese buy American refrigerators that were too large to fit into their tiny kitchens or American right-hand-drive cars for their left-hand roads?

Another American complaint was that Japanese dumped excess production abroad at prices lower than cost in order to secure a share in foreign markets. However, actual cases of alleged dumping, when examined, usually turned out to be hard to prove. Americans also criticized Japan for securing an unfair economic advantage by taking a "free ride" in defense at the American taxpayer's expense, but the Japanese responded that the American defense posture in the western Pacific was the product of American wishes and for American purposes, not Japanese, and that, in any case, Japan was contributing its share to defense through providing bases and 1 percent of its GNP for its defense budget.

Both sides had some valid arguments, but the Japanese, realizing their greater dependence on the United States, slowly gave way to many American demands, eliminating most of the red tape and detailed regulations to which the United States objected. But Japanese trade surpluses still continued to soar. In the second half of the eighties they grew to staggering sums, amounting to more than $100 billion annually, of which over $50 billion was with the United States alone. Japanese goods flooded one field after another—textiles as early as the late fifties, then cameras, motorcycles, steel, electric goods, and various types of machinery, followed by television sets, cars, and all sorts of electronic devices, and finally the products of high technology of all kinds. Japan had reached the front cutting edge of science and industry.

Already by 1980 four of the top ten automotive producers in the world were Japanese. In 1982 Dentsu became the world's largest advertising agency, and the next year four out of the top ten non-American companies in the world were Japanese. In 1988 the ten largest banks in the world and four of the top ten security houses were all Japanese. Japanese companies set up in the United States numerous ventures with their American counterparts in order to avoid tariffs and quotas, should these be placed on their products made in Japan. Factories owned and operated by Japanese began to dot the United States, Europe, East and Southeast Asia, and other areas throughout the world that were suitable for advanced manufacturing. Japanese also bought a great deal of real estate in the United States—hotels, office buildings, and choice resort areas, especially in Hawaii, to the dismay of the local population. The names of the great Japanese firms, such as Mitsui, Mitsubishi, Toyota, Nissan, Matsushita, Toshiba, Hitachi, and Fujitsu, became as familiar to Americans as Ford, Exxon, and IBM. It was a veritable economic invasion, and Americans responded with a mixture of enthusiasm, admiration, puzzlement, indignation, and fear.

The imbalance of Japan's trade, not just with the United States but with the whole world, was clearly no mere product of chance or certain unfair regulations. It was the outgrowth of a structural problem in the world's economy and as such was much more dangerous and difficult to correct. The fundamental problem was that Japan's industrial economy was simply becoming more efficient and dynamic than those of North America, Europe, or Australia.

The Japanese had several advantages, some of which have already been discussed. Virtually all of Japan's industry had relatively new and up-to-date facilities. Government and business were effectively meshed together in a system that permitted an abundance of stimulating free competition but also provided overall guidance toward desirable national objectives. Management and labor cooperated harmoniously together in a system that created loyalty to the company on the part of both groups and encouraged initiative and pride in achievement among workers as well as executives. Relatively few working days were lost to strikes, and the working week was only beginning to decline from five and a half to five days. Big business was financed largely by banking capital rather than stocks and therefore could expect stable leadership and set its eyes on long-range goals. As a result, Japanese businessmen did not need to be constantly mindful of quarterly bottom lines but could concentrate their attention on areas of long-term growth.

Another important factor was that educational standards were extraordinarily high, giving Japan perhaps the best educated work force in the world. Around 95 percent of young people completed the extremely rigorous twelve years of elementary and secondary schooling, and about 40 percent of these continued on for at least some higher education. As a consequence, Japanese were well prepared for complicated technical and scientific jobs, and factories could easily be modernized with sophisticated equipment. For example, the Japanese early became the leaders in the world in the use of robots. The efficiency of the whole economic system was enhanced by a surrounding society that was largely free of crime and drugs and emphasized the virtues of hard work and good order.

Another important point, as we have seen, was the high propensity of the Japanese to save. Even after they had achieved high levels of affluence, they continued to set aside for future needs more of their wealth than almost any other people in the world. The familiarity of the country with natural calamities, such as earthquakes and typhoons, and the relative weakness of the national social security system had conditioned them to take this precaution. The money saved by individuals, which was close to 20 percent of income, was channeled by the banks into productive ventures, making possible huge investments in the growth industries. In comparison, the rate of saving in the United States had sunk to little more than a tenth as much, slowing economic growth and making necessary heavy borrowing from abroad. All in all, Japan had a very efficient economic system.

In industrial productivity the Japanese had become virtually unsurpassed, and as a result world trade patterns were naturally altered. The magnitude of this change was increased by another closely related structural change taking place in the United States rather than Japan. This was America's tremendous budgetary debt and accompanying deficit in worldwide trade. Both soared in the eighties. The two problems of Japanese surpluses and American debt fed on each other. American indebtedness raised interest rates in the United States, which attracted Japanese surpluses. These loans from Japan then increased Japanese profits and also made it possible for the United States to go further into debt in a decade of spendthrift living on credit. Both nations had developed economic addictions that grew in the eighties to enormous proportions and were not easy to cure. Japan became by far the largest creditor nation in the world, with net foreign assets of some $200 billion, and the United States the largest debtor nation. Interest payments for their respective credits and debts grew rapidly each year, making the problem progressively harder to turn around.

The situation threatened the whole system of relatively free trade that had brought unprecedented prosperity to much of the world since the war. American resentment against Japan could conceivably lead to such harsh restrictionist reprisals that Japanese prosperity would collapse, and the United States, denied cheaper Japanese goods and the funds needed to finance its debts, would then in turn be greatly impoverished. The inevitable resulting depression in Japan and the United

States would almost certainly cause a worldwide depression and the political and military disturbances that normally accompany such economic disasters. Even without so dramatic a scenario, the great trade imbalances centering around the United States and Japan, the world's two largest industrial powers, might prove so upsetting that the whole trading system of the industrialized OECD nations might falter. Though by no means as catastrophic as a nuclear holocaust, such an economic collapse seemed a much more likely possibility.

The general outlines of the problem were clear to economists and other specialists, but they were less apparent to the average American or Japanese, whose vote was the ultimate determiner of national policies. Japan's rapid economic rise and penetration of the American market spread deep resentments in the United States and sometimes almost a sense of panic. The steel worker in Pittsburgh or auto worker in Detroit was often incensed at what he felt was the stealing of his job by Japan. There were also lingering traces of old wartime attitudes toward Japan and considerable evidence of the cultural and racial prejudices that had been prevalent only four or five decades earlier. To be deprived of employment by Japanese somehow seemed worse than if the competitors were more familiar Europeans, and Japanese cars and other goods were considered a menace to the United States in a way similar European products were not. The Japanese purchase of American real estate seemed particularly alarming, though similar purchases by Europeans had attracted little attention. It should be noted, however, that part of the reason for this was that Japanese purchases had come more suddenly and had been geographically more concentrated in a few highly visible areas.

Similar economic fears and cultural and racial prejudices were even stronger among Europeans than Americans. From the beginning Europeans had maintained sharp restrictions on imports from Japan and had shown much less interest in the country, which to them seemed indeed the "Far East," lying, as it did, out beyond the Middle East, India, Southeast Asia, and China on the one side and the American continents and two huge oceans on the other. Now that the economic strength of Japan had become enormous, Europeans were determined not to let a nascent American restrictionism shunt Japanese goods from the United States to their shores.

On the whole, American attitudes toward Japan were not as hostile as one might have expected. Most Americans eagerly bought what they considered to be superior, more reliable Japanese goods. The individual states contended eagerly for Japanese investments. Popular interest in Japan and its culture, which had been rising rapidly during the seventies, became a veritable boom in the eighties. In government circles, however, there was considerable anger over the imbalance in trade and the meagerness of Japan's contribution to defense. In some parts of the country there were also pockets of deep resentment against the flood of Japanese imports. The Japanese public was appalled in the late eighties at what it felt was a wave of "Japan bashing" and was horrified by a much-repeated television scene of a group of angry Congressmen smashing a Japanese television set with sledgehammers on the steps of the Capitol. The adoption in August 1988 of an "omnibus trade bill" that had strong restrictionist features made the Japanese government and public extremely apprehensive.

The trade problems between Japan and the United States looked very much different from the two sides. Despite their current prosperity, the Japanese felt a sense of economic vulnerability that was difficult for others to comprehend. They saw themselves as a huge mass of people forced to live entirely by their own hard work and skills on a few small islands devoid of major natural resources. Their population passed the 120 million mark in 1986 and was expected to creep up to a little more than 130 million before stabilizing at a somewhat lower level. Meanwhile the so-called NICs, or "newly industrializing countries," were taking over the industries Japan itself had once utilized to make its way into the American market. Particularly menacing were the "four little tigers" of South Korea, Taiwan, Hong Kong, and Singapore, which were following close in Japan's footsteps. Behind these four were the vast masses of China, India, Southeast Asia, and Latin America, which were beginning to industrialize on a significant scale. These newly industrialized countries would leave little room in the traditional manufacturing fields for Japan, which increasingly would have to compete with the advanced countries of the West for the rather narrow markets in the areas of high technology and the so-called knowledge industries. Since Japan was in per capita terms far poorer in natural resources than most of the countries of the West, to say nothing of the huge and richly endowed United States, Canada, and Australia, it felt itself confined to a very narrow ecological niche. Japanese believed they deserved special consideration and an ample cushion against economic disaster.

Such attitudes were strengthened by a modern history of having had to scramble hard to survive economically after the Meiji Restoration and again after World War II. The oil shocks of 1973 and 1979 and the soybean embargo of 1973 were recent reminders of Japan's vulnerability. It became popular to speak of the "hollowing out" of Japanese industry, meaning the loss of basic industrial production to the newly industrializing countries and the limitation of the advanced industries by competition with the other technological leaders, leaving Japan with a huge economic framework but very little industrial body.

Americans, on the other hand, felt that they had perhaps been too indulgent to Japan in the early postwar years and that it was high time for a rich and economically powerful country like Japan to carry more of the burdens of world peace. The Vietnam war had shaken Americans and made them realize that the euphoric days were past when the United States had stood alone among the major nations of the world, unscathed by the disaster of World War II. As the other countries had restored their economies, the United States had inevitably declined in relative terms from half of the world's GNP to less than a quarter, and it now found itself badly overextended in its worldwide commitments. It naturally felt that more of the load should be shouldered by others, particularly the Japanese, who appeared to be doing the least in terms of their wealth and strength, building instead huge trade surpluses by unclear but probably "unfair" trade practices. During the seventies and eighties, the United States became much more insistent that Japan play a larger military role and contribute more to the world's economy by reducing its trade surpluses and increasing greatly its aid to the less developed lands.

The Japanese and American governments were both fully aware of the dangers of the situation if irritation on either side were allowed to get out of hand and seriously disrupt the huge and rapidly growing economic relationship between them. Both sides made efforts to solve the problem, but without much success. Japan did accede to Western demands for liberalizing its trade policies but only at such a slow pace that frictions outran the increase of exports to Japan. The Japanese even launched official import buying drives, but the purchasing inspired by these efforts was more for high-quality European luxuries, such as perfumes and French wines, than basic industrial products from America, and in any case, the sums involved were inconsequential in terms of the trade balance. Commissions and groups of "wise men" repeatedly studied the problem, and prominent politicians and officials conferred frequently with each other but produced little but sage words. Specific trade negotiations were constantly held but all too often ended up in an angry exchange of words rather than an increased flow of goods. Particularly long and heated negotiations over opening the Japanese market further to American oranges and beef finally forced the Japanese in June 1988 to make concessions, but the net effect on the balance of trade was slight, and Australians rather than Americans appeared to be the chief beneficiaries of the new provisions regarding beef.

A more important way to limit Japanese trade surpluses turned out to be self-restrictions on exports carried out by the Japanese government in order to lessen American government pressures and keep American public attitudes below the boiling point. The Japanese government justified such restrictions to its people by using the happy euphemism of "orderly marketing." "Voluntary restrictions" of this type were first applied at American insistence as early as 1958 in textiles. The results were far from pleasing to Japan or helpful to the United States, since American textile imports simply shifted from Japan to other East Asian countries, and the Japanese then had to negotiate from a lower relative base when a multilateral agreement was later worked out. Other fields, such as steel and electronic goods, began to demand similar Japanese self-restrictions, and the Japanese felt forced to comply from time to time when pressures seemed to be reaching the danger point.

Despite various concessions, Japanese surpluses continued to grow and American resentments worsened. A particularly serious situation arose in 1969, when Nixon tried to implement his promises to certain North Carolina textile manufacturers, made in the 1968 presidential campaign, that he would get them relief from Japanese imports. He understood that Sato agreed to do this for him, and it was widely though erroneously believed that this agreement was a *quid pro quo* for America's returning of Okinawa to Japan. But there had been a linguistic misunderstanding between Nixon and Sato. The prime minister lacked the political power to force an unpopular textile agreement down the throats of a recalcitrant Diet and business world. Only after prolonged and acrimonious further negotiations was Japan finally forced in October 1971 to accept the American demands. In the meantime, Nixon had suddenly announced in August of that year a temporary 10 percent surcharge on imports and the suspension of the dollar's convertibility into gold. Both steps were aimed at bolstering the overall American trade position, but they were targeted specifically against Japan. Coming just after America's surprise rapprochement with China, they became known as the second Nixon shock.

It was a pity that so much effort was devoted to relatively minor fields of trade, such as oranges and beef, or to dying industries, like textiles, which were sure to be a shrinking element of the economy of both countries. Efforts to equalize trade in the more dynamic parts of the economy would have had more immediate and lasting effect. But the technique of "voluntary controls" was applied quite effectively in some fields, notably cars for export to the United States and other Western countries and videotape recorders for Europe. Japan, for example, agreed to a limit for exports to the United States of 1.68 million cars and trucks for 1982. A reasonable annual increase was usually permitted, and in 1985, when it was agreed that Japan would set its own self-restraints without interference from the United States, the figure was put at 2.3 million units. One result of this system, however, was that the Japanese concentrated on exporting the more expensive types of cars, with the result that the total value of Japanese automotive exports increased considerably.

Another way of attempting to bring trade into better balance was by readjusting the monetary system. In December 1971 the United States abandoned the old Bretton Woods arrangement of fixed exchange rates, which had been adopted during World War II, and shifted to a system of flexible exchange rates in which undervalued currencies would rise and overvalued ones could fall to their real value. This, it was hoped, would help the United States expand its trade, because the dollar had become greatly overvalued. In the first revaluation of the yen since it was pegged at 360 to the dollar in 1949, the dollar was allowed to fall in 1971 by 16.88 percent to about 300 yen and then to fall again, largely in February 1973, to around 230. From that point through 1985 it remained relatively stable, but starting in January 1986 it began another downward slide, reaching 121 in November 1988 before coming back to around 142 in early June 1989.

The dollar's spectacular loss of about two-thirds of its value between 1971 and 1989 seemed likely to increase American exports a great deal in the long run, but it was slow to show much effect. Many of the world's currencies remained tied to the dollar or moved generally in unison with it, and the Japanese economy was so efficient that it was able to accommodate these great changes in monetary value without much difficulty. The cost of life in Japan, however, did show some spectacular consequences. Prices in Japan became extremely high in comparison with those in other countries, and the Japanese became the richest people in the world in monetary terms, taking the place of the affluent American tourists and buying real estate and luxuries at exorbitant prices all over the world.

Americans were slow at first in accepting the idea that there were things they could learn from the Japanese economy. As late as 1979, when Ezra Vogel's provocatively titled book, *Japan as Number One: Lessons for America,* was published, it was looked on more as a curiosity than as a serious proposal for improving American business strategy. But in the course of the eighties Americans began to see the point. Large numbers of younger American businessmen and -women began to study the Japanese language, and wide attention was paid to Japanese business organization and styles of operation, for use not just in selling in Japan but for adoption by American business at home. Thousands of American workers in Japanese plants in the United States were subjected to Japanese factory organization, and many were sent for periods to Japan itself by their Japanese employers in order to study and work in a Japanese setting. Though American workers did not take to such things as company songs, they did appreciate the egalitarian atmosphere of a Japanese factory and responded well to Japan's teamwork and quality control. Many American companies found it possible to do business in Japan, sometimes with spectacular success as in the case of McDonald's and Kentucky Fried Chicken. American business penetration of Japan is still in its early phases and has been largely in the field of the services rather than in the primary industries, so it is too early to judge what overall effect it will have, but there was no doubt by the late eighties that large changes were under way. The combination of dollar devaluation and improved American business techniques had by 1988 made an appreciable dent in remedying the trade gap between America and Japan.

As Japanese and American economic relations expanded explosively during the eighties, new causes for friction between the two countries naturally increased, joining all the old resentments and long-simmering controversies between the two countries over foreign policy, defense, and a myriad other matters. So-called crises sprang up on every side, and gloomy pundits kept announcing that Japanese–American relations had never been worse since the war. But most Americans accepted with maturity the sudden exchange of roles between creditor and debtor and teacher and learner. They wisely ignored even the somewhat gleeful claims of some shallow Japanese intellectuals that the Pax Americana was being replaced by a Pax Japonica—a concept that drew far more attention in Japan than in the United States. They viewed the new relationship with Japan in a matter-of-fact way, developing relatively little irritation and a greatly increased interest in Japan. To use a trivial illustration for a significant point, *sushi* became practically a national dish along with apple pie and pizza, and an American variation utilizing avocadoes and called a "California roll" became popular in Japan as well as the United States. Japanese–American relations were clearly becoming closer and warmer.

Despite all the predictions of crises, no serious one materialized during the eighties. The economic and other relations between Japan and the United States became much more closely intertwined. Most major firms developed joint production companies or other forms of cooperation with corporations that were their counterparts in the other country. The two economies increasingly drifted toward becoming a single unified one. Instead of trade wars, a much more likely outgrowth of the eighties appeared to be a Japanese–American economic community, probably under the more attractive name of Pacific or Pacific Rim Community. It might include countries like Australia and Canada and would have room to add late industrializers, such as South Korea, Taiwan, and Mexico. But whether or not economic relations would ever grow that far, the eighties clearly laid a foundation for a much broader and more significant participation by Japan in the world economy than it had ever had before and for a very close economic relationship with the United States and some of the other industrialized nations facing on the Pacific.

In earlier periods in Japanese history, the primary divisions were defined by major political events, institutions, and leaders. By the 1980s, however, it was clear that this was no longer the case. Economic developments, especially in world trade, had become the central factors shaping the country's course. Japan had entered a new age. The struggle for political leadership continued between politicians, parties, and rival institutions; controversies over political and social issues remained remarkably constant; and individual incidents in domestic or foreign affairs still stirred the public. But these had become a sort of familiar background music, little changed from earlier years and not controlling the flow of history. The leading role had passed to Japan's economic development and its relations with foreign countries, especially its main trading partners.

Political trends remained very stable throughout the eighties. This was the result of three primary factors: The nation was prospering as never before; as a consequence, political tensions declined markedly; and voters gravitated toward the center, increasingly content with the situation as it existed. In typical Japanese fashion, this produced in the parties a greater tendency to compromise rather than to magnify their differences and to contend primarily for the support of the central floating vote.

By this time, the LDP no longer held the chairmanships of all of the committees in either house of the Diet, and its majority was so narrow that it required the cooperation of one or more of the centrist parties—the New Liberal Club, the Social Democrats, or the Komeito—to operate the Diet successfully. Actually, the LDP usually had the support of all three in passing government bills and often that of the Socialists and even Communists as well. This situation made clear that a major change in Japanese politics had taken place. There was a growing popular consensus and a marked relaxation in political tensions. The opposition parties found less and less to object to. Meanwhile, the conservatives, realizing that they must attract more urban voters to make up for their shrinking rural base, had also moved toward the center. The phenomenal economic success of the country made the LDP less insistent on growth at any price and more willing to emphasize social benefits, the control of pollution, and the improvement of the quality of life. Ideological differences on both sides declined in significance and often became meaningless to the average voter.

Japan was moving away both from the political polarization characteristic of many multiparty systems and also from the sort of one-party dictatorship found in others. The strength of the LDP had always been its conglomerate nature as a group of rival factions able to achieve consensus on a variety of differing issues and to absorb new groups into its already diverse makeup. Now that it had only a thin majority in the Diet, it was prepared to include various centrist groups in its decision-making process, and as political animosities waned, it found it increasingly possible to iron out some differences even with old enemies like the Socialists through informal, behind-the-scenes negotiations, leaving only the most divisive issues for open conflict in the committees and on the floor of the Diet. The old Japanese skill at compromise through quiet negotiations was emerging once again, though in modern, parliamentary form, taking the place of politics by confrontation, which had characterized the early postwar years. The LDP seemed destined to continue its amoebalike dominance of a ruling central coalition by absorbing or cooperating with other groups.

In a prosperous and satisfied Japan, politics became more a clash between ambitious political leaders and their factions than a contest between issues and ideologies. Right-wing demands for the revision of the constitution became further muted, and almost everyone came to accept the Self-Defense Forces and the defense relationship with the United States as these existed, though not if they were to be significantly expanded. The centrist parties sought to become the core of a new coalition but never with success, usually being co-opted instead as semimembers of the LDP coalition. Some small groups tried to increase their influence by breaking away toward the center, but all failed. Among the conservatives, the New Liberal Club survived precariously for seven and a half years before rejoining the LDP in December 1983. Among the progressives the veteran Socialist Eda Saburo established a centrist splinter party in March 1977, but it collapsed with his death two months later.

Even the Communists made it clear that they supported a multiparty parliamentary system, and in 1976 they abandoned the use of the phrase "the dictatorship of the proletariat," since few Japanese felt that they were "proletarians" and almost all hated the word "dictatorship." The Socialists had an extremely leftist ideological wing called the Society for the Study of Socialism, but its influence declined, and more moderate elements cautiously sought means to form an alliance with the centrist parties, without losing many of their leftist supporters to the Communists. The clearest sign of Socialist moderation, however, was the loss of doctrinaire political leaders and the choice of more moderate leaders to be the party chairpersons. Minobe Ryokichi was defeated for the governorship of Tokyo in 1977 after twelve years

of incumbency, and the same year the long-term moderate and pragmatic mayor of Yokohama, Asukata Ichio, was selected as the party's
chairperson, retaining the position for six years. An even more surprising choice to this post was that of Doi Takako in September 1986.
She was the first woman ever to be head of a major party, and she
proved to be a popular and moderate leader.

Mention should be made of one significant general influence of
Japan's prosperity and changing trade patterns on its politics as a
whole. Among the traditional triumvirate of power, the politicians
gained in strength, and the bureaucrats and big business lost. As Japan
grew enormously in economic power, affluence robbed the earlier
policy of growth at any price of some of its appeal. As a result businessmen no longer were seen as the country's unchallenged heroes but
came to be viewed with some disfavor as creators of crowding, pollution, and a lowering of the quality of life. At the same time, the
bureaucracy, in relinquishing some of its controls over business and
foreign trade, lost part of its influence over big business and the parties. Meanwhile, the politicians were in the best position to respond to
popular demands for an improved quality of life. The bureaucrats
followed suit, and even big business became responsive, but the parties were best able to attend to people's desires. The old model of a
triumvirate with the parties in the weakest position became progressively less valid and was replaced by a new configuration in which the
parties took the lead in supporting "residents' movements" and the
interests of the floating voters.

The lower house election of December 5, 1976, in which the LDP won
only 41.78 percent of the popular vote, proved to be the low point in
the party's fortunes. Fukuda, who succeeded Miki as prime minister
on December 24, was a stronger leader, backed as he was by a larger
faction and having a solid background as a former finance ministry
official. Some of the long-range political factors also were beginning
to take hold at about this time, and the decline of the LDP began to
bottom out. One of the many signs of this was the election in 1978 of
a conservative independent as the governor of Kyoto after twenty-
eight years of progressive rule.

Ohira Masayoshi accepts election as the prime minister on December 7, 1978. At the extreme right of the top row is Fukuda Takeo, and Nakasone Yasuhiro is the fourth from the right in the next row.

Fukuda, however, did not get to enjoy for long this shift in the tide. The LDP had adopted a new system for choosing a party president, according to which, as a means of fostering more grassroots support, all dues-paying members and contributors to the party voted as prefectural blocs for the party presidency. If no one emerged from this process with a majority, the Diet members of the party held a second vote between the top two recipients of votes. To everyone's surprise, Fukuda's old rival, Ohira, won a clear majority in the popular primary held on November 26, 1978, and accordingly was elected prime minister by the Diet on December 7. Ohira, like Fukuda, had a sizable faction behind him—Ikeda's old faction—and he also came from a finance ministry background. He happened to be a "No Church" Christian in the tradition of Uchimura Kanzo and a man of strong principles and broad international vision. He was also quite popular with the voters, who liked his low posture style and his apparently sleepy and phlegmatic mannerisms. His more centrist stance than that of Fukuda also put him in a good position to be a strong national leader, because the voters were definitely drifting toward the center. Ohira was an exceptionally skilled politician, and he might have become one of Japan's strongest postwar leaders, like Yoshida or Ikeda, had he not died early of a heart attack.

While in office Ohira faced determined opposition in the Diet by Fukuda and some of the other faction leaders. In fact, he maintained his position at first only because of the firm support of Tanaka, who, though he had officially resigned from the party because of the Lockheed scandal of 1976 and his own criminal indictment, was actually still the de facto leader of the largest Diet faction and acted as a sort of kingmaker for the next several years.

Ohira made a serious blunder when he insisted that new elections be held on October 7, 1979, against the advice of several of the faction leaders. He compounded this blunder by mentioning before the election that taxes would obviously have to be raised. In the election the popular vote of the LDP actually rose from its 1976 low of 41.78 percent to 44.6 percent, but Ohira was severely criticized because the party had been expected to do even better. A poor division of the votes also reduced by one the number of LDP seats. LDP rule was in no way threatened, since the other parties came out of the election more evenly divided than ever before, with 107 seats out of 511 for the Socialists, 57 for the Komeito, 39 for the Communists, 35 for the Democratic Socialists, and a mere 4 for the New Liberal Club. Nevertheless, a vote of nonconfidence in Ohira was passed on May 16, 1980, with the members of the Fukuda and Miki faction significantly absent from the house. This was the first time since the early postwar years that this sort of crisis had occurred. Ohira was forced to dissolve the lower house and called elections for June 22, concurrently with regularly scheduled elections for half of the upper house. The strain of the crisis proved too much for him, and he died suddenly on June 12.

In the subsequent election, sympathy for Ohira and improved apportionment of the votes combined with a large turnout because of good weather and the double election to give the LDP what is considered in Japan a landslide victory. The popular vote of the LDP rose to 47.9 percent, the highest it had been since 1967, and the party won 284 of the 511 lower house seats. In the upper house its seats rose from 124 to 135 out of a total of 252. In order to avoid a devisive fight again between strong faction leaders, the LDP decided on a relatively weak and colorless compromise candidate for prime minister. This was Suzuki Zenko, Ohira's successor as faction leader and known primarily as a fisheries expert. He was neither the graduate of a prestigious university nor a product of a powerful ministry, but he had been a lifelong politician, first elected to the Diet in 1947. Chosen prime minister on July 17, 1980, he provided two years of lackluster leadership, which well suited the Japanese system of decisions by consensus.

When Suzuki resigned as party president on October 12, 1982, a very different sort of man representing a new generation took his place. This was Nakasone Yasuhiro, the youngest of the older faction leaders and a man of great ambition and self-confidence. Big and handsome, he had always supported the direct popular election of the prime minister as favoring him with his apparent charismatic appeal. His actual winning of the post, however, was probably more the result of Tanaka's support than his own attractiveness to the public. He also differed from his predecessors in being young enough to have served as a naval officer in World War II, and as a result he had a greater inclination than they to support a stronger military establishment. His imposing appearance and outgoing personality made him more impressive to Westerners, and a great deal was made of the supposedly close "Ron-Yasu" relationship he established with Reagan. But this was largely a matter of posing, and when it came down to actual achievements, the Japanese consensus system left him little more room to maneuver than his predecessors had enjoyed.

Following Suzuki's resignation, Nakasone won the primary election of November 24, 1982. This entitled him to be chosen as party president, and two days later he was elected prime minister. He held the position for the next five years, more than twice the length of any incumbent since Sato. A general election was held, however, on December 18, 1983, at which the LDP under Nakasone did not do well. It dropped only slightly in popular votes from 47.9 percent to 45.8 percent, but it lost heavily in the number of seats from 286 to 250, while the Komeito jumped from 33 to 58, the Socialists from 101 to 112, and the Democratic Socialists from 30 to 38. Once again the LDP was forced to depend on the adherence of nine conservative independents to give it a majority. The lowest electoral turnout in history (67.94 percent) and a resulting maldistribution of the vote were probably the primary causes for what the LDP regarded as a disaster, but regardless of reasons, the result weakened Nakasone's position within the party until the next election.

At about the same time another important change in the leadership of the LDP took place. On October 12, 1983, Tanaka was sentenced to four years in prison and fined for his part in the Lockheed scandal. His influence as kingmaker began to crumble. He naturally appealed the case, but a scramble for his position as the leader of the largest faction became apparent. By April 1983 Nikaido Susumu, one of Tanaka's old stalwart lieutenants, had established himself securely enough to be made party vice president, but it was decided that Nakasone would continue another two-year term as party president and prime minister. Another of Tanaka's chief henchmen, Takeshita Noboru, also started a breakaway group in early February 1985. Tanaka, who already was in poor health, then suffered a serious stroke on February 27, which for all practical purposes removed him from the political scene.

During these same years two potentially important changes in the political system were made. On August 18, 1982, the Diet decided to have the 100 upper house members who were elected individually by the nation at large chosen instead from party slates, thus eliminating the candidates of splinter groups and the celebrities known as *tarento* ("talent"), who were able to win votes because of their personal popularity. This reform got rid of persons who were more famous or notorious than politically knowledgeable and reflected more fairly the strength of the various parties. The other change was that the Supreme Court on July 17, 1985, ruled that the lower house did not fairly mirror the result of the vote because of the extreme discrepancy between the least and most populous electoral districts. The elimination of seven rural seats and addition of eight urban ones improved the situation a little, while increasing the whole house only by one from 511 to 512 seats. Before this reform the worst discrepancy was about five or six to one, and after the reform it was about three to one. Clearly a much more sweeping change was necessary to create a truly "one man, one vote" situation, but there was curiously little demand for this, and it did not become a prime issue.

A veritable earthquake shook the Japanese political world when Nakasone on July 6, 1986, held an election for the lower house, again in conjunction with an election of half of the upper house. The results were a smashing triumph for the LDP. It won a popular vote of 49.4 percent, the highest since the election of 1963, and an overpowering 300 seats out of 512. Among the opposition parties the Socialists fell to 85 seats, the Komeito to 56, and both the Democratic Socialists and Communists to 26. The largest opposition vote was for the Socialists but was a mere 17.2 percent. The New Liberal Club did so poorly at 8 seats that it rejoined the LDP on August 15. The shock of the election was the reason why the Socialists decided to select a woman leader, Doi Takako, to become their secretary general on September 6, and after twenty years of strong leadership, Takeiri Yoshikazu of the Komeito resigned in November as party chairman.

Nakasone naturally gained great prestige from the election and, lacking an outstanding rival, was reelected party president. Since the party rules had been altered to limit party presidents to two two-year terms, this exception was made with the caveat that it should be only for one year, until October 30, 1987. With a clear date agreed to, the four chief contenders for the succession began serious infighting. Nikaido and Takeshita were the two candidates for the leadership of the former Tanaka faction, but Takeshita finally won out in July 1987. Abe Shintaro had become Fukuda's successor, and Miyazawa Kiichi emerged as leader of the former Ohira and Suzuki faction. But none of these four had a chance to win the prime ministership except through a still-unformed coalition, and therefore Nakasone continued in a strong position until the end of his term.

There seemed little to choose between Nakasone's would-be successors. Only Miyazawa stood out as being something of an intellectual with a broad international point of view. He was, in fact, the first prominent politician since the early postwar years to have a truly usable command of any foreign language, which in Japan normally means English. However, his support in the Diet was probably the weakest. Since there was a deadlock among the leading candidates, they agreed to leave the choice to Nakasone. Shortly before the expiration of his term, he chose Takeshita, who accordingly was elected party president and then prime minister on November 6, 1987.

Takeshita was an astute politician, adept at handling domestic politics, but his knowledge of foreign affairs was considered to be especially weak. There was a change of faces, but policies, both foreign and domestic, continued to flow smoothly in the directions already well established. The LDP's long decline had bottomed out in 1976, and the party appeared stronger than at any time for more than a decade. If it should again slip in the polls, the centrist parties still appeared prepared to help it out in an informal or formal coalition. No opposition party had won more than a fifth of the popular vote for almost a decade. Political issues that once were violent disputes had lost most of their venom, and typical Japanese compromise and consensus had increasingly become the rule. The LDP provided few leaders who caught the popular attention or served as dynamic leaders in the Diet, but an endless line of less colorful, consensus-minded lead-

President George Bush calling in Tokyo on Akihito, the emperor of the Heisei Period, the day following the funeral of Hirohito, the Showa Emperor, on February 24, 1989.

ers stood patiently in line waiting their chance at the prime ministership. Nakasone showed signs of hoping to recapture the position, but this seemed improbable. Younger generations of politicians might someday bring a more dynamic sort of leadership, but that seemed a long way off. Short of some international catastrophe, Japan appeared to be politically more stable than any other major country in the world—in fact, more stable then it had ever been at any time since the days of Tokugawa rule.

Although shifts in prime ministers brought few changes, a new emperor, some thought, might bring a more significant shift in direction. Emperor Hirohito died on January 7, 1989, in the sixty-fourth year of his Showa year period after the longest reign in all Japanese history. His son Akihito took his place at once under his new year period of Heisei, which might best be rendered as "Peace and Achievement." Many non-Japanese wondered if this change would not be used to revise the American-made constitution and swing Japan back toward old traditions and militarism. This, however, seemed entirely improbable. Almost all Japanese were opposed to anything of the sort, and postwar Japanese institutions had hardened into a strongly progressive, pacifistic mold. Akihito himself was a forward-looking man of 55, imbued with the democratic, peaceful ideals of postwar times and devoted to an international point of view. He and his gracious commoner empress, Michiko, were well-suited to bringing the imperial family into closer contact with the Japanese people and establishing warmer ties with foreign leaders, both roles they were eager to perform. George Bush, the new American president, underscored the strong American relationship with Japan by attending Hirohito's funeral in Tokyo on February 24, 1989.

Japanese society, tied directly as it was to the economy, was greatly affected in the eighties by the country's economic surge. Politics may have drifted with prosperity toward lessened tensions and increased stability, but society was vigorously stirred into greater diversity and liveliness. All sorts of new possibilities were opening up, which people seized upon with zest. The Japanese were also beleaguered by new problems, which baffled them but did not smother their vibrant energy. By the 1980s they seemed a different breed from the impoverished, anxiety-ridden people of a few decades earlier. For all their homogeneity, they were swept by a great many new life styles.

Most Japanese owned cars and were less bothered by their cost than by the difficulty in reaching their destinations on Japan's hopelessly overcrowded roads. They were surfeited by a plethora of wondrous electric and electronic devices, some of which were still unknown in other advanced countries. A *wapuro,* short for *wādo-purosesā,* or "word processor," was as familiar to many as a pen and pencil had been to their parents. They were living in a new world. The cities throbbed with life and cultural creativeness. People were fascinated by new styles in clothing, architecture, and objects of daily use. Probably no other people in the world spent as much of their income on fashionable apparel, decorations, and ceremonies. A Japanese insurance firm made the rest of the world gasp when it paid $44.6 million for a van Gogh painting to help decorate its corporate headquarters. Japanese travelers roamed widely abroad for business or pleasure, or simply to see what the outside world was like. In 1988 over a half million Japanese were stationed overseas, primarily for business purposes and mostly in the West, a third of the total in the United States alone; Japanese tourists had become the most numerous and richest world travelers; and nine-tenths of honeymooners made frenetic trips abroad to Hawaii, the American West Coast, or, for the less affluent, nearby Pacific Islands or Asian countries. Much did remain unaltered in Japan, but for most people life styles had changed immensely.

One simple but revealing measure of Japanese life was to be found in the statistics on longevity. Already in 1973 Japan had achieved the lowest rate of infant mortality in the world, and by 1985 it had the highest longevity for both men and women, 74.54 years for men and 80.18 for women. As with many other social phenomena, this situation had its adverse side. The population was aging rapidly. This "graying of Japan" meant a declining percentage of workers to support the aged and a larger percentage of people requiring expensive medical care and special facilities. The problem was common to all the advanced nations but was particularly marked for the Japanese, who traditionally had cared for the aged within the household or in an attached or nearby apartment. Urban crowding, however, made this solution no longer possible, and the nation faced the problem of creating a whole new system of special housing and medical care for the old.

The problem of crowding, of course, was one that affected all Japanese. Those who happened to own land in urban areas acquired great wealth, but this was not the case for the vast majority who found it virtually impossible to purchase a house or condominium and who found rentals very expensive. They were forced to live in very cramped quarters, so small that they were limited in the number and size of the excellent and relatively cheap household goods they would otherwise have bought. To find even such modest living space, millions of Japanese were forced to commute long distances, often up to two hours each way. Because of a desperate lack of space on the roads, the city of Tokyo passed a law that no one could own a car for which he did not have off-street parking facilities. The result was that many Tokyo homes came to resemble a garage with living quarters tucked behind or on top.

Despite the new wealth of landowners, most of which was soon absorbed in inheritance taxes in any case, Japan remained on the whole an economically egalitarian society with relatively small discrepancies in income. More than 90 percent of the people considered themselves middle class, and most led very similar lives. They lived

A typical Japanese family (parents and two children) at the dinner table in their crowded kitchen.

closely packed together, largely in huge metropolitan areas or at least large cities. Greater Tokyo covered the whole southern half of the Kanto Plain and then trailed westward past Yokohama along the Pacific coast, turning into a great line city that stretched with only occasional small breaks of mountains or farmland through the great urban area of Nagoya and on to the Kansai, the vast metropolitan area embracing the major cities of Osaka, Kobe, and Kyoto. From there the heavily urbanized area followed the northern shore of the Inland Sea to the metropolitan region surrounding the straits at its western end and then continued on down the north coast of Kyushu to the city of Fukuoka.

Japan's dense urban population accustomed most Japanese to being in crowds. To an average Japanese the almost deserted sidewalks and widely spaced houses of the suburbs or small towns of America seemed almost like a depopulated countryside. Used to living close together, they were forced to crowd even more closely when commuting to work, and even in their free time they seemed to prefer to be in crowds. Amusement centers in cities teemed with people drawn by a great variety of recreations, countless specialty restaurants, and, in particular, hundreds of bars, piled one on top of another in high-rise buildings and each with its loyal but exclusive clientele and special attractions, such as *karaoke* singing, in which the patrons took turns at singing individually to electronic music. Sightseeing was pursued

Youth culture, Japanese style.

avidly by large herds of children on school outings, members of village organizations, and women's groups, which at the proper season
seemed to all but obliterate the historic site or beauty spot being visited. Ski slopes in winter and summer beaches and swimming pools
were inundated by great waves of humanity. Even traveling abroad,
Japanese preferred to stick together in tight bands led by tour guides
provided with little distinguishing flags and effectively cut off from
contact with the people they were ostensibly visiting. The Tsukuba
International Science and Technology Exhibit, held in 1985 in the new
academic and science town of Tsukuba near Tokyo, drew over 20
million visitors, and Tokyo Disneyland, which was opened on April
15, 1983, on the outskirts of Tokyo, was larger in area than either its
California or Florida prototypes and from the start drew larger crowds.

Working and playing en masse can, of course, be a personal preference, but few Japanese liked their cramped living quarters. Small
urban streets usually lacked sidewalks; limited-access highways normally were only two lanes wide each way and consequently soon
became even more clogged with traffic than the normal roadways; and
the bulk of residences were still without proper sewerage facilities.
The Japanese had perhaps the highest incomes in the world in monetary terms, but in living accommodations they were still a relatively
poor people. Space, though not figured in a nation's GNP, is a form of
wealth, and this the Japanese lacked. A rough guess would be that the

average American has three to ten times as much living space as a Japanese of comparable economic and social status. The Japanese might tend his space more carefully, but no amount of work could make up for the great difference in size.

Lack of space led to the side effect of increased costs for many things. With less than 20 percent of the land suitable for agriculture and much of that being gobbled up annually by urban sprawl, Japan could not possibly feed itself. The overall cost of food was greatly increased by the long-established policy of government supports for rice and some other agricultural produce to keep the income of farmers in line with rapidly increasing urban wealth. This policy was in large part the result of the LDP's heavy dependence on the rural vote, but in Japan, as in almost every country, there was also a strong nostalgic feeling that the farmer and his family constituted the moral backbone of the nation. This attitude has become absurd in countries in which agriculture accounts for less than 10 percent of the GNP or population and most people are several generations removed from the farm, but, if Jeffersonian ideals can still run strong in the United States, it is not surprising that they are even more deeply entrenched in Japan, which historically is much closer to its rural past.

Price supports have become a heavy burden on most industrial countries, constituting a special tax on urban residents to support the farmer and the national myth embodied in him, but nowhere was the burden heavier than in Japan. In 1988 prices for rice, the national staple, were 6 times higher in Japan than in the United States, 9 times higher for beef, and 3.8 for potatoes. The situation was so extreme that supports were finally allowed to level off and in 1987 were reduced by close to 6 percent for rice in the first price cut in thirty-one years. Japan, however, still has a long way to go to achieve reasonable food costs. To do this further demographic changes will be necessary to move most of the remaining rural population to the cities or shift it to other means of livelihood, but at least a conscious decision to help this happen has been made at last.

Japan, like the rest of the industrialized world, became tied indissolubly to travel by cars, buses, and jet airplanes, with the resulting problems of clogged, snail-paced roads, dangerously crowded skies, pollution, and "public nuisances," the broader term Japanese apply to dirty air and water, toxic wastes, the incessant din of city life, and a number of other things that degrade the quality of life. The Japanese were wise, however, in not allowing rail travel to atrophy. The inadequate road system and impossible parking situation in cities did not permit many people to commute by car, and as a result the bulk of commuters were carried by the excellent national and private railways, and by subways in the larger cities, with buses used to supplement the system. Though crowded, the Japanese transportation system of the eighties was vastly superior to that of any American city.

Between cities, an equally good rail system was maintained, chiefly by the Japanese National Railway (JNR). Its numerous small feeder lines were heavy financial losers, but their services were being replaced with much cheaper bus lines. The JNR, as previously mentioned, started in the sixties an ambitious system of high-speed lines between the main cities. Officially called the Shinkansen, or New Mainline, it is often referred to as the Bullet Train in English. The first section between Tokyo and Osaka was completed in 1964 in time for the Tokyo Olympics, and it was subsequently extended down the north coast of the Inland Sea and across the straits at its western end to Kyushu, eventually terminating in March 1975 at Fukuoka (or Hakata, as the railway station is named). In June 1982 another Shinkansen was

A crowded Tokyo shopping street, temporarily closed to trucks and cars.

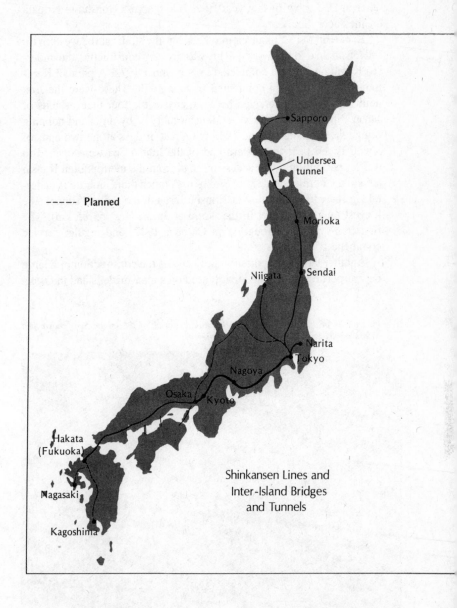

Planned

Undersea tunnel

Sapporo

Morioka

Sendai

Niigata

Narita

Tokyo

Nagoya

Osaka

Kyoto

Hakata
(Fukuoka)

Nagasaki

Kagoshima

Shinkansen Lines and
Inter-Island Bridges
and Tunnels

completed from Tokyo to Morioka in northern Honshu and still another in December of that year from Tokyo across Honshu to Niigata on the Japan Sea.

To extend the Shinkansen into Kyushu, the straits at the western tip of Honshu had to be crossed. This was done by constructing the undersea Kammon Tunnel, completed in November 1972. A parallel Kammon Bridge was also completed in June 1973. These were the first nonwater links ever created between any of the four main islands of Japan. Shikoku was linked to Honshu in 1977 by an island-hopping bridge system, and in June 1985 two great bridges at the two ends of Awaji Island near the eastern end of the Inland Sea were opened to traffic, permitting quick access by road from the metropolitan Kansai area to the northeastern tip of Shikoku. A much more ambitious undertaking linked Hokkaido with Honshu through the Seikan Tunnel, the longest undersea tunnel in the world at 35.5 miles (53.85 km). The first trains passed through it in October 1987, and regular service commenced in March 1988.

Another large transportation project was the construction of a large new airport for the Osaka area, placed on a man-made island in Osaka

Part of the bridge system crossing the middle stretch of the Inland Sea, shown just before it was opened to automobile traffic.

AP/Wide World

Bay, where its twenty-four-hour operation would not disturb people's sleep. Plans for the airport gave rise to a major dispute with the United States over the participation of foreign firms in the construction work and the supplying of equipment for the airport. The American demands ran counter to deeply ingrained Japanese prejudices against allowing foreign firms to take part in any public undertakings in Japan. The work did not get under way until January 1987, by which time it had been agreed that American firms could take part, but no one believed that this would have any significant economic effect.

The 1973 oil shock and the resulting slowdown in economic growth had delayed some of the major construction projects because the government already was running huge deficits. Japan's tax rate was slightly below that of the United States, and both were far below European averages. The result was embarrassing budget deficits for both countries, though the huge American trade deficit and the enormous Japanese trade surplus made the situation far less serious for Japan. The Japanese government, nonetheless, attempted to increase taxes but met stolid popular resistance and the reluctance of politicians, who were keenly aware of the attitude of the voters. A popular demand for lower income taxes succeeded in 1981 in cutting the nineteen brackets, which rose to a peak of 75 percent, down to fifteen brackets with a maximum tax of 50 percent. On becoming prime minister Nakasone failed in an attempt to raise government revenues through a value-added tax, which would have fallen equally on all consumers, including salaried workers, who were generally recognized as already paying more than their due share. Takeshita proved more successful in passing a value added tax but lost much of his meager popularity as a result.

A more basic budgetary problem was the heavy loss of revenue and enforced curtailment of services by the JNR and other public corporations. Inspired by the example of other advanced nations in getting rid of such costly enterprises, which were likely to be inefficient because of lack of competition, the government began as early as 1982 to give consideration to privatizing and breaking up these monopolistic public corporations. Nippon Telegraph and Telephone Public Corporation and Japan Tobacco and Salt Public Corporation were both made into private companies in April 1985, and the monopoly of Nippon Telegraph and Telephone was broken up in September 1987; JNR was split into eleven private companies, six of them regional passenger carriers, in April 1987; and JAL (Japan Air Lines) was privatized in November 1987, and its monopolistic position abroad was considerably diluted.

The eighties were economically a period of great activity in Japan, but few important new trends emerged in the social or cultural fields, except for the extraordinary rise of interest in Japanese culture in the other advanced nations, especially the United States. As has been mentioned, there was a veritable boom in interest in Japanese food, design, and culture, from the martial arts to drama and modern Japanese dance. Japan became something of a cultural world leader, and interest in studying the Japanese language increased phenomenally. This was particularly true in Australia and the United States, where the Japanese language began to be regarded along with Spanish and French as a normal subject of study.

In Japan itself, this was a peaceful, quiet time, in which Japanese tried their wings with considerable success in many avant-garde aspects of culture. Various older trends also continued, though with slowly fading force. The family continued strong, showing little of the decay that was evident in much of the West. Japan remained orderly, with virtually no drug culture or violent crime. Demonstrations occasionally occurred, but they were likely to be demands for the support of rice prices by aging farmers or sober marches against nuclear weapons and for peace, in which more middle-age persons than youths took part. The prolonged and violent opposition to Tokyo's Narita Airport continued to stir up occasional student demonstrations, the worst perhaps in March 1982, but gradually disappeared almost completely. Similar student demonstrations occurred from time to time, usually over the visit of American aircraft carriers or nuclear-powered submarines to American bases in Japan, but they became much smaller. The firing of five small homemade rockets into the spacious imperial palace grounds in March 1986 and again in August 1987 seemed like futile last sputterings of a passing age.

There was considerable concern, however, about Japanese education and trends among youth. Most Japanese were naturally proud of the excellent achievements of the educational system. Practically all young people completed the twelve rigorous years of education leading through high school and studied extremely hard during this whole period, usually driven by heavy homework and the desire to pass the examinations for entrance into the best schools at the next level. They showed the results of these efforts by ranking usually first or near the top among the advanced nations in such measurable fields as mathematics and science. In contrast, American students usually came near the bottom.

The Japanese, however, recognized that their educational system also had its shortcomings. Students were better prepared for taking examinations than thinking for themselves. They excelled at memory work but not at creative intellectual activities and self-expression. Their minds were stuffed with the same facts, attitudes, and opinions, making them even more homogeneous than they already were and less fitted for the international role history was forcing on the country. The examination cram schools that most of them attended usually worsened the situation. In some fields, such as foreign languages, Japanese performed very poorly, handicapped by a rigid, outmoded system of instruction focused on learning how to pass examinations rather than on the speaking of English. School was an unhappy experience for many Japanese children, subjecting them to painful psychological pressures and tending to stifle their spontaneity and diversity.

One thing that particularly bothered the Japanese about their educational system was the development of bullying behavior among some students aimed at weaker or nonconformist children. Those who suffered most were children who had received part of their education abroad and therefore were likely to have divergent attitudes and habits. The Japanese were particularly horrified that some of the bullying children even attacked their teachers. The number of such cases was infinitesimal by American standards, but the situation caused deep worries among the well-disciplined Japanese. It was feared that the whole race was degenerating under the corrupting influence of economic affluence and social change. The extreme styles of dress and sometimes of conduct of some young Japanese spawned a great deal of conjecture and no little anxiety about the *shin-jinrui*, the "new race."

To Westerners, however, the situation appeared very different. To them, Japanese young people still seemed too homogeneous and conformist to play the role in the world that Japan's status as an economic superpower called for. Outlandish dress and even the bullying of other children and violence against teachers all seemed to be part of a desire on the part of young Japanese to express their self-identity and also join youth in the rest of the world. From this point of view, young Japanese were making some progress, even if slowly, toward becoming more spontaneous and less suppressed. They seemed more internationally open and ready to mix with the rest of the world.

A more serious complaint about education in Japan was over text-books. Since by law these had to be approved by the central government, they were extremely uniform. A textbook by Professor Ienaga Saburo, which was felt to lean too much to the left, gave rise to a famous legal case, which started in 1965 and continued through appeals and retrials until it was finally dismissed in March 1986. In the meantime, a different sort of textbook problem had become important. South Korea, China, and other neighboring countries objected to wording that toned down the characterizations of Japanese colonial rule or conquest. Many Japanese were irritated by such foreign intervention in domestic education, but these incidents usually ended with the Japanese returning to the original wording and expressing apologies. For example, an official Chinese protest in June 1982 against the use of the word "advance" in place of what had formerly been frankly called an "invasion" of China during World War II was meekly accepted by the Japanese a few months later.

There was enough dissatisfaction with the various rigidities of Japanese education to induce Nakasone to appoint an Extraordinary Commission on Education, which issued several commendable reports. Regulations were relaxed for students who received part of their education abroad, and schools were encouraged to try out various schemes for the education of such students and the improvement of English language instruction. Several American universities set up branches in Japan, and some Japanese junior colleges and universities created campuses in the United States. Foreign students poured into Japan in greatly increased numbers, and literally thousands of native English speakers became official teachers or illegal English tutors. But despite all this peripheral tinkering with Japanese education, no basic reforms were attempted, and Japan did not come really to grips with the major educational problems forced on it by its new international status.

Japan's tremendous economic growth brought a great increase in the employment of women in industry and business, as it did in all the industrialized countries, but no great change in the position of women ensued. Although slightly more than half of women were employed outside the home, they held firmly onto their primary roles as mothers, family makers, and the dominators of the home. They paid a price for this by receiving grossly inferior wages, being paid only slightly more than half as much as men in comparable positions. This held true even after an Equal Employment Opportunities Law went into effect on April 1, 1986.

Women achieved no great gains in politics either. They were often effective through "residents' movements," as in a notable fight, largely between 1984 and 1986, in the suburban town of Zushi on the coast west of Tokyo to preserve a forest area as a bird sanctuary despite American navy requests for its use for new housing. The women won a series of local elections on the issue but in the long run got only a compromise settlement. The appointment of a woman to the cabinet in November 1984 was only the first such choice in twenty-two years, though the election of Doi Takako as secretary general of the Socialist party in September 1986 was a significant step forward for women. Perhaps the greatest advance, however, was in subtle, less visible ways. Study and employment abroad influenced many young Japanese men to treat their wives more as equals, and women increased their self-confidence in their relations with their husbands. The wife commonly drove the family car more than her husband, since he could not use it for commuting and she required it for shopping and driving their small children around. The role of women, however, still seemed very unsatisfactory to non-Japanese observers, though Japanese women appeared on the whole more satisfied with the compromise they had made among jobs, marriage, and children than were their more activist Western sisters.

Throughout the eighties there was a slow but clear drift toward more liberal ways. A good symbol of the type of change that was going on was to be seen in the persons portrayed on the bank notes adopted on November 1, 1984. Hitherto they had been great political leaders from the past, such as Prince Shotoku of the seventh century and Prince Ito, the framer of the 1889 constitution. Now they became Fukuzawa Yukichi, the first important popularizer of knowledge about the West in the nineteenth century, Nitobe Inazo, the prominent Christian educator and introducer of Japan to the West, and Natsume Soseki, Japan's outstanding modern novelist.

Japan had achieved its status as an economic giant by outstripping in industrial productivity and international trade all the countries of the world except for the United States. It would have seemed natural, therefore, if it had become self-confident in its international relations. But this was not the case. The Japanese knew full well that they depended unequivocally on the outside world for their livelihood. Long historical experience made them still feel a need to catch up with others, even though they were demonstrably ahead in most ways. They felt that they still had to concentrate on their own economic welfare. They were fearful that the other industrialized nations might conspire to undermine them and that the poor nations would expect too much from them. For many generations they had followed a reactive policy, leaving it up to others to take the lead and reacting to what they did in ways that would best serve Japan's own narrow interests. But now others looked to them for leadership and a vision that went beyond the restricted national interests of Japan itself. The country had made amazing progress in technology, economics, social organization, and political stability, but it seemed to falter in self-doubt when it faced its role in the world. What did it mean to be an economic giant and how should Japan try to play this role? The question of the *Nihonjin-ron*—what did it mean to be a Japanese?—had gripped the nation ever since the seventies. At the end of the eighties they were still groping to find an answer.

In the early postwar years, disputes over Japan's political and military position in the world had shaken the nation, and these still lingered on, though with much less fervor. Almost no one now believed in the desirability of an alliance with the communist nations; neutrality remained an appealing concept but was not seen as very practical; American bases and the Japanese Self-Defense Forces were still opposed by some but without much ardor; and almost all Japanese realized that Japan had become a part of the Western industrialized world in defense as well as economically. In 1973 the American carrier *Midway* was permitted to make Yokosuka its home port; in 1976 the government openly called for a coordinated defense policy with the United States; and in 1979 it started holding regular working-level defense meetings between the two countries. Meanwhile joint military exercises with the Americans had started, and these grew steadily in size and complexity throughout the eighties.

One flareup did occur in May 1981 when former American ambassador Edwin Reischauer mentioned to Japanese newsmen that Americans took for granted that their vessels entering bases in Japan or transitting Japanese waters did not off-load their nuclear weapons beforehand. The point had been clearly stated already in 1974 by a former American admiral, but the Japanese public did not pay any attention to it until the so-called Reischauer statement, or *hatsugen*.

The excitement, however, did not last long, since the situation as described by Reischauer was soon seen to be merely common sense. But it illustrated an old difference of interpretation that was allowed to continue. Sato, as we have seen, had himself defined Japan's three nuclear principles as being not to produce, possess, or introduce nuclear weapons. "Introduction" to Americans meant the emplacement or storage of such weapons, but to the Japanese public the corresponding Japanese term (*mochikomi*) included casual transit on nuclear-armed vessels. As late as 1983 Nakasone repeated this interpretation, but the whole subject gradually dropped out of Japanese attention.

Opposition to the veritable Japanese–American defense alliance had become largely pro forma by the latter part of the seventies, when Peking made it clear that it strongly opposed the possibility of Japan falling under Soviet influence and that it much preferred Japan having a close relationship with the United States. This old issue now raised problems only when Japanese prime ministers on visits to Washington waxed too enthusiastic or specific over their nation's alliance with the United States. There was loud criticism when Suzuki referred to an "alliance relationship" between the two countries in May 1981 and suggested the possibility in June 1982 that Japan might take part in UN peacekeeping missions, and when Nakasone in January 1983 described Japan and the United States as "allies" and referred to Japan as an "unsinkable aircraft carrier." Usually the Japanese prime minister felt compelled to "clarify" his unfortunate choice of words for the public. But none of this verbal sensitivity changed the fact that the Japanese–American alliance was growing stronger all the time and becoming accepted as a simple reality. An American suggestion that the Self-Defense Forces should take charge of the defense of the approaches to Japan up to a distance of 1,000 nautical miles shocked the public when made in May 1982, but by the end of the decade the concept had come to be accepted as only natural.

Public toleration of the Self-Defense Forces followed somewhat the same pattern. Most Japanese came to accept them at their existing strength, which, as has been noted, was generally defined as having a budget of no more than 1 percent of the nation's GNP. There was little protest when Ōhira dignified the Forces by speaking at the graduation ceremonies of the Defense Academy in March 1979. More important, the Komeito withdrew its formal opposition to the Forces in December 1981, and even the Socialists did the same "under existing conditions" in February 1984.

There was much more opposition, however, whenever plans were drawn up to exceed the traditional 1 percent limit on the military budget even by such a tiny fraction as 0.004 percent. One percent was felt to be a virtually sacrosanct figure, but it was, after all, a flexible one, capable of being calculated in many radically different ways and growing rapidly in step with the whole economy. The Japanese government figured it in a way to minimize it in the eyes of the public, but one way of counting it would have placed it as high as third in the democratic world in 1988. Since most other parts of the national budget were being held down while the military portion was allowed to keep growing with the GNP, it was also becoming a larger part of the overall budget. Because of the nation's tremendous economic growth even during the seventies and eighties, Japan came to have very sizable military expenditures, able to support a well-equipped and trained force, while also assuming a growing share of the costs of American bases in Japan. Many Japanese incorrectly came to assume that the military budget was exceeding the 1 percent limitation, but they were no longer much exercised over the point, since the "peace constitution" seemed to be holding firm.

Japanese economic ties, cultural relations, and military cooperation with the United States increased greatly in the eighties, and the "equal partnership" talked about during the early sixties, which at that time had seemed grossly overstated, had indeed become a reality. Americans now quite freely called the two countries "allies," and even some Japanese cautiously used the term. The other industrialized democracies bordering on the Pacific Ocean followed suit. The Australians had at first concentrated with bitterness on the atrocities and hatred that World War II had bred, but when they suddenly realized that Japan had become their primary market as well as source of imports, there was a great change in attitudes. The Japanese language became widely studied in schools, and contacts of all sorts proliferated. Japan and Canada also began to build close ties, and both Australia and Canada started to hold regularly scheduled meetings between their cabinet ministers and high officials and their Japanese counterparts, along the lines pioneered by the United States.

The countries of Europe were slower to change the way in which they viewed Japan. They maintained more restrictions on trade, and when the Japanese emperor and empress visited Europe in 1971, there were unpleasant incidents, in contrast to the unreserved welcome the elderly imperial couple received when they visited the United States in

October 1975. As has been mentioned, the United States insisted in 1964 that Japan be allowed to join the OECD, despite European opposition. The Japanese, however, remained in European eyes only semi-members of the community of advanced democracies, but in the seventies a great change began to take place. A nongovernmental group of political, economic, and intellectual leaders from North America, Japan, and Europe, realizing the desirability of strengthening the contacts on the third side of the triangle of great industrialized democracies, founded in April 1973 a private organization called the Trilateral Commission to help pave the way for a stronger and better balanced relationship between these three areas. An even more significant step was taken in November 1975 when Miki was included with the prime ministers or presidents of the five other largest industrialized democracies—the United States, West Germany, France, the United Kingdom, and Italy—to discuss their mutual economic problems at a "summit" conference at Rambouillet near Paris. The "summit" meetings, which soon came to include Canada, met annually thereafter in rotation in the member countries.

Japan at last was beginning to be accepted by the Europeans as a full-fledged member of the group. At first, the phrase "the West and Japan" was used to indicate its inclusion, but soon people came to speak merely of "the West," meaning to include Japan as a matter of course. Everyone, with the possible exception of some Japanese themselves, came to think of Japan as being one of the leading members of the coalition of Western democracies. Bureaucrats, statesmen, businessmen, scientists, and leaders of all kinds, including prime ministers and presidents, went back and forth between it and the other members of the group. In November 1974 Gerald Ford became the first American president in office to visit Japan, blotting out the unhappy memory of Eisenhower's aborted trip in 1960. President Jimmy Carter visited Japan for a few days before the fifth "summit" conference held there in June 1979 and returned in July 1980 for the memorial service for Ohira in an unprecedented show of personal respect and international solidarity. President Ronald Reagan in November 1983 was the first American president to address the Japanese Diet.

By the late eighties, no one any longer had any doubt about Japan being a full member of the community of "Western" democracies. At the same time, there was considerable resentment of Japan's flooding the world with its exports and some strong suspicions that it was doing this through unfair means. There was also a general perception that

Japan was failing to carry its share of the load in maintaining world security and peace. Other causes for irritation were often not as substantial but could reach a high pitch of feeling. For example, during the seventies many conservationists in the West became incensed that the Japanese continued to hunt down great numbers of whales, which Westerners considered to be a particularly precious endangered species. The Japanese, together with the Soviets and Norwegians, which were the only other whaling nations, held out against this criticism for several years, and the Japanese were much annoyed that people who looked on whales basically as a curiosity of nature should feel entitled to criticize those to whom whale meat was an important source of protein. Gradually whaling was reduced, however, until all that remained was only a little activity, ostensibly for research purposes. Meanwhile similar attitudes developed over dolphins, which Westerners considered with considerable affection. Japanese permitted the slaughter of dolphins because they ruined the nets of fishermen, whose work was essential for Japan's protein supply.

In a very different field, the United States was outraged in 1987 when a Toshiba subsidiary together with a Norwegian firm sold to the Soviet Union machinery designed to improve the making of submarine propellers, even though this machinery was on a list of items banned from trade with the Soviets by the group of industrialized democracies. The responsible company executives were forced to resign, and Nakasone personally apologized. Anti-Japanese sentiments in the United States were particularly strong over blatant Japanese racism. Racism, of course, is an attitude found almost everywhere in the world, but it has seemed especially virulent among Japanese, whose history has led them to look upon themselves as so unique as to constitute virtually a different species from the rest of mankind. With the exception of Chinese and Koreans, Japanese often made little distinction between the other nationalities, since the strongly felt distinction between Japanese and *gaijin,* or "outsiders," was so great to Japanese that it expressed their virtually "tribal" sense of uniqueness.

In earlier times, such attitudes had been acceptable, but they no longer were in a now closely interdependent world and especially on the part of a superpower like Japan. Only a few years earlier remarks made or published in the Japanese language went virtually unnoticed by others, but by the eighties Japanese were under close world scrutiny and therefore had to be circumspect in what they said. For example, in September 1986 Nakasone casually commented that the reason for the reputedly low intelligence levels of Americans was the large number of blacks, Mexicans, and Puerto Ricans in their population. He hastily tried to make amends by apologizing to the American people. Takeshita similarly had to apologize in August 1988 because of the statement by a member of the Diet that blacks in America did not mind going into bankruptcy because this freed them of their debts.

While Japan, despite much friction and many misunderstandings, did become during the eighties a full member of the coalition of industrialized democracies, its relations with the communist countries and its Asian neighbors grew mostly in size rather than warmth. Back in 1972, when it set up the Japan Foundation to further international cultural relations, it made Southeast Asia its second priority area, next to the United States. It continued to be the major trading partner of most of the nations of East and Southeast Asia and became the leading provider of aid to them. In fact, flushed by its huge trade surpluses, it assigned $10 billion to aid, becoming the world leader, a little ahead of the United States. It also spread its aid much more widely than before to most parts of the less developed world. It should be pointed out, however, that in terms of the percentage of GNP devoted to aid and the amount provided in per capita terms, both Japan and the United States lagged far behind some of the smaller Western countries.

Japan's relations with the Soviet Union during the eighties became on the whole a little less harsh but made no great progress. The Japanese Communist party did restore its contacts with Moscow in 1979, but the two governments failed to achieve a peace settlement to bring an official end to the war between them. During the seventies there had been high hopes for developing Siberia as a major source of oil and gas for Japan to replace Middle Eastern oil, but nothing came of this. Other joint development plans were equally unsuccessful. They would have taken enormous investments by Japan, which the Japanese were not prepared to place at the mercy of the Soviet Union. The Soviets on their side adamantly refused to discuss the four islands north of Hokkaido, which Japan claimed under the name of the "Northern Territories." Soviet suggestions that the two smaller southern islands might be treated separately drew indignant refusals from

Japan. This left the size of the Japanese catch of fish in waters the Soviets claimed the only important economic relationship between them that called for annual negotiations. Meanwhile a large naval buildup by the Soviet Union in the Japan Sea made both Japan and the United States nervous, and Japan's growing capacity to blockade the three straits, enclosing the Japan Sea and the Soviet Pacific fleet, worried the Soviets.

A peace treaty with China was held up during most of the seventies by Peking's insistence that it include a clause condemning "hegemony," which had been a term of opprobrium ever since antiquity in China and was now applied to Soviet military ambitions. Finally in 1978 wording was devised to satisfy both sides, and a peace treaty was signed. But the troublesome problem of China's claim to Taiwan remained. The island had been rapidly consolidating into a prosperous, stable country, which, like South Korea, was closely following the economic trail blazed by Japan. Both Taiwan and South Korea had the East Asian emphasis on education and hard work that had proved so important for Japan, and they also had the foundations of Japanese colonial rule to build on. China and Japan got around the Taiwan problem basically by ignoring it. Despite a large trade with Taiwan, Japan kept its relations with the island strictly informal and even took care to have Taiwanese and Chinese planes use different air fields in Japan. Since Peking felt the need for more technological knowledge and foreign contacts, it sent students to Japan in growing numbers, and Japan became by far its largest trading partner, developing by 1988 a trade with China that came to equal Japan's sizable commerce with Taiwan.

Korea remained a more difficult and less predictable problem for Japan. Sino-Soviet tensions relaxed notably in the eighties; wars continued in Southeast Asia but in confused fashion and with little threat to other regions; Peking let Taiwan be shifted to a back burner; but Korea continued to be full of explosive possibilities. North and South Korea for long had been military dictatorships, eager to achieve national unity by military conquest if a chance presented itself. North Korea, however, was entirely dependent on China and the Soviet Union, and the eagerness of both these countries in the late eighties for better political relations with each other and greatly expanded economic relations with the industrialized democracies made them strongly opposed to trouble in Korea, thus tying North Korea's hands.

During 1987 and 1988 South Korea advanced significantly toward democracy, becoming as a consequence less militarily inclined. For a while, there were fears that a dangerous incident might occur during the Olympic Games held in Seoul in September 1988, but this threat was safely surmounted.

The Koreans on both sides, however, shared deep resentments against the Japanese because of the colonial past. The presence in Japan of more than 600,000 people of Korean descent, originally brought there virtually as slave labor during World War II, did not help the situation. Although these people had been in large part culturally absorbed into Japanese life, stiff Japanese regulations on naturalization and the tribal exclusiveness of the Japanese people kept most of them from merging fully into Japanese society. Instead they remained a dissatisfied minority, usually siding with the opposition parties in Japan and the North in Korea and helping to stir up animosity between South Korea and Japan. Trade and other contacts between Japan and South Korea, however, increased enormously during the eighties, and tensions eased slightly. Joint problems of defense were discussed as early as 1979 between the Japanese and South Korean military, and in September 1984 Chun Doo Hwan, a former general and at the time the dictator in Seoul, was the first South Korean president to officially visit Japan, where he was given by the emperor himself a formal statement of regret about Japan's past relationship with Korea.

One symbolic issue loomed large in Japan's relations with its neighbors as well as in domestic politics during these years. This was the propriety of the prime minister visiting the Yasukuni Shrine, which was dedicated to the fighting men who had died in battle for Japan in its various wars. As part of the slow swing back toward nationalism, Fukuda and members of his cabinet visited the shrine in 1978 on its memorial day on August 15. The question was made politically more sensitive in 1979 by the inclusion in the shrine's roles of the names of the military men executed as major war criminals following World War II. During the next few years prime ministers continued to attend the ceremonies, despite the opposition of the parties out of power and Christians, who considered this an infraction of the constitutional separation of church and state. Nakasone actually made his visit an official act in 1985, but the Chinese joined the South Koreans the next spring in strong objections, and he gave up the practice that August, although some members of the cabinet continued to attend.

A somewhat similar situation developed in September 1986 when the minister of education published in a popular magazine his opinion that the Koreans themselves were in part responsible for the Japanese annexation of Korea in 1910 and that Nakasone should not have given up visiting the Yasukuni Shrine. The Koreans were infuriated, and Nakasone felt himself forced to dismiss the minister, the first time such a thing had happened in thirty-three years.

Japanese political problems were not only with the outside world. In 1986 Recruit, a rapidly expanding, aggressive company centering around a job-finding magazine of that name, sold shares at low prices to a number of top politicians, officials, and leading businessmen before these shares were publicly listed and increased greatly in value. These insider trading deals grew into a public scandal after they were revealed in June 1988, leading in time to the resignation of Miyazawa and two other men from the cabinet, the retirement of some leading business figures, and the tarnishing of Nakasone's reputation. The opposition parties, demanding a further inquiry, boycotted the Diet, delaying the adoption of the new budget for fiscal 1989 beyond its deadline of April 1.

On April 25, 1989, Takeshita announced his intention to resign the prime ministership because of his theoretical responsibility for the scandal. Before leaving office, however, he pushed through the adoption of the new budget without the participation of the opposition parties and settled long-standing negotiations with the United States over the building of the FSX, a new type of fighter plane for the Air Self-Defense Force, on the basis of a $7 billion project jointly undertaken by the two countries. Tensions with America, however, heightened when on May 25 the United States officially cited Japan, together with some other countries, as "unfair traders" against whom special sanctions might be taken.

On June 2, 1989, Uno Sosuke was elected by the Diet as Takeshita's successor. A member of Nakasone's faction lacking in any great distinction, Uno was selected largely because all the leading candidates had been temporarily eliminated on account of their involvement in the Recruit scandal. No one expected any major political changes, except possibly some more effective laws about the gray area of financial contributions to politicians and their parties and factions. Japan's chief problem area remained its relations with the rest of the world.

18

FACING THE FUTURE

Despite the continuing economic success of Japan in the eighties and the orderly, stable, and self-satisfied society it produced, the Japanese still seemed perplexed as to what the role of their country should be as an economic superpower. No Japanese now believed that the country could live alone or even through dominating some corner of the globe, like the Greater East Asia Co-Prosperity Sphere. Japan had become so big a fish that it needed the economic waters of the whole world in which to maintain itself. Some enthusiasts took the extreme interpretation of the phrase ''Japan As Number One'' to mean that it would succeed England and the United States as the world leader, overseeing a Pax Japonica. They failed to realize that that sort of world hegemony had always been quite restricted and was now completely impossible.

Great Britain had exercised extensive influence through superior naval power but had made no effort to control most of the great land masses of the world, even though it accidentally did fall heir to some of them because they were almost empty of people or else their inhabitants were politically disrupted or apathetic. The brief period of American domination had resulted from the destruction during World War II of the wealth and strength of all of the other major military powers. Its position of leadership naturally shrank in relative terms as these other countries recovered from the war. The United States also discovered that there were sharp limitations to its power. When the Soviet Union also came to possess nuclear weapons, the mutual de-

Japan National Tourist Organization

A typical downtown, neon-lit street.

struction of all nations became probable if these weapons were ever used extensively. As a result, military conflict between any of the great powers was virtually ruled out. The worldwide rise of nationalism also tipped the scales against the ponderous military machines of the great powers and toward the less developed countries, which typically lacked important military objectives but were richly endowed with fanatical fighters. The United States learned this lesson in Vietnam.

The role as world leaders that England and the United States had once played was clearly not one to which Japan or any other country could aspire. This was particularly true for Japan. The country had become an economic giant, not by growing to fill a rich continent but by developing massive ties of economic interdependence with large parts of the world. Poor itself in natural resources, it was more dependent on its trading partners than they were on it. Japan someday might free itself from its dependence on imported fossil fuels for energy if the hazards of nuclear energy could be reduced and the dangers of its toxic wastes eliminated, or if Japan could become self-sufficient through the development of solar energy or other nontoxic technologies at reasonable costs. But these solutions to Japan's energy problem seemed remote, and in any case would not solve Japan's dependence on the importation of vast quantities of raw materials and food.

Postwar Japan, as we have seen, had wisely turned its back on the blind alley of military might, and its people had chosen instead the broad road of world trade. They were completely committed to their "peace constitution." Military might, they realized, could never bring them security, much less world dominance. Despite Japan's great wealth, it was simply too small geographically to be a first-class military power, and even if it could, it would still lack military security. It was particularly vulnerable to nuclear attack, since its small size and mountainous terrain squeezed more than half its population into a mere 2 percent of its area. It was also incapable of extensive nuclear deployment on land. This meant that in the event of a nuclear war, the Japanese would have only the cold comfort of knowing they could retaliate from the sea, but only after Japan itself had been destroyed.

The Japanese relegated the now-empty concept of being a world military leader to the time in history to which it belonged. There was some reality, however, to the concept some Japanese held that the country could serve as the core of a Pacific Rim Community that could assume world leadership. Not only was Japan the fastest-growing large nation in the world, but some of the countries around it, like South Korea, Taiwan, and Singapore, were also growing fast. Transpacific trade had come to surpass transatlantic intercourse. A free-trade community consisting of Japan, the United States, Canada, Australia, Mexico, South Korea, Taiwan, and some other Pacific countries might well outstrip an Atlantic community consisting of North America and Western Europe. It could be that the world stood on the verge of a "Pacific age," as some people proclaimed.

But such concepts had to be kept in perspective. The population and GNP of Japan were only about half that of the United States or the European Community. The European Community also expected to achieve in 1992 a degree of solidarity that would be far greater than that possible for the countries of the Pacific, with the exception of the United States and Canada free-trade zone, which started on January 1, 1989, and possibly a Japanese and American economic union. Both an Atlantic Community and a Pacific Rim Community, moreover, would center on the membership of the United States and Canada, making them not two competing zones but rather two linked areas. In a sense, the two zones together would be simply the concept of the old Trilateral Commission turned into reality. To say this is not to denigrate the vision of a Pacific Rim Community. In fact, taking the lead in building it would probably be the most concrete and significant way in which

Japan could contribute at this point in history to the economic and political development of a peaceful, prosperous, and stable world, but it would not make Japan the economic leader of the world.

Global leadership today is not possible for any one country but clearly depends on international cooperation among several. An attempt to win military supremacy would probably lead only to mutual annihilation. An effort at economic supremacy would be almost as dangerous, because world prosperity depends on relatively free trade and willing cooperation among many countries. In the world as it exists today, Japan as an economic giant is well suited to be one of the most influential leaders. This is the ideal that most Japanese have vaguely in mind in the late eighties, though it is difficult for them to free themselves from a narrowly Japanese frame of reference and think fully in international terms.

The role Japan might play in an international world can best be envisioned by considering briefly some of the main problems that confront mankind today. The one that looms largest in the thinking of most people lies in the traditional area of military rivalry. The once-common dream of military domination of the world, however, has now become a bottomless morass of catastrophe. Modern military power is vastly expensive, the progress of costly technology rapid, and the task of controlling rebellious nationalism, especially in less developed countries, almost impossible. The larger a nation's conquests become, the closer it approaches economic ruin. The Soviet Union, like the United States in Vietnam, discovered this in its eight-year war with seemingly indefensible Afghanistan and as a result withdrew from that country in 1989.

The most a major country can hope for in the military field is security from other major military powers by balancing their strength and convincing them of their mutual nuclear destruction if serious conflict should break out between them and should this escalate, as it almost assuredly would, to full nuclear warfare. Some relief from the problem can be found in the sharing of military expenditures, as North America, Western Europe, Japan, and Australia already are doing, but this is merely a palliative. The only true solution to the problem is the development of a great deal more trust between the rival great powers and, on the basis of this, a cautious limitation and then reduction of their military weapons.

There are signs of hope that this is at last beginning to take place. Close to half a century has already elapsed since the end of World War II—more than twice the length of time between the first two world wars—and the threat of a major war seems to be receding steadily rather than growing closer. Japan probably will remain a peripheral player in this great military drama, but through its strong support of peace, coupled with its firm cooperation with the United States and championing of international cooperation everywhere, it can help tip the world away from unproductive military expenditures and toward a better utilization of human resources.

The second great problem area is that of economic cooperation, particularly among the industrialized democracies, commonly called the First World, or the West. A basic system of free trade must be maintained if the world is to retain and develop its present prosperity. A stable though flexible monetary system is also necessary, and a host of other difficulties must be faced. The economic problems of the world are huge and extremely complex, probably posing a much greater threat of global disaster than does the basically frozen military situation, which attracts so much more attention. If within the foreseeable future mankind is to come to catastrophe, a failure of the economic system in the First World would seem to be the most likely starting place. It may well be the keystone to the whole arch of modern civilization. If it falls out of place, poverty and political disorder might well follow in all the industrialized democracies, and this in turn might lead to economic conflict among them and greatly worsened conditions in the rest of the world. The situation then would be ripe for full-scale warfare, which could destroy world civilization as we know it. In this area, Japan's role as an economic giant—the second-largest and fastest-growing industrial power in the world—is sure to be enormous and crucial. Japan simply cannot avoid being a world leader.

Two other great global problems might be considered as subordinate elements of the problems of international economic cooperation among the First World countries. One is the desperate situation of the bulk of the world's people, commonly called the Third World, or the "less developed countries." The First World must provide the Third World with aid to live, technical assistance to permit it to develop, and, most important, a growing share of the world's markets so that the currently less developed countries can progress and someday take their rightful place in a unitary world. In other words, the First World must provide the Third with vastly more aid, much better organized than now and better designed for substantial and lasting economic growth, rather than largely for military support, as is at present the situation. Unless these goals are achieved, the whole world, crammed with resentful and desperate people, may someday explode and destroy civilized life for everyone. Here again is an area in which Japan has no choice but to play a leading role.

The other ancillary problem is the maintenance of a physically livable world for all people. There are signs everywhere of a dangerous deterioration of the global environment. Water and air are becoming seriously polluted. Toxic wastes are heaping up. A great increase of carbon dioxide and other gases and pollutants in the atmosphere has resulted from two centuries of industrial growth and a rapid reduction of forests, which help maintain a proper balance between oxygen and carbon dioxide. At the current rate atmospheric conditions could be changed sufficiently to overheat the world through the so-called greenhouse effect or produce dangerous holes in the ozone layer around the poles or blankets of ozone-filled smog over our cities. These are but a few samples, amateurishly stated, of a wide variety of environmental disasters that might threaten the well-being of mankind. The industrial development of the First World has been the chief reason for the environmental menace to mankind, and only the First World has the knowledge to try to avert the consequences and help the Third World avoid a repetition of these hazards. Obviously, crowded Japan has had much experience in the problems of maintaining a livable environment and, with its vast economic power, is particularly well suited to provide world leadership in solving these problems.

A final great problem area lies in the need to make the social adjustments forced by rapidly evolving technological changes in the world. New problems and attitudes are constantly arising. There is no country that is not undergoing puzzling moral and intellectual challenges. Those in the lead have the duty to help find new patterns for the future. Japan, which has changed over the past two centuries more than most countries and at a decidedly brisker rate but has achieved these changes in recent years without great disorder or confusion, perhaps has an especially important leadership role to play in this field too. The fact that it is the only major country in the First World that, like most of the Third World countries, does not have a Western cultural background makes its experience and successes all the more valuable. Here again is an area in which Japan's vast economic strength combined with its special cultural and historical background inevitably place it in an important position of leadership.

The need to solve or at least ameliorate the problems facing mankind has never been greater. Fortunately in the late eighties the conditions for dealing with these problems appear to be better than in the past. The communist countries of the Second World have come to realize that their brand of faith will not sweep the world in revolution and that their attempt to force their own economies into a rigidly planned system has stifled their economic growth, particularly in agriculture. They have learned that, however noble the ideals of communism may sound, its rigid practices have impoverished their countries and thus undermined their political stability and military strength. First China under Deng Xiaoping and then the Soviet Union under Mikhail Gorbachev have moved toward freer economies in their respective countries, and this in turn has produced some relaxation of society and thought. Both countries also seem to have become more aware of the significance of the long period of peace with the First World since World War II and as a result appear to have become somewhat less paranoid in their fears of the outside world. They seem to desire to reduce their external military adventures and build up their trade and technological contacts with the First World as rapidly as possible. One consequence of these trends has been a slight limiting and even reduction of nuclear weapons in step with the United States and a surge of popular demands for greater personal freedom and progress toward democracy.

The relaxing of tensions between the great powers may have helped to quiet some of the many conflicts between the smaller powers. The protracted war between Iran and Iraq, which brought serious turmoil to the vitally important export of oil from the Persian Gulf, came to a halt in 1988, and we may even be witnessing the passing of the peak of frustration with modern life expressed in the frenzy of Islamic fundamentalism that has inflamed the Moslem world in recent years. In 1987 and 1988 South Korea took some important and perhaps lasting steps away from military dictatorship and toward democracy and stability. It and the heavily armed and violently hostile communist state of North Korea, which earlier fought a terribly destructive war involving the United States, China, and other nations besides themselves, have made a few steps toward each other that may signify the beginning of a drift toward peaceful coexistence.

Many crises and conflicts remain in the Third World, and the course of events is unpredictable in countries like the Soviet Union and China, where a self-appointed handful of men contend in secret with each other for control over their millions of compatriots. But at no time in the past four decades have relations between the First and Second worlds looked more hopeful and the chances for true world peace seemed more promising. The late eighties and early nineties may be a key moment in history, opening great possibilities for Japan if it is ready.

If mankind is to avoid self-destruction, certain basic measures are necessary, not the least of which is the full-hearted participation of Japan. This is the true meaning of being an economic giant. The First World must remain firm in its democratic system and successful in its close-knit economic relations. On this basis, it then must make it possible for the Third World to develop and eventually join it in a prosperous worldwide community. And finally, peace must be preserved with the Second World and mutual trade expanded with it so that it too can someday become a part of a unified and prosperous trading world.

Since these goals are ardently desired by most Japanese, one might wonder why Japan does not plunge into the job of achieving them. It has already once played a very significant role in shaping the modern world when it demonstrated that modern technology and prosperity were not just Western traits, but could belong to all people. Why then should Japan hang back now from using its great potential influence in achieving these basic objectives, which are so necessary for its own existence and for the well-being of the whole world?

There are several problems that hold it up. The chief one is probably Japan's long history as an isolated, inward-looking country. When Japan mastered modern technology and economic skills, it did so for its own national survival. But to achieve these other broader goals,

Japan must now think of the interests of the whole world as well as its own specific objectives. The Japanese are not accustomed to doing this. To be a leader in the world today requires the ability to see the globe as a whole and not just one's own small corner of it and one's particular self-interests. It calls for a sense of internationalism—a feeling of being a citizen of the world as well as of a particular country—and few Japanese have this capacity. It is almost unimaginable to most of them.

The problem is complicated by two specific fears. Many Japanese, feeling sharply their cultural and racial differences from the members of the other First World countries, wonder if they will be accepted by the others as true equals. Deep prejudices do linger on. World War II, when the Japanese were so violently hated, and even the nineteenth century, when the West was maddeningly arrogant to all "lesser breeds," were historically not long ago. Westerners share responsibility for the attitude of Japanese and should do their best to help them overcome it.

The other and actually greater fear is that Japan, in developing the needed spirit of internationalism, will lose its own identity. By historical chance, modern technology and social and political organization came to Japan from the West, dressed, as it were, in Western clothes. The costume, of course, was a superficial matter, but the feeling in Japan is strong that modernization somehow is not Japanese but Western. Comparable attitudes are common throughout the world, but they fit Japan especially poorly. The rest of the modernized world has changed vastly too. An American of the 1980s is virtually as far from being an American of the 1880s as a Japanese of the 1980s is unlike one of the 1880s. Tenth-century Europeans had as far to go to become twentieth-century Europeans as tenth-century Japanese to being twentieth-century ones. But Europeans and Americans, unaware of or indifferent to foreign influence, felt no loss of a sense of identity.

It is unfortunate that the Japanese, who may have changed less because of the self-consciousness of an isolated people, should have so strong a fear of losing their Japaneseness. The fear is completely misplaced. Most non-Japanese feel that the danger is that the Japanese may have too strong a sense of self-identity. If Japanese instead saw themselves more as world citizens and had a greater sense of self-confidence, they would be in an excellent position to play a major role in shaping the world during these last few crucial years of the twentieth century. It is up to the Japanese to act, not react. In a sense, the future of the world is to a large extent in Japan's hands, depending much on what Japanese think and what they are willing to do.

If the Japanese are able to put aside their fears and take a creative, positive role in the world, there are several specific things they should attempt to do for the world and themselves. Japan should take a major role in bringing world trade back into balance. This it can help do in several ways, all beneficial to Japan itself. For one thing, it should spend a great deal more of its trade surpluses for the benefit of its own consumers. They have a great need to expand housing, living space, roadways, sewerage, and other living facilities. They require much more room for public use and amusement. They need a plan to reshape Japan extensively into a sort of technology and production park surrounded by adequate living space. To do this, the area devoted to agriculture would undoubtedly have to be reduced, but this would help balance trade and benefit Japanese consumers by cutting the horrendous prices they pay for food.

A second area in which Japan could take a major role of leadership would be in helping to create a strong and sound world monetary

Rice fields, the Shinkansen, and Mount Fuji in late summer without its crown of snow.

AP/Wide World

system, which is much needed. A third major area would be to contribute much more aid than Japan now does to the less developed nations of the Third World. More constructive investment in the Third World and much larger importation of goods from it would help balance world trade, contribute to the development of the Third World as a future trading partner for Japan, and benefit Japanese consumers, all at the same time. Increased economic relations with China, and in time with the Soviet Union, would do the same for Second World relations with the First, increasing world prosperity and making the dangers of a catastrophic war more remote.

The question remains of whether Japan will find itself psychologically able to abandon its traditional reactive attitude and take a more dynamic approach to world problems. The preference of the Japanese for group leadership and decisions by consensus makes this a particularly difficult change for them to make, but it is virtually a necessity for a world superpower. Japan as an economic giant has brought the problem on itself and can no longer be simply a reactor to initiatives of others.

Fortunately, there is reason to believe that Japan will begin to move more positively. Its leaders are intellectually well aware of the problem, and the last few years of the eighties have witnessed many stirrings in the right direction. Business leaders have joined the government in making generous gifts to American universities and other centers for the study of Japanese culture throughout the world; the powerful Keidanren (Federation of Economic Enterprises) promises a "Marshall Plan" for East and Southeast Asia in 1989; the new emperor, Akihito, spoke of working for "improved welfare of the human race" in his first public statement on January 9, 1989; aid money has been spectacularly increased, especially for Asian countries; Japanese investment and trade with China have been greatly expanded; investment and other contacts with South Korea have been much increased; efforts have been made to establish relations with North Korea; economic ties are being formed at breathtaking speed with many First World countries, especially the United States; younger Japanese look upon close relations with the West as a matter of course; this younger generation seems unconcerned by any reputed loss of Japanese identity, recognizing that culturally the rest of the world is being as Japanized as Japan is being Westernized; the old concern about the adverse effects of internationalization on Japan are becoming a problem of the past. In particular, the fear of Japan losing its identity through Westernization seems to be increasingly a problem of the old, who are really thinking of an age in history fast fading away. Young Japanese continue to be very Japanese and proud of it, eager to teach others about their country and not afraid to learn from others in return. The question is more not whether the Japanese will retain their identity, but whether they will be able to become sufficiently international to play the role in the world they are capable of and the world so badly needs.

Some people, however, still wonder if there is not a profound difference between being an economic superpower, like Japan, and a military and political superpower, like the United States and the Soviet Union. The answer probably is not nearly as much as most people think. Military superpowers tend to be muscle-bound, unable to use their vast military strength and weakened by the tremendous cost of maintaining it. The common derision of Japan as an economic giant but military midget seems largely misplaced. Under current conditions of mutual mistrust, the First World probably must possess sufficient military power to balance the Soviet Union, but maintaining the world trading system is in the long run even more important. Perhaps these two requirements should be looked on as comparable duties that should be rationally shared in the same way that free trade efficiently shares specialized economic production and tasks. Only through cooperation in the military, political, and economic spheres can the First World succeed in its task of building a successful world order.

No one can predict for certain what will happen in Japan during the nineties and on into the twenty-first century. Japan itself appears as politically stable, socially healthy, and economically prosperous as any country could hope to be, but what happens in the rest of the world is much more important in deciding the future and is far less predictable. Many entirely unexpected events may take place that will have an adverse bearing on Japan. But insofar as we can peer ahead through the fog of the future, the prospects for Japan during the last decade of the twentieth century look quite bright, and its relations with the rest of the world, particularly the First World countries, appear very hopeful.

CHRONOLOGY

(The division between years prior to 1853 is according to the Japanese lunar calendar.)

600 B.C.	Traditional date of accession of first emperor, Jimmu.
A.D. 57	First recorded Japanese mission to China.
552	(or 538) Official introduction of Buddhism from Korea.
562	Conquest of the Japanese holdings in Korea by Silla.
587–626	Dominance over the court by Soga Umako.
593–622	Prince Shotoku as crown prince.
604	Seventeen Article Constitution.
607	Revival of embassies to China.
645	Taika coup d'état and destruction of the Soga family.
663	Defeat of Japanese army in Korea.
668–672	Reign of Tenji.
669	Granting of surname Fujiwara to Nakatomi Kamatari.
673–686	Reign of Temmu.
701	Taiho Law Code.
708	First issuance of copper coinage.

710–784 **NARA PERIOD**

710 Founding of Heijo capital (Nara).

712 Compilation of *Kojiki*.

713 Compilation of *Fudoki* (local gazetteers).

718 Yoro revision of law code.

720 Compilation of *Nihon shoki*.

724–749 Reign of Shomu (d. 756).

729–749 Tempyo year period.

735–737 Great smallpox epidemic.

741 Establishment of *kokubunji* (provincial monasteries).

743 Legalizing of permanent possession of agricultural land.

749 Establishment of first estates (*shoen*).

752 Dedication of Great Buddha (*Daibutsu*) of Nara.

c. 760 Compilation of *Man'yoshu*.

764–770 Supremacy of monk Dokyo under Empress Shotoku.

781–806 Reign of Kammu.

784 Move of the capital to Nagaoka.

794–1185 **HEIAN PERIOD**

794 Founding of Heian capital (Kyoto).

801 Defeat of the Ainu in northern Honshu.

805 Introduction of Tendai sect by Saicho (Dengyo Daishi).

806 Introduction of Shingon sect by Kukai (Kobo Daishi).

810 Founding of Kurodo-dokoro (Bureau of Archivists).

838 Dispatch of the last embassy to China.

858–1160 **FUJIWARA PERIOD**

858 Fujiwara Yoshifusa as the first regent not of the imperial family.

884	Fujiwara Mototsune as the first chancellor (*kampaku*).
887–897	Reign of Uda.
889	Granting of the surname Taira (Heike) to Prince Takamochi, progenitor of the warrior Taira family.
891–901	Prominent role in government of Sugawara Michizane.
894	Decision to stop embassies to China.
905	Compilation of the *Kokinshu*.
930–949	Fujiwara Tadahira as regent and chancellor.
939–940	Revolt of Taira Masakado in the Kanto.
941	Execution of Fujiwara Sumitomo, pirate chief in the Inland Sea.
961	Granting of the surname Minamoto (Genji) to Prince Tsunemoto, progenitor of the warrior Minamoto family.
995–1027	Supremacy of Fujiwara Michinaga.
c. 1002	Writing of the *Makura no soshi* (Pillow Book) by Lady Sei Shonagon.
c. 1008–1020	Writing of the *Genji Monogatari* (*Tale of Genji*) by Lady Murasaki.
1017–1068	Fujiwara Yorimichi as regent and chancellor.
1051–1062	Earlier Nine Years' War: destruction of the Abe family of northern Honshu by Minamoto Yoriyoshi.
1053	Construction of the Byodoin by Yorimichi.
1068–1072	Reign of Go-Sanjo (d. 1073).
1069	Start of *insei* rule by retired emperors; establishment of the Kirokujo (Records Office).
1072–1086	Reign of Shirakawa.
1083–1087	Later Three Years' War: destruction of the Kiyowara family of northern Honshu by Minamoto Yoshiie.
1086–1129	*Insei* rule by Shirakawa.
1129–1156	*Insei* of Toba.
1156	Hogen War: elimination of most leading Minamoto.
1159–1160	Heiji War: destruction of Minamoto Yoshitomo by Taira Kiyomori (d. 1181).

1160–1185 TAIRA PERIOD

1167 Kiyomori as prime minister.

1175 Founding of the Jodo (Pure Land) sect by Genku (Honen Shonin).

1180–1185 War between the Minamoto and Taira (Gempei wars).

1185 Destruction of the Taira at naval battle of Dannoura.

1185–1333 KAMAKURA PERIOD

1185 Establishment of the *jito* system by Minamoto Yoritomo.

1189 Execution of Yoritomo's brother, Yoshitsune, and the destruction of the Fujiwara family of Hiraizumi in North Japan.

1190s Establishment of the *shugo* system.

1191 Introduction from China of the Rinzai branch of the Zen sect by Eisai.

1192 Assumption of the title of shogun by Yoritomo.

1199 Death of Yoritomo and assumption of control by his wife Hojo Masako and her father Tokimasa.

1203 Assumption of the post of shogunal regent (*shikken*) by Tokimasa.

1205 Elimination of Tokimasa and the assumption of the post of shogunal regent by his son Yoshitoki.

1206 Compilation of the *Shinkokinshu*.

1219 Murder of the shogun Sanetomo and end of the main Minamoto line.

1221 Jokyu disturbance.

1224–1242 Hojo Yasutoki as shogunal regent.

1224 Founding of Shinshu (the True Pure Land sect) by Shinran.

1227 Introduction of the Soto branch of Zen from China by Dogen.

1232 Issuance of the Joei Shikimoku (Kamakura law code).

1253   Founding of the Lotus or Nichiren sect by Nichiren.

1274   First Mongol invasion.

1281   Second Mongol invasion.

1297   *Tokusei*, or the cancellation of warrior debts.

1331   Revolt and deposition of Go-Daigo.

1333   Espousal of Go-Daigo's cause by the Kamakura general, Ashikaga Takauji; destruction of the Hojo at Kamakura by Nitta Yoshisada.

1336   Enthronement of a rival emperor by Takauji and flight of Go-Daigo to Yoshino.

1336–1392 YOSHINO PERIOD (or PERIOD OF THE NORTHERN AND SOUTHERN COURTS)

1338   Assumption of the title of shogun by Takauji.

1338–1573 ASHIKAGA (or MUROMACHI) PERIOD

1339   Writing of the *Jinno shotoki* by Kitabatake Chikafusa.

1368–1394   Shogunate of Yoshimitsu (d. 1408).

1384   Death of Kan'ami, developer of the Nō drama.

1392   Reunion of the northern and southern courts.

1397   Building of the Kinkakuji by Yoshimitsu.

1404   Start of tally trade with China (continued until 1547).

1439   Compilation of the last of the twenty-one imperial anthologies of poetry.

1441   Assassination of the shogun, Yoshinori.

1443   Death of Zeami, perfecter of the Nō drama.

1449   (or 1443)–1473 Shogunate of Yoshimasa (d. 1490).

1467–1568 PERIOD OF THE WARRING STATES

1467–1477   Onin wars.

1483   Construction of the Ginkakuji by Yoshimasa.

1488   Seizure of power in the provinces of Kaga and Echizen by members of the Shinshu sect.

1506   Death of the painter-monk Sesshu.

1543   (or 1542) Arrival of the Portuguese at Tanegashima and the introduction of firearms.

1549   Arrival of St. Francis Xavier in Kyushu and the start of the Christian missionary movement by the Jesuits.

1557   Destruction of the Ouchi family by Mori Motonari.

1568–1600   PERIOD OF NATIONAL REUNIFICATION

1568   Seizure of Kyoto by Oda Nobunaga.

1571   Start of Nagasaki as the main port of foreign trade; destruction by Nobunaga of the military might of the Enryakuji on Mt. Hiei.

1573   End of the Ashikaga shogunate.

1576   Transfer of Nobunaga to Azuchi castle on Lake Biwa.

1578   Conversion of Otomo Yoshishige (Sorin) of North Kyushu, the first great daimyo to become a Christian.

1580   Surrender of Osaka castle by the Shinshu sect to Nobunaga.

1582   Assassination of Nobunaga; start of cadastral surveys by Hideyoshi.

1583   Reconstruction of Osaka castle by Hideyoshi.

1585   Appointment of Hideyoshi as *Kampaku*.

1586   Hideyoshi granted surname of Toyotomi.

1587   Submission of the Shimazu family of Satsuma to Hideyoshi; promulgation of a decree ordering the expulsion of Christian missionaries.

1588   Confiscation ordered of the weaponry of the peasants (Hideyoshi's "sword hunt").

1590   Destruction of the Hojo family of Odawara in the Kanto and the establishment of Tokugawa Ieyasu at Edo as lord of the Kanto.

1592   Invasion of Korea; start of missionary activity by Spanish Franciscans.

1593   Truce with Chinese armies in Korea.

1597   Resumption of the Korean campaign; first executions of European missionaries and Japanese converts.

1598   Death of Hideyoshi and withdrawal from Korea.

1600   Victory of Ieyasu at the battle of Sekigahara.

1600–1867 TOKUGAWA PERIOD

1603   Assumption of the title of shogun by Ieyasu.

1605–1623   Shogunate of Hidetada (d. 1632).

1606   Completion of the reconstruction of Edo castle.

1609   Conquest of the Ryukyu Islands by the Shimazu of Satsuma; establishment of the Dutch trading post at Hirado.

1612   Resumption of the persecution of Christians.

1613   Establishment of the English trading post at Hirado.

1614   First siege of Osaka castle by Ieyasu.

1615   Second siege and capture of Osaka castle and the destruction of Hideyoshi's heirs; promulgation of the Laws for the Military Houses (Buke Shohatto).

1616   Death of Ieyasu.

1617   Building of the Nikko mausoleum.

1623–1651   Shogunate of Iemitsu.

1623   Abandonment by the English of their Hirado trading post.

1624   Ban on further contact with the Spanish.

1635   Formalization of the "alternate attendance" (*sankin-kotai*) system for "outer" (*tozama*) daimyo.

1636   Ban on Japanese travel abroad.

1637–1638   Shimabara rebellion.

1639   Expulsion of the Portuguese traders.

1641	Transfer of the Dutch traders from Hirado to Deshima in Nagasaki harbor.
1651–1680	Shogunate of Ietsuna.
1651	Plot against the shogunate by Yui Shosetsu.
1657	Great Edo fire.
1680–1709	Shogunate of Tsunayoshi.
1684	Assassination of the great councillor (*tairo*), Hotta Masayoshi.
1688–1704	Genroku year period.
1701–1703	Incident of the Forty-seven Ronin (*Chushingura*).
1703	Great Kanto earthquake.
1707	Last eruption of Mt. Fuji.
1716–1745	Shogunate of Yoshimune (d. 1751) of the Wakayama branch of the Tokugawa.
1720	Relaxation of the ban on the importation of Western books.
1725	Death of Arai Hakuseki, scholar and shogunal adviser under Ienobu (1709–1712).
1758	Punishment of Takenouchi Shikibu for teaching loyalist doctrines to the Kyoto courtiers.
1769–1786	Supremacy of Tanuma Okitsugu.
1779–1784	Stay of Titsingh in Japan.
1782	Compilation of the *Gunsho ruiji* (huge collection of early works).
1783	Eruption of Mt. Asama.
1787–1793	Supremacy of Matsudaira Sadanobu.
1792	Visit of the Russian Laxman to Hokkaido.
1798	Completion of the *Kojiki-den* by the Shinto scholar Motoori Norinaga (d. 1801).
1804	Visit of the Russian envoy Rezanov to Nagasaki.
1808	Visit to Nagasaki of British ship *Phaeton*.
1808–1809	Exploration of Sakhalin and Amur River by Mamiya Rinzo.

1811   Establishment of the Translation Bureau for Dutch Books.

1814   Founding of the Kurozumi sect of Shinto.

1823–1830   Siebold in Japan.

1830–1844   Tempo year period; Tempo reforms.

1837   Rice riots in Osaka led by the Confucian scholar Oshio Heihachiro; visit of the American ship *Morrison* to Edo Bay and Nagasaki.

1838   Founding of the Tenrikyo sect of Shinto.

1841–1843   Reforms of Mizuno Tadakuni (final retirement 1845).

1846   Visit of American Commodore Biddle to Uraga.

1849   Visit of the American Glynn to Nagasaki.

1853   Arrival of Commodore Matthew C. Perry at Uraga.

1854   Treaty of Kanagawa with the United States (March 31).

1856   Establishment of the Bansho Torishirabesho (Office for the Study of Barbarian Books); arrival of American Consul General Townsend Harris at Shimoda.

1858–1860   Supremacy of Ii Naosuke.

1858   Commercial treaty with the U.S. (July 29); founding of the future Keio University by Fukuzawa Yukichi.

1859   Execution of Yoshida Shoin of Choshu.

1860   Assassination of Ii Naosuke by Mito samurai; first embassy to the U.S.; death of Tokugawa Nariaki of the Mito branch.

1862   First embassy to Europe; assassination of the Englishman Richardson at Namamugi near Yokohama by Satsuma samurai; relaxation of the alternate attendance system.

1863   Visit of the shogun to Kyoto; bombardment of foreign vessels by Choshu forts at Shimonoseki; bombardment of Kagoshima, capital of Satsuma, by a British squadron; expulsion of Choshu forces from Kyoto.

1864   Bombardment of Shimonoseki forts by British, French, Dutch, and American ships.

1865   Imperial ratification of the foreign treaties.

1866–1867   Shogunate of Yoshinobu (Keiki, d. 1913).

1867   Enthronement of Mutsuhito (Meiji); return of power to the throne.

1868–1912   **MEIJI PERIOD**

1868   January 1, opening of Kobe and Osaka to foreign trade; January 3, resumption of rule by the emperor; April 6, emperor's Charter Oath; reception of the foreign envoys by the emperor; November 26, establishment of Tokyo (Edo) as the new capital.

1869   March 5, return of their domains by the daimyo of Satsuma, Choshu, Tosa, and Hizen; July 25, appointment of the daimyo as governors of their former fiefs.

1871   Abandonment of class distinctions; August 29, substitution of prefectures (*ken*) for feudal domains; November 20, departure of the Iwakura Mission.

1872   Opening of the railway between Tokyo and Yokohama.

1873   January 1, adoption of the Gregorian calendar; January 10, inauguration of universal military service; debate over an expedition against Korea; July 28, adoption of the new land tax system; September 13, return of the Iwakura Mission; founding of a political party by Itagaki Taisuke.

1874   February–April, revolt of Eto Shimpei in Saga; May, victory of the expeditionary force in Taiwan.

1875   May 7, agreement with Russia over the exchange of Sakhalin for the Kuril Islands; June 20, convening of the Assembly of Prefectural Governors.

1876   February 26, treaty with Korea; March 28, prohibition of carrying of swords by samurai; August 5, compulsory commutation of samurai pensions; October, uprisings in Kumamoto and Hagi (Choshu).

1877   February–September, Satsuma Rebellion; May 26, death of Kido Koin; founding of Tokyo University (reorganized in 1886 as Tokyo Imperial University).

1878   May 14, assassination of Okubo Toshimichi; July 22, law for elected prefectural assemblies; December 5, creation of the Army General Staff.

1879   April 4, incorporation of the Ryukyu Islands as Okinawa Prefecture.

1880   February 5, establishment of ward, town, and village assemblies.

1881   October 12, decree promising the convening of a national assembly in 1890; October, Jiyuto (Liberal party) organized under Itagaki; October 21, appointment of Matsukata Masayoshi as the finance minister and the inauguration of an economic retrenchment policy.

1882   Founding of a political party and Waseda University by Okuma Shigenobu; October 10, founding of the Bank of Japan.

1883   July 20, death of Iwakura Tomomi.

1884   July 7, creation of the peerage.

1885   April 18, Tientsin convention concerning Korea; December 22, adoption of the cabinet system with Ito Hirobumi as the first prime minister; December 26, civil service regulations.

1887   December 26, promulgation of the peace preservation ordinance.

1888   April 25, establishment of city assemblies and the reorganization of local governments; April 30, Kuroda Kiyotaka as prime minister; April 30, creation of the privy council (Sumitsuin).

1889   February 11, promulgation of the constitution; December 24, General Yamagata Aritomo as prime minister.

1890   July 1, first general election for the Diet (convened November 25); October 30, Imperial Rescript on Education.

1891   May 6, Matsukata as prime minister.

1892   August 8, Ito again prime minister.

1894   July 16, Aoki-Kimberley treaty to abolish British extraterritoriality in 1899; August 1, declaration of war on

China (Sino-Japanese War); November 22, capture of Port Arthur.

1895   February 12, capture of Wei-hai-wei; April 17, Treaty of Shimonoseki concluding the Sino-Japanese War; December 4, return of the Liaotung Peninsula after the intervention of Russia, France, and Germany.

1896   September 18, Matsukata again prime minister.

1897   March 29, adoption of the gold standard.

1898   June 30, Okuma and Itagaki cabinet of newly formed Kenseito party; November 8, Yamagata again prime minister.

1899   July 17, coming into effect of the revised treaties ending extraterritoriality.

1900   March 29, revision of the election laws; June 17–August 14, participation by Japanese forces in the capture of Taku, Tientsin, and Peking during the Boxer Uprising in China; September 13, founding of the Seiyukai by Ito; October 19, Ito again prime minister.

1901   June 2, General Katsura Taro as prime minister.

1902   January 30, signing of the Anglo-Japanese Alliance.

1904   February 9, attack on the Russian navy; February 10, declaration of war on Russia (Russo-Japanese War).

1905   January 1, surrender of Port Arthur; March 10, capture of Mukden; May 27–28, destruction of the Russian fleet in the Battle of Tsushima; September 5, conclusion of the Russo-Japanese War through the Treaty of Portsmouth; November 17, treaty of protection with Korea.

1906   January 7, Prince Saionji Kimmochi as prime minister; March 31, nationalization of the railways; November 26, founding of the South Manchurian Railway.

1908   February 18, Gentlemen's Agreement on Japanese emigration to the U.S.; July 14, Katsura again prime minister.

1909   October 26, assassination of Ito.

1910   August 22, annexation of Korea; September 30, creation of the government-general of Korea.

1911 August 30, Saionji again prime minister; end of the foreign restrictions on tariffs.

1912 July 30, death of Meiji emperor and succession of his son Yoshihito.

1912–1926 **TAISHO PERIOD**

1912 December 21–February 20, 1913, "Taisho political change" (*seihen*) ended with Admiral Yamamoto Gombei as prime minister.

1914 April 16, Okuma as prime minister; August 23, Japanese declaration of war on Germany; November 7, capture of Tsingtao.

1915 January 18, presentation of the Twenty-one Demands on China.

1916 October 9, General Terauchi as prime minister; October 10, formation of the Kenseikai.

1918 April 5, landing of Japanese forces at Vladivostok; August, rice riots; September 29, Hara Kei of the Seiyukai as prime minister.

1919 Height of great influenza epidemic; March 1, uprising in Korea; May 22, revision of the election laws.

1920 January 10, peace treaty with Germany; creation of the Japanese Mandate over the former German islands in the North Pacific.

1921 March–September, trip of Crown Prince Hirohito to Europe; November 4, assassination of Hara; November 12, start of the Washington Conference; November 13, Takahashi Korekiyo as prime minister; November 25, appointment of Hirohito as prince regent.

1922 June 12, Admiral Kato Tomosaburo as prime minister; October 25, final withdrawal from Vladivostok; November 30, signing of the agreement with China for the return of Kiaochow (Tsingtao).

1923 September 1, great Kanto earthquake; September 2, Yamamoto again prime minister.

1924   January 7, Kiyoura Keigo as prime minister; April 16, Exclusion Act by the United States banning Japanese immigration; June 11, Kato Takaaki of the Kenseikai as prime minister.

1925   March 27, elimination of four army divisions; May 5, adoption of universal manhood suffrage; April 22, peace preservation law.

1926   January 30, Wakatsuki Reijiro as prime minister; December 25, death of Taisho emperor and the accession of Hirohito.

1926–1989   SHOWA PERIOD

1927   April 20, General Tanaka Giichi of the Seiyukai as prime minister; April 21, bank crisis; May–June, armed intervention in Shantung; June 1, founding of the Minseito.

1928   February 20, first general election under universal manhood suffrage; March 15, mass arrest of Communists; April 10, banning of three "proletarian" parties; May 3–11, fighting at Tsinan in Shantung; June 4, bomb attack in Manchuria on Chang Tso-lin (d. June 21).

1929   July 2, Hamaguchi Osachi of the Minseito as prime minister.

1930   April 22, signing of the London Naval Treaty; November 14, wounding of Hamaguchi by terrorist (d. August 26, 1931).

1931   April 14, Wakatsuki of the Minseito again as prime minister; September 18, the Manchurian Incident; December 13, Inukai Tsuyoshi of the Seiyukai as prime minister; December 14, abandonment of the gold standard.

1932   January 28–March 3, Shanghai campaign; February 18, creation of Manchukuo; May 15, assassination of Inukai (5–15 Incident); May 26, Admiral Saito Makoto as prime minister; July 24, formation of the Social Mass party (Shakai Taishuto).

1933   February 24, adoption of the Lytton Report on Manchuria by the League of Nations; March 4, capture of the capital of Jehol in Inner Mongolia; May 10, disciplinary action against liberal professors at Kyoto Imperial University; July 11, discovery of the plot of the Shimpeitai ("God-Sent Troops").

1934   July 8, Admiral Okada Keisuke as prime minister.

1935   March 23, sale of the Chinese Eastern Railway by the Soviet Union to Manchukuo; July 16, reorganization of the army command aimed against the Kodoha faction; August 12, assassination of General Nagata; September 18, resignation of Professor Minobe Tatsukichi from the House of Peers; November 24, inauguration of the East Hopei Autonomous Regime in North China.

1936   February 20, general elections; February 26, assassinations and attempted coup d'etat (2–26 Incident); March 9, Hirota Koki as prime minister; November 25, Anti-Comintern Pact.

1937   February 2, General Hayashi Senjuro as prime minister; April 30, general elections; June 4, Prince Konoe Fumimaro as prime minister; July 7, outbreak of war with China; August 14, bombing of Shanghai by Chinese planes and the spread of the war to Central China; October 25, creation of the Cabinet Planning Office; November 8, end of the Shanghai campaign; December 12, bombing of the U.S. gunboat *Panay* on the Yangtze River; December 13, capture of Nanking.

1938   April 1, National Mobilization Law; July 11–August 10, battle with the Russians at Changkufeng in Manchuria; October 21, capture of Canton; October 27, capture of the Hankow area.

1939   January 5, Hiranuma Kiichiro as prime minister; April 28–July 11, fighting with the Russians at Nomonhan in Mongolia; July 27, denunciation of the 1911 trade treaty by the U.S. (effective in six months); August 30, General Abe Nobuyuki as prime minister; September 1, outbreak of World War II in Europe.

1940   January 16, Admiral Yonai Mitsumasa as prime minister; March 30, creation of the puppet Wang Ching-wei regime in Nanking; July 6–August 15, dissolution of the political parties; July 22, Konoe again prime minister; September 23, entrance of Japanese forces into northern French Indochina; September 26, embargo by the U.S. on scrap iron shipments; September 27, Tripartite Alliance with Germany and Italy; October 12, inauguration of the Imperial Rule Assistance Association; November 24, death of Saionji.

1941   April 13, Soviet-Japanese neutrality pact; June 22, German invasion of the Soviet Union; July 24, occupation by Japan of southern Indochina; July 26, freezing of Japanese assets by the U.S.; August 1, American licensing system for oil shipments to Japan; October 18, General Tojo Hideki as prime minister; December 7, attack on Pearl Harbor and start of the Pacific War.

1942   February 15, capture of Singapore; March 9, surrender of Java; May 6, surrender of Corregidor (Philippines); May 7–8, battle of the Coral Sea; June 4–6, battle of Midway; August 7–February 7, 1943, Guadalcanal campaign; September 17–25, checking of the Japanese advance in New Guinea; November 1, creation of the Greater East Asia Ministry.

1943   November 21–25, capture of Tarawa.

1944   June 15–July 7, Saipan campaign; July 22, General Koiso Kuniaki as prime minister; October 20, American landing in the Philippines; November 24, start of B-29 bombings of Japan.

1945   February 26, fall of Manila; February 19–March 17, Iwo Jima campaign; March 10 and May 24–25, great firebomb raids on Tokyo; April 1–June 21, Okinawa campaign; April 7, Admiral Suzuki Kantaro as prime minister; May 8, German surrender; July 26, Potsdam Proclamation; August 6 and 9, atomic bombings of Hiroshima and Nagasaki; August 8, Soviet entrance into the war; August 14, acceptance of terms of the Potsdam Proclamation; August 17, Prince Higashikuni as prime minister; September 2, formal surrender received by General Douglas MacArthur; October 4, release of political prisoners ordered; October 9, Shidehara

Kijuro (later of the Progressive party) as prime minister; December 15, disestablishment of Shinto; December 27, Moscow Agreement creating the Far Eastern Commission and the Allied Council for Japan.

1946   January 1, emperor's denial of his own divinity; January 4, first purge directive; April 10, first postwar elections; May 22, Yoshida Shigeru of the Liberal party as prime minister; October 21, enactment of the land reform law.

1947   February 1, banning of a general strike; April 25, general elections; May 3, new constitution goes into effect; May 24, Katayama Tetsu of the Socialist party as prime minister; December 18, enactment of the economic deconcentration law.

1948   March 10, Ashida Hitoshi of the Democratic party as prime minister; October 15, Yoshida again prime minister; December 23, execution of Tojo and six other major war criminals.

1949   January 23, general elections; April 15, report of Joseph M. Dodge on budgetary retrenchment; exchange rate of 360 yen to the dollar; May 12, end of reparations removals.

1950   April 6, appointment of John Foster Dulles to negotiate the peace treaty; June 6 and 7, Communist purges; June 25, invasion of South Korea by North Korea; August 10, National Police Reserve ordinance.

1951   April 11, dismissal of MacArthur, appointment of General Matthew B. Ridgway as SCAP; June 20, lifting of purge restrictions on 69,000 persons; September 8, signing of the peace treaty with 48 nations and the security treaty with the U.S. at San Francisco; October 24, split of the Socialist party.

1952   February 28, signing of an administrative agreement on terms for the U.S. bases in Japan; April 28, peace treaty goes into effect; May 1, anti-American riots in Tokyo; September 18, Soviet Union vetoes Japanese admission to the United Nations; October 1, general elections; October 15, National Police Reserve reorganized as the National Security Force.

1953   April 19, general elections; July 27, cease-fire in Korea; December 24, U.S. agrees to return Amami Islands to Japan.

1954   March 1, *No. 5 Fukuryu-maru* involved in Bikini nuclear fallout; July 1, National Security Force reorganized as the Self-Defense Forces under the Defense Agency; November 5, peace treaty and reparations agreement signed with Burma; December 10, Hatoyama Ichiro of the Democratic party as prime minister.

1955   February 27, general elections; August 6, first Ban the Atom Bomb World Conference held in Hiroshima; September 10, Japan joins GATT; September 13, start of Sunakawa (Tachikawa Air Base) struggles; October 13, reunification of the left and right Socialists; November 15, founding of the Liberal Democratic party.

1956   April 5, Hatoyama elected first president of the Liberal Democratic party; May 9, Philippine reparations agreement; July 8, first election of members of the upper house by the Soka Gakkai; October 19, joint statement normalizing relations with the Soviet Union; December 18, Japan admitted into the United Nations; December 23, Ishibashi Tanzan as prime minister.

1957   February 25, Kishi Nobusuke as prime minister; December 6, signing of a treaty of commerce with the Soviet Union.

1958   January 20, reparations agreement with Indonesia; May 2, Chinese Communist flag incident in Nagasaki leading to breakoff of trade relations with Japan; May 22, general elections.

1959   March 9, Asanuma Inejiro, secretary general of the Socialist party, declares in Peking that U.S. is common enemy of Japan and China; April 10, the crown prince marries a commoner; August 13, agreement for the repatriation of Koreans to North Korea.

1960   January 19, signing of the Treaty of Mutual Security and Cooperation with the United States; January 24, founding of the Democratic Socialist party; May 19–

20, treaty ratification pushed through; June 15, giant antitreaty demonstration resulting in the death of a girl student; June 16, cancellation of the visit of President Eisenhower; June 19, automatic ratification of the treaty; July 19, Ikeda Hayato as prime minister; September 5, announcement of the income-doubling plan; October 12, Asanuma assassinated; November 1, settlement of the Miike coal mine strike; November 20, general elections.

1961   June 10, agreement on the repayment to the United States of the GARIOA debts (economic assistance during the occupation period); November 2–4, first meeting in Hakone of the cabinet level U.S.–Japan Committee on Trade and Economic Affairs.

1962   January 25–31, first U.S.–Japan Cultural Conference.

1963   November 21, general elections.

1964   April 28, Japan admitted into the OECD (Organization for Economic Cooperation and Development); October 1, opening of the "New Mainline" railway (Shinkansen); October 10–24, Tokyo Olympic Games; November 9, Sato Eisaku as prime minister; November 12, first visit of an American nuclear-powered submarine; November 17, founding of the Komeito by the Soka Gakkai.

1965   June 22, signing of the normalization agreement with South Korea; July 23, loss of a Liberal Democratic majority in the Tokyo Assembly election; August 19–21, first postwar visit of a prime minister (Sato) to Okinawa; December 11, ratification of the South Korean normalization agreement.

1966   August 22, Asian Development Bank instituted.

1967   January 29, general elections; April 15, local elections in which Minobe Ryokichi, supported by the Socialists, is elected governor of Tokyo.

1968   January 19–23, U.S. nuclear-powered aircraft carrier *Enterprise* visits Sasebo; February 1, approval given by the U.S. for the election of the Okinawan chief executive; April 5, agreement for the return of the Bonin

Islands (returned June 26); October 17, Nobel Prize for literature awarded Kawabata Yasunari; November 10, Yara Chobyo, a leftist, elected chief executive of Okinawa.

1969   January 18–19, riot police evict leftist students from Tokyo University buildings; May 26, completion of the Tokyo-Kobe Expressway; July 25, first enunciation of the Guam Doctrine, later called the Nixon Doctrine; August 3, passage of the University Reform Law; November 21, Sato–Nixon communiqué announcing the reversion of Okinawa within a few years; December 27, general elections.

1970   March 15, opening of the World Exposition in Osaka; March 31, hijacking to North Korea of a Japan Air Lines jet; May 3, announcement of the complete separation of Komeito from the Soka Gakkai; June 23, expiration of the ten-year term for the Japan–U.S. Security Treaty; October 29, Sato reelected to an unprecedented fourth term as president of the Liberal Democratic party; November 25, suicide of the novelist Mishima Yukio.

1971   February 27, start of the compulsory expropriation of land for the new Narita Airport; July 15, first "Nixon shock" of forthcoming presidential visit to China; August 15, second "Nixon shock" of 10 percent surcharge on imports into the U.S. and nonconvertibility of the dollar; October 15, Japan formally accepts new "voluntary" textile quotas; December 20, agreement on the revaluation of the yen 16.88 percent upward against the dollar (308 to the dollar); Sato formulates the three nuclear principles.

1972   February 3, opening of the Winter Olympic Games at Sapporo; May 15, Okinawa reverts to Japan as the 47th prefecture; May 30, attack by Japanese student terrorists on passengers at the Tel Aviv airport in Israel; July 6, Tanaka Kakuei as prime minister; October 2, creation of the Japan Foundation; September 29, formal recognition of the People's Republic of China; December 10, general elections.

1973   February 15, revaluation upward of the yen by 16.67 percent against the dollar (264 to the dollar); August 8, abduction in Japan of Kim Dae Jung, Korean opposition political leader; November 14, opening of the Kammon Bridge (between Honshu and Kyushu); December 8, decision to locate the headquarters of the United Nations University in Tokyo; November–December, impact on Japan of the shock of the Arab oil crisis; inauguration of national pollution control measures.

1974   January 15–16, riots in Indonesia during Tanaka's visit; March 9, surrender of Lt. Onoda in the Philippines; March 15, completion of the Kammon Tunnel; April 11, transport and communications strike of 6 million workers; April 20, China-Japan air agreement signed and Japanese flights banned by Taiwan in retaliation; June 26, establishment of the National Land Agency; July 7, Liberal Democrats retain a narrow majority in upper house elections; August 15, shooting of the wife of President Park Chung Hee of Korea by a Korean youth from Japan; September 1, nuclear leak on the experimental nuclear-powered ship *Mutsu;* October 6–13, revelation by retired American Rear Admiral Gene LaRoque that U.S. naval vessels carry nuclear weapons in Japanese waters; October 10, allegations of corruption by the magazine *Bungei Shunju* against Prime Minister Tanaka; November 18–22, visit by President Gerald Ford to Japan; December 9, Miki Takeo as prime minister; December 10, Sato awarded the Nobel Peace Prize.

1975   March 10, the Shinkansen extended to Fukuoka; July 4, passage of the Political Funds Control Law; July 20, start of the International Ocean Exposition in Okinawa; October 2–13, visit by the emperor and empress to the U.S.; November 15–17, first summit meeting of the leaders of the six major industrial democracies at Rambouillet near Paris.

1976   February 2–4, revelation in U.S. Senate subcommittee hearings of scandals connected with the sale of Lockheed planes to Japan; May 4, Chisso executives indicted in the first criminal proceedings for pollution (Minamata case); May 24, ratification of the Nuclear Nonproliferation Treaty (signed February 1970); June 25, forming of the New Liberal Club by Kono Yohei; July 8, start of the Japan–U.S. Subcommittee for Defense Cooperation; July 22, completion of reparation payments with the final payments to the Philippines; July 27, arrest of Tanaka in connection with the Lockheed scandals; December 5, general elections; December 24, Fukuda Takeo as prime minister.

1977   March 26, Eda Saburo deserts the Socialists to form a new party (d. May 22); May 8, major clash at Narita Airport, with one fatality; July 10, upper house elections leave the Liberal Democrats with a majority of only 4; August 16–18, Fukuda's tour of Southeast Asia and promises of increased aid; November 28, appointment of Ushiba Nobuhiko, a former foreign ministry bureaucrat, to a cabinet post to supervise trade problems with U.S.; December 13, Asukata Ichiro chosen chairman of the Socialist party.

1978   May 20, opening of Narita Airport; October 17, enshrinement of fourteen class A "war criminals" in the Yasukuni Shrine; October 31, fall of the dollar to 175.5 yen before rising again to over 200; November 26, victory of Ohira Masayoshi in the first Liberal Democratic party primaries for party president; December 5, agreement with the U.S. for the increase of beef and citrus imports; December 7, Ohira as prime minister.

1979   January 13, first uniform national university entrance examinations; April 8 and 22, conservative victories in local elections and the recovery of the governorship of Tokyo after twelve years of Minobe's incumbency; April 22, Chisso executives found criminally responsible in the Minamata pollution case; June 24–27, President Jimmy Carter visits Japan; June 28–29, fifth summit meeting of the seven major industrial democracies held in Tokyo; July 1, 30 percent increase in oil prices;

July 25–26, director general of the defense agency visits South Korea; October 7, general elections; October 26, assassination of the Korean president, Park Chung Hee; November 8, appointment of the economist Okita Saburo as foreign minister in a reorganized Ohira cabinet; November 27, Komeito officially announces its support of the Security Treaty with the U.S.; December 27, Soviet invasion of Afghanistan increases world tensions.

1980   January 15–20, Ohira tours the West Pacific nations speaking of a Pacific Rim grouping; May 1, Ohira visits Washington; May 16, lower house votes nonconfidence in Ohira and he dissolves it; May 22, Asukata announces dropping of Socialists' opposition to the Security Treaty and Self-Defense Forces; June 12, death of Ohira from heart attack; June 22, LDP wins strong majorities in elections in both houses; July 9, President Carter attends Ohira's memorial service in Tokyo; July 17, Suzuki Zenko as prime minister; September, outbreak of Iran-Iraq war.

1981   May 1, Japan agrees to self-restraint on car exports to U.S. to 1,680,000 units in fiscal 1981; May 7–8, Suzuki visits Washington and confirms with President Ronald Reagan "alliance relationship" between the two countries; May 12, Suzuki "clarifies" this statement and foreign minister resigns on May 15; May 17, former U.S. Ambassador Edwin Reischauer's statement that American nuclear weapons pass through Japanese waters stirs up large controversy; May 27, most of budget frozen except for defense, foreign aid, and energy development; June 10–13, working-level defense consultations with the U.S. in Hawaii; July 21, Soviet Union and Japan block ban on whaling; August 15, Suzuki and eighteen cabinet members visit Yasukuni Shrine; December 1, Komeito chairman Takeiri Yoshikatsu says party recognizes Self-Defense Forces as constitutional.

1982   January 30, announcement of removal of sixty-seven nontariff barriers (more added May 28); March 13,

Tokyo Stock Exchange opened to foreign firms; March 26, U.S. Secretary of Defense Casper Weinberger calls for 1,000-mile radius of defense by Japan (accepted by Japan September 14); March 28, mass demonstrations at Narita Airport; March 29, 342 victims of PCB poisoning awarded 2.48 billion yen damages; June 8, two former cabinet members sentenced in Lockheed scandal; June 23, service started on Northeast (Tohoku) Shinkansen from Omiya (Tokyo) to Morioka; July 26, China protests wording of Japanese textbooks (agreement reached September 9); August 7, U.S. brings complaint on restrictions on baseball bats to GATT; August 16, revision of upper house elections passed; October 4–7, yen falls to 276 to dollar, lowest since June 8, 1977; October 12, Suzuki resigns as LDP president; November 24, Nakasone Yasuhiro wins party presidential primary; November 26, Nakasone elected prime minister.

1983   January 11–12, Nakasone visits President Chun Doo Hwan in South Korea and promises 4 billion dollars in economic aid; January 17–21, Nakasone visits Washington and declares Japan an unsinkable aircraft carrier; April 15, Tokyo Disneyland opened; April 21, Nakasone visits Yasukuni Shrine in his capacity as prime minister; August 6, Nakasone reasserts three nuclear principles; September 1, Korean Airlines jet with 269 persons on board shot down by Soviets over Sakhalin; October 12, Tanaka sentenced to four years in prison and fines over Lockheed scandal; October 21, package of economic measures to reduce trade surplus; November 9–12, Reagan visits Japan and is first U.S. president to address the Diet; December 18, in general election LDP falls from 286 to 250 seats and needs addition of nine independents to gain majority.

1984   April 12, Nikaido Susumu succeeds Tanaka as faction head and becomes vice president of LDP; June 13, All Nippon Airways (ANA) permitted to fly to Hawaii, later to Washington; June 25–27, Japan–U.S. working-level consultations on defense of Hokkaido;

August 3, privatization of Tobacco and Salt Public Corporation; September 5, first meeting of prime minister's Ad Hoc Committee on Education; September 6–8, Chun Doo Hwan makes first visit of Korean president to Japan; November 1, first woman cabinet member in twenty-two years; November 1, Fukuzawa Yukichi, Nitobe Inazo, and Natsume Soseki become chief figures on bank notes; November 4, housewives coalition in Zushi elects mayor opposing U.S. military housing.

1985   February 7, Takeshita Noboru founds Diet "study group" to lay base for leadership of Tanaka faction; February 27, Tanaka hospitalized with cerebral apoplexy; March 15, Mikhail Gorbachev named secretary general of Communist party in the Soviet Union; April 1, privatization of Nippon Telegraph and Telephone Corporation; May 17, bill for equal opportunities in employment for men and women passed; June 8, Naruto and Awaji bridges across Inland Sea opened to traffic; August 12–13, crash of Boeing 747 with 524 on board; July 17, Supreme Court rules distribution of seats in lower house of Diet unconstitutional; September 18, defense budget set at 1.04 percent of GNP.

1986   March 3 and 24, conservationist women win election victories in Zushi; March 11, appeal on Ienaga Saburo textbook case denied and case finally closed; March 28, radicals shoot five home made rockets into imperial palace and American embassy grounds; April 1, Equal Employment Opportunity Law goes into effect; April 4–6, group of seven finance ministers created at Tokyo summit; May 6–12, dollar sinks to 160.2 yen; July 6, LDP wins 300 seats in revised 512-seat lower house, gaining biggest margin since December 1969; July 14, Abe Shintaro succeeds to leadership of Fukuda faction; July 22, Nakasone elected party president for third term; July 28–30, South Koreans and Chinese demand apology for revisions in Japanese textbooks; August 15, Nakasone abstains from annual visit to the Yasukuni Shrine; August 15, New Liberal Club dis-

bands; September 6, Doi Takako selected as first female secretary general of Socialist party; September 8,
Nakasone dismisses education minister Fujio Masayuki
for disparaging remarks about Koreans; September 22,
Nakasone makes insulting remarks about American
minorities, apologizes September 26.

1987   January 19, dollar sinks to 150 yen; March 27, stopgap
budget adopted because of opposition to proposed
value-added tax; April 1, Japanese National Railroad
splits into eleven private railroads, six of them major
passenger carriers; April 12 and 26, LDP loses heavily
in local elections because of proposed value-added tax;
April 23, budget passes with value-added tax dropped;
May 1, record trade surplus of 101.4 billion dollars;
July 1, chairman and president of Toshiba resigns because small subsidiary sold to Soviet Union propeller
milling machine on banned COCOM list (Coordinating
Committee for Export Controls); July 9, U.S. suspends
Toshiba import license in retaliation; July 4, rice support prices cut for first time in thirty-one years; July 4,
secession of 113 members of Tanaka faction under
Takeshita; August 27, five homemade rockets fired into
palace grounds; September 3, three private companies
break Nippon Telegraph and Telephone monopoly;
October 19, New York stock crash followed by large
fall in Tokyo Stock Exchange; October 30, Takeshita
selected party president with backing of Nakasone and
elected prime minister on November 6; November 3–4,
Japan agrees to U.S. participation in construction of
Kansai Airport; November 10, Nippon Telegraph and
Telephone sells public stocks for first time; November
17, Japan Air Lines is privatized; December 4, Doi
reelected secretary general of Socialist party; December, dollar sinks to around 125 yen.

1988   February 25, Takeshita attends inauguration of President Roh Tae Woo of South Korea; March 7, Honda
ships first American-built Japanese cars to Japan;
March 13, Seikan Tunnel between Honshu and Hokkaido begins service; April 15, the Soviet Union agrees

to withdraw from Afghanistan; June 26, Uno Sosuki is first foreign minister to visit Jerusalem, urges end of "inhuman acts" toward Arabs and pullout of occupied areas by Israel; July, scandal over insider trading in stocks of real estate subsidiary of Recruit Company starts persistent criticism of Takeshita, Nakasone, and other top politicians because this is considered disguised political contributions; August 12, Takeshita sends letter of apology to American Congressional Black Caucus over slurring remarks by chairman of LDP Policy Board; August 20, a cease-fire goes into effect in the Iran-Iraq war; September 19, the emperor falls seriously ill and his death is expected imminently; November, dollar slides to around 121 yen; November 29, Japan and U.S. agree on joint production of a fighter based on the F-16; December 9, Miyazawa Kiichi, finance minister and deputy prime minister resigns because of implication in Recruit stock scandal.

1989   January 1, the American-Canadian free-trade zone goes into effect; January 7, emperor Hirohito dies and his son Akihito succeeds.

1989–   ## HEISEI PERIOD

1989   February 24, the new American President, George Bush, attends Hirohito's funeral; April 28, new budget rammed through after being delayed past April 1 deadline by Recruit scandal; April 28, United States and Japan agree on joint production of FSX fighter planes for Air Self-Defense Force; May 25, the United States labels Japan an "unfair trader"; June 2, Takeshita resigns as prime minister and is succeeded by Uno Sosuke; June 2, American dollar at about 140 yen.

BIBLIOGRAPHICAL
NOTE

Before World War II there were few good books on Japan in English, and large areas of its history and culture were scarcely covered at all, but in recent decades books have been pouring from the presses in torrents, making it difficult to choose from among them the few most worthy of being selected for this "Bibliographical Note." Better this embarrassment of riches than the desert of information that existed not so long ago. I have listed here some of the more significant and readable books. Most of them contain bibliographies, which will lead the reader still further into the various aspects of the subjects they treat. I have cited paperback editions of the books where possible.

A somewhat more detailed general history of Japan than this present volume is to be found in *Japan: Tradition and Transformation* (Houghton Mifflin, 1989) by Albert M. Craig and myself. It consists of the Japanese sections, with some amplifications, of a much larger work, *East Asia: Tradition and Transformation* (Houghton Mifflin, 1973 and 1989), by John K. Fairbank, Edwin O. Reischauer, and Albert M. Craig, in which the chapters on China and Korea afford a useful background for the study of Japan. A classic on the premodern history of Japan is G. B. Sansom's *Japan: A Short Cultural History* (revised edition, Appleton-Century-Crofts, 1962), which is delightfully written and full of illuminating insights. More institutional approaches are to be found in John Whitney Hall, *Japan: From Premodern History to Modern Times* (Delacorte Press, 1968) and his

Government and Local Power in Japan 500–1700: A Study Based on Bizen Province (Princeton, 1966). Sir George Sansom's three-volume series, which appeared under the overall title of *A History of Japan* (Stanford, 1958–1963), gives a much more detailed treatment of premodern history than does any of the above books. There is also Bradley Smith's gorgeous *Japan: A History in Art* (Simon and Schuster, 1964). A general treatment of Japanese history in brief, together with more detailed considerations of its modern society, politics, economics, and international relations, is to be found in my *The Japanese Today: Change and Continuity* (Harvard, 1988).

There is a host of fine books on Japanese art too numerous to attempt to list and an equal abundance of excellent translations of Japanese literature, ranging from the earliest classics to such recent or contemporary authors as Natsume Soseki, Tanizaki Junichiro, Kawabata Yasunari, Mishima Yukio, Abe Kobo, and Oe Kenzaburo. Special mention should be made of the beautiful translation of Japan's greatest literary work, *The Tale of Genji*, by Arthur Waley, and his *Pillow Book of Lady Sei Shonagon* and *Noh Plays of Japan*, all of which are available in paperback through Doubleday. A more accurate version of *The Tale of Genji* with equal literary merit to that of Waley has more recently been produced by Edward G. Seidensticker (Knopf, 1977).

Sources of the Japanese Tradition (Columbia, 1958) is a most useful compendium of translations of primary historical sources, with excellent introductory materials, compiled by William Theodore de Bary, Donald Keene, and Ryusaku Tsunoda. Mention should also be made of Keene's *Anthology of Japanese Literature from the Earliest Era to the Mid-Nineteenth Century* (Grove, 1955), and *Dawn to the West: Japanese Literature in the Modern Era* (Holt, Rinehart and Winston, 1984).

Particularly large numbers of books have been published on Japanese business and economics in recent years. I have been forced to limit myself to only a very small sampling of these. They are included below with some of the other outstanding works on Japanese history, politics, and society, all arranged in roughly chronological order according to the period of Japanese history with which they deal.

DONALD L. PHILIPPI, tr., *Kojiki* (Princeton, 1960).
ROBERT BORGEN, *Sugawara no Michizane and the Early Heian Court,* (Harvard, 1986).

WILLIAM WAYNE FARRIS, *Population, Disease, and Land in Early Japan* (Harvard, 1985).

PETER DUUS, *Feudalism in Japan* (Knopf, 1976).

JEFFERY P. MASS, *Warrior Government in Early Medieval Japan: A Study of the Kamakura Bakufu, Shugo, and Jito* (Yale, 1974).

HELEN CRAIG MCCULLOUGH, tr., *The Taiheiki: A Chronicle of Medieval Japan* (Columbia, 1959).

JOHN W. HALL AND TOYODA TAKESHI, eds., *Japan in the Muromachi Age* (California, 1977).

JOHN W. HALL AND JEFFERY P. MASS, eds., *Medieval Japan: Essays in Institutional History* (Yale, 1974).

MARTIN COLCUTT, *Five Mountains: The Zen Monastic Institution in Medieval Japan* (Harvard, 1980).

H. PAUL VARLEY, *The Onin War* (Columbia, 1967).

MASAYOSHI SUGIMOTO AND DAVID L. SWAIN, *Science and Culture in Traditional Japan* A.D. *600–1854* (MIT, 1978).

C. R. BOXER, *The Christian Century in Japan, 1549–1650* (California, 1967).

GEORGE ELISON, *Deus Destroyed: The Image of Christianity in Early Modern Japan* (Harvard, 1974).

JOHN WHITNEY HALL, KEIJI NAGAHARA, AND KOZO YAMAMURA, eds., *Japan Before Tokugawa: Political Consolidation and Economic Growth* (Princeton, 1981).

MARY ELIZABETH BERRY, *Hideyoshi* (Harvard, 1982).

GEORGE ELISON AND BARDWELL L. SMITH, *Warlords, Artists, and Commoners* (Hawaii, 1981).

HERMAN OOMS, *Tokugawa Ideology: Early Constructs, 1570–1680* (Princeton, 1985).

JEFFERY P. MASS AND WILLIAM B. HAUSER, eds., *The Bakufu in Japanese History* (Stanford, 1985).

THOMAS C. SMITH, *Native Sources of Japanese Industrialization* (California, 1988).

ROBERT N. BELLAH, *Tokugawa Religion: The Values of Pre-Industrial Japan* (The Free Press, 1957).

SHIGERU MATSUMOTO, *Mootori Norinaga, 1730–1801* (Harvard, 1970).

JOHN WHITNEY HALL AND MARIUS B. JANSEN, *Studies in the Institutional History of Early Modern Japan* (Princeton, 1968).

R. P. DORE, *Education in Tokugawa Japan* (California, 1965).

THOMAS C. SMITH, *The Agrarian Origins of Modern Japan* (Stanford, 1970).

C. D. SHELDON, *The Rise of the Merchant Class in Tokugawa Japan, 1600–1868* (Locust Valley, N.Y., 1958).

CONRAD TOTMAN, *Politics in the Tokugawa Bakufu, 1600–1843* (Harvard, 1967).

W. G. BEASLEY, *The Modern History of Japan* (St. Martin's, 1981).

HUGH BORTON, *Japan's Modern Century* (Ronald Press, 1970).

PETER DUUS, *The Rise of Modern Japan* (Houghton Mifflin, 1976).

RICHARD STORRY, *A History of Modern Japan* (Penguin, 1974).

MARIUS B. JANSEN AND GILBERT ROZMAN, eds., *Japan in Transition: From Tokugawa to Meiji* (Princeton, 1986).

HARRY WRAY AND HILARY CONROY, eds., *Japan Examined: Perspectives on Modern Japanese History* (Hawaii, 1983).

BOB TADASHI WAKABAYASHI, *Anti-Foreignism and Western Learning in Early Modern Japan: The New Theses of 1825* (Harvard, 1986).

W. G. BEASLEY, *The Meiji Restoration* (Stanford, 1973).

ALBERT M. CRAIG, *Choshu in the Meiji Restoration* (Harvard, 1961).

MARIUS B. JANSEN, *Sakamoto Ryoma and the Meiji Restoration* (Princeton, 1961).

EIICHI KIYOOKA, tr., *The Autobiography of Yukichi Fukuzawa* (Columbia, 1966).

CARMEN BLACKER, *The Japanese Enlightenment: A Study of the Writings of Fukuzawa Yukichi* (Cambridge, 1964).

E. H. NORMAN, *Japan's Emergence as a Modern State* (Institute of Pacific Relations, 1940).

JOHN W. DOWER, ed., *Origins of the Modern Japanese State: Selected Writings of E. H. Norman* (Pantheon, 1975).

GEORGE SANSOM, *The Western World and Japan* (Knopf, 1950).

WILLIAM R. BRAISTED, *Meiroku Zasshi: Journal of the Japanese Enlightenment* (Harvard, 1976).

J. HIRSCHMEIER, *The Origins of Entrepreneurship in Japan* (Harvard, 1964).

MARIUS P. JANSEN, ed., *Changing Japanese Attitudes toward Modernization* (Princeton, 1965).

R. P. DORE, ed., *Aspects of Social Change in Modern Japan* (Princeton, 1967).

DONALD H. SHIVELY, ed., *Tradition and Modernization in Japanese Culture* (Princeton, 1971).

WILLIAM W. LOCKWOOD, ed., *The State and Economic Enterprise in Japan* (Princeton, 1965).

ROBERT E. WARD, ed., *Political Development in Modern Japan* (Princeton, 1968).

ROBERT A. SCALAPINO, *Democracy and the Party Movement in Prewar Japan* (California, 1953).

GEORGE AKITA, *Foundations of Constitutional Government in Modern Japan* (Harvard, 1967).

ROGER F. HACKETT, *Yamagata Aritomo in the Rise of Modern Japan 1838–1922* (Harvard, 1971).

IVAN HALL, *Mori Arinori* (Harvard, 1973).

ALBERT M. CRAIG, ed., *Japan: A Comparative View* (Princeton, 1979).

JOSEPH PITTAU, *Political Thought in Early Meiji Japan* (Harvard, 1967).

IRWIN SCHEINER, *Christian Converts and Social Protest in Japan* (California, 1970).

JOHANNES SIEMES, *Hermann Roesler and the Making of the Meiji State* (Tuttle, 1968).

TETSUO NAJITA, *Hara Kei and the Politics of Compromise 1905–1915* (Harvard, 1967).

PETER DUUS, *Party Rivalry and Political Change in Taisho Japan* (Harvard, 1967).

ALBERT M. CRAIG AND DONALD H. SHIVELY, eds., *Personality in Japanese History* (California, 1970).

ROBERT M. SPAULDING, *Imperial Japan's Higher Civil Service Examinations* (Princeton, 1967).

WILLIAM W. LOCKWOOD, *The Economic Development of Japan: Growth and Structural Change, 1868–1938* (Princeton).

RUTH BENEDICT, *The Chrysanthemum and the Sword* (Meridian World).

HENRY SMITH, *Japan's First Student Radicals* (Harvard, 1972).

AKIRA IRIYE, *After Imperialism: The Search for a New Order in the Far East, 1921–1931* (Princeton, 1965).

TATSUO ARIMA, *The Failure of Freedom: A Portrait of the Modern Japanese Intellectual* (Harvard, 1969).

ROGER DINGMAN, *Power in the Pacific: The Origins of Naval Arms Limitations* (University of Chicago, 1976).

BYRON K. MARSHALL, *Capitalism and Nationalism in Prewar Japan: The Ideology of the Business Elite 1868–1941* (Stanford, 1967).

FRANK O. MILLER, *Minobe Tatsukichi, Interpreter of Constitutionalism in Japan* (California, 1965).

GEORGE O. TOTTEN, *The Social Democratic Movement in Prewar Japan* (Yale, 1966).

JAMES B. CROWLEY, *Japan's Quest for Autonomy: National Security and Foreign Policy, 1930–1938* (Princeton, 1966).

DAIKICHI IROKAWA (tr. and ed. by Marius B. Jansen), *The Culture of the Meiji Period* (Princeton, 1981).

CAROL GLUCK, *Japan's Modern Myths: Ideology in the Late Meiji Period* (Princeton, 1985).

ANDREW GORDON, *The Evolution of Labor Relations in Japan: Heavy Industry, 1853–1955* (Harvard, 1985).

HARU MATSUKATA REISCHAUER, *Samurai and Silk: A Japanese and American Heritage* (Harvard, 1986).

RAMON H. MYERS AND MARK R. PEATTIE, eds., *The Japanese Colonial Empire, 1895–1945* (Princeton, 1984).

DOROTHY BORG AND SHUMPEI OKAMOTO, eds., *Pearl Harbor as History* (Columbia, 1973).

HERBERT FEIS, *The Road to Pearl Harbor* (Princeton, 1950).

JOSEPH GREW, *Ten Years in Japan* (Simon and Schuster, 1944).

JON LIVINGSTON, JOE MOORE, AND FELICIA OLDFATHER, eds., *The Japan Reader: Imperial Japan 1800–1945* (Pantheon, 1973).

YALE C. MAXON, *Control of Japanese Foreign Policy: A Study of Civil-Military Rivalry* (California, 1957).

JAMES W. MORLEY, *Dilemmas of Growth in Prewar Japan* (Princeton, 1976).

RICHARD J. SMETHURST, *A Social Basis for Prewar Japanese Militarism: The Army and the Rural Community* (California, 1974).

THOMAS R. H. HAVENS, *Farm and Nation in Modern Japan: Agrarian Nationalism 1870–1940* (Princeton, 1974).

ROBERT J. C. BUTOW, *Tojo and the Coming of the War* (Princeton, 1961).

F. C. JONES, *Japan's New Order in East Asia* (Oxford, 1954).

JOHN TOLAND, *The Rising Sun: Decline and Fall of the Japanese Empire 1936–1945* (Random House, 1971).

THOMAS R. H. HAVENS, *Valley of Darkness: The Japanese People and World War Two* (Norton, 1978).

ROBERT J. BUTOW, *Japan's Decision to Surrender* (Stanford).

AKIRA IRIYE, *Power and Culture: The Japanese-American War, 1941–1945* (Harvard, 1981).

JOHN W. DOWER, *War Without Mercy: Race and Power in the Pacific War* (Pantheon Books, 1986).

KAZUO KAWAI, *Japan's American Interlude* (University of Chicago, 1960).

JOHN C. PERRY, *Beneath the Eagle's Wings: Americans in Occupied Japan* (Dodd, Mead, 1980).

EDWIN O. REISCHAUER, *The United States and Japan* (Compass).

MASATAKA KOSAKA, *100 Million Japanese: The Postwar Experience* (Kodansha, 1972).

ZBIGNIEW BRZEZINSKI, *Fragile Blossom: Crisis and Change in Japan* (Harper & Row, 1972).

JOHN EMERSON, *Arms, Yen and Power: The Japanese Dilemma* (Dunellen, 1971).

ROBERT C. WARD, *Japan's Political System* (Prentice-Hall, 1978).

J. A. A. STOCKWIN, *Divided Politics in a Growth Economy* (Norton, 1975).

JON LIVINGSTON, JOE MOORE, AND FELICIA OLDFATHER, eds., *The Japan Reader: Postwar Japan 1945 to the Present* (Pantheon, 1973).

T. J. PEMPEL, *Japan: The Dilemmas of Success* (Foreign Policy Association, 1986).

FRANK GIBNEY, *Japan: The Fragile Superpower* (New American Library, 1985).

ROBERT WARD AND YOSHIKAZU SAKAMOTO, eds., *Democratizing Japan* (Hawaii, 1987).

ROGER BUCKLEY, *Japan Today* (Cambridge University Press, 1985).

EZRA F. VOGEL, *Japan as No. 1: Lessons for America* (Harvard, 1979).

JARED TAYLOR, *Shadows on the Rising Sun: A Critical View of the Japanese Miracle* (Quill, 1983).

ARDATH W. BURKS, *Japan: A Postindustrial Society* (Westview, 1984).

KURT STEINER, *Local Government in Japan* (Stanford, 1965).

ARTHUR TAYLOR VON MEHREN, ed., *Law in Japan: The Legal Order in a Changing Society* (Harvard, 1963).

GEORGE R. PACKARD, *Protest in Tokyo: The Security Treaty Crisis of 1960* (Princeton, 1966).

NATHANIEL P. THAYER, *How the Conservatives Rule Japan* (Princeton, 1969).

HARUHIRO FUKUI, *Party in Power: The Japanese Liberal-Democrats and Policy-Making* (California, 1970).

GERALD CURTIS, *Election Campaigning Japanese Style* (Columbia, 1971).

ALLAN B. COLE, GEORGE O. TOTTEN, AND CECIL H. UYEHARA, *Socialist Parties in Postwar Japan* (Yale, 1966).

AKIRA KUBOTA, *Higher Civil Servants in Postwar Japan* (Princeton, 1969).

PAUL LANGER, *Communism in Japan* (California, 1972).

JOSEPH A. MASSEY, *Youth and Politics in Japan* (Lexington Books, 1976).

I. I. MORRIS, *Nationalism and the Right Wing in Japan* (Oxford, 1960).

T. J. PEMPEL, *Policy Making in Contemporary Japan* (Cornell, 1977).

ROBERT A. SCALAPINO, *The Japanese Communist Movement 1920–1966* (California, 1967).

J. W. DOWER, *Empire and Aftermath: Yoshida Shigeru and the Japanese Experience, 1878–1954* (Harvard, 1980).

GERALD L. CURTIS, *The Japanese Way of Politics* (Columbia, 1988).

BRADLEY M. RICHARDSON AND SCOTT C. FLANAGAN, *Politics in Japan* (Little, Brown, 1984).

RONALD J. HREBENAR, *The Japanese Party System: From One-Party Rule to Coalition Government* (Westview, 1986).

MARGARET A. MCKEAN, *Environmental Protest and Citizen Politics in Japan* (California, 1981).

STEVEN REED, *Japanese Prefectures and Policymaking* (University of Pittsburgh Press, 1986).

KURT STEINER, ELLIS S. KRAUSS, AND SCOTT C. FLANAGAN, eds., *Political Opposition and Local Politics in Japan* (Princeton, 1980).

KOZO YAMAMURA AND KOMAKICHI YASUBA, eds., *The Political Economy of Japan. Vol. I. The Domestic Transformation* (Stanford, 1987).

R. P. DORE, *Land Reform in Japan* (California, 1958).

EZRA F. VOGEL, *Japan's New Middle Class: The Salary Man and His Family in a Tokyo Suburb* (California, 1971).

KOZO YAMAMURA, *Economic Policy in Postwar Japan: Growth vs. Economic Democracy* (California, 1967).

JAMES C. ABEGGLEN, *Management and the Worker: The Japanese Solution* (Kodansha, 1973).

R. P. DORE, *British Factory, Japanese Factory: The Origins of National Diversity in Employment Relations* (California, 1973).

SHELDON GARON, *The State and Labor in Modern Japan* (California, 1987).

ROBERT CHRISTOPHER, *The Japanese Mind* (Faucett Columbine, 1984).

TADASHI FUKUTAKE, *Japanese Society Today* (Tokyo University Press, 1981).

TADASHI FUKUTAKE, *The Japanese Social Structure: Its Evolution in the Modern Century* (Tokyo University Press, 1982).

TAKEO DOI, *The Anatomy of Dependence* (Kodansha, 1971).

CHIE NAKANE, *Japanese Society* (California, 1970).

R. P. DORE, *City Life in Japan: A Study of a Tokyo Ward* (California, 1958).

R. P. DORE, *Shinohata: A Portrait of a Japanese Village* (Pantheon, 1978).

GAIL L. BERNSTEIN, *Haruko's World: A Japanese Farm Woman and Her Community* (Stanford, 1983).

HERBERT PASSIN, *Society and Education in Japan* (Columbia, 1965).

THOMAS P. ROHLEN, *Japan's High Schools* (California, 1983).

MERRY WHITE, *The Japanese Educational Challenge: A Commitment to Children* (The Free Press, 1987).

KOZO YAMAMURA, *Economic Policy in Postwar Japan: Growth vs. Economic Democracy* (California, 1967).

HUGH PATRICK AND HENRY ROSOVSKY, eds., *Asia's New Giant: How the Japanese Economy Works* (Brookings, 1976).

ELEANOR M. HADLEY, *Antitrust in Japan* (Princeton, 1970).

M. Y. YOSHINO, *Japan's Multinational Enterprises* (Harvard, 1976).

ROBERT E. COLE, *Japanese Blue Collar* (California, 1971).

KUNIO YOSHIHARA, *Japanese Economic Development: A Short Introduction* (Oxford University Press, 1979).

G. C. ALLEN, *The Japanese Economy* (St. Martin's, 1982).

CHALMERS JOHNSON, *MITI and the Japanese Miracle: The Growth of Industrial Policy, 1925–1975* (Stanford, 1982).

KUNIO YOSHIHARA, *Sogo Shosha: The Vanguard of the Japanese Economy* (Harvard, 1982).

RODNEY C. CLARK, *The Japanese Company* (Yale, 1979).

MICHAEL A. CUSUMANO, *The Japanese Automobile Industry: Technology and Management at Nissan and Toyota* (Harvard, 1985).

W. MARK FRUM, *Kikkoman Company, Clan, and Community* (Harvard, 1983).

THOMAS PEPPER AND MERIT E. JANOW, *The Competition: Dealing with Japan* (Praeger, 1983).

THOMAS K. MCCRAW, ed., *America versus Japan: A Comparative Study* (Harvard Business School Press, 1986).

DANIEL I. OKIMOTO, ed., *Japan's Economy: Coping with Change in the International Environment* (Westview, 1982).

ROBERT A. SCALAPINO, ed., *The Foreign Policy of Modern Japan* (California, 1977).

I. M. DESTLER, HIDEO SATO, AND PRISCILLA CLAPP, eds., *Managing an Alliance: The Politics of U.S.-Japanese Relations* (Brookings, 1976).

I. M. DESTLER, HARUHIRO FUKUI, AND HIDEO SATO, *The Textile Wrangle: Conflict in Japanese-American Relations, 1969–1971* (Cornell).

FRANKLIN B. WEINSTEIN, ed., *U.S.-Japan Relations and the Security of East Asia* (Westview, 1978).

MARTIN E. WEINSTEIN, *Japan's Postwar Defense Policy 1947–1968* (Columbia, 1971).

ROBERT S. OZAKI AND WALTER ARNOLD, eds., *Japan's Foreign Relations: A Global Search for Economic Security* (Westview, 1985).

CHARLES E. NEU, *The Troubled Encounter: The United States and Japan* (Wiley, 1973).

WILLIAM I. NEUMANN, *America Encounters Japan: From Perry to MacArthur* (Johns Hopkins, 1963).

HOLLAND HARRISON, *Managing Diplomacy: The U.S. and Japan* (Hoover Institution, 1984).

EDWIN O. REISCHAUER, *My Life Between Japan and America* (Harper & Row, 1986).

ALBRECHT ROTHACKER, *Economic Diplomacy Between the European Community and Japan, 1959–1981* (Gower, 1983).

WOLF MENDEL, *Western Europe and Japan Between the Super Powers* (St. Martin's, 1984).

TSOUKALIS LOUKAS AND MAUREEN WHITE, eds., *Japan and Western Europe* (St. Martin's, 1982).

ALAN RIX AND ROSE MOUER, eds., *Japan's Impact on the World* (Canberra Japanese Studies Association of Australia, 1984).

JOSHUA D. KATZ AND TILLY C. FRIEDMAN-LICHTECHEIN, eds., *Japan's New World Role* (Westview, 1985).

KENICHI OHMAE, *Triad Power: The Coming Shape of Global Competition* (The Free Press, 1985).

ALBERT M. CRAIG, ed., *Japan: A Comparative View* (Princeton, 1978).

EZRA F. VOGEL, ed., *Modern Japanese Organization and Decision Making* (California, 1975).

ELLIS S. KRAUSS, THOMAS P. ROHLEN, AND PATRICIA G. STEINHOFF, eds., *Conflict in Japan* (Hawaii, 1984).

KENT E. CALDER, *Crisis and Compensation: Public Policy and Political Stability in Japan, 1949–1986* (Princeton, 1988).

INDEX

Korea (*Cont.*)
  trade with, 56, 77
  in World War II, 170
  Yamato in, 13–14
Korean war, 200, 202, 220, 221,
    224, 241, 258, 331–332
Kublai Khan, 44
Kukai, 50
Kwantung Army, 158, 179
Kyodoto (*see* Cooperative party)
Kyosanto (*see* Communist party)
Kyoto, 23, 37, 250, 305
  during feudal period, 38–40, 43
    bakufu in, 57–58
    decline, 53–55, 61, 62
    emperor at, 44
    faith sects in, 63
    Taira usurpation of power, 46
  local government of, 296
  opening up of trade and, 97, 99
  reunification and, 65, 66
  in Tokugawa period, 80
  in World War II, 178
Kyoto University, 151
Kyushu, 10, 13, 53

Labor movement, 138, 147, 248,
    285
  American occupation and, 194–
    195, 198
  and the economy, 207–208
  exploited, 209
  and internal organization of in-
    dustry, 228–229
  in political demonstrations, 243
  Socialist party and, 216–217,
    254
Labor supply, 132–133, 246
Land, Sea and Air Self-Defense
    Forces (*see* Self-Defense
    Forces)
Land ownership, 21–22, 33–35,
    61, 105, 195
Landscape gardening, 59

Language and writing, 8, 28–31
  Chinese, 24–26
  study of, in foreign countries,
    312, 318
Laos, 172
Law codes, 23, 41, 123
Laws for the Military Houses, 69
LDP (*see* Liberal Democratic
    party)
League of Nations, 148, 159, 201
Liaison Conferences, 164
Liberal Democratic party (LDP),
    231
  decline of, 264, 273–276, 296
  as majority, 240, 241, 244,
    253, 257, 276–277
  and political tensions, 237–238
  and the rural vote, 307
  and the Socialists, 255–256
  strength of, 294–301
Liberal party (Jiyuto), 124, 125,
    212, 214, 215, 218
Literacy, 82, 137, 138
Literature, 28–30, 32, 37, 89,
    145, 248
  Buddhist, 48
  Chinese, 59
  of feudal period, 48, 51, 59–60
  modernization and, 139
  Tokugawa, 85–87
Lockheed Corporation, 276, 298,
    299
London Naval Conference, 159
Longevity, 304
Lotus Sutra, 51

MacArthur, General Douglas, 178
  dismissal of, 200
  and Japanese constitution, 208,
    219
  and the occupation, 187–188,
    191, 193, 226
  and reform of Japan, 198, 203
  surrender of Japan to, 181